KT-525-395

BEING A SCOT
SEAN CONNERY
and Murray Grigor

Design and art direction Teresa Monachino

WEIDENFELD & NICOLSON

To all the past and present trustees and staff of the
Scottish International Education Trust I salute all of you.
Words cannot begin to do justice to your 'efforts' for the Trust.

SEAN CONNERY

CONTENTS

FOREWORD

The lyres of time sang softly,
I cared not how I fared,
For free with the strength of ignorance,
How could I have been impaired?
My armour bright and virile
Entombed a passionate heart,
That nurtured dreams of fire,
But to where, to where to start.
  Sean Connery 1951

My three great passions in life, apart of course from Micheline, my wife since 1970, are acting, sport (especially golf) and Scotland. Of the three I would put Scotland and Scottish politics first. For many years I campaigned for the reinstatement of Scotland's ancient Parliament and put my weight behind the second Scottish referendum of 1997. I had a great affection for John Smith, who referred to devolution as 'unfinished business' and rigorously promoted it before his untimely death, as the 'settled will of the Scottish people'.

Fountainbridge, where I grew up, sounds rather Arcadian but it was far from that. Our industrial district was something of a grim no-man's-land far away from Edinburgh's historic Royal Mile, running down from the castle to the Palace of Holyroodhouse and the classical crescents and squares of the New Town. 'Auld Reekie' was the old Scots name for Edinburgh, called that for the amount of smoke that reeked from its huddled chimneys, trapped often by the sea fog known locally as the haar. The reek we savoured daily was at once sweet, porridge-like and pungent, as it poured out from the combined chimneys of a toffee factory, brewery and rubber mill where my dad put in long hours. When I came to form my own

Hollywood production company, I named it Fountainbridge Films – an idyllic-sounding name derived from that less than salubrious district which I still remember with great affection.

It's only in retrospect that you know anything about deprivation. As Craigie Veitch, my Fountainbridge neighbour all those years ago, told me recently, 'Looking back, we were disadvantaged because we grew up in an area of social deprivation. But since we didn't have social workers to tell us that we were deprived, we were all as happy as pigs.'

My first big break came when I was five years old. It's taken me more than seventy years to realise that. You see, at five I first learnt to read. It's that simple and it's that profound. I left school at thirteen. I didn't have a formal education. And yet there I was, accepting the thirty-fourth American Film Institute's Life Achievement Award in the summer of 2006. I told the glittering Hollywood audience that without the lust for reading instilled in me all those years ago by my teachers at the Bruntsfield Primary School in Edinburgh, I would not have been there with them that night. It had been a long journey to that star-studded event, from my two-room Fountainbridge home in the smoky industrial end of Edinburgh near the McCowans' toffee factory.

In 1991 I had the honour of receiving the Freedom of the City, which would have made my hard-working folks very proud. To follow in the footsteps of such earlier Edinburgh Freemen as Benjamin Franklin, Charles Dickens and now Nelson Mandela is very humbling indeed. Although I was much reassured to spot, among the other honoured recipients, Greyfriars Bobby, that faithful old dog who never left his master's grave. It's that essential quirkiness which endears me so much to Edinburgh.

When I took a taxi during a recent Edinburgh Film Festival, the cabbie was amazed that I could put a name to every street we passed.

'How come?' he asked.

'As a boy I used to deliver a milk round here,' I said.

'So what do you do now?'

That was rather harder to answer.

Sean Connery

Sean Connery, June 2008

Page 1: To be dubbed a Knight Batchelor in 1999 by the Queen, in the Palace of Holyroodhouse's long Picture Gallery of Scottish monarchs, meant a great deal to me, all the more so because it happened in Scotland.

Page 2: With my father and mother Joe and Effie and grandparents Neil and Helen at the Edinburgh Opening of *From Russia with Love*.

Page 4: At the Forth Bridge in the fifties.

Page 6: Around three years old with my mother Effie and grandmother Helen.

Page 7: Receiving the American Film Institute's Life Achievement Award in 2006.

Above: I received the Freedom of Edinburgh from Lord Provost Eleanor McLaughlin in 1991. To become a Freeman of Edinburgh was one of the greatest honours of my life. None of its ancient privileges remain, and claims that a recipient of this ancient accolade can drive sheep down the Mound are also just a Scotch myth.

1 MY EARLY DAYS IN EDINBURGH
Fountainbridge, step by step, to the screen

I was born on 25 August 1930. We lived at the top of a tenement at 176 Fountainbridge. There was no hot water and no bathroom. The communal lavatory was outside, four floors down. For years we had only gas lighting. Sometimes the light in the shared stairway would be out after some desperado had broken the mantle, to bubble gas through milk for kicks. We were the smallest family in the building. We knew most of the others, especially the elderly. 'Better go and see if Mrs Corrigan needs to run a message,' my mum would ask me. Then you didn't walk, you ran for her groceries – bread, firewood or briquettes. We moved three times within the one building and each time was an advancement. We ended up on the second floor with a view on to the street. I remember my excitement at seeing the length of Fountainbridge from the window. Diagonally across the street from our home was a pub at the entrance of McEwan's brewery. As a boy it always puzzled me why the workers piled into that pub at the end of the day to pay for the beer they were being paid to brew, since drinking free 'pauchy', or unfiltered beer, was always allowed at work.

When I was young, I didn't know that I lacked anything, because I had nothing to compare it with. There's a freedom in that. I had a very hardworking mother and father and I still think about them both a great deal.

Joe Connery met my mother Euphamia Maclean at a dance in Edinburgh. She was known as Effie by my father's family and as Phemie by her own. They were married on 28 December 1928 at Tynecastle Parish Church, when my father was twenty-six and my mother twenty. For the wedding party my mother cleared all the furniture out of the house in time for my father to roll in a firkin of good strong beer to provide seventy-two pints as chasers for all the other drinks that would materialise. The Connerys and the Macleans lined up at opposite ends of the kitchen. It wasn't a very cohesive gathering. After a few glasses, Neil Maclean, my Scottish grandfather, began to annoy Tommy Connery, my Irish grandfather. Tommy's father was a poor itinerant pedlar from County Wexford in Ireland who had first settled down in Glasgow with the mill worker Jennie Macnab. Neil began to dress Tommy down in Gaelic, which he knew Tommy couldn't understand. Then Tommy told Neil to 'shut his face' or he was going to have to sort him out. It was that kind of evening. Before it became too much of a barney, Neil took Jennie aside, encouraging her to go home for her own safety, which she took very badly.

Tommy made something of a living as a recycler by driving a horse and cart around the poorer neighbourhoods of Edinburgh, collecting old clothes and anything the hard-up would sell him. He took everything he could get to the rag-and-bone man Asa Was, who operated out of a courtyard a few doors up from us in Fountainbridge. Beyond a narrow pend, or archway, big barricade doors were open seven days a week to receive whatever goods people brought him. Asa paid more for woollens than for rags, which he weighed on large scales and then sorted into piles. He was a striking figure wearing a long fur coat to his ankles. Some thought that he was a Yorkshire Quaker, others had the idea that he was just an eccentric Jewish merchant who had come into money. 'Ach no,' he would always say, when anyone accused him of being rich, 'if only I was'. And the name stuck. 'Is he as he always is?' the kids would sing. 'Or is he as he was?'

Pages 10/11: With my mother Effie at the beginning of the James Bond era.

Left: In my Fountainbridge Films production of *Finding Forrester*, directed by Gus Van Sant, 2000. Rob Brown plays the young writer. Although he had never acted before, he immediately struck me with his presence. Rob Brown now combines an acting career with studying to be an engineer.

Right: The end of the day shift at the Castle Mills Works of the North British Rubber Company in Fountainbridge where my father worked, though his 12-hour shift seldom finished before 10 o'clock at night.

In the Scottish tradition I was called Thomas after my father's father, which was shortened to Tam by my friends. I had great affection for the old rascal, who was always getting into scrapes. He fought boxing bouts in public parks, encouraged by my grannie Jennie, who often kept his corner. His major money-making 'job' was working as a bookie's runner. In those days you had to be at a race course to place a bet on a horse. Few working men could take time off for that, so they would write their bets on slips of paper and the runner would run them to a bookie. This was against the law so you chose a daft name like 'Desperate Dan' to prevent being found out and possibly arrested. Tommy would pay out the day's winnings each evening in a pub lavatory. From time to time he got 'lifted' by the police, but the bookies would always pay his fines. Fifty years later I modelled much of Jesse McMullen, that streetwise career criminal in *Family Business*, on my tough old wily granddad.

'My other grandfather, Neil Maclean, was a stonemason who later became a foreman, so I suppose the Macleans were better off and more successful than the Connerys. The Connerys were Catholic but none of them were churchgoers; my father certainly wasn't. My mother's side was Protestant, but they were not religious either. I think they rather looked down upon the Connerys, a bit embarrassed about them being rag-and-bone men, going around the streets with a horse and cart. Nor did Neil have a high regard for the Irish labourers he hired. 'Now listen Mick,' he would say to one, 'unlike the others, you're a good worker. But I have to tell you I pay you more than the rest. Now not a word.' Mick would walk away thinking what a fine gentleman my granddad was. He never knew that Neil told all the labourers the same thing. None of them told each other, so no one ever knew that they were all getting the same wage.

The Stewart Terrace school gang. That's me second from the left in the front row; but why am I the only one who is wearing a tie?

During the World War II down on Stewart Terrace, along the Gorgie Road, everyone had an allotment to grow vegetables. Once you started to get half-decent vegetables people would steal them. Neil came up with an ingenious idea to protect the family crop. He unravelled the different-coloured strands from old electric cables. He then wound them around stakes, zigzagging a red wire past the lettuce, a blue one over the cabbages and a green wire across the potatoes. When the biggest blabbermouth in the neighbourhood came over and asked him what on earth he was doing, my granddad looked up at him and said, 'You know all this stealing that's going on. I just hope those buggers try to steal my vegetables.'

'Why?'

'All this goes straight to the police,' he said, pointing to the web of coloured wires.

Nobody ever touched his vegetables.

On Saturday evenings many of the Fountainbridge worthies would don their bunnets, or flat hats, and 'hing oot' of their windows, resting their arms on a pillow, to watch the street's comings and goings. From such 'high hings' I've often wondered if that American expression 'Where do you hang out?' had its origins way back in urban Scotland.

In those days there was no television. Radio was then the big thing. Movies featured the Wild West with goodies and baddies in Westerns and cowboy stars like Tom Mix rode the range. Scary weekly serials such as *The Amazing Exploits of the Clutching Hand* with the mad scientist Dr Paul Gironda were special favourites. Few of us could afford the ticket prices so we pooled what money we had for just one of us to go in. At an appropriately spooky moment, perhaps when the clutching hand reached out of the darkness, our designated mole would scamper out of his seat and rush to the emergency exit to let us all in.

On the corner fifty yards up the street was the rubber mill where my father worked. He used to go there at ten in the morning and work until ten at night. I didn't see a lot of him so there was little talking time in our home. He gave my mother all the money, as she dealt with all the real decisions. She was very tough: the engine in the family. During the war she too worked long hours, cleaning for Polish officers billeted in grand old Edinburgh houses. Always carrying briefcases and wearing long tailored overcoats, these Poles with their suave haircuts cut a dashing presence in wartime Fountainbridge. As kids we all liked them, especially when they put on exotic cabaret shows at the Palladium and handed out distinctive lead lapel badges of Polish Eagles.

In a district where only two homes had their own phone, you could contact the police in emergencies through a direct line installed inside cast-iron police huts. All you had to do was to open a small hinged door to talk directly to the police station. One of them was strategically placed across the street from our home. As a boy I learnt what was happening in the neighbourhood by watching how a policeman approached that hut. How he walked told you everything. You knew that nothing was afoot if he'd stroll along his beat and then slowly unlock the metal door. But when he rushed down the street, tore off his helmet and dived through the door, you knew something serious was up. When I came to play the Chicago cop Jimmy Malone in *The Untouchables*, I drew on my memories of those

Edinburgh Police box. Edinburgh's city architect Ebeneezer J. Macrae rejected the standard British police box. A Greek temple-like design, complete with heroic wreath, was thought more appropriate, especially for the classical streets of the New Town. Sadly the position of a city architect was scrapped years ago with a dire effect on Edinburgh's architecture.

Although most cities have removed their police boxes, Edinburgh has listed many of them as historic monuments. Nearly a hundred have survived in various states of preservation. Some have even been converted into coffee bars. Try asking for a 'copuccino'.

Fountainbridge policemen. Sadly, those classically designed Edinburgh police boxes no longer function, even though they would still provide a useful community role in emergencies. Many still survive around Edinburgh, dressed up in various garish colours as booths serving coffee.

Playing soccer with a tanner ball all the way up the street to school is my strongest memory of growing up in Edinburgh in the Thirties. A tanner was a mere sixpence, worth only a couple of pennies today. After school we battered that tanner ball endlessly up and down the back green behind our home. In reality the green was grey. The grass had been concreted over years before, but that made it perfect for playing headers. On the tenement walls we chalked up goalposts and headed that ball back into goal for hours, day after day, all year round. When hungry I could always call up to my mum for a jammy piece. She'd hurl one down from a window at the back of the building. The trick was to catch the sticky sandwich before it splattered on the ground.

We were all soccer-crazy. When our school was temporarily closed down during the war, it didn't upset us at all. No lessons meant more time to perfect our soccer. We all dreamed of a professional career and one day playing for Scotland.

At twelve I passed my qualifying exam and was offered a place at Boroughmuir High School, probably thanks to my mother. This was the school for high achievers. But I found out that they played rugby there rather than soccer. Since soccer was second only to breathing for me, I passed up the good school and went to the Darroch Secondary in Upper Gilmore Street near the Union Canal. It was far less academic than Boroughmuir, but there they took soccer seriously and I was soon playing for the school team. Miss Rosie, my English teacher, was a stickler for accuracy and kept alive my love of words. Since most of the pupils hoped for jobs in the technical and craft trades, we got a good grounding in mathematics. Strangely enough, Mr Brown's freehand drawing skills in geometry I still remember to this day. He would deftly chalk up the squares on the sides of a right-angled triangle, then drum into us that famous theorem of Pythagoras, that the sum of the areas of the two small squares equals the area of the large one.

But it was the right-angled rectangle of our soccer pitch that was my overriding interest in school. At the same time, I was thrilled to have a job earning money. I couldn't wait to work. Work was very important to me. I collected bottles for the deposit and I became a part-time butcher's boy. At the end of the week I was given a 'pochle' of odd ends of pork, lamb, chicken leftovers. My mum would be very pleased and I would be so pleased that she was pleased. From the age of nine I would be up at six in the morning to deliver milk for Kennedy's dairy before school. Out of my pay packet of three shillings and sixpence a week, only 20 pence in today's money, I gave my mum the three shillings and put the sixpence into my Post Office savings box. To encourage you to read, the box was shaped like a book. Only the Post Office had a special key to open it when whatever money you had would be put into your account to earn interest. The entrance slot had teeth, which closed as the coin went in. When I was caught short I learnt that I could fiddle out coins by wiggling two knives backwards and forwards in and around the slot.

During the war our school was requisitioned by Civil Defence. We were told to present for lessons in a grand manor house in Morningside, Edinburgh's poshest district. When the lady of the house spotted that I was her milk boy, she said, 'No. I don't think so', in the 'refined' accent of a Miss Jean Brodie, and closed the door. Those were the days. It really didn't bother me that much at the time. I never grasped that it was arrant snobbery. For me it just meant more time off for soccer.

My mother lost two brothers in the war and although we couldn't afford it she adopted Donald, the love-child of a doctor and a maid she knew. My great escape from the confinement of Fountainbridge was to visit my Maclean grandparents who had retired across the river to Fife. What a thrilling adventure it was to cross the river over the great cantilevers of the Forth Bridge. Since the first German air raid over Britain had narrowly missed this strategic bridge, huge barrage balloons then encircled its high girders like giant flying Dumbo elephants. Artillery emplacements were deployed on the islands all round. Some had their guns poking out of ancient fortifications, which gave them the look of decoy battleships.

My uncle had bought a Church of Scotland manse and farmed the smallholding in the rather run-down coalmining village of Lassodie, north of Dunfermline. He offered my grandma and grandpa the manse's low shed-like extension, which he soon converted into a cosy home by building rooms and installing a great wood-burning stove. I so well remember feeding logs into the hungry letterbox of its open grate on cold winter nights and feeling the instant warmth thrown out, as the draught pulled the heat up its tall chimney.

For town boys like us Lassodie was our little home on the prairie. Through our city eyes the open fields, under the wide horizons, loomed like the open range in cowboy films. Even the pigs and chickens looked exotic. As the war drew to an end

Barrage balloons were deployed around the Forth Bridge during World War II to foil low-level Luftwaffe bombing raids. In the Sixties, when a company director from Germany visited the Hewlett-Packard computer plant at South Queensferry overlooking the Firth of Forth, he was asked if he had ever seen the bridge before. 'Only through a periscope,' he replied.

My grandparents Neil and Helen with their Scottish wolf-hounds on their smallholding at Lassodie, across the Firth of Forth in Fife.

my young brother Neil and I spent glorious summers there. Now it was his turn to deliver the milk by collecting it still warm from the farm. I was even able to ride our neighbour's Clydesdale cart-horse, whose day job was drawing ploughs or dragging chains across the fields. It would have towered over the Highland garron pony that pulled my milk cart back in town.

I was much intrigued by my grandpa's ingenious system for keeping hens on the lay. He had built a large rectangular-framed hutch on two shafts with a floor of wire mesh snug on the grass so that the hens could peck through it for corn. Every few days he would move the mobile hutch to a different part of the field. It allowed the hens to forage contentedly and encouraged them to produce more eggs. Two could lift the hutch up and then move it to a different patch. It both protected the hens from foxes and prevented them from wrecking the grass. It all came about because of the war, but it would still work today. Recently I encouraged my son Stéphane to construct a version of that mobile hen hutch at his home in Bedford, Connecticut.

As I approached my thirteenth birthday in August 1943 I couldn't see the point of returning to school. I wasn't learning much. I wanted to work, earn money and play soccer. Since it was wartime, somehow I got away with it. Most of the working men were in the forces, so I soon got a job at St Cuthbert's, the local dairy of the Co-operative Wholesale Society. Like most families in Fountainbridge, we were members of the Co-op. Every time you bought anything, you gave in your number. I have never forgotten mine: 26245 Connery. But you had to make sure that it was recorded, or you missed out on your dividend. In those days it could amount to the dizzy sum of £45. And to think that they might pay that out to you twice a year.

My first official job title at St Cuthbert's was the Corstorphine Dairy barrow worker. I only learnt this recently on a visit to the National Library of Scotland. After I saw some of the great documents in their archives, including letters by Charles Darwin and Lord Byron, and the heartbreaking last letter of Mary Queen of Scots written only six hours before her execution, I was shown one of my first pay slips. By some extraordinary sleuthing, an archivist had found it among thousands of documents in the stacks. It recorded my starting salary in 1944 as a guinea, or twenty-one shillings a week (£1.05p). I was reassured to see that it also recorded my promotion to the position of full dairy transport worker, which meant that I was then a junior horseman with a horse of my own.

I remember that day so well. To be like the big boys I ran out to buy moleskin trousers. The horse I groomed was a Highland garron pony called Tich and I loved her dearly. I bought her rosettes and chains, which looped down from each ear, along with a martingale or bracelet, which hung down her front. I added 'birlers', roundels which birled or twirled in the wind, or when she trotted. I was so proud of Tich that I entered her in the annual horse and cart competition for the best-dressed horse and she won a Highly Commended.

Left: My pay slip from the St Cuthbert's Dairy, collection.

Right: In the stacks of the National Library with the archivist David McClay.

Years later, as a fledgling actor, when I began to read books seriously and study plays, I tried to recapture the emotional moments of the first day I left home to trot my own milk cart out of the dairy into the Edinburgh dawn. At the time I must have been reading *Portrait of the Artist as a Young Man*, James Joyce's warm-hearted evocation of his early days in Dublin, though the title I gave the piece must owe more to Dylan Thomas's version, *Portrait of the Artist as a Young Dog*. Here it is, just as I slowly tapped it out on my portable typewriter all those years ago:

PORTRAIT OF THE ARTIST AS A YOUNG HORSE

I remember when I'd just turned fourteen, a horse of my own to drive! ME!

I couldn't grasp it I was so elated.

That night as I tried to go to bed I was sure my heart was going to leap up and choke me. I told not a soul.

Ma and Dad were intrigued that I could polish my well-worn studded boots: forever the cause of dung carpeted rows.

In shirt-tail I scrambled into bed, 'Yes I shall always polish my boots if it makes me feel like this,' I lied pleasantly to myself.

After winning show after show, polishing miles of harness, breaking in all the new horses…I slept.

Awakening to the chimes of the brewery clock (can't remember hearing 5 a.m. before) curse those laces. I'll buy a new pair on Thursday payday – Driver – Connery – 271.

Creeping through the kitchen whispering to my mother so not to waken Dad, I made a cup of tea in the breathy wet gaslight of the lamppost outside our window – in the dark shadow of the press door I silently poured my tea through the dishcloth down the sink, slunk out the kitchen door with a throbbing cheerio to my astonished mother.

My armpit wrapped around the banister I spiralled down the three landings and bounded out into the deserted street, thinking how can people complain about the weather when you must have rain for the grass for the horses, seems straightforward enough for me.

Watching my grotesque shadow growing bigger and bigger in time with the ringing clip of my boots, I entered the dimly lit salty stable-yard, up the gangway past the steaming dung heap into the men's harness room and bothy. Hullo the 'Carter' has arrived said old Jock Luke acidly, the others laughed as he went about trimming and fixing his lamps, his lard-like face sunk into his bent shoulders, and red wet lips pouted as though to whistle, which he never did, and the roaring crackling wood fire reflecting on his well-worn greasy moleskins. 'Well ma son here's your curry-comb and dandy, see and use it,' chirped old Comby the head stableman. I mumbled a thank-you; pushing both his hands into the bib of his brown dungarees to tuck in his white collarless shirt he reminded me, 'A healthy horse is always a clean horse'. His snow white moustache flicked up as if to kiss his clear blue eye – giving me a wink, as I left the bothy.

Pages 20-21: With my grandfather Neil in the Fifties, who is doing much to dispel the air of gloominess of the Lassodie pub. In its run-down state this bar was a strong candidate for what Hugh MacDiarmid described as being for 'connoisseurs of the morose'.

Above: St Cuthbert's Co-operative Association Dairy continued to deliver milk by horse and cart well into the Eighties.

Brushing and combing, wheeze-breathing through clenched teeth till my sweat was pinging on my spine, I gave her smoke grey skin the final hessian rub. I stood looking at her and I could feel Comby's words – Birdie told me herself with her mouse soft nosing gestures. I pretended to scold and argue with her like old Tam in the next stall with his bull-necked Belgian mare.

With the last of my mother's black shoe polish and dad's army-famed boot brushes I shined up her hooves.

With a throbbing heart I drove out the yard and up Fountainbridge as proud as Punch.

Coming towards me I spotted Old Jock Luke with a full load, sitting head sunk in his shiny collar. Praying that he would acknowledge me, I tried to relax as we came nearer and nearer, then just on passing with a sudden flick of his head, 'Lousy morning son'. I don't know what I replied but I know it could never have told what I felt.

The rain almost made an excuse for the wet hotness in my eyes as I trotted off up the bridge – so happy…

In my milk delivery days I took few photographs, but here's one of Joe Ritchie driving his horse.

Tich, my faithful companion on those early-morning milk rounds, together with the Wild West antics of Tony, Tom Mix's wonder steed on the silver screen, may have kindled my special relationship with horses. Or was it riding that massive cart-horse over the fields next to my grandfather's home in Fife during school holidays that really bonded me with horses, which lingers to this day. I still feel comfortable in the saddle and have never had any fear of horses. Within reason I am always up for tackling the film stunts dreamt up by screenwriters in the safety of their own garrets. Yet in the films I've made involving horsemanship, from *Zardoz* to *The Untouchables*, some of my more spectacular action sequences resulted from unplanned accidents. When I was riding full tilt in *Highlander*, Russell Mulcahy the director signalled a turn, but when I reined my charger round, my sword got entangled in my cape and dug sharply into the horse's flank. The panicked beast veered suddenly sideways at the gallop, menacingly close to a dangerous drop. 'More of that!' was all the delighted director shouted back.

Any horse that I'm asked to ride in movies, I like to take out for an early-morning canter, so that the two of us get to know each other before any of the action begins. In *The Wind and the Lion* I rode quite a small horse, which was quick and much more flexible for filming dialogue than a bigger horse would ever have been. The script called for a rider to charge through a first-floor window into a courtyard below. I was playing the impressive-sounding Mulay Achmed Mohammed el-Raisuli the Magnificent, so clearly this was a stunt too far for me. We were in good hands, filming around Seville where, without question, live the world's best horsemen. In order to persuade the horse, against its better reason, to defenestrate, it was first taught to approach an opening obscured by tissue paper and then gradually introduced to slashed transparent plastic sheeting. After a number of false starts the horse gave up shying and wouldn't hesitate to charge straight through.

Left: *Shalako*, 1968, directed by Edward Dmytryk, shot on spaghetti western locations in southern Spain. I played Shalako, a freebooting gunfighter riding in Apache country to the rescue of such European aristocrats as Brigitte Bardot.

Right: In *The Wind and the Lion*, 1975, directed by John Milius, I play the Berber brigand Mulay Achmed Mohammed el-Raisuli the Magnificent, who kidnaps Eden Perdicaris and her two children and causes the American president to launch an armed rescue mission.

Opposite: The Fet-Lor Amateur Soccer Club, 1949-50. I am third from the right in the second row.

On the actual day of shooting it was led upstairs into a first-storey living-room facing the specially constructed French windows. A sandbank had been piled up in the courtyard below, calculated to be long enough to break the horse's fall with its rider on top. With four poised cameras ready to go, the horse sensed the excitement and in a terrified flash took off like a bullet, charging straight through the windows into the air – so far that it totally missed the sand, throwing the stunt rider on to his head. Everyone thought that the American was dead. They rushed him by helicopter to a Malaga hospital, but having been given two aspirins in flight he arrived, miraculously, totally recovered. It took over four hours to find the startled horse, which had bolted miles away. Only two cameramen were quick enough to catch its unrepeatable action.

In *Shalako* I had my own excitement. At short notice I was given Brigitte Bardot's standby white horse. This would save time unbuckling the special harness of her number one horse since she was riding side-saddle. With the light beginning to fail there was no time for my usual practice run. As I rode through the Almería orchards the horse reared up. I was lucky enough to get one leg out of the stirrup, for if a horse comes back flat and its whole weight falls on you, it's goodnight sweet prince.

Such future dangers were far from my thoughts as I settled Tich back in her stables at St Cuthbert's, for the rest of the day was then free to practise soccer at the Fet-Lor Club. Although I delivered milk to Fettes College it was only recently that I had made the connection that this enterprising club had been founded after World War I by Edinburgh's two leading boarding-schools, Fettes and Loretto. Soccer was my passion, but the Fettesian–Lorettonian Boys' Club had rooms near the High Street where they also offered gymnastics, boxing, billiards, an extensive library and the then rare luxury of a hot bath. Before the days of the Welfare State, the club aimed 'to take poor underfed and underclothed boys off the street by offering them a friendly meeting place with something to eat and a hot drink'. Certainly for me, and other Fountainbridge kids, the public soccer pitches of Saughton Park lured our tanner-ball antics off the streets and propelled some of us into playing professional soccer.

Even though I was so happy in my job, practising soccer daily with my pals and living contentedly with my family, I had an ever-increasing desire to experience the wider world. Since I had already joined the Royal Navy's Sea Cadets, on a sudden impulse at seventeen, I signed up for twelve years as a Royal Navy Volunteer with five years in the Reserves, and began training in Portsmouth on the shore-based HMS *Formidable*. One night ashore, I fell in with my shipmates to carry out that old naval ritual of getting tattooed. As the old saying goes, a sailor without tattoos is like a ship without grog. But instead of the erotic fantasies favoured by many, I chose to have 'Mum and Dad' on one arm and 'Scotland Forever' on the other. Although now much faded, they still evoke memories of life at home and my passion for the old country.

Within two years I was an able seaman on the battleship HMS *King George V*. But in reality as a seaman I was most unable-bodied, with worrying stomach cramps. Diagnosed with duodenal ulcers, I spent eight weeks in Hassler Hospital without one single visitor. Forced to 'swallow the anchor', as they say in the Royal Navy, I was discharged with a 20 per cent disability pension. This amounted to 11 shillings and 9 pence (approximately 59p) per week. I cashed it in immediately and with the £87 bought an ex-army Norton motorbike. Strangely, I have never had ulcers since.

Looking back, it was probably my inability to take orders from the officers, especially from those I found had reached their position largely through privilege, that gave me ulcers. Over twenty years later my experiences below deck put fire into my performance as Joe Roberts, the picked-upon courtmarshalled sergeant major in *The Hill*, Sidney Lumet's astute exposure of merciless punishment in the British Army.

Back in Edinburgh I took on a bewildering number of odd jobs, before the British Legion came to my rescue. As a disabled ex-serviceman I was offered training as a tailor, barber or French polisher, among other trades. I chose polishing and was sent to Johnstone in the West of Scotland for a rapid induction course. After training in this hard-to-master skill, I was soon polishing for a cabinet-making firm run by Mr Stark in Haddington, east of Edinburgh. Since his main business was supplying coffins to the local undertakers, most of my days were spent polishing them, which always struck me as a real waste of time. Stark appeared to be a kindly man, visiting old people when they were ill, but his real purpose was mentally to measure them up. If a family preferred an oak coffin Mr Stark would have us bleach a mahogany one. In really busy times I'd bring in a flask of tea and save myself the fare home by kipping overnight in one of the coffins. I can't really say I ever mastered the craft of French polishing. On the other hand my fellow apprentice Peter Moran became an expert and ended up maintaining all the furniture in Edinburgh's North British Hotel, now renamed The Balmoral.

1951 was the year of the Festival of Britain exhibition, and a cousin of Peter's in London invited us south to see what all the fuss was about. As soon as we hit the South Bank we were caught up in its sense of optimism that a new era was beginning. The gravity-defying rocket of the Skylon alongside the flying-saucer-like Dome of Discovery, with splashes of colour everywhere, made a dazzling impression on us, after those drab postwar years. What Old Labour achieved in those penny-pinching days was a sense of a better future. How ironic, then, that Herbert Morrison, the minister responsible for the event, saw it successfully through to completion in 1951 and then some fifty years later his New Labour grandson, Peter Mandelson, would promote that vacuous Millennium Dome, all puff and no content. As Stephen Bayley, the creative director of the 'Millennium Dome Experience' (for a brief six frustrating months), said, 'The Festival of Britain offered escape from the age of austerity; the Millennium Dome was a pitiable memorial to an age of excess.' Costing close to £1000 million, it's now been saved for blockbuster exhibitions. The one worth saving, the £11 million Dome of Discovery, was summarily destroyed by Churchill's vengeful incoming Tory government. Together they can be read as a barometer between probity and fatuousness marking the sad decline of the Labour Party's values under Tony Blair.

Back in Edinburgh I had taken up body-building at the Dunedin Amateur Weight Lifting Club. Its name made the club sound grand and it sported its own blazer, yet it operated out of a disused air-raid shelter with bare electric bulbs and the minimum of facilities. There I met Archie Brennan, a talented weaver at the

Opposite, top left: Happy doing my 'dhobey', as they call washing your kit in the Royal Navy.

Top right: Here, as Able Seaman Connery, I am trying to look my most 'tiddly', the naval expression for sartorial elegance. The more bleached the stripes were the more tiddly you became. Folding your bell-bottom trousers into seven parts provided your night-time pillow.

Bottom left: Time off with my mates from gunnery school on Whale Island, Portsmouth, 1948.

Bottom right: Training break on land-based HMS *Excellent*, Portsmouth, 1948.

Above: *The Hill*, 1965, directed by Sidney Lumet. The sadistic torture of carting sand daily up an artificial hill in the blazing sun at a British Army military Detention Camp during World War II caused me to explode as I confronted Staff Sergeant Williams played by Ian Hendry.

BATHING POOL, PORTOBELLO.

A.4127

Dovecote Tapestry Company and the Edinburgh College of Art, who told me about posing as a model for easy money. It wasn't all that easy remaining motionless for fifty minutes. The professional model was Mancini, who could hold his pose for the exact period, before taking his ten-minute break. Years later Richard Demarco, by then a freebooting cultural commando in the arts, reminded me that I had posed for his group of students and I fear he has the paintings to prove it. There wasn't that much money in it, but it was an entry into another world. I soon found a far better-paid job installing the heavy, curved printing plates on to the rotary presses of the *Edinburgh Evening News*.

For a time I worked as a lifeguard at the Portobello Outdoor Swimming Pool. It still had the wave-making machinery which helped prepare troops for the D Day Landings. In my down time I made such good use of the high-diving boards that I was soon invited to join a travelling troupe of demonstration divers. Before I could consider that, I was asked, along with two other tall lifeguards, to dress up for walk-on parts in Anna Neagle's *Glorious Days* at the Empire Theatre. All we had to do was to don a Guard's uniform and a busby, which really was easy money. Other times I did real guard duties outside dance halls. During a Musicians' Union strike I became a bouncer for fund-raising jazz bands at Oddfellows in the Old Town. When I barred a rowdy bunch from entering, one of them menaced me.

'It's just because we're foking Irishmen.'

'No,' I said, 'it's just because you're foking drunk.'

All this time I continued to play soccer for clubs around Edinburgh like the Carrick Vale Juniors and Oxgang Rovers. At twenty-one I turned professional for Bonnyrigg Rose in the Scottish Junior League and earned £35 (paid in the toilet). It would be the only payment I ever earned for playing professional soccer.

Along with a number of Edinburgh friends I entered the Mr Universe contest in London. Despite what many claim, I never won any awards. There were far too

Opposite, top left: Grasping the cliché at the Festival of Britain. If there aint any seegar store Indians around, find yourself a Highlander in full tartan fig, but where have all his pipes gone?

Top right: Ricky Demarco's oil sketch of me posing at the Edinburgh College of Art, 1949.

Bottom left: Portobello open-air swimming pool opened in 1936. With room for well over a thousand swimmers, it had a wave-making machine and was heated by the nearby power station. Demolished, 1980.

Bottom right: By the left-step forward lifeguard Connery dressed as a guardsman for Anna Neagle's *Glorious Days* – a celebration of the life of Queen Victoria. Neil Murray on the right became the manager of Edinburgh's Empire Theatre.

Left: Pictured here with my competitors during the Mr Universe competition of 1953 at the Lyceum, London. My blazer sports the badge of the Dunedin Weight Lifting Club, Edinburgh.

many massive real musclemen from around the world to take care of the medals. I appeared ridiculous standing next to the eventual winner, an American called Bill Pearl, with a physique like Arnold Schwarzenegger. Beside him I looked like one of those seven-stone weaklings in a Charles Atlas ad. But it was during this competition that I first heard Joshua Logan was casting for the British run of the American musical *South Pacific*. One of the body-builders was Stanley Howlett, who was leaving its London run. He told me that I should try for an audition since Vic Harmon, one of the marines, had emigrated to Canada. All you had to do was to look like an American and do a couple of handsprings. I got Vic's part cutting up wood on stage before springing up and singing, 'There Is Nothing Like a Dame'. Since they were guaranteeing £12 per week, which was as much as I had ever earned, I signed up for the two-year national tour. I had no ambition then to be an actor – it was purely the money and the fun that got me hooked.

During the tour we formed a *South Pacific* soccer XI and played all comers: any amateur, police team or anyone else who would take us on. When we had a match against a Manchester United junior team, their legendary manager Matt Busby was among the spectators. Busby came to the show and presented us all with soccer strips. Best of all, I was spotted as a promising player by one of the scouts and offered a trial. The thought of being a Busby Babe and playing for Manchester United was then every young footballer's ambition. My affection for the theatre took a sudden swerve stage-left to a soccer field's left wing. Could I still be that footballer of my dreams?

When I got back to my digs I ran my exciting offer of a soccer trial past my new friend Robert Henderson, one of the leading American actors in the show. 'But you told me how much you were enjoying being an actor,' he said, stalling my enthusiasm in its tracks. The advice which this remarkable man then gave me would change my life. 'You've shown that you have talent in these two very different worlds,' he said. 'If you choose soccer you may have another ten years, but as an actor you could go on till you drop. But if you choose acting you still have two real problems. The first concerns your near-impenetrable Scots burr.' I realised that I had a problem here since another cast member, Millicent Martin, later famous in *That Was The Week That Was*, had thought that I was Polish. 'Secondly,' Robert went on, 'you have to educate yourself. If you're really serious about acting I will help you.' Up until this moment I had never contemplated acting as a career. I just thought it was a great way of earning more money. My week's pay had recently been upped to £14 a week, which seemed a fortune in 1953. For the first time in my life I had been given a definitive direction to do something in life and have half a chance to be somebody.

So now it was decision time. I bought a reel-to-reel Grundig tape recorder for a hefty £60 and began to hear for myself how heavily accented my voice really was. Of course I wanted to be clearly understood. I practised articulating my words more distinctly. Yet at the same time I wanted to retain the personality of my own voice and to be honest to my Edinburgh roots. I didn't care much for the declamatory style that actors were then expected to bring to a part, especially in Shakespeare plays. For me it separated the head from the heart. When I recorded

Striking poses for the photographer Bill Green, the Vince Studio photographer for *Health and Strength* magazine.

With the *South Pacific* soccer team on tour in 1953.

Opposite: On the town in Liverpool, with cast members Carol Sobel, Susan Yu and Victor Spinetti.

myself on tape, declaiming Hamlet in the received Shakespearean manner, it rang utterly false to me. How could I ever bring an emotional dimension to a part if I would always be enunciating clipped elocutions as though I were stuck up there on the battlements of Elsinore? I wanted to keep my own natural voice and remain true to myself. I wanted to sound like me, not someone else, yet to be clear and understandable. I never wanted to imitate that staccato precision of perfection achieved by such masters of the articulated vowel as the incomparable John Gielgud. I felt that I couldn't be honest with myself or express any emotions truthfully if I tried to re-invent my speech patterns in an actorish declamatory way. Or proclaim like Dylan Thomas's 'men from the BBC who speak as though they had the Elgin Marbles in their mouths'. I was going against the fashion of the times, since then all actors, regardless of their background, delivered their lines in the well articulated plummy vowels of Standard English. All this would change in the Sixties when actors of similar backgrounds to mine, like Michael Caine and Albert Finney, took to the stage and screen. Recently the screenwriter Buck Henry told me that I was the only one he knew who could play characters as diverse as a Russian submarine commander, James Bond, an Arab sheikh, a medieval Northumbrian priest or a Chicago Irish cop, and still be totally believable in the part speaking with a Scottish burr.

Robert Henderson's second problem with me was that I was clearly uneducated. He handed me a formidable list of books to read, starting off with Ibsen's *Hedda Gabler*, and followed it up with *The Wild Duck*. The plays were a revelation to me and we discussed them long into the night. I didn't buy the books he recommended: I couldn't afford them, and anyway I had nowhere to keep them. All I had in life was a padlocked wicker basket, which was shipped ahead with the

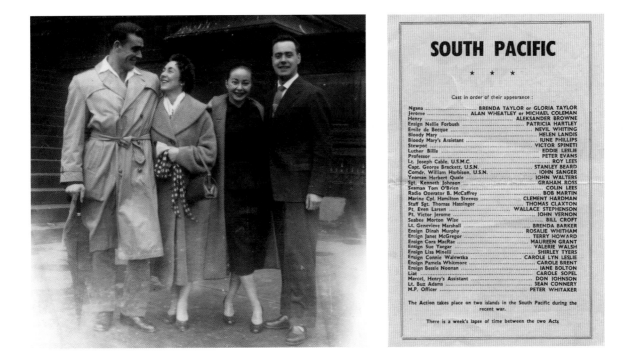

SOUTH PACIFIC

★ ★ ★

Cast in order of their appearance :

Ngana .... BRENDA TAYLOR or GLORIA TAYLOR
Jerome .... ALAN WHEATLEY or MICHAEL COLEMAN
Henry .... ALEKSANDER BROWNE
Ensign Nellie Forbush .... PATRICIA HARTLEY
Emile de Becque .... NEVIL WHITING
Bloody Mary .... HELEN LANDIS
Bloody Mary's Assistant .... IUNE PHILLIPS
Stewpot .... VICTOR SPINETI
Luther Billis .... EDDIE LESLIE
Professor .... PETER EVANS
Lt. Joseph Cable, U.S.M.C. .... ROY LEES
Capt. George Brackett, U.S.N. .... STANLEY BEARD
Comdr. William Harbison, U.S.N. .... IOHN SANGER
Yeoman Herbert Quale .... IOHN WALTERS
Sgt. Kenneth Johnson .... GRAHAM ROSS
Seaman Tom O'Brien .... COLIN LEES
Radio Operator B. McCaffrey .... BOB MARTIN
Marine Cpl. Hamilton Steeves .... CLEMENT HARDMAN
Staff Sgt. Thomas Hassinger .... THOMAS CLAXTON
Pt. Even Larsen .... WALLACE STEPHENSON
Pt. Victor Jerome .... IOHN VERNON
Seabee Morton Wise .... BILL CROFT
Lt. Genevieve Marshall .... BRENDA BARKER
Ensign Dinah Murphy .... ROSALIE WHITHAM
Ensign Janet McGregor .... TERRY HOWARD
Ensign Cora MacRae .... MAUREEN GRANT
Ensign Sue Yaegar .... VALERIE WALSH
Ensign Lisa Minelli .... SHIRLEY TYERS
Ensign Connie Walewska .... CAROLE LYN LESLIE
Ensign Pamela Whitmore .... CAROLE BRENT
Ensign Bessie Noonan .... IANE BOLTON
Liat .... CAROLE SOPEL
Marcel, Henry's Assistant .... DON IOHNSON
Lt. Buz Adams .... SEAN CONNERY
M.P. Officer .... PETER WHITAKER

The Action takes place on two islands in the South Pacific during the
recent war.

There is a week's lapse of time between the two Acts

scenery as I followed the tour of *South Pacific* on my bike. In every town we visited, after finding my digs, I would make straight for the nearest public library. I was astonished to discover that they were free. You just filled in the form, handed it in and you got your book. I did all the libraries up and down the country. From then on I was never without a book. The excitement of the written word, imbued in me when I was five, and which had remained dormant during all my years as an odd-job man, now came rushing back. I got through Stanislavsky's *An Actor Prepares* and *My Life in Art*. They made me aware of the physiology of acting, which I had never thought of before. I remember wondering how you could play an intelligent person if you were stupid, and vice versa. For their emotional truth Robert recommended the novels of Thomas Wolfe. I thought he was a wonderful writer on the grand scale. *Look Homeward, Angel* still haunts me, I felt such real sympathy for the predicaments of the Gant family who reminded me so strongly of life in our own home in Edinburgh.

> And again, again, in the old house I feel beneath my tread the creak of the old stair, the worn rail, the white washed walls, the feel of the darkness and the house asleep, and think, 'I was a child here; here the stairs, and here was darkness; this was I, and here is time.'
>
> Thomas Wolfe, *The Return of Buck Gavin*

There I was, in some obscure provincial digs transported back to 176 Fountainbridge, tiptoeing down those dark stairs once again into the morning darkness to start my milk round.

I went on to *A Movable Feast by Ernest Hemingway*. I read Russian novels by

Turgenev and Tolstoy's *War and Peace*. I got through three volumes of Proust's *Remembrance of Times Past*, but balked at the next four. There were a lot of references that I didn't understand, but I ploughed through most things before moving on to another book. I had to buy a big dictionary and look up words all the time. I worked my way through Shakespeare and Dickens. I tried T.E. Lawrence, though I never finished *The Seven Pillars of Wisdom*.

By the time *South Pacific* reached Sheffield, my book of the week was James Joyce's *Ulysses*. The librarian raised her eyebrows and asked me how old I was, but she was only joking. The book was restricted and not out on the public shelves. Since it was up to the discretion of the librarian she allowed me to sign the book out. *Ulysses* was retrieved from the stacks and handed to me wrapped in a plain cover. All this fuss made a big impression on me and I wondered how rules like that were made. Back in my digs when I finally opened the book, I saw that the last half a dozen pages were still uncut. So I was the first person ever to have read that copy. I had to take a razor to slice open those final pages. It was a struggle enough to get through *Ulysses* without that, though I had to admit that it added a certain extra frisson to Molly Bloom's monologue, as I turned the now separated pages down to its last 'Yes'.

Above: The actor-director Robert Henderson played Captain George Brackett, the head of the US base. Off stage this remarkable man changed my life, as he steered me, step by step, towards a career in acting.

Opposite: On the ropes as Mountain McLintock in Alvin Rakoff's live BBC television production of *Requiem for a Heavyweight*, 1957.

I was a Flower of the mountain yes when I put the rose in my hair like the Andalusian girls used or shall I wear a red yes and how he kissed me under the Moorish wall and I thought well as well him as another and then I asked him with my eyes to ask again yes and then he asked me would I yes to say yes my mountain flower and first I put my arms around him yes and drew him down to me so he could feel my breasts all perfume yes and his heart was going like mad and yes I said yes I will Yes.

And to think there was still *Finnegans Wake* to come.

Getting through these books and engaging with them was hugely important to me. The fact that I read them, learning new words as I went along, greatly increased my confidence and self-esteem. It gave a balance to my life and a better identity, just as body-building had done for me physically at an earlier time.

In the theatre Robert encouraged me to be a second understudy, to learn the part and shadow the actor who was the first call. He encouraged me to see plays at matinées on my free afternoons. I began to hang out with actors and realised how articulate they all were. When the part fell vacant the ever helpful Robert had me promoted from the chorus line to the speaking role of Lieutenant Buzz Adams. What a thrill it gave me on stage that first night, stepping forward to inform Robert as Captain Brackett that the Japanese had just landed in the Pacific. I felt at last I was now on my way to becoming an actor myself.

When the *South Pacific* tour ended I found how hard it was to be an out-of-work actor. Once again the all-providing Robert stepped forward, offering me small parts in three productions he was directing at Richmond's Q Theatre. I started to take on bit parts in films, but the creative roles for actors in those days were in what we are not allowed to call today, the golden age of television.

By the end of the Fifties a number of innovative Canadian directors were working for the independent commercial television network as competition to the BBC. They had no problems with new faces or, more importantly for me, new voices. When Jack Palance dropped out of Alvin Rakoff's *Requiem for a Heavyweight*, Rakoff went out on a limb to cast me in the leading role of Mountain McClintock. The BBC reluctantly contracted me for £35. It was my first major role. The play was a hit, with rave reviews in the popular press. Even *The Times* conceded that I 'displayed a shambling and inarticulate charm'.

This wouldn't be the last time I would be thankful to a talented Canadian.

2 MACBETH
Mac Bethad mac Findláich 1005-1057

History, Stephen said, is a nightmare from which I am trying to awake.

James Joyce, *Ulysses*

I was in bed one weekend morning when the phone rang and in my half-awake state I was offered the title role in a television production of *Macbeth* in Canada. The fee would be $500 Canadian, which was generous by early-Sixties standards.

Of all the plays in the world, Shakespeare's major tragedy is the only one that dares not speak its name. So deeply drenched in sorcery is this occult masterpiece that even today actors shiver superstitiously if anyone dares to say its title on a theatre stage. Coyly the acting profession refers obliquely to *Macbeth* as 'the Scottish Play'. For centuries it has been considered an unlucky work, with injury, fire and other trouble following in its wake. It seems that the evil portrayed is drawn so powerfully that it still threatens anyone who acts in it. There are those who still believe that the witches' song has the power of working evil, though we know this was just an invention to flatter a witch-fixated king four hundred years ago.

Dreaded myths began to circle around performances of *Macbeth* from its opening night in 1605, when the young Hal Berridge, playing Lady Macbeth, literally died on stage, or so it's told. Following a staging in 1672, the deed was well and truly done when Macbeth picked up his less than visionary dagger and plunged it into the very real heart of the poor actor playing King Duncan. At a London performance in 1703 the heavens opened as thunder and lightning ushered in a tempestuous storm, which raged on through the night. Even Verdi warned the impresario of the Teatro San Carlo in Naples that his opera *Macbeth* either did generally well or could be a complete disaster. Then, after fans protested when the role of Macbeth went to the English actor William Charles Macready

Playing Alexander the Great in Terence Rattigan's *Adventure Story* in Rudolph Cartier's BBC production of 1961. 'Who is to succeed me to the throne of Asia?' Alexander asks at the play's end. 'Who shall I condemn to death?'

Born in Austria in 1904 as Rudolph Katscher, Cartier became an outstanding director with over 120 memorable productions to his credit for the BBC.

instead of the American Edwin Forrest, a riot erupted outside New York's Astor Theatre, causing over twenty deaths. It's also said that Lincoln read *Macbeth* the night before his assassination in Washington's Ford's Theatre.

Every actor seems to have suffered injuries, or has a bad story to tell when playing Macbeth. Ralph Richardson told me that if actors refused to perform in one of his productions he would spread the word that they had acted in his own disastrous *Macbeth*. The young Laurence Olivier was nearly taken out when a lead weight crashed down from the lighting rig at an Old Vic rehearsal of *Macbeth* on the eve of World War II. Duncan and two of the three witches in John Gielgud's wartime production died in the Blitz. Charlton Heston's tights burst into flames at an outdoor performance in Bermuda when a strong breeze got up; a well-wisher had given them a dip in paraffin. Many performances of the play have been disasters in themselves. When Peter O'Toole, covered in bloody 'Kensington Gore', proclaimed that the deed was done to the echoing siren of a passing ambulance outside the Old Vic, it was the last straw for an audience already stunned by Bryan Forbes's concept of *Macbeth* as a Victorian melodrama. Never mind, I thought, what good luck it would be to have the challenge of playing the lead in Shakespeare's notorious tragedy of bad luck.

'Just fly me there and find me a room with a good bathroom,' I asked, without checking anything with my agent.

For this offer I had to thank a young Canadian director, Paul Almond. Paul had been head-hunted by Granada in Manchester to direct *The Dumb Waiter*, Harold Pinter's first televised play. He had played a leading part in student theatre when he was up at Oxford, where he had seen a remarkable performance of *Macbeth* at the Playhouse. He had the idea of casting a Scot to play Macbeth, which back then

As King Pentheus in *The Bacchae* by Euripides at the Oxford Playhouse, 1959, directed by Minos Volanakis.

Opposite: To achieve this realistic severed head of King Pentheus meant a gruelling session with my face buried in plaster.

was considered rather radical. When he asked his agent, the ex-actress and playwright Elspeth Cochrane, to help him, she recommended me on the strength of my television performance as Alexander the Great.

One of my great regrets had been being unable to play Macbeth in Joan Littlewood's touring company when my girlfriend was dangerously ill. So I leapt at this second chance, dropped everything and flew to Canada.

Macbeth is a challenge even for the most experienced actor. On the plane I began to plot out what I could bring to the role. It was certainly a far cry from my first night on stage singing as a Seabee in *South Pacific*. But in the ensuing years I had taken on increasingly complex roles. I had come through the petrifying terror of acting in live television dramas, an altogether unnerving experience, totally unknown to actors today. For Alvin Rakoff's live TV production of *Requiem for a Heavyweight* I had drawn on everything I knew about boxing and body-building, which gave me my first real success. My first Shakespearean role was the challenge of playing Hotspur to Robert Hardy's Prince Hal in the first four episodes of the BBC's memorable series *The Age of Kings*. Based on *Henry IV Part I*, this ground-breaking series was a trial by fire for any actor, as those episodes were all transmitted live. I played Count Vronsky opposite Claire Bloom as Anna Karenina, most movingly directed by the outstanding Rudolph Cartier.

Around this time I was cast in a stage production of *Anna Christie*, Eugene O'Neill's play which Garbo had made famous in her first talkie. The title role was played by the accomplished Australian actress Diane Cilento, who had studied at RADA. Diane told me how she was still benefiting from movement classes devised by the Swedish dancer Yat Malgrem and she urged me to join her. Yat had been a dancer with the Kurt Joos Ballet Company and had studied with the Hungarian Rudolf Laban, who had developed a theory of movement and was a pioneer of time-and-motion study.

Although at first I was only able to afford floor lessons three times a week, Yat's approach was a revelation to me. Up to that moment I had never had a single acting lesson. My training as a body-builder greatly helped me play the many tough parts I was offered. But here was a system applicable to all roles. Yat had developed Laban's teachings into a method to which he gave the rather odd name of 'cohesive terminology'. This articulated the factors actors need in creating a character into the four main categories of Weight, Space, Time and Flow. Learning about the dynamics of Weight, the Space which you occupy, the reach of Time and the emotion of Flow soon provided me with the essentials in creating a character, and I have used his system ever since.

I applied Yat's technique to good effect in a repertory season at the Oxford Playhouse in 1959. The talented Greek-born director Minos Volanakis cast me as the young King Pentheus in *The Bacchae* by Euripides. The part called for my dismemberment in the last act, which meant that a plaster cast had to be taken of my head. When my body parts were carried on stage and my severed head was held aloft on a pole, a roar of anguished disbelief erupted from the pit. My murder had been all too realistic for an African visitor who left the theatre howling in abject terror.

I also played an Italian consul in the Pirandello play, *Vestire gli Ignudi* (literally, 'to dress the naked'), which Minos and Diane Cilento translated as *Naked* under the name of Simon Nedia, an anagram of their first names. I could never have played such roles without the depth of understanding instilled in me by Yat Malgrem.

Macbeth was a big part to learn in ten days, apart from its tough production schedule. When I arrived at the CBC building in Toronto there were eight plays being rehearsed all at once. I found that actors in Canada were paid to rehearse by the hour, like periods at school. This meant that you were seldom able to run your lines together with other actors, as they left one play to rehearse in another. This was unlike London, where as often as not you just hung around all day doing nothing.

To give my best I realised that I would have to allot myself a strict schedule of work. I would get up each morning at five to rehearse Macbeth in the shower, shouting my lines over the cascades of splashing water ricocheting off the tiles. I would then take the long walk to the studio, talking to no one, with the lines tumbling around my head. There was a corner café on the way where I often stopped for breakfast. One day I looked up and there was Len D'Agostino, an old friend from Leith Walk, Edinburgh.

'What on earth are you doing here?'

'I'm playing Macbeth for CBC,' I said, breaking my vow of silence.

Len thought nothing of that, though he knew enough about theatre superstitions not to wish me good luck in 'the Scottish Play'. Paul Almond kept close to Shakespeare's text, as the project was first conceived as a five-part education series for Canadian schools. He was very accommodating and accepted my idea of doing some of the key speeches as soliloquies, as though Macbeth were in a trance. With great ingenuity the Austrian set designer Rudi Dorn created gaunt abstract shapes, reminiscent of the Expressionist movies of Thirties Vienna.

He had been an architect there before the war and was a master at handling space and light. Paul had him create a great symbolic staircase and throne to give expression to the play's upward and downward action. When lit with raking light the menacing shadows fulfilled Paul's desolate vision of a primeval eleventh-century Scotland out on the edge of Dark Age Europe.

Paul had expected me to have studied *Macbeth* at school, like all schoolchildren do in Canada, but I had neither read the play before nor had I ever seen it performed. Paul liked that because he said that I had nothing to unlearn, unlike actors who come to the part having seen twenty-seven *Macbeth*s and want to base their performance on aspects of past productions. As I came to the role fresh I was open to Paul's suggestions and his ideas for setting the mood. With nothing to base Macbeth on I was free to think this way or that. I had grown my beard and began to reshape my physical bearing according to Yat Malgrem rules. Once I had learnt the lines (and it's one helluva part to learn) I would think through my performance. My only problem was that I then developed a vicious form of flu. Zoe Caldwell recommended a surefire Australian remedy of breathing in hot menthol and eucalyptus under a towel. But successful as her remedy was in clearing out my tubes, it had the drastic side effect of somehow blocking my remembered lines. Zoe was kind enough to judge my sometimes hesitant delivery as giving an extra dimension of considered thoughtfulness to my performance.

One night walking home dead-tired, muttering a long speech, I was dazzled by flashing lights and pulled over by the police. I had been taken for a bearded and perhaps demented vagrant. The sceptical traffic cops took some persuading to believe that in my present state I was really in Toronto to play Macbeth. The King of Scotland, I tried to assure them, was truly a man of peace.

This modestly funded *Macbeth* was an unforgettable experience. There I was in Canada, each day transported back to a bleak foreboding vision of my homeland,

Macbeth, 1961, with Zoe Caldwell as Lady Macbeth, Michael Blodgett as King Duncan and Powys Thomas as Malcolm. Originally produced for the school broadcast department of CBC and transmitted in five episodes in 1962, introduced by the director Paul Almond.

The director Paul Almond was an actor's director who used minimal sets and moody lighting to create symbolic levels of meaning. His first feature film *Isabel*, with Geneviève Bujold, initiated a new Canadian Cinema in the Sixties.

Although Paul has now retired from the cinema to concentrate on writing, his innovative television series *Seven-Up*, which he created and directed in the fifties, is still with us.

In the incident known as The Gowrie Conspiracy of 1600, John Ruthven, 3rd Earl of Gowrie is killed while trying to assassinate James VI, later James I of England. Or was it all just a put-up job by James?

Opposite: Raphael Holinshed's *Chronicles of England, Scotlande, and Irelande*, 1587.

preyed on by supernatural forces. Could Scotland ever have been so dark? Few can now imagine the historical reality of medieval Scotland, other than through the swirling myths of overpowering weirdness bestowed on it by Shakespeare through his legendary Macbeth. So powerful is his vision that the one Scots king the world knows is now remembered only as a murderous thug. To compound the gore, the one Scots Queen known abroad is Mary, whose dreadful execution was the subject for one of the world's first fiction films, a half-minute of Grand Guignol of 1895, for Edison's kinematograph company.

Back in London after the Canadian television production, Macbeth returned to haunt me. Knowing then so little about the history of my own country, I began to research the sources of Shakespeare's play. In a second-hand bookstore I picked up an old copy of the compendious Variorum Edition of *Macbeth*, exhaustively edited by the American Shakespearean scholar Horace Howard Furness. Here each line comes under the most intensive scrutiny. Scholar battles scholar over interpreting every fact. Pages are devoted to the 'Source of the Plot' and such questions as 'Was Shakespeare ever in Scotland?'

There is tantalising evidence of the comings and goings of English theatre troupes in Scotland in the late sixteenth century. We know that the Lord Chamberlain's Men, a troupe much favoured by King James, was playing in Aberdeen in 1597 when twenty-four witches were burnt at the stake for sorcery. The Scottish records single out the actor Laurence Fletcher as James's special favourite. But there is no mention of his colleague William Shakespeare. If the bard had never been to Scotland, he could have certainly learnt a lot from Fletcher. From the all-pervading sense of Highland gloom Shakespeare conjures up, and from the accuracy of all those place-names and descriptions that are strewn through the stage directions of *Macbeth*, it is hard not to imagine that Shakespeare crossed the Scottish border. Although he does have Inverness and Fife within a medieval stone's throw of each other, Shakespeare peppered his medieval play with intrigues that recall many incidents in late-sixteenth-century Scotland. Historians have speculated that both the cast and much of the action of *Macbeth* were drawn from the eerie goings-on around the court of James VI, the King of Scots. With such plotting and murder in high places, Scotland's recent past must have seemed to Shakespeare like just one bloody Jacobean drama before its time.

King James, believing that God had appointed him to rule England and Scotland, saw it as his divinely appointed role to defend his new united kingdoms. He became obsessed with witches, especially when a demonic pact was said to have been devised against him, 'that another might rule in his place'. When storms had forced back his young Queen Anne of Denmark in 1589, James imagined that witches had targeted her ship. The Devil's evil helpers can 'rayse stormes and tempestes in the aire, either upon land or sea', he wrote in *Daemonologie*, his three-part diatribe against sorcery in all its forms. So when Anne at last reached Scotland, James had two defenceless women rounded up as suspected witches and supervised their trial. 'Convicta et combusta' was their predictable sentence: to be burnt at the stake alive, as per the King's book. So, to please his majesty:

> Thunder and Lightning. Enter three witches.
> *Macbeth* I.i.

Apart from being tormented by the witches in his mind, James had lived through real times of terror. His father Henry, Lord Darnley, survived a bomb before being strangled in an Edinburgh back garden, when James was one year old. His mother was imprisoned by his aunt Queen Elizabeth in 1568 and eventually dispatched to the scaffold at Fotheringay in 1587. His cousin the Earl of Bothwell was condemned for scheming to kill him by witchcraft, and fled the country.

In 1582 when James was only sixteen he was kidnapped by William Ruthven, the ambitious 1st Earl of Gowrie, and held for ten months under house arrest. James was rescued and Ruthven was ordered to leave the country but was executed for high treason in 1584. In one of the more bizarre encounters of his final years in Scotland, James was invited by Alexander Ruthven to Gowrie House in Perth, where John Ruthven, the 3rd Earl of Gowrie, was said to be detaining a foreigner with a great deal of money. In James's authorised version (which was widely circulated after the event, but little believed) James was lured into a room, held at knifepoint, and cried for help, shouting 'Treason!' The King's armed escort, which just happened to be standing beneath his window at the time, raced up the turret stairs to save him. As they burst through the door, a hunting falcon flew off one of his defender's arms and began to flutter and circle the room, as Gowrie and his brother were stabbed to death. But stranger things were still to happen. Out of Gowrie's pocket fell a 'little close parchment bag, full of magical characters and words of enchantment'. Only when they were all removed did the stricken corpse begin to bleed. It was the final sign James needed to prove that Gowrie was a 'conjurer of devils'. The day itself, Tuesday 5 August 1600, would also be remembered in one of the greatest tragedies ever told.

OLD MAN
On Tuesday last
A falcon, towering in her pride of place
Was by a mousing owl hawk'd at and kill'd.
Macbeth II.iv. 11–13

Since the King owed Gowrie a considerable sum of money, there were few in Scotland who believed that he had been in any mortal danger. Many thought that the Gowrie Conspiracy (as it soon became known) was the King's revenge on the Ruthvens who he believed were not loyal to the Crown. It was no surprise that James ordered the House of Gowrie hauled down and the name Ruthven abolished for all time. This he did not quite achieve, either in fiction or in reality. Centuries later, rather spookily, Lord Ruthven would flutter back to blood-sucking life in the pages of *The Vampyre* written by John Polidori, the doctor to Lord Byron. Equally surprisingly, when my son Stéphane joined Sotheby's I met theirchairman, who turned out to be a living Earl of Gowrie. The rather Byronic-looking Alexander Patrick Greysteil Ruthven had inherited the title of the 2nd Earl of Gowrie. When asked about the tragedy of his murdered Scottish ancestor, Grey Gowrie shrugged off any family connection with those dark times in Scotland, maintaining firmly that his revived Gowrie title was 100 per cent pure Irish.

Within months of his coronation in 1603 James elevated his favourite theatre troupe, the Lord Chamberlain's Men, to the King's Men. The troupe inadvertently offended the monarch with *The Tragedy of Gowrie*, a play based on the events at the House of Gowrie. As the King's Men's principal playwright, surely Shakespeare must have been its author and, just as intriguing, since he was one of the most popular actors, how could Shakespeare not have resisted playing the role of the King himself? We shall never know. After two performances to full houses the curtain fell for good. It was said that the King was not amused and the play was banned.

The Tragedy of Gowrie was never performed again and no copy has survived. The play had breached the royal protocol, which then held that princes in their lifetime should never be portrayed on stage. Had the Gowrie tragedy been drawn too close to the royal bone? Had the King's conscience been reawakened with pangs of guilt over what had really happened that day at the House of Gowrie? If there were to be a Scottish play of treason to curry favour with the King of Scots on the English throne, it had better be distanced further back in time, Shakespeare must have thought. It was time for the bard to dust down his copy of Raphael Holinshed's *Chronicles*.

In Holinshed's *Chronicles of England, Scotlande, and Irelande*, first published in 1587, 'Makbeth' and 'Banquho' first encounter 'three weird sisters' who wear 'strange and wild apparell, resembling creatures of elder world', on their way

across the moor to visit King Duncan. 'All haile Makbeth, that herafter shalt be king of Scotland,' the third sister proclaims. Shakespeare renames the weird sisters as witches to impress King James, who republished *Daemonologie*, his extended book on witchcraft, the year before *Macbeth* was performed at court in 1605. Since James was proud of his descent from a long line of Scots kings including Banquo, his role in Duncan's murder, as described in Holinshed, is suppressed in Shakespeare's play. Holinshed's description of Macbeth's victory over the Danes is also dropped, since James's queen, Anne, was born in Denmark.

Holinshed's history of the Scots was loosely based on a much earlier Latin text by the Scots writer Hector Boethius, who filled many of his pages with spells and premonitions of dire dread. This supernatural element would chime with James, who believed that the purging of witches was as beneficial to society as psychiatry is today. After all, James had written his *Daemonologie* to refute *The Discovery of Witchcraft*, the first book in English to argue that a belief in witches was 'contrarie to reason, scripture and nature'. Its author, the Kent landowner Reginald Scot, had advanced the view that those who were thought to be possessed by demons, and therefore accused of practising witchcraft, were probably just the victims of mental illness. The same disturbing condition could equally explain the fanaticism

Opposite: *Macbeth and the Witches*, Henry Fuseli, (Johann Heinrich Fussli), 1741-1825.

Below: *Macbeth*, John Martin, 1789-1854.

of their accusers. Such an enlightened attitude held no favour with the king, who ordered all copies of Scot's book burnt, and instructed Parliament to toughen up the punitive laws against all witches.

Given Shakespeare's skill in wrapping topics of the day back into a distant past, the tragedy of *Macbeth*, set in an ancient half-remembered Scotland, would surely make for an intriguing diversion for the proudest Stuart king. The idea that Shakespeare's *Macbeth* is not a play of the eleventh century at all, but a real-life Jacobean tragedy pivoting on the King, gave me the idea of directing a film set in those uncertain times of religious rivalry, when witches stalked the land, at least in the mind of James.

I discussed with the writer Eddie Boyd how we would bring out the intrigues and politics of his reign that Shakespeare had embedded in *Macbeth*. Eddie had a refreshingly wry take on history and had stamped his own surrealist style on a number of visually evocative plays for BBC Scotland. He was a formidable scotcher of myths and had recently caused uproar in a Fife fishing village with his television play *The Lower Largo Sequence* – right from its very first lines.

Robinson Crusoe, rumour is rife, was born in Lower Largo in Fife.
About his sex life it's rather bleak,
He had a Man Friday, but what did he do every other day of the week?

Eddie and I had just begun to draft our approach when Roman Polanski leapt ahead of us with his own blood-drenched cinematic vision of a Dark Age *Macbeth*. And so our own very different brainchild fell sadly stillborn on the blasted heath.

No one can diminish Shakespeare's genius in the writing of his greatest tragedy. But I learnt early on that the bard's brilliant depiction of the evil self-destructing 'butcher and his fiend-like Queen' had maligned the real Macbeth, who was considered a most capable and resourceful king for his times. During his reign of seventeen years, Scotland remained a far more peaceful country than England. Unlike Edward the Confessor, who was then trapped holding down his rebellious warlords, Macbeth had even made a pilgrimage to Rome, where, according to the Irish monk Marianus Scotus, he had 'scattered alms like seed'.

Legends die as hard in Scotland as they do in the American West. 'You're not going to use the story?' Jimmy Stewart asks the newspaperman in *The Man Who Shot Liberty Valance*, one of my favourite John Ford Westerns. 'This is the West, sir,' replies Carlton Young of the *Shinbone Star*. 'When the truth becomes legend, print the legend.' Just like in the Highlands, I could add. When Shakespeare printed the legend of Macbeth, it too became fact.

So Cawdor Castle, built over three hundred years after the reign of Macbeth, continues to attract its hordes of puzzled visitors. The late Earl of Cawdor used to wave a blunderbuss at anyone who dared mention Macbeth crossing his drawbridge. Yet tourists today still follow the false trail of fictional tragedy to Cawdor Castle. Meanwhile, only a trickle of the better-informed ever reach the woody grove of nearby Lumphanan, which marks the spot where the real Macbeth fell bravely in battle around 1056.

While I was pursuing my ill-fated *Macbeth* I met Alastair Dunnett, writer and charismatic editor of the *Scotsman* newspaper, who would soon become one of the driving forces in the early days of our Scottish International Education Trust. His wife Dorothy was by then the established author of a series of highly successful – especially in the USA – historical novels. After six publishers in London had knocked back Dorothy's first novel, Alastair wrote to his New York friend Lois Cole, who had discovered Margaret Mitchell and her *Gone with the Wind*. 'How would you like to see an astounding story?' he wrote to Lois, 'written by the wittiest woman in Scotland?'

A dozen or so successful historical novels later, Dorothy was asked by her American publisher for a novel featuring a famous Scot and suggested either Mary Queen of Scots or Charles Edward Stuart. Since so much had been written about these two rather tragic figures, Dorothy's proposal was to rescue the historical Macbeth from his maligned anti-hero status of Shakespeare's greatest tragedy. Having signed a contract to complete it within a year, she soon discovered that it was an era few historians had ever written about.

So began an extraordinary journey of discovery through libraries and archives at home and abroad. Ferreting through manuscripts and poetry in the UK, Italy, Austria, Normandy and the Celtic Library at Harvard, Dorothy's richest find came when she realised the importance of the much overlooked contemporary Orkney sagas of the Vikings. When she found that there were so many parallels in the life of Macbeth's half-brother, the mighty Earl Thorfinn, she came to the controversial conclusion that everything made perfect sense if they were one and the same person. After six years' work, her own saga *King Hereafter* was an instant success and hailed by many as her masterpiece.

Historians were divided. Their comments ranged from the dismissive 'utterly preposterous' to the more tentative 'intriguingly possible'. The licence of a novelist can sometimes get closer to the truth. If her findings are judged as fiction, her historical research, unlike Shakespeare's, was at least founded in the right historical period. As soon as I read *King Hereafter* I could see it as a startling saga for a movie, and I still do.

Left: Lumphanan, North East Scotland, the grove where the historical King Macbeth fell in battle around 1056.

Right: Cawdor Castle, fourteenth century. Although this castle was built over three centuries after the reign of King Macbeth, Shakespeare chose to feature it in *Macbeth*. 'I wish the bard had never written his damned play!' said the 5th Earl of Cawdor, who was known to repel tourists who mentioned Shakespeare.

Because Shakespeare's play is so full of sorcery, unbridled ambition and murder most foul, it has coloured the wider world's impression of Scottish history. All that is hardly a boost to Scottish morale. I even think that the fictional tragedy of Macbeth's success in failure continues to haunt us today in Scotland. This didn't go unnoticed on the thousandth anniversary of Macbeth's birth in 2005. Alex Johnstone, the Member of the Scottish Parliament whose constituency includes the battlefield where the historical Macbeth was slain, attempted to raise a motion in the Scottish Parliament to lay the evil myths to rest. His initiative to clear the name of the historical Macbeth managed to raise only a handful of votes.

Of course, catastrophes lose nothing in the telling. In this extract from *The Simpsons* even Homer nods:

Ian McKellen: Please, take these free tickets to my play!
Homer: What? What play?
IM: We thespians believe it's bad luck to mention the name of this particular play out loud.
H: You mean *Macbeth*? (A car splashes McKellen.)
IM: Quiet, you plundering fool! You'll curse us all!
H: What, by saying *Macbeth*? (An anvil falls on McKellen's foot.)
IM: OW! Stop saying it!
H: Saying what?
IM: *Macbeth*!! Oh, now I've said it. (McKellen is hit by lightning.)
Bart: This is cool! *Macbeth, Macbeth, Macbeth.* (McKellen is hit by lightning each time Bart says *Macbeth*.)
Marge: Bart, stop saying *Macbeth*! (McKellen is hit by lightning.)
Lisa: Mom, you said *Macbeth*. (McKellen is hit by lightning.)
H: Mr Macbeth, I'm really sorry. (McKellen is hit by lightning.)
IM: That's quite alright. You didn't know.
Bart: Good luck.
IM: It's also bad luck to say that. (Sign falls on top of Ian.)

In 1996 *The Simpsons* hit the Edinburgh Festival in Rick Miller's award-winning *MacHomer*, in which he played a one-man *Macbeth*, impersonating the entire cast in a non-stop cascade of Simpson voices.

This tour de force injects Matt Groening's wry critique of our contemporary world into Shakespeare's bloody tale. Homer Simpson attempts to play Macbeth, but hunger makes him stumble on his soliloquies. 'Is this a dagger I see before me?' he falters. 'Or a pizza?' 'I wear the pants in this family,' says Marge as Lady Macbeth, who fares no better. Krusty the Clown plays the porter, and the egregious Montgomery Burns, descended from the great-great-grandson of Robert Burns's dog, appropriately dies the death as Duncan. With such memorable cross-platform lines as 'He really put the whoa! in Banquo!' how can such a double whammy of a show fail? D'oh! Macbeth's sorcery will never die.

Miller returned to the Edinburgh Festival in 1999 with an even slicker production of *MacHomer*, using smoke, videos and back-projected portraits of the

Simpsons in sixteenth-century garb. But when he noticed that Matt Groening was giving a masterclass at the Television Festival along with his screenwriters, he was more than alarmed over what the Fox Broadcasting copyright lawyers might make of his Simpson impersonations. His worries were quickly dispelled when he fell in with a Simpson's cast party. 'Matt Groening was extremely kind,' Miller said, 'and gave me his blessing', and the show continued on the Fringe to packed houses.

In 1735 when Thomas Blackwell, professor of Greek at Aberdeen University, published *An Enquiry into the Life and writings of Homer* he revealed the importance of the ancient bard to the thinkers of the Scottish Enlightenment. Nearly three hundred years later at Edinburgh's Napier University, Alistair McCleery, professor of literature, offers a lecture on 'Having the Donut and Eating it: Self-Reflexivity in *The Simpsons*'. We live in interesting times.

In 2003, the 'Scottish Play' featured in 'The Regina Monologues' episode of *The Simpsons*, directed by Mark Kirkland and written by John Swartzwelder.

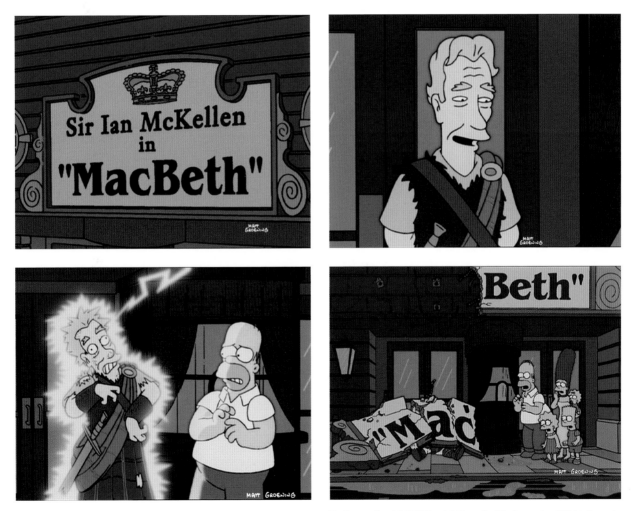

The Simpsons™ and © 2008 Twentieth Century Fox Film Corporation. All Rights Reserved.

3 SCOTCH MYTHS AND REALITIES
Fragments of ancient poetry

O Caledonia! stern and wild
Meet nurse for a poetic child!
Land of brown heath and shaggy wood
Land of the mountain and the flood…

This was Sir Walter Scott's take on Scotland and he was some poetic child. As for me, well, 'stern and wild' – yes. If you were born here, out on the edge of Europe, you had better be made of stern stuff and look on the wild side.

The early Irish chronicle, the *Lebor Gabála Érenn* (*The Book of Invasions*), tells how Scota, the daughter of a pharaoh, married a Babylonian called Nel. Their son Goídel Glas was expelled from Egypt, around the time of the exodus of the Israelites. After many wanderings Goídel settled in the south of Spain before reaching Ireland to become the ancestor of all Gaels, even down to inventing the Gaelic language. There's a Scottish version of Scota and 'Gaedel' Glas in the *Scotichronicon*, a history of Scotland written in Latin by Walter Bower, the abbot of Inchcolm Abbey, in the 1440s. Scota gave her name to a marauding Ulster tribe known as the Scotii by the Romans, who never managed to placate them. Although the Romans never colonised Ireland, the Scotii, or Scots, successfully colonised the Western Islands and Highlands, where Gaelic is still spoken to this day. In the ninth century, when the Scots under King Kenneth MacAlpin subdued the indigenous Picts and unified both east and west, the whole country then became known as Scotland.

Because I grew up in Edinburgh during the Depression of the 1930s I've always considered adversity, rather than necessity, to be the mother of invention. To survive in Scotland from the earliest times you were driven to invent. Who, for instance, on a sunny Greek island, would have had much need for a raincoat?

On the wet west side of Scotland the mac was just destined to be invented by a man called Macintosh.

My mother Effie was a Maclean from the the island of Mull in the Gaelic-speaking Western Highlands where the going was often tough and few knew what the future held for them. If you were really worried, and knew your Scottish history, you could always try Taghairm. This ancient Gaelic rite required wrapping yourself up in a fresh bullock's hide, before plunging in behind a roaring waterfall. As you showered you might be lucky enough to hear a Celtic oracle proclaim your future. If you emerged unenlightened but soaking wet, well, it probably didn't matter too much, for the chances were it would be raining anyway. After all, Scotland is still the land of the mountain and the flood and nobody else does wet like we do wet. The Scots language is drenched in a deluge of 'weet', 'weetie', 'wat' and so many words of sheer onomatopoeic wetness, from the light drizzle of a 'dreep' to a plummeting 'dooncome'.

It's probably no coincidence that the earliest traces left by our ancestors over five thousand years ago are carved rings closely resembling the radiating ripples of raindrops on water. They left us no image of themselves, only such incised markings as these circular patterns. If they don't represent raindrops, what else could have been in the minds of those early people who carved so many concentric rings on the rocks of Achnabreck on the wet west coast of Scotland?

James Hutton's observations of the atmosphere at his Berwickshire farm led to the development of his 'Theory of Rain' in the late eighteenth century. Hutton proved that the amount of moisture held in the air grew as the temperature rose. He then observed that when the temperature dropped, as it often tends to do in Scotland, the air released its moisture. And that of course meant yet more rain.

Today we know Hutton not so much for his theories of wetness, but for being the father of modern geology, based on the literally ground-breaking study of his *Theory of the Earth*. 'Man is not satisfied, like the brute, in seeing things as they are,' he wrote. 'He seeks to know how things have been, and what they are to be.' Farming apart, Hutton was a medical doctor whose long-term patient was the Earth. He saw that the fertility of soil depended upon its loose state, from the particles, which arose from the erosion of rock. He turned his mind to such imponderables as how the Earth began. Hutton had grasped that the present was the key to the past. He saw that the Earth had risen from the wreck of a former world. He looked at mountains for signs. He read their rocks as evidence of past incidents, frozen in time. Lavas, fossilised ripple marks of ancient tides, were for him chapters in the Earth's history, extending back into the abyss of deepest time.

Hutton realised that forces of nature, like erosion and mountain building, were never-ending. 'Speak to the Earth and it shall speak to thee,' he said. 'Time is to Nature endless and as nothing.' Hutton's field observations challenged Bishop Ussher's precise dating of the world's creation to 4004 BC, and were judged heretical in England. Hutton propelled Earth's beginnings back into the furthest reaches of time. 'I see no vestige of a beginning,' he famously wrote, 'and no prospect of an end.' These words should be carved in huge letters on a cliff of

Edinburgh University's School of Scottish Studies is still wringing out Scots words for every shade of rain from Highland and Lowland skies.

scuff **seepin** shore **shour** skail **skiff** smirr smizzle **smuchter** smook **sowp** spark **spate** spleiter **sump** sup **swirl** teem **thicht** upple **wak** feechie **hail** watter **lash** leck **mak** mug **outpour** pani **peel** rushich **pelsh** pewl **thunder-plump** plowtery **plump** plunge **plype** pour **rap** rash **saft** scapple **scour** scowder **spleiter** skimmer **skite** snifter **spleuterie** sklent **bletter** drabble **spitter** blatter **driffle** seeper **ding** lauchin **pelsh** leash **plooterie** dag **pish-oot** dawk **deval** drabble **drow** spitter **smizzle** ure **weet** weetie **wat** bicker **black** weet **brack** brash **dash** dish **dissle** dooncome **drap** dreep **dribble** driggle **eident** evendoon

Opposite: The Falls of Foyers, Loch Ness, Chromolithograph, 1900s.

Top: The Ship of Scota from Bower's *Scotichronicon*, 1440s.

Bottom: Achnabreck, Argyllshire: the largest collection of Neolithic concentric ring marks to be found in the British Isles, around 3000 BC.

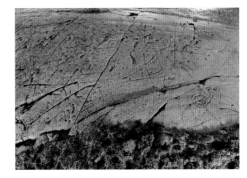

Lewisian gneiss in the Hebrides. Around 2300 million years old, these strata are now known to be amongst the oldest rocks in Europe, half the age of the Earth itself. Such free thinking was the hallmark of the Scottish Enlightenment, which attracted scholars from England and abroad to study in Scotland. What Isaac Newton did for space, James Hutton had now done for time.

Hutton made a number of geological forays round Scotland collecting evidence for his theory, accompanied by his brother-in-law, the artist John Clerk of Penicuik. Illustrating what Hutton saw, Clerk's drawings combined art with science in the true spirit of the Scottish Enlightenment. The poet Robert Burns could fuse lyrics with the heat of scientific discoveries and turn them into popular songs. 'My Luve's Like A Red, Red Rose' pledges love back into the far reaches of geological eternity:

> As fair art thou, my bonnie lass,
>   So deep in luve am I:
> And I will luve thee still, my dear,
>   Till a' the seas gang dry.

'Till a' the seas gang dry' could hardly have better described James Hutton's cycle of deserts in geological eras. Although Burns and Hutton shared seemingly different worlds, such a coming together of poetic imagination and scientific inquiry typified the era.

Opposite: Aeneas Silvius Piccolomini visits King James I in 1435, as imagined by Pintoricchio, whose fabulous depiction of the Scottish Court in the Siena Cathedral Library, c.1509, portrays Scotland as a nation of the imagination.

An equally fantastic vision of Scotland is this one dreamt up by Vincente Minnelli and his Holywood set designers when Tommy Albright (Gene Kelly) meets the bridegroom Charlie Chisholm Dalrymple (Jimmy Thompson) in the MGM musical, *Brigadoon*, of 1954. The reality of Scotland lies off-screen and off-fresco.

Till a' the seas gang dry, my dear,
   And the rocks melt wi' the sun:
O I will luve thee still, my dear,
   While the sands o' life shall run.

'And the rocks melt wi' the sun.' What leaps of millennia are summoned here, extending love far into the future, a cyclical repeat of those molten magmas of the Jurassic which Hutton determined had made the rocky crags and Edinburgh's Arthur's Seat. 'No prospect of an end', indeed.

Thoughts, then, could soar across disciplines. There were no boundaries or compartments between the arts and sciences. Restricting bulkheads, the poet Hugh MacDiarmid would say two centuries later, are only useful if your ship is sinking.

Despite its climate, visitors were attracted to Scotland. And there were always those who came to foment a little trouble with neighbouring England. This was certainly the reason why the Italian Aeneas Silvius Piccolomini led a delegation to the court of King James I in the stormy winter of 1435. Out on the edge of old Europe Scotland was then an almost legendary land. Piccolomini had read up on some of the country's more bizarre myths and knew that Scots enjoyed a conscience-free alternative to fish on Fridays. It was thought that those strange beaked crustaceans, which still to this day are called goose barnacles, sprang from tree cones falling on Scottish rivers before hatching into flying geese. After all, no one had ever seen those geese nesting and who would have known then that they were annual immigrants from Canada?

Piccolomini's visit failed to persuade King James to invade England. He returned to Italy and became the first humanist Pope. As Pius II he transformed his hometown of Corsignano, near Siena, into an ideal Renaissance city and its grateful citizens renamed it Pienza in his honour. Siena Cathedral built a library to receive his gift of books and commissioned frescoes to celebrate the key chapters of the Pope's life. One of these pictures his visit to the court of King James in 1435. Painted by Pintoricchio and his assistants fifty years after the event, it is the earliest large-scale painting of Scotland we have. But could the court of James I in 1435 have ever been as luxurious as this artist's depiction, with the King attended by so many exotic courtiers?

The marble-columned palace framing jagged rocky crags capped by the spiky turrets of a Dracula-like castle, with groves of trees leading down to a stretch of water, looks more like a vision of Transylvania transposed to the Umbrian shores of Lake Trasimeno than the reaches of the Firth of Forth. Neither Pintoricchio nor his assistants had ever left Italy. So all the painters had to go on were descriptions of Scotland in Piccolomini's biography. Take away all those half-imagined elements and you see something like the undulating coastline of the Firth of Forth close to Edinburgh. It's a view that I should recognise, because I sailed from here when I joined the Royal Navy as a seventeen-year-old in 1947.

More than twenty years before Hutton's *Theory of the Earth* was read to the Royal Society of Edinburgh and twelve years before Sir Joseph Banks' expedition

The artist Pintoricchio would have read about the castles of the Forth from Piccolomini's biography. But his purple-turreted fantasy with those exotic spires high up on a cliff is a far cry from the reality of the much knocked-about castle of Rosyth. In his fresco he got the stretch of water of the Firth of Forth almost right. The hills are more or less in the correct place. I know them well because I sailed down river here when I joined the Royal Navy in 1947.

Pages 56/7: *A loch north of Hadrian's Hall,* Walter Severn, 1830-1904. Along with poets and writers, Macpherson's Ossian enraptured artists to shroud our perceptions of the Highlands and the Western islands forever in romantic mists, like this scene, presumably of Loch Coruisk on the Isle of Skye.

'discovered' the architectural wonder of Fingal's Cave, an imaginative but headstrong young Highland schoolmaster called James Macpherson transported the Irish mythological character Fiuhn MacCoul from medieval Ulster to Scotland's Western Isles in his *Fragments of Ancient Poetry*. In this collection of ancient Gaelic tales published in 1760 Macpherson renamed the Irish hero Fingal, and Oisín, his blind harp-playing teller of tales, became Ossian. Together Ossian and Fingal would soon make waves far beyond the rocky columns of Fingal's Cave, to help usher in the Romantic Age. The world seemed ready for an epic from the North, for here was an alternative Atlantic pantheon of heroes to rival the Mediterranean gods of ancient Greece.

Macpherson grew up in Badenoch in the shadow of the Grampians in a Gaelic-speaking home, where storytelling and songs around the fireside celebrated ancient heroes. Since it was less than two days' march south from Culloden, where Prince Charles's army was massacred in 1746, his community experienced the savage reprisals wrought by the victorious army which set out to destroy Highland culture. In acts of Hanoverian high-handedness the government banned the wearing of kilts and the playing of bagpipes, and greatly restricted the speaking of Gaelic. The systematic repression of the Highland clans made a deep impression on the young Macpherson.

Macpherson's tutor at Aberdeen University was the pioneering classical scholar Thomas Blackwell, who had recently translated Homer's *Iliad* and was promoting the ancient bard as the greatest writer of all time. Macpherson would have been particularly struck to learn that Homer had written the *Iliad* in times of strife, when ancient Greece was also racked by war. Blackwell explained how this masterpiece had come down to us through generations of Greek storytellers and singers, before it was written down centuries after Homer's death. Surely here was a model to frame the fragments of the songs and stories he had listened to as a boy? Could Blackwell's eager student of the *Iliad* reconstruct these shards of Gaelic poems and augment them in the classical rolling prose of eighteenth-century English? Could Ossian become the Homer of the North?

Corruisk Skye
1894

James Macpherson, 1736-96, Scottish poet and author of the Ossian cycle, first published as *Fragments of Ancient Poetry Collected in the Highlands of Scotland*, in 1760.

Previous pages: *A loch north of Hadrian's Hall*, Walter Severn, 1830-1904. Along with poets and wrtiers, Macpherson's Ossian enraptured artists to shroud our perceptions of the Highlands and the Western islands forever in romantic mists, like this scene, presumably of Loch Coruisk on the Isle of Skye.

When Macpherson returned as a teacher to his Highland home in Badenoch he was now doubly driven to collect Gaelic tales. Through listening to stories retold around the hearths of crofting friends and hearing songs and music from Gaelic singers, harpers and pipers who passed through his broken Highland community, the wild seeds of Ossian were sown in the mind of the young man.

Macpherson enrolled at Edinburgh University to become a minister of the Kirk of Scotland. By chance, during a half-term break at a spa in the Border town of Moffat, he met John Home, one of Edinburgh's best-known literary figures. Hearing his Gaelic poetry, he encouraged Macpherson to English his 'wild Highland flowers' so that a wider world might gain something of their worth. Macpherson published his *Fragments of Ancient Poetry* in 1760 in English translation. His heroic tales set in the then remote mountain ranges of misty Scotland chimed with a deep yearning in the eighteenth century for a return to nature. Ossian, to whom he attributed the original stories, was seen to evoke the innocence of the philosopher Rousseau's primitive 'noble savage', a defenceless artist uncorrupted by the modern world and surrendering to his senses in preference to reason. The melancholic adventures of Ossian, set in a far distant past, were seen to extol the values of human goodness judged to be increasingly lacking in modern so-called civilisation.

In Scotland the elegiac tone of Ossian echoed the sense of loss felt among Macpherson's fellow Gaels. At the same time, Ossian instilled in Scots a pride in a distant and heroic past, far beyond the shame of the disastrous Jacobite Rising. With Ossian's success Gaelic culture entered the world stage for the first time.

Ossian has appeared amongst us as the greatest poetic revelation of our age. His work is sublime - the echo of a noble soul. This ancient bard appears to have been endowed by nature with an exquisite sensibility of heart. A sensibility prone to that tender melancholy which is so often attendant on great genius.

This glowing assessment from Hugh Blair, the first professor of Belles Lettres and Rhetoric at Edinburgh University and the minister of St Giles, catapulted Macpherson's reputation from the humble bothies of Badenoch to the coffee houses of London's Strand. Samuel Johnson, an admirer of Blair's sermons, objected to his Ossianic effusions. 'No poet knew better how to seize and melt the heart,' wrote Blair. 'Our rude Celtic bard has such virtuous feelings of every kind that not only the heroes of Homer, but even those of the polite and refined Virgil, are left far behind by those of Ossian.'

Dr Johnson found Macpherson's claims that he had recovered original third-century Gaelic texts on his Highland jaunts preposterous. When Johnson accused Macpherson of fakery, the impetuous Highlander hardly helped his cause by recklessly threatening the physically infirm doctor with his hefty cudgel.

Mr James Macpherson – I received your foolish and impudent letter. Any violence offered to me I shall do my best to repel, and what I cannot do for myself the law shall do for me. I hope that I shall never be deterred from detecting what I think a cheat by the menaces of a ruffian. What would you have me retract? I thought your book an imposture. I think so still. For this opinion I have given my reasons to the public, which I dare you to refute. Your rage I defy. Your abilities, since your Homer, are not formidable; and what I hear of your morals induces me to pay regard not to what you shall say, but to what you shall prove. You may print this if you will − [signed] Sam. Johnson.

Johnson's dismissal still echoes to this day in Britain, where Ossian is mostly banished to the bookshelves of irrelevant curiosities. This has never been the case abroad, either then or now. 'Ossian has superseded Homer in my heart,' said the doomed hero to his lover in *The Sorrows of Young Werther*, Goethe's hugely successful sad romantic fiction. Rejected by the beautiful Charlotte, Werther is hastened to his end by reading Ossian crouching on the rocks above a waterfall. 'Where is the bard,' he quotes to his lover, 'where is the illustrious son of Fingal? He will walk over my tomb.' Charlotte flees from Werther as his pistol fires. The shot ricocheted round Europe, as distraught young men in love killed themselves, clutching their leather-bound volumes of Ossian.

'I am not ashamed to own that I think this rude Bard of the North the greatest poet that ever existed,' Thomas Jefferson wrote from America. 'Merely for the pleasure of reading his works, I am become desirous of learning the language in which he sung, and of possessing his songs in their original form. Mr Macpherson, I think, informs us he is possessed of the original.'

Jefferson would not be alone in claiming Ossian as the greatest poet of all time. Composers too fell under the seductive spell of the ancient bard. Schubert's Ossian lieder led to such melancholic odes as 'Darthula's Dirge' by Brahms, which soon tolled their doom and gloom through the drawing-rooms of Victorian Europe. The twenty-year-old Felix Mendelssohn was so entranced by all things Ossianic that he travelled by coach, cart and steamship to the Western Isles. There on stormy seas approaching Staffa, the seasick composer set down the opening bars of his Hebrides Overture. Without Ossian, could Mendelssohn ever have dreamt up his haunting theme, forever evoking those waves rolling relentlessly into Fingal's Cave?

That a future president of the United States sought to learn Gaelic, in order to read Ossian in the original, was an extraordinary compliment. But Jefferson's request presented Macpherson with a serious problem. He was possessed of the originals, but they were mostly works of his own originality. He had set what word-of-mouth fragments of Gaelic poetry he had found in the Highlands and combined them with passages transcribed from surviving manuscripts. These he then framed in a rhythmically rolling prose of his own invention, much in the style of the King James VI's translation of the Bible, or of Blackwell's recent translations of Homer's *Iliad*.

'The eagerness with which these poems have been received abroad, is a recompense for the coldness with which a few have affected to treat them at home,' wrote an aggrieved Macpherson in a preface to his Ossianic tales towards the end of his life. He had some reason to be bitter. Apart from the impact of his epics

abroad, a strong case can be made for Macpherson as an oral archaeologist, disinterring Gaelic verses from folk memories. This was at a time when the very existence of the language was under threat; some of the fragments he wrote down might otherwise have been lost for ever.

Linking medieval fragments with classical prose of his own invention was surely just what Robert Adam had achieved at the same time in architecture. The wonder of Culzean, perched high on a rocky Ayrshire coast, was re-invented by incorporating classical interiors within the fragments of a derelict medieval castle and capping them with mock defensive battlements.

What was once the original castle of Culzean's dank and gloomy courtyard Adam transformed into a sunny oval staircase, which rose elegantly in an unprecedented curve to a classically detailed circular drawing-room above. Here classical motifs, derived by Adam from Hadrian's Villa outside Rome, punctuated the windows to frame the islands of the Clyde ready to catch the Atlantic's setting sun. Surely this classical treatment of a medieval past was just what Macpherson had achieved with Ossian. Yet who has ever called Adam's unprecedented fusion of the classical and the romantic a fake or a forgery, as London literati have disparaged Macpherson's Ossian?

Ossian became central to Sir James Clerk's vision of Penicuik House. Following his father Sir John Clerk's success in building Mavisbank, the original dream of the great collector and amateur architect was to fill its spacious rooms and ceilings with paintings of classical themes, and to this end he sent two young and promising Edinburgh artists, John and Alexander Runciman, to Rome. But when Alexander returned (sadly, Sir John died in Naples) all classical themes for its Great Hall were abandoned for the newly discovered 'Homer of the North'.

Ossian's Hall survives today only in a few sketches and watercolours, because a devastating fire consumed Penicuik House at the turn of the nineteenth century. No more would the enthroned blind bard sing to his youths and maidens. Only the blackened husk survives today; Penicuik's windows now stare back as blinded eyes, its sense of loss as tragic as any tale of Ossian.

The fame of Ossian has largely faded from Scottish memory, yet his name today has crystallised in place-names scattered across the map of Scotland. There's Oisean's or Ossian's Mound; Carn Oisean or Ossian's Cairn; Rudha na h'Oisinne or Ossian's Point, and Loch Ossian. Clach Ossian, the Stone of Ossian, is a large erratic glacial block at the top of the Sma' Glen in Perthshire. Apart from the naming of natural features, monuments to the bard were erected, of which the Duke of Atholl's near Dunkeld was the most evocative. Visitors flocked from far and wide to experience Ossian's Hall's 'agreeable horror or pleasing melancholy'. On the banks of a rushing stream they would discover a romantic bridge spanning a rocky chasm leading to a classical temple above the cascading Falls of Braan. On entering the temple visitors would first find themselves in a small, dark chamber. As their eyes adjusted they would come face to face with a painting of the blind bard singing to Malvina, the wife of his son Oscar. Then, over the murmur of the falls, a tune called 'Ossian's Hall' would strike up on a fiddle. It was the cue for a startling surprise, as Calvin Colton, an American visitor, describes: 'On a sudden,

Opposite above: Culzean Castle, the medieval fortified keep of the Kennedys on the Ayrshire coast before 1772.

Below: Culzean Castle, as re-envisioned by Robert Adam for the Earl of Cassilis, 1777.

How does Adam's classical re-invention of Culzean's medieval fragments differ from Macpherson's achievement in extending his fragments of Gaelic poetry with the classical prose of his own invention?

This Victorian watercolour of Ossian's Hall in Penicuik House gives some hint of Runciman's twelve dazzlingly painted ceiling panels celebrating Ossianic themes. Runciman's Great Hall of Ossian became the instant marvel of the Scottish Enlightenment.

The Hermitage, Dunkeld, on the River Braan. This engraving, after a pastel by George Walker, from James Cririe's *Scottish Scenery*, 1803, depicts the romantic bridge leading to the small classical temple of the Hermitage which was converted and renamed 'Ossian's Hall'.

Opposite, left: Calum Colvin based his 2008 installation in Ossian's Hall on his inventive cycle of innovative photo-collages, Fragments of Gaelic Poetry.

Opposite, right: Douglas firs near Ossian's Hall along the River Braan near Dunkeld. The tallest tree in the British Isles is now claimed for the Dughall Mor, a Douglas fir which has reached a tow'ring 210ft or 64m in the Reelig Glen Woods of Inverness-shire.

in the twinkling of an eye, by some invisible machinery, the painting was withdrawn. The space occasioned by it opened into a splendid but small saloon, the farther end of which again opened directly on a cataract.'

To create this startling effect a guide pulled on a hidden pulley. The painting parted and each half slid into wall recesses on either side to reveal a mirrored chamber. To the pounding of the waterfall, visitors were now struck with a stunning visual display. Defying gravity, cascades of darting water rushed this way and that, over mirrors on the walls and ceiling. Seen through panes of coloured glass, the swirling white foam crashing over fragments of black rock became red and green by turn. When visitors reached the centre of the room, the roar of the waterfall grew to a crescendo, reverberating off the walls and windows, as they watched in awe the natural wonder of the falls.

Of course there were some who condemned Ossian's Hall for its sheer vulgarity, like the formidable Mrs Elizabeth Grant of Rothiemurchus. 'It's more like a boudoir than a Hermitage. The whole development of the Braan with its summer houses and peep-bo places destroys the proper character of the wild torrent.' Another visitor objected to the coloured glass, blaming it for 'turning water into a cascade of verdigrease'. But Dorothy Wordsworth thought that Ossian's Hall was 'almost dizzy and alive with waterfalls'.

Only a hint now remains of its eighteenth-century Ossianic glory. Not a trace of the original kaleidoscopic mirrors, which made the waters dance, survives. The stabilised shell of Ossian Hall, now known as the Hermitage, has loomed above the natural beauty of the cascading Falls of Braan with all the enchantment of a municipal lavatory in a provincial seaside town. The National Trust for Scotland, which has looked after the Hermitage for over half a century, has attempted to catch something of the excitement of the original monument. 'We are not attempting to recreate the original design complete with the mirrors and furniture,' said Ben Notley for the Trust. 'There would be too much conjecture in its reconstruction.' Such an attitude is unusual in Scotland, a land where historical buildings are so often revamped pastiche. The artist Calum Colvin was commissioned to reconfigure some of his innovative images from his National Galleries of Scotland Ossian exhibition. But this inventive artist, who uses mirror so effectively in his work, should have been given a freer rein to capture the spirit of this magical place. Painting the walls a deep wine red shows little understanding of the original spirit of this temple built in Nature. It was the emergence from the dark vestibule into the dazzling bright light of all those reflecting mirrors, to the sound of the falls, that entranced visitors in the eighteenth century.

If Ossian's Hall is now sadly diminished, the landscape around it has since grown abundantly. In 1797, when Robert Burns visited the banks and falls, he found their effect was much impaired through an absence of trees and shrubs and wrote a poem as a 'Humble Petition' to the Duke of Atholl:

Would then my noble master please
    To grant my highest wishes,

He'll shade my banks wi' tow'ring trees,
  And bonnie spreading bushes.
Delighted doubly then my Lord,
  You'll wander on my banks.
And listen mony a gratful bird
  Return you tuneful thanks.

The trees around Ossian's Hall are now truly 'tow'ring'. The Duke was so inspired by Burns's poem that he planted some of the first Douglas firs in Europe to create today's 'bonnie banks of Braan'. Brought back from the west coast of North America by the pioneering plant collector David Douglas, the trees have flourished. Nearly two hundred mild winters and moist summers later, this towering woodland now boasts some of the tallest trees in the British Isles.

Burns, like other major Romantics from William Blake onwards, was deeply affected by Ossian. This 'Prince of Poets,' he said, 'is one of the glorious models after which I endeavour to form my conduct.' Burns even called his dog Luath, after Cuchullin's hound in Ossian's Fingal. *Luath* in Gaelic means swift or nimble, which is an appropriate name for an impetuous collie, who tripped Jean Armour into Burns's arms. When poor Luath met a violent death, Burns immortalised him in his poem, 'The Twa Dogs'. This witty dialogue between Luath, the 'ploughman's collie', and Caesar, the incomer labrador 'o' high degree', allowed Burns to explore fraught allegiances to do with class and language within a Gaelic- and English-speaking Scotland.

The first I'll name, they ca'd him Caesar,
Was keepit for his honour's pleasure:
His hair, his size, his mouth, his lugs,
Show'd he was nane o' Scotland's dogs:
But whalpit some place far abroad,
Whare sailors gang to fish for cod.
…

The tither was a ploughman's collie,
A rhyming, ranting, raving billie,
Wha for his friend an' comrade had him,
And in his freaks had Luath ca'd him,
After some dog in Highland sang,
Was made lang syne – lord knows how lang.

For his Ossian exhibition Calum Colvin updated Burns's 'Twa Dogs' by exploring sectarian allegiances in present-day Scotland. Colvin, at once sculptor, painter and photographer, involves himself in a complex journey to create his imagery. He has given Ossian a contemporary spin by photographing fragments of found objects and arranging them into sculpted and painted constructions, before manipulating them digitally into large-scale high-definition multilayered images. These photographed tableaux are compounded out of everyday found objects as visual equivalents to Macpherson's found fragments of Gaelic poems. Taking Ireland's claim to the historical Oisín and England's long-standing indifference, Colvin's work questions where Scottish culture stands today. He maintains that 'Scots have to define themselves between two cultures – the lure of Ireland and the pull of England. Ossian seems to me to be the struggle of Highlanders making a comeback and trying to define themselves culturally between an English or Irish identity.'

But it was in Napoleon's France that *Ossianisme* reached fever pitch in the arts. For Napoleon the poems of Ossian were 'the purest and most animating principles and examples of true honour, courage and discipline, and all the heroic virtues that can possibly exist'. The Emperor commissioned the most celebrated artists of the day to embellish his palaces with Ossianic themes. And it is said he carried Melchiorre Cesarotti's Italian translation with him into battle.

Anne-Louis Girodet's Ossianic fantasies were shown to have clearly influenced the sets for one of the greatest operatic successes of the early nineteenth century, *Ossian, ou Les Bardes* by Jean-François Le Sueur, which premiered at the Paris Opéra within two months of Napoleon proclaiming the Empire in 1804. The Emperor was so entranced with the opera's double chorus and its orchestra, augmented with a dozen Ossian harps, that Le Sueur immediately became the most fêted composer of the new regime. In a scene which not even Macpherson could have imagined, the imprisoned Ossian dreams of his soul rising up from a dungeon to be embraced by naked maidens and the dead heroes of his race. Clearly we are now well on our way to Wagner's *Ring of the Nibelung*.

Twa Dogs – from Calum Colvin's Ossian series, Fragments of Gaelic Poetry. In this tableau 'The Twa Dogs' of Robert Burns's poem are derived out of the most unlikely objects and set down in a bizarre Highland kitchen. A Nike trainer becomes the snout of Luath, nosing its way amongst the soccer kitsch.

The fact that Ossian was so central to the flowering of Western Romanticism in art and literature you might have thought would have been of special interest to Scotland. Yet the National Gallery of Scotland has never mounted an exhibition devoted to the impact of Ossian on Western culture. Provincial prejudice may explain why London rejected the revelationary Hamburg Kunsthalle Ossian exhibition, which went on to fill the Grand Palais in Paris in 1974. But what explanation can be offered for Scotland's rejection of an exhibition which so imaginatively explored the overwhelming influence of Macpherson's Ossian in the Western world? Is this just another example of what the writer Neal Ascherson diagnoses as the 'St Andrews Fault', the national psychological fault line which so often defers sycophantically to the foibles of South Britain?

Colvin's exhibition of Ossian tableaux at the National Portrait Gallery of Scotland was invited to the UNESCO gallery in Paris to coincide, appropriately, with the Louvre's Girodet exhibition. The combined events inaugurated an international conference on Ossian's influence in all the arts, as dominating a presence in this little gallery as was Napoleon's once in France.

Although James Macpherson's literary achievements were scorned in London, it didn't stop him advancing his career. In 1764, still under thirty, he was appointed secretary to the Governor of the newly created British West Florida. London wags wagered that there he would soon unearth fragments of ancient Indian poetry. Like Sir Pertinax MacSycophant in Charles Macklin's notoriously anti-Scottish play, *The True-Born Scotsman*, Sir James 'bowed and bowed again' to become spin doctor to Lord North's government. Soon an MP, he was rewarded with the lucrative post of London agent to Mahommed Ali, nabob of Arcot.

Left: *The Dream of Ossian*, 1811, by Jean-Auguste-Dominique Ingres, Montauban, Musée Ingres. Le Sueur's opera inspired Jean-Auguste-Dominique Ingres to create this massive canvas for Napoleon's Palace of Monte-Cavallo in Rome. But the battle of Waterloo intervened.

Right: *Ossian Receiving the Ghosts of French Heroes*, 1802, by Anne-Louis Girodet de Rousy Trioson, Salon doré, Malmaison, Musée National du Château.

Left: Balavil, Kingussie, by Robert Adam, 1790-5, the last home of James Macpherson.

Right: For Balavil, the home of his romantic client, Robert Adam chose the austere Hanoverian classicism of the Lieutentant-Governor's house on the right of the parade ground in Fort George, Ardersier, which, as an aspiring architect, he had worked on in the 1750s.

Opposite: Receiving the Academy Award for Best Supporting Actor for *The Untouchables* in 1987. The award is much better known as the Oscar, the name Macpherson transformed for Ossian's son.

'Rise, Ossian, and save my son; save Oscar, prince of men...' Fingal Book IV.

The crofter's son now had high ambitions, and soon commissioned Robert Adam, Scotland's greatest architect, to build him a chateau in sight of his beloved Grampian mountains. He would call it Balavil, or sometimes Belleville, to impress the French. What Adam built for such a romantic was an altogether dour classical monument. The façade of Balavil has a severity of design that gives Macpherson's Highland home more a military than domestic air. Ironically, Balavil resembles the Lieutenant-Governor's house on the parade ground of Fort George where Robert Adam's career began, supervising the construction of this vast military barracks built to pacify the Highlands for all time to come.

In 1796 Macpherson was interred in Westminster Abbey at his own expense. He now lies, with some poetic justice, just outside Poets' Corner, where the bust of his formidable adversary Dr Johnson forever bears down on him with a stony stare. The neighbour of Badenoch's bard is Robert Adam, who may well wish to be remembered for other works than James Macpherson's Balavil.

In the wake of Ossian's international fame, towns sprang up from America to Australia throughout the eighteenth and nineteenth cenuries, bearing names derived from Macpherson's tales. There are Morvens in Georgia, North Carolina and Virginia. It was from Selma that the great march for civil rights left for Montgomery, Alabama. And there's a Temora in New South Wales. Oscar, the son of Ossian, gave his name to two crowned kings of Sweden and Norway, and then there's Oscar Fingal O'Flahertie Wills Wilde. 'Is not that grand, misty and Ossianic?' wrote Lady Jane Wilde to a Scottish friend, announcing the birth of her second son who would become a very famous Oscar. No one is quite certain who the Oscar was who gave his name to Hollywood's Academy Awards, but what is certain is that the first Oscar sprang from Macpherson's Ossian who had transformed the original Gaelic Osgar, just as he had englished his father from Oisin to Ossian.

A gargantuan mountain carving of Oscar dying on his shield, cradled in a rock-hewn amphitheatre in the Morven peninsula, has been the ambition of the sculptor Alexander Stoddart for many years. This massive undertaking would rival in scale the head of Mount Rushmore's Thomas Jefferson who had taken Ossian to his heart.

I met the sculptor when I unveiled his memorable monument to R. L. Stevenson in Edinburgh. This was a refreshingly down to earth portrayal of David Balfour and Allan Breck Stewart from 'Kidnapped'. That rattling great adventure of intrigue upon intrigue, set in the Highlands and Lowlands when Jacobites were still on the run, was always a favourite of mine. Perhaps the artist should just don that bullock's hide and slip under a waterfall in Morven to ask the Highland oracle of Taghairm what chance he has of carving his mountain Oscar.

I have to admit that I only stumbled on the ancient powers of Taghairm quite recently, and it wasn't in Scotland. During a golf tournament in California I fell by chance on the Taghairm Practitioners' Convention in Redwood City: a whole event devoted to the antediluvian art of the Highlands. For a quick induction in this ancient art, the hotel lobby had a portable waterfall in a shower cabinet with an ample supply of oxhides. A poster advertised a group seminar on 'Learning to Listen to the Voice of the Spirit That Lies Within'. It was time to leave. Ancient Scots myths never die. They merely emigrate.

4 THE FORGING OF SCOTLAND
The reassembly of cultural ruins

O wad some Pow'r the giftie gie us,
To see oursels as others see us!

Robert Burns, *To A Louse. On seeing one on a lady's bonnet at church.*

As Ossian ebbed into obscurity with Napoleon in 1815, Scott's first novel *Waverley* rose to fill its place of influence in the world. Instead of Macpherson's misty heroes, Scott's historical characters were of flesh and blood, seemingly living through real incidents of Scotland's past. 'It is, then, sixty years hence,' *Waverley* begins, with an added footnote: 'The precise date (1745) was withheld from the original edition, lest it should anticipate the nature of the tale by announcing so remarkable an era.' The wounds of the Jacobite Rising, the defeat of Prince Charles at Culloden and the humiliations that followed were healed in *Waverley* as Scott dealt Scotland a noble, if not a Highland, past. His subsequent novels were read from Moscow to the American frontier. The *Waverley* novels were translated into all major languages and performed as plays, operas and eventually films. As tourists, Scott's readers came in thousands to see the landscape of his mind. And his works today still fuel the presentation of Scotland to the world.

I saw a great part of the border country spread out before me and could trace the scenes of those poems and romances which had bewitched the world. I gazed about me for a time with mute surprise, I may almost say with disappointment. I beheld a mere succession of grey waving hills…monotonous in their aspect and destitute of trees…and yet such had been the magic web of poetry and romance thrown over the whole that it had a greater charm for me than the richest scenery I beheld in England. I told Scott that he had a great deal to answer for on that head, since it was the romantic associations he had thrown by his writings over so many out-of-the-way places in Scotland that had brought in the influx of curious travellers. Scott laughed and said I might in some measure be right and recollected a circumstance in point. He recalled an old woman who kept an inn at Glencross who recognised him as the gentleman who had written a bonnie book about Loch Katrine. She begged him to write a little book about their lake too, for she understood his book had done the inn at Loch Katrine a muckle deal of good.

Washington Irving, *Abbotsford and Newstead Abbey*, 1817

'Sir Walter Scott, you are the man in Scotland I most wish to see,' was the welcome King George IV gave to the drenched author of *Waverley* as he stepped aboard the royal yacht at Leith on a tempestuously rainy August day in 1822. And for good reason too, for Scott had masterminded the Edinburgh royal visit into one vast unprecedented Highland gathering of the clans. There would be levées at the Palace of Holyroodhouse, a state procession to Edinburgh Castle and a command performance of Scott's own *Rob Roy*, which the King had preferred to a staging of *Macbeth*.

And there the King stands in bronze today, cloaked in some confusion (is it a toga, or is it a plaid?) astride Hanover and George, the crossing of two Edinburgh

David Wilkie, *George IV at the Palace of Holyroodhouse*, 1822. It was the first visit of a British monarch to Scotland since the coronation of King Charles II at Scone in 1651.

Right: *Alexander, Third King of Scotland.
Rescued from the fury of a stag by
the intrepidity of Colin Fitzgerald*,
Benjamin West, 1738-1820.

Opposite: *The Monarch of the Glen*,
Sir Edwin Landseer, 1802-73.

New Town streets honouring the Hanoverian dynasty. The King's elegant leggings suggest something of the excesses of his 1822 visit, when the kilted monarch sportingly wore a pair of pink under-tights as a modest precaution against revealing too much royal leg to his Scottish subjects. He certainly wouldn't have known from Sir Walter Scott that most Scots were as unused to wearing tartan as he was. The Act of Proscription of 1746, which had the power to transport any wearer of tartan to the colonies, had only been repealed a generation before. Although the Lowlands had never worn the stuff, Sir Walter's vision of an all-tartan Scotland has remained the dominant national image of Scotland ever since.

George was a corpulent sixty when he first discovered his northern kingdom. So how come that youthful face and elegant light-footed poise of his statue? Was it an act of flattery by the sculptor Francis Chantrey? Not so. George's bold Roman stance (middle name, Augustus) was struck to front the many splendid pleasure domes of the Brighton Pavilion. To thank the dashing Prince Regent for putting their seaside town on the tourist map, when he was just past twenty-one, the citizens of Brighton raised over £3000 for this statue. Forty years later Edinburgh ordered another cast. So today we can view his cloaked majesty either as he revels in a vision of an India that never was, or struggling to make sense of an equally fabricated Scotland, hastily forged for a royal occasion. In Augustan splendour, sceptre in hand, he still stares across from Edinburgh's classical New Town to the scribbled Gothic skyline of the romantic Old Town.

Appropriately, Scotland's National Gallery of Art lies in a Greek temple on the debatable lands beneath the castle. Inside, an Edinburgh Festival soirée is in full swing. In spirit, and even costume, it must be close to the levée attended by the King in 1822, as captured by Turner in historical smudges of misty tartan proto-Impressionism. The gallery is dominated by Benjamin West's colossal canvas with

its appropriately extended title, *Alexander, Third King of Scotland. Rescued from the fury of a stag by the intrepidity of Colin Fitzgerald* (and it goes on). Tonight by its side hangs Edwin Landseer's *Monarch of the Glen*. Close by is John Martin's sketch for a painting of the witches meeting Banquo and Macbeth on the blasted heath, a painting that Sir Walter yearned to have for his home at Abbotsford. To the world at large all these works evoke a mythological Scotland, yet the artists are either Anglo-American or English.

If West's mythic vision of Scottish history struck a blow for the new Romanticism, then stampeding across Europe on medieval white chargers, it would be Landseer's noble beast, over fifty years later, that would consolidate the prevailing image of Scott's 'Land of the mountain and the flood'. Appropriately his *Monarch of the Glen* was commissioned for the House of Lords refreshment bar, but because their lordships failed to meet the artist's asking price it was sold privately. The stag was eventually bagged by Tommy Dewar, that Promethean whisky myth distiller, then bent on making scotch the drink of monarchs everywhere.

At the 1993 Edinburgh Festival fancy dress party at the National Gallery, Landseer's royal stag had a special resonance as Dewars was part of the Distillers' Company. Stalking in front of the *Monarch of the Glen* was Ernest Saunders, chairman of the Distillers' Board, along with his fellow directors, then in the throes of corrupt dealings over the Guinness takeover. In the current parlance of art criticism we could call the event something between installation and performance art. The artist of this provocative work was the then gallery director Timothy Clifford, who had for long brought a sense of much criticised fun to those more used to dousing their appreciation of art in Scotland with dour solemnity. When the new board of Diageo (*née* United Distillers) scotched its long-held promise to keep the world's largest scotch whisky concern's headquarters in

Colonel Alasdair MacDonell c.1812, Sir Henry Raeburn. Colonel Alasdair MacDonell of Glengarry was a clan chief who tried to live the life of his feudal forebears. Raeburn paints him against a wall of his ancestral castle in an over-the-top theatrically inspired Highland dress. Such an historical throwback had great appeal for Sir Walter Scott.

Scotland, the Edinburgh branch office got custody of Landseer's *Monarch.* Then Her Majesty got custody of Ernest Saunders and two of his directors, who were convicted on counts of conspiracy, false accounting and theft, and sent to jail. A third director escaped prison due to ill health. *The Monarch of the Glen* remains in Scotland today as a poignant souvenir of such out-of-fashion corporate business practices in contemporary Britain as probity.

What is the fascination in these heroic but essentially mad depictions of Scotland? West's *Fury of a Stag* was surrounded in the gallery by a series of ruddy-faced bigger-than-life portraits by Henry Raeburn. Yet even here, in the work of one of Scotland's finest painters, well known for his portraits of Edinburgh's men-about-town, the mythic past creeps back. Perhaps inspired by the description of Fergus Mac-Ivor in Scott's *Waverley*, Raeburn depicts Alasdair MacDonell of Glengarry as a Highland chieftain, bristling with anachronistic weapons and garlanded improbably in swags of tartan. Or could it have been the other way round, as suggested by the perceptive art historian Lindsay Errington? Since this swashbuckling portrait of 1812 predates Scott's novel, it could have been this fantasy by Raeburn that fired the imagination of the 'Wizard of the North', the true inventor of tartan Scott-land.

Pages from Scott's novels were to provide historical scenes to fuel the romantic imagination of Scotland's artists throughout the Victorian era. The influence of his romanticism on Scottish artists was so overpowering that it seems to have driven out any interest in artists belonging to the real Scottish tradition of scientific innovation and industrial invention. Ironically Scott was something of an innovator himself, for Abbotsford was one of the first homes in Scotland to be lit by gas.

In a major exhibition celebrating the arts and sciences in Glasgow, in its year as European City of Culture, only four paintings out of over sixty could be found that had anything at all to do with Scotland's celebrated engineering prowess and industry in the city which became the Victorian workshop of the world. Even the Forth Bridge, that engineering wonder of its age, was left unchallenged by artists. Was it because that arbiter of Victorian taste, John Ruskin, had said that the bridge made him wish he had 'been born a blind fish in a Kentucky cave' or because William Morris had spitefully called it 'the extremest specimen of all ugliness'? When compared to those daring high girders and overreaching cantilevers across the Forth, the Eiffel Tower was but a flagpole. Yet even during its construction it had fired the imagination of Georges Seurat. In the following decades the Eiffel Tower became a symbol of modernity for the avant garde. As an axiom of abstraction it inspired poets like Guillaume Apollinaire, film-makers, photographers and such innovative painters as Bonnard, Chagall, Dufy, Signac, Utrillo and Vuillard. For Robert Delaunay the girders of the Eiffel Tower became a generator of Cubism, suggesting to him a near-infinite number of Cubist variations. But what cubistic delights those diagonal girders of the Forth Bridge would have held had there been artists in Scotland inspired enough to tap them.

To celebrate Sir Walter Scott's remarkable achievement as the author of the *Waverley* novels, a competition for a monument yielded two notable proposals.

One was a towering obelisk by the rising classical architect William Playfair. The other was a soaring Gothic rocket ship, crewed by statues of characters from his poems and novels, by George Meikle Kemp, who had never built anything in his life before. Kemp's design won first prize, but the poor man would never see his masterpiece, as he was drowned in a freak accident in 1844; a tragic irony that might have fallen from the pages of a *Waverley* novel. The Scott monument, one of the largest ever raised to a writer, now dominates Prince's Street Gardens. Once again the Romantic had triumphed over the classical. It was Scott's love of the Middle Ages that had helped create the romantic Gothic Revival in the first place. When Edinburgh's main railway station opened in 1854 they called it Waverley after his shelf-ful of novels, a wonderful salute to a writer. I'm so outraged that it's recently been renamed Edinburgh Waverley by some railway bureauprat. Why can't it still be called Waverley?

The Hanoverian vision that brought about the Scots Baronial pepper-pots of Balmoral generated the vogue for all things Jacobite in Scottish painting. The young Queen Victoria and Prince Albert inspired Landseer and such Scottish artists as the one-time theatrical scene painter Horatio McCulloch and the portraitist John Pettie to paint their louring glens of gloom, Bonnie Prince Charlies and Chieftains' Candlesticks. Their potent pictures of dreich landscapes, crumbling castles and costumed tableaux dominate tourist brochures and scotch whisky advertising to this day.

Left: *Champs de Mars/La Tour Rouge*, 1911, Robert Delaunay,1885-1941. The Eiffel Tower as a generator of cubism.

Right: The high girders and soaring cantilevers of the Forth Bridge, which far excel the engineering of Eiffel's giant flagpole, failed to excite the painters of Scotland.

Antonio Canova, 1757-1822. The Stuart Monument designed in 1817 in memory of the last three members of the Royal House of Stuart, James Francis Edward Stuart, his elder son Charles Edward Stuart, and his younger son, Henry Benedict Stuart. It was only when the triumphant Hanoverian King George III paid for it that this Jacobite monument was executed in white marble and installed in St Peter's Basilica, Rome, in 1829.

Right: *The Poet's Dream, The Minstrel at Lincluden*, 1840, David Octavius Hill, 1802-70 from *The Antiquities of Scotland* by Francis Grose. The dream of Robert Burns embraces the ancient blind Ossian above and many a bogle below, as the antiquary Francis Grose straddles the gallery writing his great book on Scottish antiquities.

The bridge that connects the realities of Scottish history to the battle scenes in movies like Mel Gibson's *Braveheart*, rises from the banks of Victorian Romanticism across the great woven images of Skeoch Cumming. This artist depicted such highly wrought chapters of Scottish history as the defeat of the English at Bannockburn on high-definition wide-screen tapestries. To achieve these forerunners of Hollywood epics, Cumming had his gamekeepers and ghillies pose in a variety of Highland fancy dress out of the pages of *Vestiarium Scoticum* and its sequel *The Costume of the Clans* by the brothers John Sobieski Stuart and Charles Edward Stuart.

In the 1830s these two plausible Welsh-born brothers persuaded Lord Lovat and much of Edinburgh society that they were the direct descendants of the Young Pretender. Lovat awarded them more than Highland hospitality by giving them generous quarter at Eilean Aigas, a spare home he had on a sliver of an island on the River Beauly. As artists they soon made its modest rooms both huge and famous. Their wide-angled imagination portrayed a Highland castle embowered in Jacobite memories. They exaggerated the size of their re-invented living-room by painting themselves on a much diminished scale, and if reality ever returned, they would have been the size of table-top tartan dollies. But they also recorded much genuine Highland culture at a time when it was rapidly disappearing. Just like James Macpherson, whose Ossian has for too long been dismissed as worthless, the Stuart brothers have been consistently ridiculed and underrepresented in Scottish histories. They created much of value, including remarkable high-backed Gothic chairs and other furniture that has never properly been represented in museums. No museum in Scotland bought their high-backed chairs when Eilean Aigas was sold.

Surely this is where folklore and fakelore meet; the perfect place to ponder the imponderables of Scottish representation. To help fire their imaginative powers the museum and gallery directors in Scotland I think should contemplate *The Poet's Dream*, D.O. Hill's mythic collision of imagery derived from Macpherson's Ossian and Burns's *Tam O'Shanter* for the frontispiece of *The Land of Burns*. Best of all, why don't they combine an exhibition on Burns, Macpherson's Ossian and Charles Edward Stuart as an exploration of the real, the unreal and the surreal in Scotland? The French might lend their mythic *Dream of Ossian* by Ingres, from Montauban; the Italians could offer a reconstruction of Canova's classical monument to the last Stuarts in St Peter's Basilica, in the Vatican in Rome.

The Americans could fill in any Burns gaps from the world's second-largest collection of Burnsiana in Washington's Masonic Temple of Scottish Rites. Of course, all this might be of little interest to London critics who make a habit of displaying their Little England provincialism and ignorance of most things Scottish as a regular silly-season whinge at each year's Edinburgh Festival. But it might set the heather afire at home, and on the Continent meet with great acclaim.

> O what a tangled web we weave,
> when first we practise to deceive!
> Walter Scott, *Marmion*

LAND OF BURNS,

VOL. I.

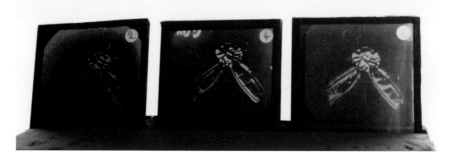

Tartan was chosen by the great scientist James Clerk Maxwell, 1831-79, to demonstrate the principles of colour photography in 1861 through his 'trichromatic process'. Three black and white photographs, taken through red, green and blue filters, were superimposed using the same colour filters to produce this tartan rosette. Although the orthochromatic photographic emulsions at that time were insensitive to red light, Clerk Maxwell was lucky that the ribbon reflected enough ultra-violet light to register the red.

No more tangled a web was ever woven than that Scottish fabric of historical threads which the world knows today as tartan. The great weaver of yarns himself, Sir Walter Scott, not only promoted the wearing of tartan for King George IV's visit to Scotland in 1822, but he was partly complicit in its re-invention. Now it's impossible to unpick the factual warp from the fictional weft of tartan's extraordinary weaving; from its misty origins right up to the present day when new tartans can be concocted by the yard. The scientific fame of James Clerk Maxwell may rest with his equations linking electricity with magnetism, which led to Einstein's general theory of relativity and quantum physics. But he was also the first to bring colour to photography, in 1861. And what was his subject? A tartan rosette, of course.

In 1998 the US Senate and the Canadian government established Tartan Day on 6 April, the day chosen to commemorate the Declaration of Arbroath when fifty-one noblemen signed a letter to the Pope confirming Scotland's independence in 1320. The event soon grew to embrace many aspects of Scottish culture and now includes art exhibitions, fashion shows, film screenings and talks by writers. But central to the celebrations is the march of ten thousand pipers down 6th Avenue in kilts. There were over eighteen hundred participants in 2007 and over one hundred thousand spectators watching the largest pipe band in the world. I remember the surge of some great collective longing as Micheline and I joined an earlier parade with all the crowds applauding from the sidewalk.

How can we explain the enigma of the Highland bagpipe? How is it that such a simple instrument, one that is so primitive that it can be varied neither in pitch nor in volume, can express so many emotions? It can convey rapture at weddings, impel soldiers to feats of courage in the height of battle, or help assuage inconsolable grief around the graves of loved ones. When New York marked the anniversary of the 9/11 catastrophe, five pipe bands of firemen expressed the rage and grief of the many relatives and friends at Ground Zero, lamenting the senseless deaths of near three thousand who perished there. And to think it took the primitive Highland bagpipe to console the citizens of one of the world's most sophisticated cities.

Thanks to the number of Highlanders who emigrated, Scots Americans have always had an infatuation with tartan. No one showed more ancestral pride of his family tartan than the American astronaut Alan Bean, who stole a swatch of MacBean tartan aboard Apollo XII (against strict NASA rules) and flew it to the moon.

Tartan Day, New York City, 2 April 2002. To massed pipe bands and close to 10,000 marchers, Micheline and I led the Tunes of Glory parade down ten blocks, keeping pace with our flag-waving granddaughter, Saskia.

5 THE FREEDOM OF EDINBURGH
Shades of the Enlightenment

Edinburgh is the visible expression of [its] history. With the Enlightenment a new town arose, suitable to the enlarged ideas of the age, separated from the old town of Mary Queen of Scots, Mary of Guise, John Knox and the Covenanters only by a little valley. New town and old town lie side by side, and the life of the city is the life of both.

A.J. Youngson, *The Making of Classical Edinburgh*

Moving from street to street through Edinburgh's New Town in a horse-drawn cart was the pace at which people moved when it was built. The speed of my horse-drawn milk delivery cart allowed me plenty of time to appreciate the elegant buildings of the New Town. New, that is, up to a point; for like most things called new in Edinburgh, the New Town is really very old. In 1767 the first streets and squares were laid out in open fields north of the castle by the twenty-seven-year-old James Craig. Then Robert Adam, whose original plan for Charlotte Square was a masterfully created urban space with neoclassical architecture of the highest order, was followed by architects of genius such as Thomas Hamilton, William Playfair and Enric Miralles.

You really get to grips with streets in winter when your horse slips back on the ice. I remember once having to get behind my horse Tich's arse to push her and the cart up a slippery slope from the Dean Village. On better days I would be offered spectacular sunrises over Comely Bank with the brooding silhouette of Fettes College posing against the Forth like a chateau of the Loire. As Tich and I trotted from street to street on my daily milk runs, perspectives could shift dramatically. My favourite was the turn from Queensferry Road into Melville Street in Edinburgh's West End, where those long neoclassical terraces climax in the soaring Gothic spires of St Mary's Episcopal Cathedral.

The quaint method of delivering the morning milk by horse and cart survived well into the 1980s. It came in handy when Murray Grigor and I made our film on Edinburgh. One of the first drop-offs was in Charlotte Square, which glowed that morning in the early sun. The façades were raked in sharp light and shade, marvellously capturing what Adam called 'architectural movement', the very essence of his style. Alas the street is blocked off half way round, and cannot be seen as Adam intended. Did I catch the eye of an Adam sphinx on the rooftops scowling down in disbelief?

Opposite: Replacing the straggle of industrial buildings of the old Holyrood brewery, the campus of the Scottish Parliament by Enric Miralles in 2004 brought Edinburgh's historic Royal Mile to a triumphant conclusion. Thomas Hamilton's neoclassical masterpiece of the Royal High School of 1828, and William Playfair's never completed Parthenon on Calton Hill above, give Edinburgh the look of the Athens of the North.

Left: Melville Street, Edinburgh, West End, architect Robert Brown, 1814. This harmonious vista of contrasting architectural styles allows the restrained classicism of Melville Street to come to the Gothic close of Gilbert Scott's St Mary's Episcopal Cathedral of 1874-1917.

Centre and right: Robert Adam's masterful palace front of Charlotte Square, 1785-1820. Adam's rooftop sphinxes, proud symbols of immortality, must now deplore the present state of Charlotte Square, with its tarred-over cobbles and traffic dead-ends.

Left: Fettes College, David Bryce, 1864-70. The commanding baronial presence of Fettes College faces classical Edinburgh from the North. Bryce's masterful architectural bouillabaisse fuses elements of Scottish Baronial with French Gothic, derived in part from Castle Fyvie in Aberdeenshire and his scholarly studies of the châteaux of the Loire and the Hotel de Cluny in Paris.

Centre: The builders of William Playfair's Parthenon of 1822 erected fewer than a quarter of the required fifty columns of the Greek temple. But twelve columns were just enough to present a film-set illusion as an affordable acropolis to claim for Edinburgh the title 'Athens of the North'.

Right: Thomas Hamilton's Royal High School, 1825-9, with its Doric columns derived from the Temple of Theseus in Athens, delivered a Greek Revival masterpiece.

When Scottish devolution was first seriously discussed in the 1970s, Edinburgh's finest neoclassical building was proposed for the Assembly. The Greek Revival Royal High School by Thomas Hamilton commands the east end of the city under that fragment of the Parthenon on Calton Hill which gives Edinburgh its filmset claim to be the Athens of the North. Hamilton's masterpiece was chosen since it fronted the government offices of St Andrew's House, the Scottish art deco building designed by Thomas Tait in 1939. The Royal High School was converted at great expense, but when the Scottish voters failed to reach the 40 per cent majority in the referendum demanded by Westminster, devolution was scrapped. I took part in a lively pre-referendum gathering in September 1997 at the Royal High School. That time there was an unassailable 74 per cent in favour of a Scottish parliament

The First Secretary Donald Dewar deemed the Royal High School unsuitable as a parliament despite the millions spent on its conversion. He admitted that it had 'enormous attractions in terms of symbolism'. A group of nationalists kept a day-and-night 'vigil for democracy' outside its gates, a vigil which would last for an astonishing 1,980 days. So perhaps it was the symbolism of independence that turned the First Secretary against the Royal High School.

Soon an international competition was announced for a new building opposite the Palace of Holyroodhouse at the end of the Royal Mile. The winner out of the seventy submissions was Enric Miralles, a charismatic Catalan who entranced Dewar and the judges with his beautiful renderings and collages of his ideas for the Parliament, which included displays of leaves and broken twigs. But it was his gnomic English that really won their hearts. 'In the end the parliament,' said Miralles, 'should be a mental place.' And this must surely have appealed to Dewar's sense of the absurd.

Miralles also brought with him a deep knowledge of Scottish architecture, from William Adam to Charles Rennie Mackintosh. As a student he had studied English in Edinburgh and had written a dissertation on the baroque of William Adam. Adam was the architect who followed William Bruce at Hopetoun House, Scotland's greatest country house. Miralles saw that the rounded towers of Bruce's seventeenth-century extension to the Palace of Holyroodhouse would face the site finally chosen for the Scottish Parliament. There were few architects, either here or abroad, who knew as much about the Scottish building tradition as did the young maestro from Barcelona. The Scottish Parliament was now in the

Top left: Boat sheds, Holy Island, Lindisfarne, Northumberland. Miralles stumbled on these upturned boats on an outing to the Holy Island of Lindisfarne on the coast of Northumbria. For the romantic Catalan these creatively reused boats provided a telling symbol for seafaring Scots and when expressed in steel would stand for the Clyde's past prowess in shipbuilding.

Top right: From the air the skylights suggest a small harbour of jostling boats.

Centre left: In the Parliament's pivotal Garden Lobby the spars of Miralles's steel-clad boat-shaped sky-lights frame the seventeenth-century Queensberry House.

Below: The MSP Building. Visiting the Parliament during the last months of its construction was a revelation. I thought that this complex of buildings expressed a Scotland in the world. Details like the windows of the MSP Building were inspired by both Charles Rennie Mackintosh and Antonio Gaudí.

Enric Miralles had a special affinity with Charles Rennie Mackintosh. They both could illustrate their ideas with great fluency, shared a love of plant and organic forms and they even looked alike. For Miralles, Mackintosh was the hero architect of Glasgow, just as Antonio Gaudí was of Barcelona.

Above centre: One of many corbie or crow-stepped gables in the Canongate.

Above right: C.R.Mackintosh's witty reverse corbie steps, under the cantilevered plant house of the Glasgow School of Art. Miralles continues this allusion in the window openings of the MSP building and the stairways inside.

creative hands of someone who not only was knowledgeable and cared about Scotland's past, but was also a world-renowned architect at the cutting edge of international design.

Miralles insisted that 'the Scottish Parliament should neither pivot on a central dome nor indulge in any French Revolutionary grandeur. It should avoid surrounding itself in columns from ancient Greece, for Edinburgh already has enough of these.' He wanted to present the city and the country he loved with architecture in forms of his own invention, in the true spirit of Scottish innovation. Above all he wanted to avoid the idea, so prevalent in many of the short-listed architects' proposals, for a glass bowl of a debating chamber, which many of the competitors thought would symbolise political transparency. Miralles's idea was that a parliament should be a place for looking out from. So he set about designing framed views to connect the parliament with the city, to the crags of Arthur's Seat and beyond. He wished to bring the land into his building in order to express his notion of a 'gathering' of people from all of Scotland. 'The Scottish Parliament should not be a colossal building, but more like a university campus, or a series of buildings around a cloister; its spaces ordered like a monastery.'

To give flight to his imaginative solution Miralles chose to launch his novel ideas in the form of metaphors. A row of upturned boats on the Holy Island of Lindisfarne triggered his imagination for the shapes of roofs. 'Enric charmed us as judges with his sketches,' said the architect Andy MacMillan. 'He developed the idea of upturned boats and brought the organic forms of plants into his thinking, very much like Mackintosh had done a century before. For me the two had much in common.' Even more astonishingly, Miralles derived the shape of the window frames for the MSPs' office block from the abstracted profile of the curving poise of Raeburn's famous painting of the skating minister, the Reverend Robert Walker, gliding over the ice of Duddingston Loch. 'See the landscape around the minister skating over the ice,' Miralles once told an audience of architects. 'For me this is the icon for Scotland. Look close at the arc and curve of his silhouette. It will be a module for the new Scottish parliament.' Now instead of rows of mundane rectangles MSPs have their windows framed by the reverend's curves, fused with a zigzag design derived in part from the corbie-stepped gables of the Canongate and Mackintosh's Glasgow School of Art. Miralles, like Mackintosh, was a total architect, involving himself with every aspect of design.

Miralles also brought to his design inspiration derived from his deep understanding of international Modernism. For him the curving sweep of Le Corbusier's chapel at Ronchamp was the first modern building to recapture the spiritual in architecture since classical times. When Dewar insisted on the preservation of the derelict Queensberry House on the Royal Mile, Miralles was inspired by the Venetian architect Carlo Scarpa's great dialogue with history in his innovative rejuvenation of the Castelvecchio in Verona.

Miralles aimed to rebuild the spaces in his own designs. Sadly, this innovative approach was thwarted by the massive bomb-proofing demanded by the MSPs in their self-deluded paranoia in the wake of the 9/11 destruction of New York's World

Opposite, centre: *The Reverend Robert Walker, Skating on Duddingston Loch.* Attributed to Sir Henry Raeburn 1790s. This emblematic figure of the skating minister was already an icon of Scottish art before Miralles derived the outline contours of the window frames and stairway openings of the Members of the Scottish Parliament Building from the curves of his body gliding over the ice. Not only is it the National Galleries of Scotland's bestselling postcard, but it is also to be seen on the shuttle bus skating between the four main Edinburgh galleries daily on the hour. When Stephen Lloyd of the National Portrait Gallery claimed in 2005 that the unsigned icon was not Scottish at all but was painted by the French neoclassicist Henri-Pierre Danloux, his findings shook the Scottish arts establishment. After several rounds between Lloyd and Duncan Thomson, his ex-director at the National Portrait Gallery, cracks appeared in the ice of Lloyd's thesis and the minister now seems to be gliding back into the Raeburn fold.

Below: The Palace of Queensberry House, 1681. After the departure of the Duke of Queensberry, following the signing of the Treaty of Union in 1707 (for which he received £10,000 to steady his hand from the English Government), the Palace of Queensberry House began its long decline. Stripped of its carved decoration, marble mantelpieces and fine furnishings, it became a hospital. An additional storey was added in 1808 when it was converted into an army barracks. Its days were nearly ended when it closed as a geriatric hospital in 1996. In his rejuvenation of the building Miralles restored the original roofline by removing the additional storey. Instead of installing bogus reconstructions so prevalent in Scottish restorations, he designed new interiors in the Style Miralles to complement the damaged spaces. Work on this was soon thwarted by the post 9/11 demand for bomb-proof windows and doors. The interiors are now only a shadow of what the architect intended.

Left: Parliament Hall was commissioned by Charles I and completed in 1639 as a permanent home for the 314 members of the Scottish Parliament when aristocrats claimied 247 of the seats. Following the 1707 Treaty of Union with England, the Great Hall was eventually transferred to the High Court of Justiciary. Today marble sculptures of legal worthies look down as solicitors walk up and down instructing their advocates.

Right: Parliament's debating chamber, with its innovative roof-trusses, echoes the intricacies of the hammer-head oak beam ceiling of the original Scottish Parliament. To span the 30 metres of the Debating Chamber without supporting columns, Miralles devised an intricate roof structure of triangular laminated oak beams, clasped in stainless-steel connecting nodes. Everything down to the carpet was designed by Miralles, including the seats and desks, laid out in a semi-circular sweep. MSPs face a wall of glass panels featuring cut-out abstracted profiles of people, or are they the architect's bottled-up references to the land of whisky?

Trade Center. His overall aim was for a parliament framed by both history and place, a suitable neighbour of our times to front the Palace of Holyroodhouse, under the spectacular backdrop of Holyrood Park and the rocky bluffs of Arthur's Seat.

When the first Scottish Parliament rose for the last time on 25 March 1707, the hammerbeam rafters of the old Parliament Hall echoed to 'ane auld sang' memorably described by the Earl of Seafield. Three hundred years later Miralles's forest of roof trusses in his debating chamber resounded to the new song of Scotland's Parliament reborn. When I was invited to see over the building, in the final stages of its construction, I had to marvel at the architect's sheer inventiveness. John Gibbons, the Scottish Executive's supervising architect, told me how much Miralles had been influenced by Mackintosh and his love of that other city's hero architect, Barcelona's Antonio Gaudí. Tragically, neither Donald Dewar nor Enric Miralles would ever see their building finished.

In 2005 the Parliament became the second most visited public building in Scotland, after Edinburgh Castle at the other end of that great street of history, the Royal Mile. If the new Parliament has done nothing else it has made contemporary architecture in Scotland news again. It has also breathed new life into the narrow closes, or alleys, of the Canongate near where my grandparents once lived.

It was only during a recent Edinburgh Festival, when my friend the industrial magnate David Murray re-ran our Edinburgh film in his Charlotte Square headquarters, that I realised we were sitting next door to the building we had filmed twenty-five years before. It was strange to see that little milk cart parked outside on David's screen, and at the same time to look down at the tented pavilions crowded into Charlotte Square Gardens hosting the Edinburgh Book Festival, one of the largest in the world. David Murray went to Fettes and has a great line at parties claiming that we all went to the same school as Tony Blair. 'That's true,' I always have to reply, 'but I went there only to deliver milk.' That's before David tells them how Ian Fleming sentenced his lusty sixteen-year-old fictional James Bond to two years at Fettes, expelled as he was from the garden of Eton for the sin of making love with a college maid. We made some play of that in the Edinburgh film, comparing the education of the 007 commander with milk-cart driver 271 who left school at thirteen.

One summer I went back to Fettes with David on Founders' Day. As BMWs, Jaguars and other top-of-the-range cars were disgorging fashionably bedecked parents, he told me that the school was originally built for the children of indigent parents. The school's founder, Sir William Fettes, a hugely successful entrepreneur who became Lord Provost of Edinburgh, had made his pile out of the Napoleonic Wars and left most of it to found his school. Later David showed me the conditions of Sir William's generous bequest. 'I stipulate,' it read, 'that this endowment is for the maintenance and education of young people whose parents have either died without leaving sufficient funds, or who, from innocent misfortune are unable to give suitable education to their children.' There were few signs of innocent misfortune in evidence that day at Fettes. David had to leave this school at sixteen when his father's business went belly-up. My folks never had 'sufficient funds' for private schooling. So I guess both of us then qualified for entry under the terms of the original endowment. Unwittingly I did benefit from Fettes as a boy as a member of the Fet-Lor soccer club, set up by Fettes and Loretto to encourage sport among the less fortunate Edinburgh kids. This was indeed fortunate for us, as the fee-paying rugby-playing pupils of both these schools were denied soccer.

It took thirty years for the Fettes trustees to agree on the right architect, unlike the commissioning of our new Scottish Parliament. Were they being paid annually? I wonder. In the end they chose David Bryce, who was an easy choice to deliver the trustees' dreams for an imposing college. Bryce was the master builder of Scotland's grandest Scottish Baronial country houses, like the turreted and crowstep-gabled Castlemilk in the Borders. He had just returned from a summer in France filling his sketchbooks with details drawn from the castles of the Loire. For Fettes, he fused these drawings with details derived from Highland castles around the River Dee. Ever since the time of Mary Queen of Scots, French building styles had influenced Scottish architecture, no more so than in its castles. What Bryce dished up in 1870 was a heady stew of French Gothic and Scottish Baronial. A *bouillabaisse écossaise*; a celebration in stone of Scotland's early pact with France – L'Alliance Vieille – the Auld Alliance of 1295 – the oldest political treaty in the Western world.

For the cloisters at the school's entrance, Bryce shuffled pages from his French and Scottish sketchbooks. He drew up dumpy versions of the columns of the Château de Blois to book-end a hefty version of the famous Apprentice Pillar, derived from the tiny Chapel of Rosslyn a dozen miles south of Edinburgh. Before he left for France, Bryce had spent a year restoring Rosslyn's exuberantly decorated fifteenth-century choir. Perhaps it was because he was a practising freemason, and the architect of Edinburgh's Freemasons' Hall, that Bryce was drawn to Rosslyn. A descendant of its founder was the first Grand Master of St John's Kilwinning No. 2, the oldest purpose-built masonic lodge in the world. An earlier Rosslyn 'restoration', by William Burn, had drawn the wrath of such

The cloisters of Fettes College by David Bryce owe much of their inspiration to Rosslyn Chapel which Bryce restored in the 1860s.

Left: The Collegiate Chapel of St Matthew, or Rosslyn Chapel, was founded in 1446 by Sir William St Clair, third and last St Clair Prince of Orkney. Although only part of the choir of his proposed collegiate church was ever completed when St Clair died in 1484, Rosslyn remains as one of the world's most enigmatic buildings, its symbolic carvings craving meanings from millions of visitors.

Centre: Rosslyn Chapel. The candles on Rosslyn's Victorian altar reveal the true size of this remarkable choir.

Right: The Mosteiro dos Jerónimos in Belém, Portugal, founded in 1502, displays carvings remarkably similar to work in Rosslyn, although the chapel was begun in 1446, over fifty years earlier than the Portuguese monastery.

artists as David Roberts, who much preferred the 'dim religious light' and the 'green mossy vegetation' which grew then all over the half-ruined chapel. When Bryce ordered its famous carvings to be 'sharpened up', another wave of outrage arose. The Maltese crosses, five-pointed stars, the seals of the Lamb of God, the olive branches carrying doves, the engrailed crosses, all got the sharp attention of his masons' chisels.

Rosslyn Chapel has puzzled generations down the ages and remains one of the great unsolved architectural conundrums of Old Europe. There is simply nothing resembling the profusion of its Gothic decoration anywhere else in the British Isles. Built in 1446 for Sir William Sinclair (St Clair), the 3rd and last Prince of Orkney, Rosslyn has come down to us as the proverbial 'riddle, wrapped in a mystery, inside an enigma', as Churchill might have said had he not been writing about Russia. It remains one of the world's most enigmatic buildings, its symbolic carvings craving meanings from millions of visitors. Yet this jewel-like church always had a reputation twice its size. This was sometimes literally so. A French painter in the 1820s, who always thought big, took the fame of Rosslyn to new heights. With more than a little artistic licence he placed robed Knights Templars in the choir, which he doubled in scale (unless the knights were wee folk well under a metre tall). The artist was Louis Daguerre, who went on to invent the Daguerrotype system of photography. But before that he made Rosslyn the talk of Paris as a theatrical event. By employing enormous back-lit translucent screens, pivoting on revolving floors, he created one of most successful illuminated theatrical dioramas ever.

Daguerre's exaggerated height of Rosslyn's choir eerily matches the scale of the Cathedral of Belém of the Mosteiro dos Jerónimos in Greater Lisbon, Portugal, which has similar Gothic carvings. Could Rosslyn's masons have come from Portugal? And there's another mystery. Belém Cathedral was begun over

During the filming of *The Name of the Rose,* Umberto Eco and I had time to reflect on the re-invention of Scottish history and the sheer daftness of Knights Templar lore.

fifty years after Rosslyn. That is a fact that would be grist to my friend Umberto Eco's mythic mill. In *Foucault's Pendulum* he has a character imagine the Templars leaving the castle of Tomar in Portugal only to reappear as masons in Kilwinning, Ayrshire. Did Portuguese stonemasons also fetch up there? Or did Scots masons journey south? These were the unanswerable questions which Umberto and I would distract ourselves with, as our arses froze to the stone pews of the monastery of Kloster Eberbach, waiting for the cameraman and the director to stop bickering over shots on *The Name of the Rose.* I've often wondered what Umberto Eco would make of Rosslyn, for its symbols are as mysteriously dense to me as are the scholarly illusions he plants in his novels. In fact I am beginning to think that Rosslyn should be read as an Eco novel carved in stone.

I had read *The Da Vinci Code* before it became such a tearaway success, when I was looking for a follow-up film to produce after *Entrapment.* I liked the idea of a complicated quest ending with a Scottish twist, and Rosslyn's connections with the Knights Templars and the Holy Grail were new to me. Provided we filmed *The Da Vinci Code* with buckets of irony, I thought it would have all the makings of a popular fast-paced thriller. But I was thrown back on my heels when Fountainbridge tried to option it, for the rights were going, or had already gone, for well over $10 million.

It then began to puzzle me why there was nothing mentioned about the Templars or freemasonry in my own well thumbed Rosslyn guidebook. As Dan Brown's *Da Vinci Code* began to break bestseller records, other books appeared to encumber Rosslyn with yet stranger myths. Soon there were even books on *The Da Vinci Code,* attempting to decode the undecodable. It all seemed to have started with *The Holy Blood and the Holy Grail* in 1982. Despite the unsuccessful outcome of the court case, brought by two of its authors, accusing Dan Brown of plagiarism, it was clearly their book that had set Brown's novel on its way, and the

The Wonder of Sir Walter Scott in Rosslyn
Chapel, by John Adam Houston, 1854.
'The wondrous blaze' described in 'The
Lay of the Last Minstrel' on the night of a
St Clair's death is captured here playing
around the chapel pillars.

Opposite: The Apprentice Pillar. The
pivotal generator of many of Rosslyn's
myths, especially the quite recent one of
the jealous mason slaying his talented
apprentice, a legend which echoes the
murder of Hiram Abiff, the architect of
Solomon's Temple. That alone may have
brought in its wake all the phoney
fakelore of the Knights Templars.

At the base of the twisted Apprentice
Pillar lurk the dragons of Viking lore,
guarding Yggdrasil, the great ash tree
which binds Heaven, Earth and Hell
together. Could this be an allusion to
Rosslyn's founding Earls of Orkney?

subsequent stampede of tourists to Rosslyn's door. Then along came *The Rosslyn Hoax?*, written by Robert Cooper, the Curator of the Museum and Library of the Grand Lodge of Scotland, the home of Scottish freemasonry. This scholarly investigation seems the most level-headed and thoroughly researched historical analysis so far. Not only does Cooper scatter the myths and legends of Rosslyn to the winds, he has also finally put to rest all those claims made for Rosslyn on behalf of freemasonry and the Knights Templars.

Of all the Border castles, keeps and abbey ruins that Sir Walter Scott brought back to life, it was his magical depiction of Rosslyn, near the ballad's end, which led his readers to beat a path to the little church above that leafy glen.

> To Roslin's bowers young Harold came,
> Where, by sweet glen and greenwood tree,
> He learn'd a milder minstrelsy…

Dan Brown's fictional 'Rose-line' is a mistranslation of Rosslyn's Gaelic roots from 'ross', a promontory and 'lynn', a pool of water. And this is just the start. I can now see Umberto summoning up a detective to solve the mysteries of the chapel. But could even this master of post-modernity ever have dreamt up that the present Earl of Rosslyn is just such a person. Peter St Clair-Erskine is a senior police officer in the London Metropolitan Police Service, a commander with the special brief to protect Her Majesty the Queen. To add to his sleuthing skills he is married to the art historian Helen Watters, whose own detective work brought together an extraordinary range of pictures and photographs in the exhibition she co-curated with Angelo Maggi, called *Rosslyn: Country of Painter and Poet*, at the National Galleries of Scotland.

Little is known about the foundation of Rosslyn, as the records of the St Clair family are lost. Fortunately some information was transcribed in the seventeenth century by Father Hay, a priest who has left us a tantalising reference to the chapel's foundation by William St Clair: so that 'he might not seem altogether unthankful to God for the benefices he receaved from him, it came to his mind to build a house for God's service, of a most curious worke'. Building began in 1446 for a collegiate church in the shape of a cross, but when St Clair died in 1484 only a quarter of the plan had been completed. Rosslyn today is a choir in search of a church. Yet it's a choir whose richness of decoration has no equal. There are enough carvings of all descriptions within its walls for a building ten times its size. Many are ahead of their time, like the rib vault, which soars upwards with Europe's earliest-known stone carvings of the Dance of Death.

The dancers are drawn from all walks of life, a farmer, an abbot, a ploughman and a child, each partnered with a skeleton, evoking not the grim reaper but the state that awaits them all after life's last waltz. They are as arresting a reminder of our immortality as that grim medieval epitaph, 'What you are now, I once was. What I am now, you'll one day be.' This macabre Dance of Death might well have inspired the great sixteenth-century poet William Dunbar to write his disturbing 'Lament for the Makaris' with its haunting refrain: 'Timor mortis conturbat me' ('The fear of death disturbs me'). There's plenty more to disturb in Rosslyn and even to suggest other Dunbar poems. A carved lintel is devoted to the Seven Deadly Sins, which depicts a procession of doomed sinners strutting towards the open jaws of Hell. Dunbar's 'Dance of the Sevin Deidlie Synnis' begins with Pride.

> 'Lat se,' quod he, 'Now quha begynnis;'
> With that the Fowl Sevin Deidlie Synnis
> Begowth to leap at anis.
> And first of all in dance was Pryd,
> With hair wyld bak and bonet on syd…

For pilgrims of the esoteric, Rosslyn is the chapel of a thousand myths and undeciphered codes. Many who make the pilgrimage come believing that the chapel harbours the most unfathomable secrets, or guards the most precious relics of the world. The list is legion, but here are just a few of their wilder claims. Rosslyn Chapel

> …enshrines the lost scrolls of the Temple
> …hides the Ark of the Covenant in a secret vault
> …conceals five Arks of the Covenant
> …has a fragment of the True Cross within its walls
> …enshrouds the head of Christ below the Apprentice Pillar
> …holds the sanctuary of the Black Madonna
> …awaits the White Goddess within to awaken the Celtic world
> …cloisters the tomb of Merlin
> …is the sanctum sanctorum of the Holy Grail
> …hides the Holy Treasures of Scotland
> …guards Scotland's real Stone of Destiny.

Top: The apprentice (or so they say) with his scar. Or is it Robert the Bruce? Or Hiram Abiff? Or just the result of Victorian chisellers?

Centre: Green Men abound in Rosslyn. Pagan fertility symbols were readily embraced by the early Church.

Below: Rosslyn's puzzles even extend to its decorative vegetation. What are we to make of these cobs of maize ascending this Gothic arch, carved years before the discovery of the New World? Or are they merely stalks of Old World celery?

And there are those who hold that Scotland's 'Stone of Destiny' actually is the Holy Grail. Some even think that it is concealed between the Apprentice Pillar and the Mason's Pillar. With its luxuriant spiral of foliage, Rosslyn's most famous pillar has attracted the chapel's most enduring legend. Rosslyn's master mason, it's said, was so struck by the exquisite work of his apprentice that he slew him in a raging fit of envy. A guide will point out the knife wound on his face carved on the wall behind. Yet you are just as likely to hear from another guide that this is the head of King Robert the Bruce, with the scar on his temple explained by the leprosy he contracted on the Crusades. Or is it the head of the murdered Hiram Abiff, the architect of Solomon's Temple? More likely than not, none of these claims hold true, since the scar could have been added during Bryce's Victorian 'restoration' when many of the carvings were 'sharpened up'. Others see the Apprentice and Mason's Pillars as Boaz and Joachim, the guardian cherubim of Solomon's Temple. They believe that Boaz and Joachim, standing for strength and beauty, are the biblical pillars of eternity on which all creation rests. For them Rosslyn is the Temple of Solomon born again.

Rosslyn sports many other puzzles. Ambiguous plant forms luxuriate everywhere. There are cascades of stone celery. Or is it maize? If so, this New World vegetable was carved here forty years before Columbus ever set eyes on American corn. But the Scots Templars have an answer to that. They got there first. The only snag is the Scots Templars were never connected with Sir William's church. Rosslyn's symbols are no more than a Rorschach test for a seemingly infinite number of interpretations. An engrailed Sinclair cross may wrongly suggest the Holy Grail by its words alone. To many, the profusion of leafy green men conjure up pagan rites. Yet the early Church fused many ancient beliefs into Christianity, which must explain the abundance of them in so many English country churches.

'The Rosslyn Chapel Trust claims to promote what's known of the chapel's real history,' says the historian Louise Yeoman, 'yet the Trust still perpetuates the myth of the Templars on their interpretation boards.' Yeoman is well known for publishing real documents from Scottish history and has no truck with what I call fakelore. 'This gloriously enriched collegiate church should honour its founder, who built it for the sake of his soul and the souls of his family. Surely visitors should learn how this ornate Catholic church connects with Scottish medieval piety.' Instead, Yeoman claims, 'the Rosslyn Trust seems to encourage the most ludicrous conspiracy theories'. Many really do believe that Dan Brown's book is the Gospel truth and some have even asked Stewart Beattie, the Trust's project director, to lift the chapel carpet to prove that there really is no Star of David underneath. *The Da Vinci Code* is clearly on display in the Trust's bookshop, along with the dubious and spurious books on the myths and legends of the Templars and freemasonry. Impulse buys on offer include a range of expensive masonic jewels and accessories in precious metals. They even sell a sterling silver replica of the fabricated masonic pendant I wore in John Huston's movie *The Man Who Would Be King*. It's time to flee Rosslyn's shop of junk history before they stock a book claiming that the tomb of Alexander the Great lies buried under Dan

Brown's imaginary Star of David on the chapel floor. If Indiana Jones is to have yet another sequel, then let's have Junior lay off the Holy Grail and rescue Rosslyn from all this gimcrackery.

In Scotland, where the invention of tradition is in itself a tradition, the Knights Templars were brought out of fiction in 1808 by the ambitious Edinburgh engraver Alexander Deuchar. By 1815 Knights Templars had become the Royal Grand Conclave, with Deuchar appointed Grand Master for life, through the dispensation of the Order in England. Inspired by *Ivanhoe* and other fictions of Sir Walter Scott, he piled myth upon myth to claim that the Templar cavalry came to the last-minute rescue of Robert the Bruce to defeat the English army at Bannockburn in 1314, of which no historical evidence exists.

The man who is really credited with reviving the order in Scotland was James Burnes, a relative of the poet Robert Burns. Out of veiled allegories and half-remembered truths Burnes, in the chivalrous spirit of Victorian Romanticism, forged non-existent connections between the Templars and freemasons. Now, a group of very unwarlike knights, rechristened the 'Militi Templi Scotia', conduct a ceremony each year at Rosslyn to celebrate the day when the King of Scots offered the Knights Templars refuge in Scotland, which they call, in suitably

Left: The 'green mossy vegetation', so much admired by the Edinburgh-born painter David Roberts, returned recently to cover the constellation of stars carved on Rosslyn's vaulted ceiling. This was the result of a catastrophic Fifties restoration programme, which trapped in moisture. Although the chapel is now protected from rain, it will take many years to dry out. Since the success of *The Da Vinci Code* the situation is further exacerbated by the breath of a ten-fold increase in visitors.

Right: To protect the chapel from rain and to allow the stonework to dry out, the innovative engineer and restoration specialist John Addison created this ingenious canopy. As some compensation to this architectural disturbance, visitors are now able to view the roof details from a catwalk.

The Masonic Lodge of Canongate Kilwinning No 2, 1845, by Stewart Watson, 1800-70. This gathering in Edinburgh celebrates the initiation of Robert Burns as Poet Laureate, an honour which was not created until nearly forty years after the bard's death. Although he was once a guest here, Burns's Lodge was at Tarbolton which he entered as an apprentice in 1781. The painting on the upper right is of Sir William St Clair of Rosslyn.

mysterious Templarese, 'The Lifting of the Veil'. It reminds me of a character in Umberto Eco's *Foucault's Pendulum* who says, 'If somebody brings up the Templars, he is almost always a lunatic.'

With twenty million copies of *The Da Vinci Code* sold worldwide and over two million of them in the UK, Rosslyn's visitor numbers leapt over tenfold from fewer than 10,000 visitors in 1995, to well over 100,000 ten years later. Ron Howard's film of the same title was so digitally manipulated that cinema-goers may now be searching for Rosslyn perched high up on an isolated forest hilltop, like some exotic temple in Yucatan. Sadly, what they find when they arrive is a little church crouching under an umbrella of scaffolding, erected to help the stonework dry out from years of misguided restoration work.

The algae, which had so delighted the artist David Roberts as 'green mossy vegetation', had returned by the 1950s. It soon received the disastrous attention of the Ancient Monuments branch of the Ministry of Works. Draconian measures were put to work involving solutions of ammonia and scrubbing with stiff bristle brushes, followed by a coating of a 'cementitious slurry of magnesium fluoride'. With a combination of rusting Victorian iron repairs in its roof and residual water now sealed in by that impermeable slurry, the church was destined to decay. Now, with its protective rain-shedding roof, the vaulted stonework has a chance to dry. When the process is complete the roof's stone slabs will be sealed with lead. All the interior cement will be flaked off by hand. The present restoration is estimated to cost in excess of £11 million. But as visitor numbers continue to grow to help fund this, their breath increases condensation in the cold chapel, slowing down the drying-out of the masonry.

The work has already lasted ten years. No one can yet forecast when Rosslyn's own 'lifting of the veil' will occur. Or will the Trust have to face the same solution that saved the cave paintings of Lascaux in southwestern France and build a tourist replica of Rosslyn? Perhaps when the restoration is complete William St

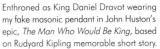

Enthroned as King Daniel Dravot wearing my fake masonic pendant in John Huston's epic, *The Man Who Would Be King*, based on Rudyard Kipling memorable short story.

Clair's 'most curious worke' will finally be seen for what it is: Scotland's jewel of Gothic architecture, with all those silly myths finally set aside. After all, nearly three hundred years would pass before Rosslyn had any real associations with freemasonry. As Robert Cooper has pointed out, earlier claims connecting Rosslyn with freemasonry arose because 'Charters of Masons' (meaning stonemasons) were taken to stand for masons meaning freemasons. It wasn't until 1736 that William St Clair of Rosslyn was elected Grand Master of the Grand Lodge of 'Antient, Free and Accepted Masons'. His portrait still hangs in Edinburgh's St John's Canongate Kilwinning No. 2. When the Earl of Elgin was Deputy Grand Master of St John's, the Queen, long believing that the Brotherhood was exclusively male, was quite taken aback when she was told that as 'King' of Scots, she was in fact Grand Master.

6 AN EDINBURGH TOO FAR
Door of the seas, the key of the universe

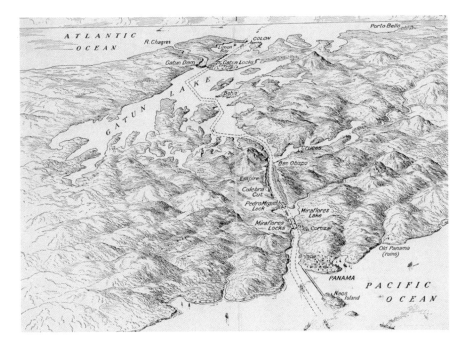

Opposite: Inspecting the Panama Canal from the command post with David McGrath, the Honorary Panama Consul to the Bahamas.

Left: The isthmus of Panama in Central America where Scotland planted its unsuccessful colony in 1698.

In 2003 my wife Micheline and I, along with our friend David McGrath, the Honorary Panama Consul to the Bahamas, were invited to celebrate the centenary of Panama's independence from Colombia by President Mireya Moscoso. We were taken to the command post of the fifty-one-mile-long Panama Canal, a marvel of engineering when it was completed in 1914.

Panama's go-ahead young Mayor Juan Carlos Navarro told us about the plan to double the canal's capacity by constructing a third lane of locks to allow the passage of the new generation of cargo ships and supertankers. Eighty per cent of Panamanians voted for the $5 billion plan, the work to be completed by the centenary of the original canal in 2014. 'We must capitalise on our geographical position between the world's two great oceans,' said the mayor. 'We knew all about that in Scotland three hundred years ago,' I told him, 'but like many of our ideas it was a little ahead of its time.' On that, Juan Carlos arranged a trip to the Darien Peninsula to visit the site of New Edinburgh at Punta Escoces.

'As the seventeenth century drew to a close,' the historian Tom Devine recounts, 'Scotland was in desperate straits. Seven years of crop failure called for heroic measures. An act for "Encouraging Foraigne Trade" was passed by Scotland's Parliament.' So in 1695 the Company of Scotland, trading to Africa and the Indies, was granted the right by the Scottish Parliament to create a colony on the strategic Darien isthmus between the Pacific and the Atlantic in today's Panama.

The Darien Scheme's chief promoter was William Paterson, a Scot of great financial vision who had already founded the Bank of England in 1694. Darien, Paterson claimed, would 'hold the key of the commerce of the world'. His notion of 'free trade' was formulated years before the economic theories of Adam Smith. For Paterson, Darien would be the 'door of the seas, the key of the universe'. Transferring cargoes from the Atlantic to the Pacific would take half the time and

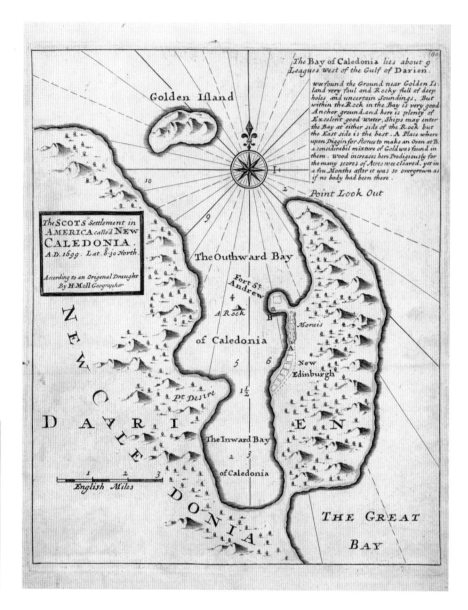

Leith Harbour, around the summer of 1698, when a small flotilla of ships sailed with 1200 Scots on board, to found New Caledonia in the swamps of the Panama peninsula.

The Colony of New Caledonia at Darien on the isthmus of Panama, Central America.

expense of navigation to China and Japan, and bring peace to both oceans without the guilt of war. Impoverished Scotland would rise again as one of the richest of nations.

It was certainly a great idea to connect the traders of the Pacific with the Atlantic, and Scotland could surely have prospered greatly. All differences of race or religion were to be ignored. But there were just a few snags. Darien was already claimed by Spain; and England had sent a proclamation to her colonies in North America and Jamaica demanding that they should withhold any assistance to the Scots. Worse still, the lands, which were promoted as a paradise on earth, were in reality vast stagnant reaches of malarial swamps, riddled with yellow fever.

Without a proper survey ships were bought, built and chartered in Holland and Hamburg. The Company's warehouses at Leith and Glasgow were slowly filled with a bizarre collection of goods which, it was confidently believed, could be exchanged for the spices, silks and gold of the Orient. In July 1698, the population of Edinburgh poured down to the piers of Leith to see five ships with such proud Scottish names as *Caledonia*, *Unicorn* and *Saint Andrew* unfurl their sails. Paterson and his family joined the little fleet of settlers for the Atlantic crossing.

The flotilla made landfall off the coast of Darien in November, and claimed it as the Colony of Caledonia. But already many of the would-be colonists were dead from flux and fever. Their leaders came totally unprepared for what faced them. The harbour chosen was a trap for vessels, which were unable to sail to windward. Ambition, pride and envy, aggravated by ignorant stupidity, destroyed the spirit of those who survived the killing fevers. Paterson's wife and child died within a few days of the landing, and he went slowly out of his mind with despair. The town of New Edinburgh was never more than a few palmetto huts, and the ramparts of Fort St Andrew were washed away by the pitiless rain.

Scotland had assembled another expedition of four ships, and it was already at sea before the failure of the first landing was known. It reached Caledonia in November 1699, to be welcomed by four hundred lonely graves. Despite the bitterness of famine, the shortage of money and supplies, and finding only a 'vast, howling wilderness', the new arrivals rebuilt the huts and reoccupied the fort. The Spaniards blockaded the colony by sea and land, and advanced their guns and trenches to the rotting ramparts of the fort. The Scots resisted bravely for a month and then surrendered. On 12 April 1700, Caledonia was finally abandoned to the Spanish. Only three hundred of the colonists, soldiers and seamen ever got back to Scotland. Paterson returned, 'looking more like a skeleton than a man', leaving his wife and child buried in Darien. Two thousand men, women and children had been sacrificed, drowned at sea, buried in the fetid earth of Darien, abandoned in Spanish prisons or indentured as servants in the English colonies. A number of luckier ones made their way to New England. It would be altogether too ironic to think that the town of Darien in Connecticut, now one of the most affluent communities in the United States, was founded by those unfortunate Scots. The Darien Historical Society prefers to think that it was named by an intinerant sailor who had returned from Panama. But why not print the legend?

Where the Scots had staked out their colony is even today unreachable from the pan-American highway running from Alaska to Patagonia. We had to fly there over the rainforests by helicopter. As we circled in to land it was clear that the tropical vegetation had totally obscured any visible vestige of the Scottish colony. A fifty-strong archaeological expedition of young students and local native Kuma helpers had recently discovered the extent of Scotland's lost settlement. The expedition was led by the ex-army engineer and adventurer Colonel John Blashford-Snell for the Royal Scottish Geographical Society, who had been fascinated by the whole doomed Darien episode ever since he drove an expedition of Land Rovers successfully through the then roadless Panama isthmus in 1970.

After hearing about Blashford-Snell's ambitious plans at a lecture, I had agreed to be the Darien expedition's patron and to help fund the young archaeologists. In their first year they had unearthed a line of graves, which only hinted at the number that

William Paterson, 1658-1719, founder of the Bank of England, promoter of Scotland's Darien Colony in Central America.

doubtless extended back into the uncleared jungle. Only traces of the ramparts of Fort St Andrew remained, which were probably washed out years ago by the relentless rains of Panama. At another New Edinburgh site traces of the settlement's wooden huts and a pitiful array of artefacts were found, including broken tools, parts of churchwarden clay pipes and a few eroded Scottish coins. Marine archaeologists had located the wreck of the *Olive Branch*, one of the relief ships which had burned and sunk in the bay before it was able to unload any of its vitally needed cargo. To relieve the gloom surrounding the tragic remains of that disastrous chapter of Scottish history, we were taken into the jungle for a picnic close to a recently discovered waterfall which some wit had already named Connery Falls.

There is now a moving exhibit on New Edinburgh and Scotland's doomed colony in Panama, arranged by the mayor. I told him about the empty Darien oak treasure chest with its thirteen locking bolts, which is now one of the most poignant exhibits in the New Museum of Scotland. Perhaps one day it could be exhibited in Panama. Back in Old Edinburgh I asked my friend David Murray what he would have done at the time.

'Well, I think I would have first checked out the site,' he said. 'I've never bought anything blind. Perhaps if Paterson had spent as much caution on the expedition as they did on the ingenuity of the Darien chest's complicated locks, the colony might have turned out a little differently.'

The Darien iron money chest, with its complicated lock of fifteen spring bolts, was inherited by the Royal Bank of Scotland, and since gifted to the National Museum of Scotland. In the wake of the Darien Disaster the Royal Bank was founded on half of the doomed venture's remaining funds. The chest may remain empty but the Royal Bank of Scotland is now one of the largest banking groups in the world.

Opposite: Lauriston Castle was built around 1590 by the father of John Napier, the inventor of logarithms. A later owner, John Law of Lauriston, exploited Napier's mathematics into realms unknown.

John Law of Lauriston, 1671-1729, was the Jekyll and Hyde of mental arithmetic, at once brilliant economist and hell-bent gambler; the father of finance and the promoter of the Mississippi disaster, the Enron of its day.

'Do you think the disaster of Darien engendered a national fear of risk-taking, which is still with us today?' I asked.

'Whether Darien left a psychological scar, I'm not so sure, unless it jumped a few generations, for Scottish enterprise blossomed in the nineteenth century with industrial innovators, inventive engineers, and shipbuilders to the world. But you're right, today we do seem to have a fear of risk-taking, though Darien was certainly a risk too far.'

Yet, had things been better thought through, perhaps the Scots of New Edinburgh might have flourished. A canal, for a start, would have been a good idea, but the Panama Canal was still two hundred years away in the future.

Through the disaster of the Darien Scheme Scotland lost nearly a quarter of its liquid assets and its economy was ruined. There had been no glory, no valour. Few nations could have withstood the terrible loss of pride and money. Scotland's exchequer and storehouses were empty, and its challenge to the mercantile power of England was now a mockery. Compounded with years of poor harvests, the Darien misadventure had brought Scotland to its economic knees. To get Scotland back in business after this disaster, Parliament was offered an enterprising scheme by a successful Edinburgh entrepreneur called John Law, to create a council of commerce. He made a proposal to Parliament for the establishment of a national bank to issue promissory notes on the value of land. Law further proposed an allocation of state revenues to be placed in the hands of a national council approved by Parliament to improve, capitalise and develop national industries. In effect the nation was to go into business. But in the wake of Darien's heroic failure, Law's speculative, untried plan seemed too unacceptably risky.

On 1 May 1707, the Treaty of Union was voted through between the two kingdoms of Scotland and England. By Article XV, the Company of Scotland was dissolved and the dream of a Scottish colony was finally laid to rest. Led by Andrew Fletcher of Saltoun, there were many who had pressed for better terms with England, and who foresaw the Union leading inevitably to Scots subordination to England. 'I ken, when we had a king, and a chancellor, and parliament – men o' our ain,' Walter Scott has one of his characters lament in *The Heart of Midlothian*, 'we could aye peeble them wi' stones when they werena gude bairns – but naebody's nails can reach the length o' Lunnon.'

In the end the Treaty had been sweetened a little by the 'Equivalent', the payment of £398,000 to compensate for the Darien losses and to support Scottish industries. After twenty years half the remaining Equivalent stock went to found a new bank. Few realise today that the Royal Bank of Scotland, now one of the largest in the world, owes its birth to Scotland's failure in the humid jungle of seventeenth-century Panama and that it was an idea first proposed by John Law.

Who knows what Scotland's fortunes might have been had the Scottish Parliament adopted Law's other more ingenious scheme for a council of commerce? John Law was an unbeatable gambler who would become one of the most famous bankers ever. His father was a goldsmith who took over Lauriston Castle, once the home of the mathematician John Napier, the inventor of Napier's Logs, a logarithmic calculating system providing rapid solutions to mathematical problems. The young Law's mind was honed on such devices and further ingenious systems derived from other Scots 'geometers'.

John Law would soon put his calculating skills to profitable use in the fashionable London gaming-houses of the early eighteenth century, to win vast fortunes at card games. He focused his mathematical brain on the game of hazard, the original name for what the Americans now call 'craps'. Law mastered the odds of gambling. He was probably the first card counter; a skill he combined with an acute understanding of complex probability theory. He was the first to discover a system that, where 7 is the 'main' and 4 the 'chance', the odds against the croupier are enhanced. What he had learnt on the baize tables would soon make him one of the most famous financial speculators of all time.

Following a duel in April 1694, Law was imprisoned in the Tower for murder. He soon escaped and fled to the Continent. Safely in France, Law now continued to develop his theories on banking and commerce from lessons won as a gambler. He had seen how wealth accumulated through pushing heaps of coins across tables. The inconvenience of manoeuvring such large heaps of gold gave him the idea of introducing counters, each of which would be worth eighteen gold Louis coins. With such piles continually falling into his lap, Law got the idea that currency itself could be a motor for the production of wealth. He introduced the modern idea of extended credit.

Law presented himself to King Louis as the financial saviour of France, whose national debt was then proportionately as large as Scotland's. After Louis's weary wars, a ruined agriculture and languid trade, he offered the beleaguered king salvation. Law, or Le Sieur Lass, as the French pronounced his name, now took Paris by storm. He became known as the *seigneur écossais* who daily substituted his two sacks of gold coins with gambling counters. He became so successful he was asked to leave the country for knowing 'too much of the games he played'.

After the death of Louis XIV, Law returned and was granted a licence in 1716 to establish a Banque Générale in which he invested much of his own money. With an initial capital of six million livres, divided into 120 shares each of 5000 livres, it was a bank of discount and deposit based on a fixed weight of gold, with the right to issue notes payable on demand. It was an immediate success. Law became the first modern speculator. In effect he had created modern banking. He became a Catholic convert and through his fellow Scot, the Chevalier Andrew Ramsay, Law became a close friend of the playboy Regent of France the Duc d'Orléans, who soon dubbed him a Chevalier. He established his new status in the regal splendour of 23 Place Vendôme, that most elegant of all Parisian squares, where the fountains still play over the sensuous sculptures of nymphs and satyrs. Law's salons soon gained a licentious reputation and it was even said that he had read the lascivious works of François Rabelais in church.

Law liked to live some distance from his work, so for his bank he chose the Rue Quincampoix, a small street near Les Halles. He then founded the Compagnie de la Louisiane ou d'Occident to exploit the apparently limitless resources of the area of North America watered by the Mississippi and its tributaries. These included the

The medallion of the Compagnie de la Louisiane ou d'Occident which portrayed the Mississippi as a land rich in gold and silver, precious stones, fertile lands where fortunes were to be made from the pelts of wild animals. The offer was irresistible to the war-worn peasantry of German states who sailed to Louisiana to escape the eternal conflicts of Europe.

Missouri and the Ohio Rivers – the French had laid claim to a vast area, which included territories also claimed by the British. To make the company show a profit, Law knew that he had to develop the Mississippi swamplands. That would take some doing, for few émigrés had ever settled there.

Law devised a seductive company medallion of a Mississippi river god dispensing a cornucopia of golden coins. Throughout Europe, his handbills proclaimed that the river god's treasuries awaited Louisiana's happy settlers. Investors stampeded to the Rue Quincampoix to buy their shares. This little narrow street, where the share brokers worked all day and night, soon became the goal of speculators. The share price of the Compagnie de la Louisiane ou d'Occident rose dramatically in a frenzy of speculation. Shares of 50 livres rose to 10,000 livres in a year. In everything but name he was the Prime Minister of France. When the Compagnie issued a 40 per cent dividend in 1720, the share price rocketed to 18,000 livres. People became rich beyond their dreams. Law coined the term 'millionaire' to match his fortune, and the word immediately entered both the French and English languages. Even Law's valet became a millionaire. Prince Charles, the Young Pretender, who by then was a ridiculous rather than a romantic figure, came to Law for funds and left with riches.

Chevalier Law undertook to repay the national debt of France in return for the control of national revenues and the French mint for a period of nine years. At this point speculators took their profit. The shares tumbled. In panic, investors sought to redeem their promissory notes, but the Compagnie had insufficient coin. Then, just like the collapse of Enron, which turned coin into paper in our own times so disastrously, Law's Mississippi venture collapsed into bankruptcy. Meanwhile, Louisiana settlers died in their hundreds on the fever-wracked banks of the Mississippi, cursing with their last breath John Law and his shining lies. It became the 'Louisiana Purchase' when Napoleon sold it for $15 million to Thomas Jefferson, the third President of the United States of America. That worked out at roughly 4 cents an acre. Jefferson informed Congress the morning after clinching the deal.

Centuries later the gold Law's scheme promised was discovered under the slack waters of the Bayou Boeuf swamps. Black gold. To this day Louisiana owes much to the Scot John Law. Some leading economists now consider him to have been one of the most remarkable financiers of all time. Chased out of France by his creditors, he died near-penniless in Venice in 1729. Under a pompous Latin dedication he now lies in the central aisle of the suitably pompous Venetian church of San Moise.

John Law's brother William stayed on in France, and a descendant of his, Madame Lily de Lauriston, saved the famous champagne label of Bollinger through the dark days of World War II. That raised a smile for me, as Ian Fleming made Bollinger James Bond's favourite champagne. And then I read that Bollinger was also the first choice of Thomas Jefferson, that discerning founder father of the United States. And to think that it was Jefferson who bought Law's Mississippi for America. Surely we can raise a glass to that and to the Auld Alliance between Scotland and France. And if it's not too much, perhaps we should raise another to that extraordinary adventurer, the Chevalier John Law – Slainte to Le Sieur Lass!

Beyond the soaring column of La Place Vendôme, John Law held court in great luxury, promoting his financial schemes.

7 THE STRANGE CASE OF JAMES VI OF SCOTLAND AND I OF ENGLAND

James Stuart 1567–1625

You might wonder why we are devoting a whole chapter to this Stuart king. But it's my belief that the inequalities between Scotland and England hark back to 25 July 1603 when James VI of Scotland was crowned James I of England. As Tom Devine says in *The Scottish Nation*,

> The difficulties had their origin in the Regal Union of 1603 when James VI of Scotland had succeeded Elizabeth I to the crowns of England and Ireland. James had been eager to go much further, and in 1604 commissioners from England and Scotland discussed a union of parliaments and a scheme of common citizenship. Despite James's keen support the idea foundered.

King James believed that God had ordained him to unite the two kingdoms of Scotland and England as equals, under the Crown of Great Britain, not of England. He had proposed free trade between the nations and a true United Kingdom. Had England agreed to his proposals, much of the strife of the next hundred years might have been avoided. The English Parliament saw the Union of the Crowns solely as a way of absorbing Scotland under southern rule. Wales had been subsumed centuries before under the English Crown, and England claimed dominion over Ireland, not to mention France. 'The State of monarchy is the supremest thing on earth,' James proclaimed to Parliament in 1604, before adding in questionable theology, 'For kings are not only God's Lieutenants upon earth and sit upon God's throne, but even by God himself they are called gods.' The Stuarts believed in the divine rights of kings, so James sidestepped the dissent of Parliament and proclaimed himself King of Great Britain, a title that held no sway in England. And that's where Scotland's unequal partnership began.

Basilikon Doron by King James VI, 1599. Of the seven copies of the original edition printed privately for the King, only two are known to survive. This plate is reproduced from the copy in the National Library of Scotland, the other is in the Grenville Collection in the British Museum.

James Stuart was born in 1566, the son of Mary Queen of Scots and her cousin Henry Stuart, Lord Darnley. At a touching ceremony in the Chapel Royal of Stirling Castle which Darnley refused to attend, the future king was baptised a Catholic. Less than two months later Darnley would die at Kirk o' Fields, murdered at the hands of Scottish nobles. In reckless haste, Mary married the Earl of Bothwell, one of the prime suspects in the plot. The nobles then turned on her, marooning Mary in a castle on an island in Loch Leven. The Queen of Scots was forced to abdicate the crown; thus one-year-old wee James became the King of Scots.

A series of regents ruled the troubled land. James's education began when he was three years old, and from then on he would be raised a Protestant. His tutor, the Renaissance scholar George Buchanan, was one of the most learned men in Europe, teaching James Greek and Latin and instilling in him a love of classical poetry. Although Buchanan had once dedicated a book to James's mother, he implicated Mary in Darnley's murder. He railed against her Catholic faith, tormenting her with anti-Papist rhetoric. James would hear little humanism from the great scholar, least of all concerning his now incarcerated mother. This was mitigated somewhat by Peter Young, another of James's tutors. He imbued in James a love of contemporary literature, poetry and theatre. He encouraged the young scholar to read books from his mother's library, which included shelves of romances and lighter works in French. With Buchanan's gravitas and Young's lighter touch, James was soon well on his way to becoming an accomplished poet and a respected author in his own right.

Since both his mother and father were grandchildren of Margaret Tudor, the eldest daughter of England's Henry VII, James was in line for the English throne. Contemplating his future responsibilities, he began to think seriously of his ultimate accession to the two crowns. In 1590 he sailed to Oslo to marry Anne, the fourteen-year-old daughter of the King of Denmark. Back in Edinburgh a fabulous coronation awaited the royal couple. At the Mercat Cross on the Royal Mile, the Goddess of Corn and Wine blessed the marriage so propitiously that six children quickly followed. When Henry, his first-born, was only five years old James wrote a treatise on government, *Basilikon Doron* (Greek for 'the Kingly Gift'), dedicating it to 'Henrie my dearest sonne and natural successor'.

THE ARGUMENT OF THE BOOKE.
SONET.
GOD gives not Kings the style of Gods in vaine,
For on his throne his Scepter do they swey:
And as their subjects ought them to obey,
So Kings should feare and serve their God againe.
If then ye would enjoy a happie raigne,
Observe the Statutes of your Heavenly King;
And from his Lawe make all your Lawes to spring:
Since his Lieutenant hear ye should remaine.
Rewarded the just, be steadfast, true, and plaine:
Repress the proud, maintaining ay the right,
Walke alwaies so, as ever in his sight
Who guardes the godly, plaging the prophaine,
And so ye shall in princely vertues shine.
Resembling right your mighty King divine.

James's broad Scots accent, made all the broader by his over-sized tongue, and his bisexuality, made him an awkward king for the English to embrace. Recent assessments, concentrating on James's wise statesmanship and remarkably peaceful reign in times of trouble, have been kinder. He ruled until he died, in 1625, without ever taking his now 'united kingdoms' to war.

Antonia Fraser traces the orphaned James's 'inability to resist love' back to his adolescence and a 'search to recapture the golden youthful quality of his early passion'. In her sympathetic biography, Fraser sees thirteen-year-old James's romance with Esmé Stuart, his dashingly handsome older French male cousin, as the love event of his life, in an over-confined upbringing deprived of affection; a love James touchingly recaptured in one of his earliest sonnets.

First Ioue [Jove], as greatest God aboue the rest,
Graunt thou to me a pairt of my desyre
That when in verse of thee I wryte my best,
This onely thing I earnestly require…

Despite fathering many children, the King was sneeringly mocked as 'Queen James' at court. 'I am neither a god nor an angel, but a man like any other,' James said provocatively, defending his love for George Villiers before ennobling him as

James VI King of Scotland, 1567-1625. King James I of England 1603-25. This portrait by the Flemish artist John de Critz was painted soon after James had acceded to the throne of England in 1603. Although the flamboyant jewelled 'Mirror of Great Britain' in his hat was commissioned to commemorate the union of the Scottish and English crowns, the Parliament of England refused James the title, King of Great Britain.

Duke of Buckingham. 'For Jesus Christ did the same, and therefore I cannot be blamed. Christ had John, and I have George.' Such pleadings have made him one of the earliest defenders of gay rights, a claim which has stirred both Roman Catholic and Protestant fundamentalists to fire salvoes at each other across the ether.

The website of the American 'Bible Church' makes a spirited defence against inferring James's homosexuality from his writings. It maintains that it is a misunderstanding of the wider meaning of 'love' as interpreted in Jacobean times. This is countered by the 'Catholic Apologetics', who not only besmirch the King in an intemperate homophobic rant, but also go on to trash the translation of the Bible commissioned by King James. They achieve this not without some irony, since several of their Old Testament quotations, condemning homosexuality, are lifted word for word from James's Authorised Version. Then there is the more brotherly-loving intervention of the Internet's 'Liberated Christians', who whole-heartedly back the King for 'promoting intimacy' within the Church.

All this apart, the King had to withstand the anti-Scottish detractors. There was much resentment when James filled the royal household with Scots within a month of his arrival in London. The most vociferous of his critics was the venomous Sir Anthony Weldon, who had bad-mouthed him ever since James had excluded him from court. Scots in their droves – from the talented to rascals down on their luck who would soon be on the make in London – had followed the King south. A storm of Scotophobia erupted. Gangs of thugs, calling themselves the 'Swaggerers', beat up any Scots found sleeping rough. They took their lead from the swashbuckling Sir Edmund Baynham, who was later implicated in the Gunpowder Plot of 1605.

James certainly deserves better than to be dismissed as the 'wisest fool in Christendom' by the Duc de Sully, although the quip is now usually attributed to Henry, King of France. He was certainly the most scholarly king ever to sit on the Scottish and English thrones. He ruled in peace and his king-craft (as he called it) ended the war with Spain in the first year of his reign. This enabled England to found her own colonies, a quest for long solely the preserve of the Spanish and Portuguese.

My American friends are usually surprised when I tell them that their country owes its foundation to a Scot. It's always puzzled me why so many know so little about the role played in the creation of America by Scotland's James VI, the first Stuart King of England. After a number of unsuccessful attempts to establish a foothold in the New World, the first English colony in North America to survive was founded at Jamestown, Virginia, in 1607 through a charter granted by King James.

An enterprising Suffolk explorer, Bartholomew Gosnold, who had already charted the New England coast, naming Cape Cod and Martha's Vineyard as he sailed south, was the prime mover in settling the colony of Virginia, together with such an unlikely partner as the swashbuckling adventurer John Smith, who had recently escaped from imprisonment in Turkey. James granted a royal charter to their Virginia Company in the hope of discovering gold and a lucrative passage west to India. He sent them God speed across the Atlantic with fulsome prose – that 'it shall please God to send you on the coast of Virginia, you shall do your best endeavour to find out a safe port in the entrance of some navigable river, making choice of such a one as runneth farthest into the land'.

The sea-weary 'venturers' finally sailed up a river in Virginia to found a settlement which perfectly matched the royal objective. They called their new 'cittie' Jamestown, on the James River, in honour of their King. James's instructions had urged the colonists to grow hemp and mulberry trees for the manufacture of silk, but the settlement would have foundered had it not been for crops of an improved strain of tobacco introduced by John Rolfe from the West Indies some years later. After a disastrous first year, when over half the colony died, Jamestown would eventually blossom into the first successful English colony in America. But it would be through the gold of Virginian tobacco that it prospered, much to the distaste of the anti-smoking King.

At the height of the American Civil War in 1863 Lincoln made Thanksgiving a national holiday in the hope of uniting the country. Two years later, after the defeat of the Confederate South, the founding of America would for ever shift north from Virginia to Plymouth, Massachusetts. After all, wouldn't a country founded on religious freedom be better than one which had begun as a commercial venture and was only brought to success through indentured teenage apprentices, slaves shipped in from Africa, and through the export of tobacco?

During the 2007 celebrations of the four-hundredth anniversary of the founding of Jamestown, I learnt that even the ceremony of Thanksgiving began there two years before it was taken up in Plymouth. 'On December 4, 1619 settlers stepped ashore at Berkeley Hundred along the James River,' reads the new National Park sign on the James River, 'and, in accordance with the proprietor's instruction that the day of our ship's arrival ... shall be yearly and perpetually kept as a day of thanksgiving, celebrated the first official Thanksgiving Day.' This all makes better sense to me. When I think of all my American friends, especially the very successful ones, it's hard to see how they could have descended from those fun-denying pilgrims. Much more likely they sprang from that strain of freebooting entrepreneurs. I feel much more akin to those not so godly Jamestown adventurers, who would eventually steer the colonies towards American independence. James must have regretted that his first successful colony had flourished through the export of that pernicious weed, for tobacco more than got up King James's nose. It infuriated him that by 1612 the largest tobacco exporter to London was Jamestown, the 'cittie' founded in his name.

But through tobacco Virginia flourished. When the British government later prevented the Virginians from selling their tobacco to other nations, the enraged farmers protested furiously. In 1776 two Virginia tobacco growers would register their fury more decisively with a later Hanoverian king. They were Thomas Jefferson of Monticello and George Washington of Mount Vernon.

In the first full year of his reign, in 1604, King James had rushed out a medically accurate 'counterblaste' against smoking, or 'drinking' as it was then curiously called. In seeing the dangers of tobacco-smoking, James was centuries ahead of his times.

Introduced to England by Sir Francis Drake, smoking was already highly fashionable. Sir Walter Raleigh had even persuaded Queen Elizabeth to light up. In his searing attack on the habit James saw the importance of educating the young, who are drawn to smoking by copying their elders, or 'like Apes, counterfeiting the manners of others, to our own destruction'. His 'Counterblaste' took no prisoners: 'Have you not reason then to be ashamed and to forbear this filthy novelty... a custom loathsome to the eye, hateful to the nose, harmful to the brain, dangerous to the lungs, and in the black stinking fume thereof nearest resembling the horrible stygian smoke of the pit that is bottomless.' James's devastating conclusion is as relevant today as it was four centuries ago. Extracts from his fulminations could easily double as mandatory health warnings on cigarette packs today.

King James's greatest achievement was the commissioning of a new translation of the Bible, which remains as the one work of literature written by a committee. Before leaving Scotland James had proposed such a translation to the General

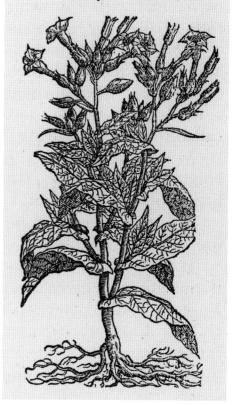

† 1 *Hyoſcyamus Peruvianus.*
Tabaco, or Henbane of Peru.

Tobacco was smoked by the Incas in the Ecuadorean and Peruvian Andes and by Native Americans for at least the last two thousand years. Introduced to Europe by the returning ships of Columbus and others, 'drinking' tobacco (as smoking was then called) soon became a fad and a life-saver to the early settlers in America. John Rolfe, a leading light in the Jamestown colony and an 'ardent smoker', learnt the skills of growing and curing tobacco from the local people of the Powhatan Confederacy, before marrying the Chief's daughter, Pocahontas. In 1611 Rolfe is credited with bringing a more fully flavoured tobacco plant from the Caribbean island of Tobago (hence the name tobacco). Successful annual crops then provided an economic basis for America's first colony which would soon yield centuries of slave-driven profit for the Southern United States.

The Authorised Bible of King James of 1611 would become the most printed book in world history.

Assembly of the Kirk of Scotland at Burntisland in 1601, but the scholars and resources were then unavailable for such an extended project. 'I could never yet see a Bible well-translated,' he told an assembly of churchmen and scholars at the Hampton Court Conference in 1604, when he initiated what has since been called 'a monument of English prose'. His deep knowledge of the classics, and his inquisitive turn of mind, challenged some of the greatest linguists and writers of their day to translate the Bible into an English that could be understood by anyone who could read.

Before the committee could begin, the King graciously lifted the penalty of death, which still threatened anyone who translated the Bible into English. At the beginning of James's reign in 1603, the authorised Bible was St Jerome's fourth-century version in Latin, which only the highly educated could ever have understood. Early in the sixteenth century the scholarly priest William Tyndale began a translation in secret, but he had to flee to Germany to have his Bible printed. 'Lord, open the King of England's eyes,' were Tyndale's last words, before agents of Henry VIII tracked him down in 1536, then strangled and burnt him for heresy.

Tyndale's courageous translation provided the groundwork for the fifty-four scholars and clerics who translated the King James version. But in addition to Tyndale's Greek texts they also had access to the Old Testament in Hebrew. Working unpaid in six separate working groups at Westminster and the university colleges of Oxford and Cambridge, they delivered the King James Bible within six years, in 1611. It immediately became a model of writing for generations of English-speaking people to come and the bestseller of all time, with over a billion printed.

The young Henry Frederick Stuart was nine when James took over the throne of England. Quick-witted, a fine horseman, tutored in military history, the handsome young Henry became the very model of a prince and future king. 'I know what becomes a prince,' he said, comparing himself to his scholarly father. 'It is not necessary for me to be a professor, but a soldier and a man of the world.' Loved in Scotland as the Duke of Rothesay and Lord of the Isles, in England he was made the Duke of Cornwall; at sixteen he was invested as the Prince of Wales – a combination of Scottish, English and Welsh titles that male heirs to the British throne still carry to this day.

Henry had inherited his father's love of literature and theatre, and shared his eye for art and architecture. Unlike his father, Henry promised to be a man of action, a warrior king. With this in mind the playwright and poet Ben Jonson mounted a masque in which Merlin likens the young Prince Henry to King Hal at Agincourt:

Yet rests that other thunderbolt of war,
Harry the Fifth; to whom in face you are
So like, as fate would have you so in worth.

Then, in November 1612 the Prince recklessly took a swim in the open sewer that the River Thames then was. He fell desperately ill, probably with typhoid, and died within days, aged just eighteen. James would never recover from the death of the golden son he had groomed as the future king, and neither would his country. What Henry would have achieved as King remains one of the great 'ifs' of British history. Would he have accommodated Parliament and prevented the Civil War? Or would he, as a staunch Protestant, have waged war against Catholicism in Europe?

The role of King was now thrust on Charles, the younger brother who had been brought up in his shadow. Charles I had impeccable taste in the arts, but he grew into a king who was by turns both reckless and indecisive. He harboured his

Below: The Banqueting House, Whitehall, London, 1619-22. This Palladian hall of state was commissioned by King James VI and I and designed by Inigo Jones for royal receptions and performances of masques.

Opposite: The nine ceiling paintings of 1635 by Sir Peter Paul Rubens, 1577-1640, glorifying the reign of King James, were commissioned by his son King Charles I.

There is no more moving monument to the hopes and fortunes of the Stuart kings than the Banqueting House in London's Whitehall. As you enter its Great Hall and look up at the heroic ceiling by Rubens, James, the King of Scots, celebrates the Union of the Crowns of 1603. Half-clad allegories of Scotland and England embrace the infant union, symbolised by James's naked baby Charles, who had been born in Dunfermline only two years before. Minerva, the goddess of wisdom and a thousand works, holds the twin crowns of the two nations above the child's puzzled face.

The lower central panel depicts the Union of the Crowns.

The upper central panel, The Peaceful Reign of James I, celebrates King James as Solomon. The King is enthroned in Solomon's Temple, in homage to the decisive powers bestowed on him by Sir Francis Bacon, who described James as the Solomon of his times.

Detail: In the great central oval panel Rubens revels in the King's apotheosis. Cherubs playing trumpets beckon him to God's right hand in Heaven. Those who question the theology must remember that King James believed that he had been appointed by God to rule the destinies of a United Kingdom of Scotland and England. It was his son's belief in the divine rights of Kings which would eventually demand that he walk under this painting, of his father's ascent into heaven, to his death on the scaffold mounted on the balcony outside.

father's fatal belief in the divine rights of kings over Parliament, which would not only cost him his kingdom, but also his life.

Dying in 1625, James never saw the nine masterful baroque pictures in his Great Hall, glorifying his peaceful reign. His son Charles grew up to be an even greater connoisseur of the arts. In one of the most enlightened acts of royal patronage in Britain, he commissioned the ceiling of the Banqueting House in London from the Flemish artist Sir Peter Paul Rubens. In the cruellest of ironies, King Charles I had to pass under the *Apotheosis* of his father into the heavenly heights, as he left the Great Hall for the scaffold in 1649. The divine rights of God's Lieutenant were denied Charles by his mortal accusers. 'I am the martyr of the people,' he said. 'I go from a corruptible to an incorruptible Crown, where no disturbance can be,' were his final words.

Early in his reign, James VI of Scotland and I of England had opened the royal court to artists, writers, poets and architects. He made John Donne his Chaplain in Ordinary before nominating the poet as the Dean of St Paul's. The witty playwright Ben Jonson was encouraged to collaborate with the architect Inigo Jones to write and design ever more elaborate masques. These would often open with the utterings of a holy fool and the antics of comics in a world turned upside down. For the second half of the performance the audience would join with the actors to sing and dance to 'musick fyne'.

With such revelry and fusion of the arts, James had put a thoroughly Scottish spin on an evening's entertainment. Such occasions were probably close in spirit to the good night out delivered by John McGrath's enterprising 7:84 theatre company in Scotland which I remember so well from the 1980s. Shows like *The Cheviot, the Stag and the Black Black Oil* would take over a Highland village hall and end up inviting the whole audience to reel and sing in a joyful ceilidh well into the night. I imagine it to be just like the fun of an all-singing, all-dancing Banqueting House Stuart masque. At least that makes for an altogether happier conclusion to remember James's peaceful reign by.

8 SCOTCH GOTHIC
Shadows of the Endarkenment

Up the close and down the stair,
In the house with Burke and Hare;
Burke's the butcher, Hare's the thief,
Knox, the man who buys the beef.
                    Edinburgh children's song

Marnie, 1964. Alfred Hitchcock always liked to keep his actors on their toes. When I had apparently speeded up my dialogue, after many takes on a tricky back projection sequence with Tippi Hedren, Hitch said to me, 'The puppy's feet,' in his plumy voice. This puzzled me because the line was nowhere in the screenplay. 'Pause,' he said.

Edinburgh's contrasts fascinated me as a boy. I grew up between the classical New Town of Dr Jekyll and the Gothic closes of Mr Hyde's Old Town. Perhaps that's how Robbie Louis Stevenson might have described our industrial limbo land in what he called the precipitous city of his birth. Leaving school at thirteen, I got to know the divided selves of Edinburgh almost building by building on my morning milk rounds.

'Eerie.' 'Gruesome.' 'Weird.' 'Warlock.' Strange, isn't it, how these gloomy or supernatural words all derive from the Scots language? They are Scotland's Gothic gift to English. If you clamber up the worn stone steps of Edinburgh's Outlook Tower at the top of the Royal Mile, they just jump out at you. Especially when you reach the gloomy uppermost room of the Camera Obscura and peer down in the eerie half-light. There, dished up on a giant platter, the ordered streets of Edinburgh's classical New Town slowly take shape before your eyes. Beyond the twin Greek temples of the National Galleries, it is not hard to imagine Stevenson's Dr Jekyll living down there in the civilised refinement of the Scottish Enlightenment. Then, as the operator steers the Victorian periscope lens across the rooftops of the Old Town's Gothic huddle, it is just as easy to conjure up the good doctor's demonic alter ego, the evil Mr Hyde, scuttling along the dark closes of the Royal Mile. 'Few places, if any, offer a more barbaric display of contrasts to the eye,' wrote Stevenson of his own hometown. This was not lost on Alfred Hitchcock, who

Camera Obscura, Royal Mile, Edinburgh. The visionary town planner and polymath Patrick Geddes,1834-1932, acquired this camera obscura in 1892, renaming the building The Outlook Tower. From the moving lens in the tower above, visitors can still observe the sweep of the city naturally projected on a flat dish in a darkened room. And they can also experience something approximating what Geddes called the 'Inlook Room' to ponder what they have seen and learnt.

told me during the filming of *Marnie* that he had always wanted to film the perfect murder on those Edinburgh rooftops. It intrigued Hitch that an assassin would never have known that his seemingly unobserved murder would have been seen by all those watchful eyes inside the Camera Obscura's darkened chamber.

The lens of the Camera Obscura has now panned over the rooftops of the Old Town to dish up a fleeting presence in the shadows. Down in a narrow close, a student is hectoring a huddle of tourists. Hired by one of the many spooky Edinburgh lore and gore tours to retell the spurious fakelore of haunted Edinburgh, he's dressed for the part in an ill-fitting gravedigger's trench-coat. As he drones on, no one seems to have noticed a menacing shadow edging up the wall. But when a hand reaches out from a hooded figure, a startled tourist turns and shrieks on seeing the charade of a head painted as a gruesome skull. The wails of others soon echo into nervous laughter, as the essential daftness of the ghastly tourist scene returns them back to sanity. But is this all such harmless fun?

Around St Giles' Cathedral posters now compete in grimness, promising 'gruesome and bloody entertainment'. 'Let our costumed guide take you back to Edinburgh's grisly past,' proclaims one hoarding. Another adds a worrying disclaimer that their 'Mackenzie Poltergeist can cause physical and mental distress'. Leaflets are handed out advertising witch trial re-enactments in a nearby ruined castle with the challenging slogan, 'Dinnae come if you're feart.' I was shocked to see such a dreadfully depressing event promoted by Historic Scotland, especially since I had seen a monument to one of the last persecuted women burnt as a witch earlier in the day in rural Perthshire. That a government agency, set up to conserve buildings of national importance, is now driven to increase its visitor earnings by celebrating sixteenth-century misogyny is surely unacceptable. In Spain I learnt that they call such corruption of heritage in the name of tourism *la putería*, or the 'whoring', of the culture.

I might be open to the charge of encouraging such dark tourism myself, for there is a scene set in Mary King's Close in the film I hosted and David Murray ghosted (without any mention of spooks) on the cramped conditions of seventeenth-century Edinburgh. When what became the City Chambers were

With so many hoardings and placards now pitching dark tourism, Edinburgh's Royal Mile around St Giles Cathedral promotes the heresies of the Scottish Endarkenment with the shrouded look of a nightmare on Elm Street.

built in the eighteenth century the closes were all levelled off and sealed from above, leaving shops and rooms below intact. The public is now able to visit this subterranean part of the city. But instead of being able to appreciate how people then lived, they have to go along with a Disneyfied haunted-house experience. Just as well that Edinburgh Council's jurisdiction doesn't extend to re-enactments among the ruins of Pompeii, at least near those notorious bordellos.

For those who live above the routes of Edinburgh's ghost tours, a summer of shrieking can unhinge even the sanest, especially if you have small children. One night a fearsome yell awoke a baby into a crying fit, just after his young mother had got him back to sleep. She snapped, and rushed down screaming in her nightdress. The tour group thought it was all part of the act they had paid for, until she grabbed the ghost's stick and began beating everyone back up the close. Upstairs, her partner, thinking that her life was threatened, grabbed a meat cleaver from the kitchen and joined the fray. It all ended in court with the woman receiving an £80 fine and her husband a three-month jail sentence, for 'attempted grievous bodily harm'. 'Nightmare on Victoria Terrace' was the headline in the local paper. Is 'Dark Tourism' not going too far?

Fact or fiction, the Old Town of Edinburgh was just destined to play a leading role in the birth of the Gothic Movement: from the castle straddling the rocks of an extinct volcano, down the fishbone of the Royal Mile, with its ribs of dark closes splayed out on either side, all the way down to the ruined abbey of Holyrood. Could there ever be a better backdrop than that for Gothic drama? I well remember rounding the castle rock during the Edinburgh Film Festival with the German film producer Joachim von Mengershausen. Looking up at the clouds scudding over the floodlit battlements, he turned to me in astonishment. 'Your city was surely built by the set designers of *Dracula* for Hammer Films.' And who could disagree? After all, *The Body Snatcher*, Hollywood's version of Stevenson's retelling of the murderers Burke and Hare, opens on the castle esplanade where a shepherd, somewhat inappropriately, is gathering in his flock of sheep.

The eeriest of Gothic tales seems to have arisen effortlessly out of Scotland's native earth. From Edinburgh's dank closes to Ayrshire caves or Border hills, Scotland can more than stake its claim to hold the psychic low ground of Gothic yarns. Even America's number one shocker, Edgar Allan Poe, spent his formative years in Ayrshire on the west coast of Scotland. He was born in Boston, and by the time he was two his father had left and his mother had died. John Allan, a rich tobacco trader from Scotland, and his wife Frances rescued the children and returned to his hometown in Ayrshire where Edgar would attend the old Burgh School at Kirkgatehead.

The local Gothic folk stories which Robert Burns drew on so creatively in such tales of the supernatural as *Tam O'Shanter* must surely have alerted the young Edgar to those mischief-making bogles, to places 'where ghaists and houlets nightly cry'. As a schoolboy, he was free to wander among the gravestones of the old Laigh Kirk, with their grim skull-and-crossbones and other carved symbols of death. Nearby were the ruins of Castle Dean, where old folk still remembered the night when a catastrophic fire had shattered its walls in half to reflect a fiery

Left: Symbols like these were often read as works of magic compiled by sorcerers. The Rylands Library inherited manuscripts from the library of the Earls of Crawford, the Bibliotheca Lindesiana named after Lady Anne Lindsay – a Poet Laureate of Scotland. Could such a page have sprung from the hand of Michael Scott?

Right: Advocate's Close from Old and New Edinburgh by James Grant, 1880s. The closes, or alleys, running down from the Royal Mile were a gift to Gothic fictioners.

wedge on to the still waters of the loch. Could this have inspired the red-hot walls of the condemned man's cell in 'The Pit and the Pendulum', one of Poe's greatest Gothic tales?

The supernatural has a long tradition in Scotland, at least as far back as the Middle Ages. Sir Walter Scott, in 'The Lay of the Last Minstrel', wrote:

> In these far climes it was my lot
> To meet the wondrous Michael Scott
> A wizard, of such dreaded fame…

Michael Scott was one of the greatest minds of the early thirteenth century. Yet his real achievements in the arts and sciences became so overlaid with legends of dark sorcery that he soon became Scotland's un-godfather of the Gothic. As a philosopher, doctor and mathematician, Scott sought out the greatest scholars of his age in Spain and Sicily, where he translated Arab and Jewish texts. His books on algebra and esoteric sciences were comprehensible only to a few. Given that he dressed in Arab robes, many read his texts, with their the mysterious algebraic symbols, as books on magic.

Michael Scott returned to Scotland, where he died around 1235. People believed that if his great books were ever opened they would let loose a gaggle of malignant fiends. Legend has it that his books were buried with him in Melrose Abbey to ensure they were never opened again:

> When Michael lay on his dying bed,
> His conscience was awakened…
> I swore to bury his Mighty Book
> That never mortal might therein look…

But a mortal might therein look again, for there are still some who claim that a medieval treasure in the rare manuscript collection of the John Rylands Library in Manchester is Michael Scott's magic 'Mighty Book'. Its pages of algebraic equations still read as occult hieroglyphs and reek of magic to me. To the few who can crack the codes, this book is more likely a work of medieval mathematics, fathered on Scott by less informed and more fanciful minds many centuries ago.

Michael Scott lives on in the Borders. The magic of the Wizard was seen to be so powerful that he is credited with cleaving the Eildon Hills in three, despite them being known locally as Trimontium since Roman times. With his supernatural powers, Scott is said to have caused the bells of Notre Dame to peal in Paris as he prayed in a cave in Spain. His sorcery became so notorious that Dante in his *Divine Comedy* has him marching backwards into the Inferno, giving this brilliant intellectual the singular distinction of being the only Scot to win a place in Hell:

Quell'altro che ne' fianchi è così poco,
   Michele Scotto fu, che veramente
   de le magiche frode seppe 'l gioco.

Ché da le reni era tornato 'l volto,
   e in dietro venir li convenia,
   perché 'l veder dinanzi era lor tolto.

The next to come was short and skinny
Michael Scott, true master wizard,
A magician of the occult arts.

Arsey versey all were turned
And backwards had to walk
Never looking to the front.

Inferno, Canto XX vv.5, 39

The occult would gather force in Scotland, in the centuries to come, gripping the minds of the people who believed that the evil force of Satan vied with the divine goodness of God. We have already seen how the belief in the powers of sorcery overcame the mind of King James VI, whose witch obsessions became part of the fabric of Shakespeare's *Macbeth*. Towards the end of his life, the long tormented history of Scottish sorcery began to enthral Sir Walter Scott. When the shadows of night and death were gathering around him in his Gothic home of Abbotsford, he became obsessed with the forces of the supernatural. Ghosts, demons, elementals, poltergeists and all forms of magic and the occult captured his imagination. He began a series of letters on demonology and witchcraft to his son-in-law, J. G. Lockhart, a writer who would eventually become his biographer. Scott's short story of the supernatural, 'Wandering Willie's Tale', was inspired by the shocking story of Major Weir.

Major Thomas Weir was a pious retired lieutenant in the Scottish Puritan Army. He was a forbidding figure and a respected preacher among the Bowhead saints, the Presbyterians who lived in the steep winding street of the West Bow. At seventy-six, Weir appeared to fall ill, confessing incest and sorcery, a confession that was confirmed by his sister Jane. Scott writes, 'Weir was seized by the magistrates on a strange whisper regarding vile practices.' Weir claimed that he was of the Devil's party. His sister, whom many took to be a kindly old spinster, claimed that her brother's depravities had overwhelmed her. The pair were arrested together and were convicted and executed on charges of witchcraft. He died, 'stupidly sullen and impenitent,' wrote Scott. Weir's thornwood walking-stick was consigned to the flames with the Major, and it was said to have writhed like a satanic snake. The Weirs' home in the West Bow was believed to be haunted. Heads of spectral calves were said to appear at night along with other phantoms, and eventually the whole building was pulled down.

   Robbie Louis Stevenson, who was well versed in Edinburgh's pious and demoniacal past, chose to call his last unfinished novel 'Weir of Hermiston'. His Weir was another wielder of the stick. Major Weir would be neither the first nor the last Scot to live a double life. Stevenson always wanted to write a story about a fellow who was two fellows. 'I have been doomed to such a dreadful shipwreck: that man is not truly one, but truly two,' Dr Jekyll confesses, in his final 'Full Statement

Dante's *Divine Comedy*, Canto XX of *Inferno*, illustrated by Sandro Botticelli, 1445-1510. Led by the poet Virgil, Dante descends through successive circles of Hell. For his alleged sins of sorcery Michael Scott is condemned to have his head twisted permanently backwards as he is marched into hell.

of the Case'. 'It was on the moral side, and in my own person, that I learned to recognise the thorough and primitive duality of man…' Stevenson himself felt 'that strong sense of man's double being which must at times come in upon and overwhelm the mind of every thinking creature'. If Stevenson distanced the haunts of Dr Jekyll and Mr Hyde from Edinburgh to London, could he not have disguised the potion which turned the doctor's polite civility into monstrous brutality? What if that altering draught came not from white powders but was the purest whisky, 100 per cent alcohol, unattainable through distillation, but won by the doctor in the experimental laboratory of his 'changing' room. Stevenson had often observed in Edinburgh how easily the spiritual in men surrendered to the spirituous. He had witnessed many respectable Scots drink themselves by day into a stupor of staggering aggressiveness by night. And he was never shy of a glass himself.

One of strangest things about Scotland's capital is that its grimmest historical realities often transcended the wildest imagination of its Gothic fictioners. Who could have dreamt up the real-life duplicity of one town councillor, a much respected member of Edinburgh society by day and a villainous ne'er-do-well by night? As deacon, or chief, of the Wrights and Masons William Brodie was skilled in cabinet-making, a master locksmith and a convivial man-about-town. He had inherited the business from his father, one of Scotland's greatest cabinet-makers whose work can be seen today in Dumfries House along with such English masters as Chippendale and Hepplewhite. Brodie's position allowed him entry to the most fashionable Edinburgh homes where he was often a welcome dinner guest. Such hospitality he would ruthlessly exploit. After casting an eye over the valuables of his hosts, he would find an absent moment to slip outside and press their door keys into bars of soap. Then in the dead of night, donning his burglar's clothes, he would cry: 'Well, the day for them, the night for me…On with the new coat and into the new life! Down with the Deacon and up with robber!…I'm a man once more till morning.' Or at least those were the lines given to him by Stevenson in *Deacon Brodie — or the Double Life*, the forgotten melodrama he co-authored with his friend William Henley.

Living high by day and low by night, Brodie cruised the lower depths of Edinburgh life. Gambler, philanderer, drinker and cock-fighting aficionado, he was clearly heading for a fall. Brodie and his gang were caught red-handed robbing the Excise Office in Chessel's Court off the Royal Mile. Friends in high places secured Henry Erskine, the Dean of the Faculty of Advocates, for Brodie's defence. 'Now we have got the best cock that ever fought,' the Deacon boasted. But when his key accomplice turned King's evidence, Brodie was dispatched to the newly improved gallows which he himself had designed and his firm had only recently rebuilt. At his public execution a question hovered over the crowd, as Brodie's body was hurriedly spirited away: could this deceitful master of his craft not have engineered a mechanism to allow him to escape his fate? Some thought that he had been rushed aboard a ship at Leith for a new life in Virginia.

Straddling good by day and evil by night, Deacon Brodie presented Stevenson with an archetypical character of the divided self. The strange case of this master

Dr. Jekyll and Mister Hyde, 1932, directed by Rouben (Zachary) Mamoulian. 'I do believe the cinema is in imagery, not in words,' Mamoulian once said. Nobody has surpassed Frederic March as the ultimate 'double', who won an Oscar for his performance of R. L. Stevenson's kindly doctor and evil Hyde. James Cruze, Sheldon Lewis, John Barrymore, Spencer Tracy, Paul Massiek, Anthony Perkins and Mark Redfield are among the many who have played the double title roles.

cabinet-maker had probably fascinated Stevenson ever since his childhood days, as his bedroom included a striking piece of furniture by Brodie. It's not hard to imagine the young writer's impressionable mind wandering beyond the counterpane, especially on stormy moonlit nights.

Stevenson himself lived a double life in Edinburgh; a 'respectable' practising advocate in the lawcourts by day and devil's advocate by night, whoring with his 'Highland Marys'. Suavely dressed in his velvet jacket, he would leave his elegant Heriot Row home in the classical New Town at dusk to entrance the 'wee hoories' in the Gothic Old Town. 'I have been all my days a dead hand at a Harridan,' wrote Stevenson later, 'I never saw the one yet that could resist me.' Yet he could still look back to the lost opportunities of his Edinburgh youth, in a letter to Henley, 'If I had to begin again…I believe I should honour sex more religiously. The worst of our education is that Christianity does not recognize and hallow sex.'

By the beginning of the nineteenth century Edinburgh had won an international reputation for teaching medicine, based on practical observation and a thorough understanding of anatomy. This was at a time when bodies for dissection could only be legitimately acquired from the hangman, in the shape of executed criminals. The academic question was how could the law of supply and demand maintain the teaching of medicine, in the city that was once home to Adam Smith, that wise philosopher and father of economics?

The 'resurrection men', as they soon became known, would dig up the newly buried by night and deliver them in the morning to the anatomy department of Edinburgh University. William Hare, the landlord of a decaying lodging-house, fell upon an alternative supply. When one of his lodgers died, he filled his coffin with bark and sent the body up to Surgeon's Square to be seven and a half pounds the richer. Such a sum eclipsed what a fellow lodger, William Burke, could have earned in a year as an itinerant carter. So together they formed a grisly partnership bent on suffocating any poor wretch that came their way. Over a period of nine months they had smothered eleven women and five men. All were delivered still warm to the ambitious anatomist Dr Robert Knox, who asked no questions. But when his students recognised the kindly face of 'Daft Jamie' – a local character they often ran across in the streets of Edinburgh – the anatomical tables began to turn on Knox. Then, when the body of Marjory Docherty was found under a bed by fellow tenants, the body-snatchers were caught by the police dead-handed. Hare offered to turn King's evidence. Burke was sent to the gallows in the most notorious public hanging that Edinburgh had ever seen.

Knox was denounced vehemently as 'a foul trader in human flesh' by Sir Walter Scott, who felt that the lofty ideals of his alma mater had been vilely disgraced. Yet Knox was neither brought before the law nor censored by the university. He didn't regard the Burke and Hare murders as criminal acts. On the contrary, Knox looked upon them as an enlightened method of disposing of worthless derelicts for the bettering of humanity through the study of anatomy. Clearly Knox had left the light of learning for the dark side of the Scottish Enlightenment, what the historian Bill Zack so aptly calls the Scottish Endarkenment. At least the anatomy department denied him Burke's corpse. This was first exhibited by public demand

William Hare from *West Port Murders, or an Authentic Account of the Atrocious Murders Committed by Burke and his Associates*, 1829. The serial murderers William Hare and William Burke, in collusion with the anatomist Dr Robert Knox, were the embodiment of the Scottish Endarkenment. At their trial Hare turned King's evidence condemning his accomplice Burke to be hanged and dissected in 1828.

Robert Louis Balfour Stevenson, 1850-94, by John Singer Sargent, 1856-1925 (detail). 'The most intense creature that I had ever met.' – J.S. Sargent.

In the Department of Anatomy of Edinburgh University, Burke's skeleton is still displayed among others for medical study. My deerstalker is a reminder that Conan Doyle studied medicine here under the analytical Dr Joseph Bell, who did much to shape the famous diagnostic skills of his fictional detective, Sherlock Holmes. From *Sean Connery's Edinburgh*, 1981, directed by Murray Grigor, produced by Lynda Myles and Penny Thomson.

and then dissected by Knox's rivals in front of crowds. As I stood beside Burke's skeleton for a sobering sequence in the Edinburgh film, I felt a twinge of Gothic horror that this gruesome exhibit of a murderer was still displayed here in the guise of advancing medicine.

Despite this outrage, Edinburgh's reputation for medicine grew. One of its most outstanding students was William Polidori, who graduated as a doctor at the precociously young age of nineteen, writing his thesis on sleep-walking. He became Lord Byron's personal physician and accompanied him to Switzerland in 1816, where the poet summered on the shores of Lake Geneva with Mary and Percy Bysshe Shelley. Stormy weather drove the friends indoors for days and nights. To get over their collective depression, Byron came up with the homeopathic remedy that everyone should write a haunting Gothic yarn as an entertainment. Polidori, whose patience with Lord Byron was beginning to fray, conjured up unexpectedly what was to be the first ever vampire story. His lurid tale clearly caricatured Byron as the unscrupulous Lord Ruthven. By night he had his lordship transformed into a swooping vampire, flying through windows to suck the blood out of beautiful women. The young doctor created both the noble vampire and a potent Gothic tale. But it would be the young and seemingly retiring Mary Shelley who would take her inspiration from the scientific experiments of James Lind, a retired Scots doctor. She wrote *Frankenstein* after

These ruins of the sixteenth-century Slains Castle, which now embody the very essence of Gothic gloom, date only from 1925 when the insanity of British tax laws eliminated annual rates for roofless buildings. Ironically Slains Castle, which inspired Bram Stoker's *Dracula*, was intact in 1890 when the 19th Earl of Errol had the Irish author over for a round of whisky, which makes Stoker's achievement uncannily prophetic. But the Gothic haar may soon be dispelled, as plans are now afoot to turn the ruins into holiday homes.

overhearing Shelley talking to Byron about Lind's scientific experiments. Through the mysterious power of electricity Lind had brought a frog back to life, or at least had caused its back legs to twitch and jump. As Mary listened to them endlessly discussing such imponderables as the essence of life, she wondered if electricity could impart the divine spark of life to reanimate a human corpse. 'I saw the hideous phantasm of a man stretched out, and then, on the working of some powerful engine, show signs of life, and stir with an uneasy, half vital motion' (*Frankenstein, or the Modern Prometheus*).

In the wake of Mary Shelley's *Frankenstein* and Polidori's *Vampyre* would come a stream of Victorian penny-dreadfuls, gruesomely illustrated with the crudest of woodcuts. One of the bestsellers was *Varney the Vampire* by Preskett Prest. But soon, far outselling them all, was Prest's retelling of the life and crimes of Sawney Beane, Scotland's most notorious highwayman, who fed his ever-growing family on his murder victims.

The wellsprings of Scotch Gothic run deep. While on holiday around Cruden Bay on the Aberdeenshire coast in the summer of 1890 Bram Stoker was inspired by the ruins of Castle Slains. In the gloaming of the dying day its dark cliff-top silhouette became the menacing Gothic fortress of the blood-sucking Transylvanian Count Dracula, as he wrote it up that night in the Kilmarnock Arms Hotel.

But no tales of the divided self, of internal battles between good and evil, of doubles or doppelgängers, have ever been better explored than in James Hogg's portrayal of the power of evil in his masterpiece, *The Private Memoirs and Confessions of a Justified Sinner* (1824). Set in early-eighteenth-century Scotland, Hogg's novel recounts the corruption of Robert Wringhim, a boy of strict Calvinist upbringing, by a mysterious stranger. Under the influence of this stranger Wringhim commits a series of murders in the belief that the 'Elect of God' can do no wrong. The reader, while recognising the stranger as the Devil, is prevented by Hogg's subtlety from deciding whether he is more than a figment of the imagination. Many talented writers have since tried to bring Hogg's masterpiece to the screen. For me the best screenplay was written by Bill Douglas; he developed his masterful trilogy out of his own experiences, growing up in a far bleaker Scotland than I could ever have imagined. Revelling in the purposeful ambiguities of Hogg's novel, Douglas's version might well have turned out to be that elusive first masterpiece of the Scottish cinema, if only funders had known so at the time.

Once, when flying back over the Border hills to Edinburgh, I fell into conversation with a student reading *Crime and Punishment*. She was just completing a course in English literature at Edinburgh University. Since one of my first television roles was in a Dostoevsky adaptation, we began discussing the force of evil that powered the murderous Raskolnikov. 'You'll have read *The Confessions of a Justified Sinner*,' I asked. But she had heard neither of the book nor even its author, because Scottish literature had its own department. If a four-year course in English literature in Scotland can accommodate Dostoevsky, then why not Hogg?

'A thin wiry man with a high nose, angular shoulders and penetrating eyes,' was how Conan Doyle described his mentor Dr Joseph Bell at Edinburgh University's medical school. 'You see, but you do not observe,' was one of Bell's famous remarks, the eager seventeen-year-old student who would one day write the *Adventures of Sherlock Holmes* remembered.

Joe Bell, as he was known, had the uncanny ability to reveal a patient's predicament even before they had spoken a single word. Bell showed a group of students a beaker full of a powerful drug. 'It's bitter to the taste,' he told them, dipping his finger in and tasting it, before passing the beaker round his students. Bell watched each one of them taste the liquid in turn, before dressing them down. 'Gentlemen, I am grieved that none of you has developed the power of perception which I have always stressed is so vital a part of diagnosis. If you had observed me closely you would have seen that I placed my forefinger in the medicine, but it was my middle finger that found its way to my mouth.' When Sherlock Holmes declares to Watson, 'the art of criminal deduction comes from the science of observation', his author Conan Doyle is only quoting the advice of his tutor from his student days at Edinburgh University.

In a book-crammed room in Glasgow's West End lives the literary alchemist, artist and writer, Alasdair Gray. Of all his works his most Gothic is *Puir Things*, which pivots on the creation of a female Frankenstein monster. But as the author says, it's really much more complicated than that. In the smoggy Glasgow of the 1880s (the word 'smog' first came into existence to describe Glasgow's fusion of soot and fog), Gray's Doctor Archibald McCandless falls under the spell of his colleague Godwin Baxter, a performer of advanced medical procedures. Baxter brings a dead woman back to life by giving her the brain of her unborn child. The result of his transplant is the recreation of a mature and sensual woman, but with the brain of an infant child. Gray weaves a variety of voices and approaches through his beautifully designed and illustrated novel to bring a fusion of science,

GODWIN BAXTER

Illustration for his *Puir Things* by Alasdair Gray, b.1934. An artist of genius with a multitude of strings to his bow: writer of fantasy, realism and science fiction, master of typography and book illustration, painter of murals and much more. Gray's first novel *Lanark*, 1981, was hailed by the *Guardian* as 'one of the landmarks of 20th-century fiction'.

sex, art and politics which has breathed new life into the deep waters of the Scottish Gothic novel.

James Robertson, with his first novel *The Fanatic*, chases its Gothic themes backwards and forwards over three centuries. He ingeniously weaves the killing times of Scotland's religious wars of the Covenanters in the seventeenth century with the banal distortions of history performed nightly in Edinburgh by the tourist-tat pedlars of the present. The weird Andrew Carlin, a feckless failed PhD mature student, is hired to play the tourist-baiting ghost of Major Weir, that staunch pillar of the Kirk by day but sorcerer by night, who was burnt at the stake in 1670. His fatuous role as the caped crusader, complete with demonic walking-stick and performing plastic rat, reactivates Carlin's interest in history. So begins a rewardingly serious quest to untangle the myths from the realities of Scotland's fanatical past which leads Carlin to James Mitchell, another 'justified sinner', who was imprisoned in 1674 for the attempted assassination of the hated Bishop Sharp of St Andrews. Robertson's first major work came as a reviving shot in the arm for the Gothic novel. It makes our perception of the past in the present seem a very foreign country.

Muriel Spark, like Stevenson, never lost sight of her Scottishness, though she never returned to write in the country she had left as a teenager. Spark was the daughter of two outsiders. Her father was a German engineer and an agnostic Jew. Her mother was High Church English. So by living in predominantly Presbyterian Edinburgh the young Miss Camberg grew up straddling three traditions. She attended the douce Edinburgh Merchant School of James Gillespie's. There she won literary prizes, becoming one of the cleverest 'gurls' chosen as *la crème de la crème* by the misguided teacher she would fictionalise so mordantly in *The Pride of Miss Jean Brodie*.

Keeping the name of her husband from a failed marriage, Spark converted to Catholicism. In her first published novel, *The Comforters* (1957), she explored this transition by ingeniously creating an alter ego who realised that she was also a character written into her own fiction. Spark's obsessions began to chime with the concerns raised by another Catholic convert, Graham Greene, who saw in her writing 'the drama of doubt' he explored in his own novels and 'entertainments'. Great moral dilemmas drove her stories, as her characters struggled over the nature of evil before veering into the Gothic and supernatural, like the satanic Dougal Douglas in *The Ballad of Peckham Rye*. Despite being a devout Catholic, her feelings about religion were nothing if not critical. In *The Abbess of Crewe* she explored the evil imbued in those elected to power in the Church. In the end, Spark has her abbess spying on her nuns through an electronic bug she has planted inside a devotional figure of the Infant Jesus of Prague.

Living happily in exile in the village of Oliveto in Tuscany, Spark's companion of many years, the sculptor Penelope Jardine, recalled how happy she was in the months before she died, discussing the poems of the Book of Job with the local priest. One of Spark's greatest admirers was Ian Rankin, who embarked on a literary thesis on the novels of Muriel Spark at Edinburgh University. Although he soon abandoned the pursuit of his doctorate, Rankin was so inspired by her

'I am Scottish by formation,' Muriel Spark always maintained. Despite spending her creative life abroad, her novels have their psychological footings in Scotland, especially *The Prime of Miss Jean Brodie*, one of the most witty and sinister characters in modern fiction.

'Such a beautiful city,' she said. Rebus tried to agree. He hardly saw it any more. To him, Edinburgh had become a state of mind, a juggling of criminal thoughts and baser instincts…'I never tire of this view,' she said, turning back towards the car. He nodded again, disingenuously. To him, it wasn't a view at all. It was a crime scene waiting to happen. – Ian Rankin, *The Falls*.

Muriel Spark, 1918-2006.

Ian Rankin, b.1960.

work that he paid her the greatest compliment of all by becoming a Gothic writer himself. He too has transfused new red blood into the long tradition of the Gothic crime novel. His dour Presbyterian cop, John Rebus, is a man always coming to terms with himself in a city of light and darkness, as he pursues crime in Edinburgh wearing the doubled-sided mantle of Jekyll and Hyde. The name Rebus derives from a puzzle, someone Rankin thought he'd never encounter in real life. Then of course he met a Rebus in his local pub. 'Are you a cop?' he asked him. The truth was stranger than fiction. This real Mr Rebus was a heating engineer, but he happened to live in Rankin Drive.

The Rebus plots seem to arise seamlessly out of Edinburgh from the genius of the place. In Rankin's thrillers Edinburgh's dark secrets surface effortlessly, continually sending Rebus off in new directions. That certainly was the case when Rankin was shown over the reconstruction of Queensberry House, during the building of the new Scottish Parliament. He learnt that a most gruesome incident occurred there on the day the Treaty of Union between Scotland and England was signed in 1707. The Duke of Queensberry had received £10,000 from London to steady his hand into signing the enabling document. His Lordship invited his household to witness the momentous day outside the old Parliament on the Royal Mile. This left Queensberry House empty, except for a young kitchen helper and the Duke's severely handicapped son James. In the non-politically correct usage of the day, James was described as being 'an idiot of the most wretched kind, as rabid and as gluttonous as a wild animal, who had grown to an enormous size'. For years 'daft Jaimie' had been confined to the basement of Queensberry House, with boarded-up windows to prevent him ever being seen. But on that fateful day he managed to break out and lurched his way wildly from room to room until savoury smells drew him lumbering down into the vaulted kitchen. There he saw the young servant boy roasting a side of meat on a turnspit. James grabbed the skewer, stripped the boy, then kebabbed him over the coals. The Duke returned in time to see his son devouring the kitchen helper. Soon the horror of it all reached the crowds outside. Shouts rose up that this dire deed was God's judgement on the Duke's odious role in selling Scotland down the river.

This extraordinary event inspired a key chapter in *Set in Darkness*, where Rebus investigates the discovery of a body found during the restoration of the Duke's old kitchen. Today this vaulted room still retains traces of the cannibal's oven. I hope its cooking days are over, as it now processes the expense accounts of the members of the Scottish Parliament.

If visitors to the Old Town are still plagued by cultural charades of witches and warlocks, a more contemporary take on all things Gothic now unfolds in Edinburgh's port of Leith. 'Trainspotting' tours now cruise the haunts of Sick Boy and his cronies, to the dismay of its author, Irvine Welsh. 'You feel that you should've been dead a hundred years before that kind of thing happens,' he said. 'I'm flattered, but I'm no Robbie Louis Stevenson.'

But for some, like Ron Dean, the bogeymen of childhood live on. Dean grew up along the Galloway coast that the Sawney highwayman Beane is supposed to haunt. 'Look out!' his dad would threaten him. 'It's Sawney Beane, and he's gonna eat yees all.' Ron so believed in Beane that he spent years trying to find the notorious cave where Beane's clan lived. If anyone now asks him, Ron leads visitors to a perilous sheep track down the cliffs of Bennane Head, a few miles north of Ballantrae. Whoever wrote the original account of Sawney Beane, whether he is myth or not, the narrow cleft that leads into this cave seems drenched in buckets of dread and gloom. As Ron's torch picks out dripping rocks and darts its beam down to the odd bone on the cave floor, the sound of the groaning sea echoes into a terrifying growl. Given the generous tourist grants handed out for promoting any gruesome aspect of our heritage these days, I am sure Ron Dean has as lucrative a future as Sawney Beane once had – before, that is, he was forced to surrender his taste of Scotland.

Let Stevenson have the last word. His books have always been more popular in America, where they have never been out of print. So when the time came for his Edinburgh admirers to commemorate his life, appropriately they commissioned a memorial from Stevenson's friend, the American sculptor Augustus Saint-Gaudens. The wall space in St Giles Cathedral allowed the artist to display the original full length version of his famous portrait roundel. When the large bronze relief was unpacked it revealed Stevenson as the teller of tales lying comfortably stretched out on his chaise longue in Samoa in the South Seas, balancing a writing pad. But – good heavens – between his fingers dangled a cigarette in a holder. No doubt the church elders, if not his friends, found the notion of the great writer holding a smoke sacrilegious in a kirk. So with skilful subterfuge the cigarette was fudged into a very unlikely pen, held unconvincingly in an impossible writing position. In the end resolute righteousness triumphed over dissolute bohemianism. Such a face-saving outcome would surely have wrung a wry smile from the wee man in the velvet jacket.

Bronze memorial, 1888, of Robert Louis Stevenson by Augustus Saint-Gaudens, 1848-1907. St Giles Cathedral or the High Kirk of Edinburgh

After numerous sittings in New York, Saint-Gaudens depicted the author who was ill with tuberculosis, reclining in bed, holding a cigarette. R.L.S. pronounced it as a 'speaking likeness'. But the cigarette was smudged into a pen for the memorial in the High Kirk of Edinburgh.

9 BROCHS, BARONIAL AND BEYOND
The architects of Scotland

'Wall out the Barbarians,' was the Emperor Hadrian's verdict as he surveyed the prospect of ever civilising the northern tribes of Britain in the early second century. I've often thought what an opening that would make for an epic sword-and-sandal movie. Hadrian had embarked on a fact-finding expedition to eliminate the trouble spots from his vast multi-ethnic Roman Empire. He had already formulated an exit strategy for Mesopotamia which would pull his legions out of what is now Iraq. As for the even more troublesome northern tribes, the Emperor judged them well beyond the pale.

Hadrian's eighty-mile-long barricade was built to protect the now civilised Roman province of Britannia from the barbarian raiders of the north. Today the ruins of Hadrian's Wall, meandering over the hills from the River Tyne to the Solway Firth, remain as a worrying reminder of our troublesome past. Yet it was this monument to our 'barbarity' that would eventually delineate the ancient nation state of Scotland. The border may have been beaten north in the ensuing seven centuries, but Kenneth MacAlpin finally united the warring tribes of Caledonia under the flag of Scotland around 843. It was architecture – the Wall – that first defined the land of Scotland.

Today the dominant vision of Scotland, as promoted by tourist agencies, is an empty land of bare mountains and ruined castles. The lone silhouette of a crumbling ruin against a gaunt landscape may fire the purple prose of brochure writers bent on luring visitors north, but in reality these scenes of desolation may owe more to our industrial enterprise than to the clash of warring clans. The felling of the Caledonian forests for charcoal to fire the iron smelters of the eighteenth century left the Highlands almost treeless. Despite this, the vision of the ruin is now zealously protected by 'ruinists'. Extraordinary as it may seem, their desolate view of architecture is endorsed by Historic Scotland, the government-appointed agency for the protection of ancient buildings.

Evocative of melancholy as they often are, how differently do we perceive ruins reflected in the distant waters of a loch from the silhouettes of such rebuilt castles as Eilean Donan or Kishimul at Castlebay on the Isle of Barra in the Outer Hebrides? Is our experience of these born-again castles in any way diminished by the pleasure we get from contemplating ruins?

Duart, along with Eilean Donan further up the west coast, is everyone's idea of what an ancient Scottish castle should look like. Yet both of them were built up from rubble less than a hundred years ago. Given Scotland's turbulent history, few medieval castles or churches now exist in their original state and most of them are now reduced to fragments. Glasgow's medieval cathedral was the only one left intact after John Knox's Reformation, until Victorian reformers decided to fell its Gothic towers. There couldn't be a more Scottish castle than Duart, out there on a headland overlooking the Sound of Mull in the Inner Hebrides. This is the fortress of the Macleans, my mother's clan. Lachlan, the clan chief, is a cousin of my old friend the late Fitzroy Maclean, the great adventurer and war hero, who was one of Ian Fleming's models for a certain James Bond. I first saw this castle as a teenager in that weirdly haunting movie *I Know Where I'm Going*, Michael Powell's romantic escape to the Hebrides. I fled there myself to hide from Catherine Zeta-Jones in my own production of *Entrapment*.

Hadrian's Wall, early second century, meandering over the Northumberland hills. Today many Scots see Hadrian's Wall as a monument to a nation never defeated by the might of Rome, rather than a worrying reminder of our past barbarity.

Left: Duart Castle on the Isle of Mull dates back to the thirteenth century. The castle had become completely ruinous by 1911 when the Macleans commissioned the architect J.J. Burnett, 1857-1958, to rebuild Duart as the castle we see today.

Right: Castle Tioram, Loch Moidart, fifteenth century. Unlike Castle Duart, which was born again, the derelict and roofless ruins of Tioram are destined to moulder with plans for its restoration opposed by Historic Scotland.

My aim was to bring the remoteness of that ancient Highland stronghold into my portrayal of Robert MacDougal, plotting his elaborate hare-brained heists so far-flung from the realities of the world. From the island of Mull to the Petronas Towers in Malaysia, *Entrapment* was quite some logistical challenge to bring to the screen. 'Impossible, but do-able,' as Mac in the movie would have said. It was only through the nuts and bolts know-how of the Scots line producer, Iain Smith, that the impossible in the end proved in any way do-able. Iain is used to moving crews and film gear round the world in double-quick time. But in Scotland it doesn't matter who you are, or how important you think your mission is – nothing moves any faster in the Hebrides than the ferries of Caledonian MacBrayne. The cast and crew just had to surrender to those ferries' arrival and departure times. Yet when they first caught sight of Castle Duart, louring down on them from across the Sound of Mull against a mackerel sky, there was not a soul who worried about delays. Everyone agreed that it was by far and away the most naturally dramatic location for *Entrapment*.

Duart is a fine example of thick-walled architecture, a tradition which goes back over two thousand years in Scotland to those ancient defensive towers, or brochs. Brochs are a uniquely Scottish building type which developed out of prehistoric roundhouses. Recent research has distanced their origins back into prehistory, to some time between the fourth and second centuries BC. Standing proud on headlands, they were defiant symbols of local power to deter hit-and-run raiders coursing up and down the sea lanes. Imagining those early people living within the walls of these stark towers, hunkered down in their dark recesses, might explain those traits of collective paranoia in our national subconscious when everything seems to be going against us. I have often thought that the real fear of the Scots paranoid is 'Am I paranoid enough?' Yet these tall protecting towers were a match even for the might of Rome.

The Duart Castle you see today is mostly the work of one of Scotland's most innovative Victorian architects, Sir John James Burnet. Perhaps it's harder to realise that Eilean Donan, that great generator of Scottish tourism, is itself a twentieth-century construct. During the first Jacobite Rising in 1719 three ships of the Royal Navy bombarded the thirteenth-century stronghold. The Highlanders were forced to surrender, along with a small detachment of Spanish soldiers.

Twenty-seven kegs of gunpowder then reduced Eilean Donan to a pile of stones in the waters of Loch Duich. A vision of this now most photographed castle came back in all its medieval glory to Farquhar MacRae in a dream. It was a dream so vivid that it inspired his fellow clansman Lt Col. John MacRae-Gilstrap to spend a fortune over fifteen years to recreate the castle down to the last stone of its causeway bridge. First opened to the public in 1928, Eilean Donan became an instant icon for the Highlands.

Ever since a boy, Lex Brown had been entranced by Castle Tioram on its rocky promontory on the shores of Loch Moidart. Encouraged by the Highland Council, he bought the ruins to rebuild it as his home. Brown found that the battles that once reduced castles to rubble now rage to prevent them being rebuilt. Historic Scotland prefers Castle Tioram in ruins. A public inquiry took all of 174 pages to condemn Brown's proposal. In the ten years that have passed since he bought the castle of his dreams, one of Tioram's curtain walls has fallen.

'Scotland needs fewer ruins,' insists Magnus Linklater, the author and former Scottish Arts Council chairman, 'I much prefer a living building to a dead one. Instead of encouraging people to revive buildings Historic Scotland seems to exist to fine those who try to make them liveable again.' When Chris Ruffle spent well over £1 million of his own savings reconstructing in stone the derelict ruin of Dairsie Castle in Fife, he was taken to court by Historic Scotland for inserting a few upper-storey window surrounds in reconstituted stone.

'To do as our fathers did, is not to do as our fathers did,' was the historian Kenneth Clark's favourite saying. And as for that curse of present-day 'restorers' who talk of their work as 'fitting in', just look what that great Scot James Gibbs achieved next to Cambridge's King's College Chapel around two hundred years later. He complemented that fan-vaulted masterpiece with a library in a restrained classical style as foil to the earlier Gothic.

Perhaps Brown's plans to re-inhabit Tioram may have fallen short of the quality of work that has rejuvenated such great Italian buildings as the Castelvecchio in Verona. Here the architect Carlo Scarpa had no desire to fudge the past, but added his own brilliant contemporary designs to complement what had survived and to make a dialogue across time. Surely a statutory body should exist to advise, but not prohibit? Instead of being offered professional advice to assist the planned

The Castelvecchio, Verona, Italy. The Castelvecchio has had many lives before it was rejuvenated by Carlo Scarpa; medieval castle, Napoleonic barracks and a pastiche palazzo art gallery. Now visitors are never confused with what's old and what's new in Scarpa's incomparable modern additions. His master stroke was to present the equestrian sculpture of Cangrande della Scala on a cantilevered plinth at the junction of two buildings, overlooking the bridge crossing the Adige. Scarpa's innovative approach inspired the architect Michael Spens to rejuvenate Cleish Castle, Kinross-shire, with a nickel-plated steel-supported minstrels' gallery and a ceiling by his friend Eduardo Paolozzi. This award-winning scheme only lasted a decade, but the ceiling is now part of the Paolozzi collection at the Dean Gallery, Edinburgh.

One of the best-preserved fourteenth century castles in Scotland, thanks to an extensive restoration in 1833. Doune is now famous for the generosity of the Earl of Moray who gave quarter to Terry Jones and his band of merry medievalists for the filming of *Monty Python and the Holy Grail*. Historic Scotland, the inheritor of the agency, which had refused access to other castles in 1975, now promotes the hysteric Scotland of the Pythons with questionable souvenirs to boot.

Opposite: As a wholly modern construct, complete with mannequins, the Stirling Castle kitchen is surely more suited to a theme park presentation than to be an adjunct to what remains of one of the great renaissance palaces of Scotland. Oh Kitschfinder General, where are you when we need you most?

rebuilding of Tioram on to a higher architectural level, Brown was disparaged for having the effrontery to tamper with this castle's slowly eroding walls.

Terry Gilliam and Terry Jones, being serious medievalists, selected a carefully chosen range of castles in Scotland to match specific sequences for *Monty Python and the Holy Grail*. 'Then just as the crew was about to drive north,' Terry Jones recalls, 'we got this message from the Department of the Environment for Scotland, saying that they wouldn't let us use any of their castles because we were doing things that were not consistent with the dignity of the fabric of the buildings. These places had been built for torturing and killing people; you couldn't do a bit of comedy? It was ridiculous. So Terry and I ended up going off to find new locations a week before filming.' Fortunately Douglas, the 20th Earl of Moray, was sporting enough to offer the Monty Pythons the free range of his recently inherited Castle of Doune. By carefully choosing different angles the film crew were able to give the impression of a variety of castles, and the great banqueting hall, although freezing cold, became the perfect background for all those diaphanously dressed girls.

In 1984 the Earl gifted Doune to the nation and it's now under the guardianship of Historic Scotland, the Department of the Environment under a new name. So 'the dignity of the fabric of the building' can now echo to a tattoo of a thousand thundering hooves, courtesy of this responsible government agency, which specially imported hampers of coconut shells to promote authentic *Monty Python* re-enactments in the national interest. Now fans of *The Holy Grail* account for up to a third of Doune's 25,000 visitors each year. Many are young Americans encouraged by Historic Scotland to shout from Doune's battlements such immortal Arthurian lines as 'I fart in your general direction. Your mother was a hamster and your father smelled of elderberries.' 'We are the Knights Who Say "Ni!" a bunch of schoolkids from California, down amongst the shrubbery, shout back. Dignity has surely been restored to the fabric of Doune.

The theme of the unicorn appears in the Stirling Castle tapestry inventories of the reign of James V. Perhaps they were similar to the *Hunt of the Unicorn* tapestries now hanging in the recreated Cloisters of the Metropolitan Museum of Art in New York City. Historic Scotland commissioned reproductions of these fine tapestries, shrunk by ten per cent to fit the Queen's Presence Chamber, in a coarser weave of four warp threads per centimetre instead of the seven of the originals, and woven, not in naturally coloured wools, but in the bright colours of chemical dyes. Their costs of over two million pounds are being largely met by the Quinque Foundation of America. Couldn't this generosity not have bought genuine tapestries? But then they wouldn't have made a technicolor splash in tourist brochures. It strikes me as rather odd that the genuine Unicorn tapestries can be seen in the fabricated medieval Cloisters of New York, whereas their modern cruder copies will now cover the walls of the genuine historic monument of Stirling Castle.

Sir William Bruce, 1630-1710, started building Kinross House in 1685, although he had begun planting out the terraces, parterres and orchards of his magnificent formal garden six years earlier in the contemporary Franco-Dutch style. Bruce aligned his formal garden to contrast the restrained classicism of his Palladian home with the ruins of Lochleven Castle as a romantic eye-catcher across the water.

By the late seventeenth century the fad for castle-like excesses was waning. There is nothing mock-miltary about the formal symmetry of Kinross House, designed by the aristocratic architect William Bruce in 1685 as his own home. Bruce, as the founder of the classical school in Scotland, signalled new directions in Scottish architecture.

But classical as his architecture was, he still had an eye for the Romantic. Kinross House was aligned, across a spectacular French garden of parterres, to face the island ruins of the medieval Loch Leven Castle, where Mary Queen of Scots was imprisoned in 1567.

After the Union of the Crowns of 1603, when James VI of Scotland went south to become James I of England, most of the Scots nobles and notables left with him. Such an exodus left few opportunities for architects in Scotland. James had promised to return to Scotland every three years, but he came back only once, in 1617. Two generations would pass before King Charles II would initiate such large-scale projects as the extension of the Palace of Holyroodhouse in Edinburgh. He commissioned William Bruce in 1671 to balance Holyrood's ancient Gothic towers, and the architect obliged by mirroring them in his symmetrical extension to front a quadrangle of classical façades.

For the historian Charles McKean Scotland lost its cultural memory in architecture as a result of the modernising forces of the Scottish Enlightenment. Old tower houses of the Stuart era were seen as old-fashioned, and many in Scotland were completely abandoned. Architects like Colen Campbell, who had already built classical homes in Scotland, took the road south to seek lucrative work in England. To help drum up commissions, Campbell published a lavishly illustrated book of outstanding country houses with the grand title, *Vitruvius Britannicus*. Amongst the handsomely engraved plates Campbell craftily included his own quite modest design for Shawlands House in Glasgow, based on the pure, simple lines of the classical villas that the great Renaissance master Andrea Palladio had built in Italy. But it would be his far grander scheme for Wanstead, a country house in Essex, which would soon be perceived as 'the purest, most classical building of its age'. Campbell's influential book could not have been better timed. It placed him where he wanted to be – right at the centre of the country-house building boom of the 1720s.

Left to right: Church of Mary-le-Strand,
1714-17, James Gibbs, 1682-1754.

Church of St Martin-in-the-Fields, 1721-
26, James Gibbs.

St Michael's Episcopal Church, 1751-61,
in Charleston, South Carolina, USA.
Through his published pattern books
Aberdeen-born James Gibbs set the
standard for eighteenth-century British
and American church architecture. His
St Martin-in-the-Fields was the model for
St Michael's in Charleston, South
Carolina, and many others.

Today the clean classical lines of Campbell's Houghton Hall have domes, which
were added after Campbell's death in 1729 by James Gibbs. Unlike his English
contemporaries, the Aberdeen-born Gibbs had studied in Rome and was
determined 'to introduce the temple beauties of Italy' to private buildings. For his
church of Mary-le-Strand in London Gibbs found inspiration in the Palazzo
Branconio dell'Aquila in Rome. He included a handsome engraving of it in his
illustrated *Book of Architecture*, which he had devised as a 'pattern book for districts
remote from architectural advice'. Gibbs claimed that his designs could be
'executed by any workman who understands lines'. His great book soon became
the most widely influential architecture book of the century, making his London
church of St Martin-in-the-Fields (1721-6) one of the most copied buildings of its
time in the English-speaking world. Gibbs-inspired churches can now be found
across New England, and the greatest American colonial church, based on St
Martin-in-the-Fields, is St Michael's in Charleston, South Carolina (1752-61).
St Paul's Chapel, Broadway, the oldest church in New York City, where
Washington worshipped, was designed by Thomas MacBean, one of Gibbs's
most talented apprentices, from Aberdeen.

There was one important architect who remained in Scotland. William Adam
became the country's 'universal architect', inheriting the classical legacy of
William Bruce. Adam's greatest commission came from the first Earl of
Hopetoun, who had benefited financially from the union with England. By creating
an imposing colonnaded east façade for Hopetoun House, in the wake of James
Gibbs Adam transformed William Bruce's original rather restrained French-style
double-pile house into an altogether more flamboyant and grandiose Italianate
structure. Following Colen Campbell's success with *Vitruvius Britannicus*, Adam

Top: Fort George, 1750s, William Skinner with James and Robert Adam. To placate the Highlands the Government built the largest defended garrison in Europe.

Below: Duff House, Banffshire, was built between 1735 and 1740 by William Adam for William Duff of Braco, who became Earl Fife in 1759. Since 1995 it has been part of the National Galleries of Scotland, displaying pictures from the national collection.

published *Vitruvius Scotticus*, in which he too included his own designs, like his grandiose Duff House on the Banffshire coast. It is now the most northerly outpost of the National Galleries of Scotland.

At Duff House Adam created a great temple façade as a centrepiece, in the spirit of the baroque. This sturdy, if somewhat unoriginal, composition took its inspiration from the towers of Houghton Hall, not as designed by Colen Campbell but from the domes added later by James Gibbs. As a builder-architect Adam became an important contractor to the government, serving from 1730 as Master Mason to the Board of Ordnance for North Britain. Following the massacre of the Jacobites at Culloden in 1746, he became a key player in the massive Hanoverian building programme launched to subdue the Highlanders who had risen to restore the rightful Stuart line to the British throne. To this end William Adam was awarded lucrative government contracts for roads, bridges and fortifications, which his sons took over after his death in 1748. For the next ten years John, James and above all Robert would gain their own architectural training through physically building such gargantuan defences as Fort George, where they would learn the rudiments of architecture literally from the foundations up.

By the beginning of the eighteenth century neoclassicism had come to symbolise Scotland's new place in Europe. This was no better on display than at Mavisbank, the home created by the architect William Adam for his enlightened client Sir John Clerk. Its classical façade inspired by the villas of Palladio, its French mansard roof and its two distinctively Dutch pavilions, all celebrated the culture of an outward-looking country confident of its place in Europe.

Clerk was a powerful and influential thinker, who held that Scotland should return to the Classical Age. The Roman remains which abounded in Scotland were for Clerk 'the last tangible links with civilisation before it was engulfed in the long medieval twilight'. In the spirit of the Scottish Enlightenment, the poet Allan Ramsay addressed his learned friend in a witty ode:

> Amongst all these of the first Rate
> Our learned CLERK blest with the Fate
> Of thinking right, can best relate
> These beauties all,
> Which bear the marks of ancient Date,
> Be-North the Wall.

But there was enough of the romantic in Clerk to call his Arcadia on the banks of the River Esk, Mavisbank, after the mavis, the Scots for a song thrush. In his poem 'The Country Seat', he wrote:

> On Esca's flowery Bank there is a grove
> Where the harmonious Thrush repeats its love,
> There Ile observe the Precepts you indite
> But never any more attempt to write.
> Sir John Clerk, 'The Country Seat'

Now only the mavis sings within what remains of the walls of Mavisbank, because Clerk's masterpiece was gutted by fire in 1973. It lies as derelict as Hadrian's Villa. At least its shell has now been secured by Historic Scotland, with the restoration architects Simpson and Brown still optimistic about saving one of the greatest houses of the Scottish Enlightenment.

If the Emperor Hadrian defined Scotland geographically in the second century with his wall, the excavations of the ruins of Hadrian's Villa at Tivoli outside Rome in the eighteenth inspired Scots architects and artists to define neoclassicism in art and architecture. Charles Cameron's illustrated study of the baths of Rome so delighted Catherine the Great that she invited the young Jacobite architect to Russia to work at her Summer Palace outside St Petersburg.

Mavisbank House, 1723-36, by William Adam (1689-1748) and Sir John Clerk (1676-1755). Plate 47 from *Vitruvius Scotticus* by William Adam. Adam was called in to assist in the design of Mavisbank, Midlothian, in 1723 by Sir John Clerk of Penicuik who later claimed most of its design as his own, 'however the Architecture may please or displease' he wrote, 'it is owing chiefly to myself.' The overall design was in fact inspired by an amalgam of elements from Colen Campbell's *Vitruvius Britannicus* of 1715.

Mavisbank, its forecourt strewn with abandoned cars. Mavisbank was reduced to ruins by a fire in 1973 under the ownership of a scrap dealer who broke cars up in its forecourt. The structure was stabilised in the 1980s by Historic Scotland, although it remains a roofless, derelict and deteriorating shell. This jewel of the Scottish Enlightenment is culturally as important a monument to Scotland as were the war-ruined palaces of Catherine the Great to Russia. The Summer Palace at Tsarskoe Selo, along with Catherine's Cameron Gallery by Charles Cameron, were meticulously restored in the Soviet period. If a then impoverished USSR could restore the works of a Scots architect as a key part of its patrimony, surely Mavisbank deserves similar respect from the State. An organisation devoted to preserving cultural monuments, which cannot fund the restoration of Mavisbank, is really one that's not worth having.

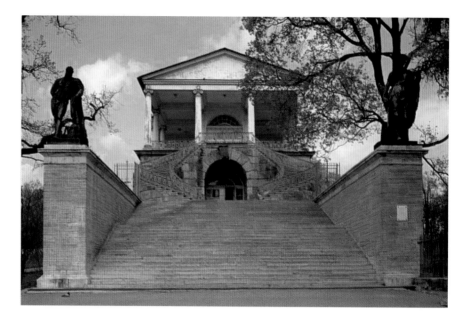

The Cameron Gallery, Charles Cameron, 1740-1812, Tsarskoe Selo, Catherine the Great's Summer Palace outside St Petersburg, Russia.

His greatest monument there was the Cameron Gallery, one of the few world-class buildings to be named after its architect. So powerful an influence was Cameron's neoclassicism that it would remain the dominant architectural style in Russia up to the time of Stalin.

When Robert Adam returned home from Italy in 1757, he was fully armed as a neoclassical architect from studying the ruins and antiquities in Rome and Tivoli. The refinement of his style would make him one of the most sought-after architects of his generation. But only an architect of Adam's genius could have grafted the lessons of classical Rome on to a rambling medieval cliff-top castle to create his Scottish masterpiece of Culzean. From between the castles of the Middle Ages and the classical world emerged Scottish architecture.

If there had been architectural thought police preventing or halting any new work in old buildings in the eighteenth century, Culzean Castle would never have come into being. What genius it was for Robert Adam to take a near-ruined medieval keep on the Ayrshire coast, envelop it with battlements, add a great round tower and then to bestow upon it one of the finest classical interiors of its time. There was no precedent in Scotland for anything like this. What Adam did was to innovate from what he had learnt from studying the great buildings of classical and medieval Rome. 'I wanted,' he wrote to his young client the 10th Earl of Cassilis, 'to bring a little Italian sunshine into a Scotland that can be so dull at times.' And so a new architecture was born; a masterpiece of romantic and neoclassical re-invention that is now the National Trust for Scotland's greatest visitor attraction. Inspired by Hadrian's Villa, Adam's circular drawing-room seamlessly combines two architectural styles fused into one harmonious whole. To see the sun set into the sea off the Ayrshire coast, as its glow magically bathes Adam's round room in golden light, is to relive a sublime moment of the Scottish Enlightenment.

Born in Kirkcaldy in 1728, Robert was the son of William Adam, Scotland's 'universal architect'. In London he had quickly established himself as an artist of the world who was provincial neither in place nor time. At thirty he was a member of the Royal Society of Arts, which commissioned him in 1772 to build its new premises in John Adam Street off the Strand.

Sir Joseph Banks, the president of the Royal Society, had just returned from a scientific expedition studying the geological riddles of Iceland. When their ship was becalmed on their journey north in the Inner Hebrides, the party had stumbled upon a 'cathedral of the seas'. Pillars of rock, stacked like classical colonnades, retreated before them into a dark vault that Banks thought worthy of ancient Rome. The cave's rocky canopy arched above them like the ribs of a Gothic cathedral, supported by natural columns as in a classical temple. 'Compared to this,' Banks asked, 'what are the cathedrals or the palaces built by men…where now is the boast of the architect?' Where indeed?

Through the happy accident of tides, what the locals had known for centuries the world would soon discover as the architectural wonder of Fingal's Cave. 'Nature is here found in all her possession,' continued Banks. 'Is not this the school where art was originally studied?' Such descriptions, and drawings by John Miller, the expedition's draughtsman, struck Adam 'with all wonder and amaze'. The artist and architect Joseph Gandy was astounded too. He chose to feature 'Nature's cathedral' as one of his first paintings in his ambitious series, *The Origin of Architecture*.

If the Gothic and the classical could coexist in nature, why could they not be built together? Had Robert Adam not just been following nature at Culzean? The great promoter of neoclassicism had worked in the Gothic style before, most notably for Horace Walpole at Strawberry Hill. He would follow Culzean with over fifty country and other houses in the castellated classical style that was now

Left: *The Origin of Architecture*, 1838, by Joseph Gandy, 1771-1843, Sir John Soane Museum, London. Gandy celebrates nature as the world's first architect. In front of Fingal's Cave's cathedral-like columns an orang-utang shows his architectural prowess in the building of a brushwood hut, as a beaver admires its animal-made dam.

Right: *Fingal's Cave*, by John Miller, 1772. 'As the first light of day stole over the ruins of nature's own antiquity…this cave's classic order of symmetry – its simplicity of style stretching back into a twilight gloom – the play of reflected light, the echo of the measured surge rising and falling, the transparent green of the water, the profound and fairy solitude of the whole scene – could not fail to impress any mind gifted with a sense of beauty in art or nature.' – Sir Joseph Banks, Royal Society of the Arts.

all his own. The most entrancing Scottish chateaux were for his extended family. Seton House on the east coast was a masterpiece of Adam's final years, a wedding present for his favourite sister Mary when she married the young army officer Alexander Mackenzie. Seton's interiors displayed such witty motifs as a Scottish version of the ancient Roman ox-skull frieze, which Adam transformed into an antlered stag derived from the arms of Clan Mackenzie.

Adam's eclectic fusion of the antique with the exuberant tower houses of the Scottish Renaissance inspired the up-and-coming generation of architects and became the foundation for Scottish Baronial. David Bryce embellished and exaggerated the castle style into full-blown Scottish Baronial. He was invited by the Duke of Atholl to restore the grandeur of Blair Castle, which had lost its tower and much of its warlike air in the civilising 'improvements' of the previous century. Bryce re-invented a new entrance tower with pepper-pot turrets drawn from Fyvie Castle, further north in Aberdeenshire. But the granddaddy of all Bryce's Scottish Baronial country houses was Castlemilk, built in 1863. Its decorated battlements and mock fortifications now guard the peaceful Water of Milk in Dumfriesshire. Castlemilk's military air was all for show – a Victorian manifestation of all things Scottish, tamed for effect. Its massive round entrance tower looked back to Castle Fraser in Aberdeenshire. But even in the early seventeenth century when this castle was rebuilt, battlements were already more ornamental than defensive. The gun-loops on the ground floor were for providing light rather than for shielding muskets. The large protecting gardens were more for pleasure than defence.

So much of Scotland's architectural past has been lost or ruined. Of the seven thousand Renaissance houses built in the sixteenth and seventeenth centuries in Scotland, only around one thousand remain today. In contrast to the large-windowed English houses of the period, Scottish country houses had small defended openings on the lower storey but blossomed into flamboyant

Seton House, 1790, Robert Adam. With its Palladian windows and castellated towers, including 'corbie' or crow-stepped gables, Seton was an entirely romantic conception, a 'gothick' ideal breaking into a classical age. The result was a triumph of the Adam castle style.

Detail: The antlered stag skull and targe frieze was invented by Robert Adam to celebrate the Mackenzie's crest of his brother-in-law's clan.

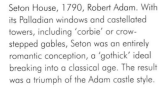

architectural devices corbelled or cantilevered off their upper storeys, like the Castle of Crathes in Aberdeenshire built towards the end of the sixteenth century. Crathes was a castle only in the French sense, which the historian Charles McKean expands in his book appropriately titled *The Scottish Chateau*:

> With all their turrets and overhanging battlements they have the look of heavily defended buildings, but in reality these devices were more for pageant than for war. Such architecture was part of the culture and society of its time. Imitation fortifications and gun loop window slots were proof of Scotland's warlike past. They chimed well with the British notion of a Scotland of fierce soldiers and as the suitable homes for romantic if not primitive warriors. Castles like these were imposing masks boasting past military traditions. At the same time they were the proud tower houses of a culture which was fully participating in contemporary European life. In essence the Scottish Chateau was a castle of dreams.

When Walter Scott chose the Gothic style for his new home in the Borders, the hugely successful author of the *Waverley* novels had William Atkinson rebuild the old farmhouse of Cartley Hall into a romantic evocation of a Scottish past. Abbotsford soon became a portrait of Sir Walter Scott in stone. Historical fragments, swords, targes and armour were collaged on to the walls to evoke a Scotland that Scott had almost single-handedly re-invented. The Scottish Baronial became one of the first national styles in Europe. From rich men's castles to suburban villas, from factories to town halls, from railway stations to dog kennels, all had to have their share of mock turrets, towers and battlements.

Just as Scottish Baronial grew out of Adam's restrained castle style, twentieth-century Scottish architects chose severity over decoration. Despite the castle-like appearance and rubble walls of Formakin in Renfrewshire, this was no restoration.

Formakin, Renfreweshire, 1912, Robert Lorimer. Just as Scottish baronial grew out of Adam's restrained castle style, twentieth-century Scottish architects chose severity over decoration. Despite the castle-like appearance and rubble walls of Formakin in Renfrewshire, this was no restoration. It was built from scratch in 1912 by Robert Lorimer for the eccentric self-made art collector Johnnie Holms. When the editor of *Country Life* mistook Formakin for a 'cold Scotch house of the seventeenth century,' Holms was delighted.

Below left: Castlemilk, Dumfriesshire, 1867, by David Bryce. This Scottish baronial mansion was inspired by the late 16th-century Castle Fraser, Aberdeenshire.

The Hill House, Helensburgh, 1902,
Charles Rennie Mackintosh, 1868-1928.
Mackintosh's clean white harled walls
and randomly placed windows derive
from his deep understanding of such
Scottish vernacular buildings as Stenhouse
Mansion, 1613, Saughton, Edinburgh.

It was built from scratch in 1912 by Robert Lorimer for the eccentric self-made art collector Johnnie Holms. When the editor of *Country Life* mistook Formakin for a 'cold Scotch house of the seventeenth century', Holms was delighted. Lorimer believed in stripping back the accretions of history. In the restoration of his own home, the sixteenth/seventeenth-century Kellie Castle in Fife, he had all the harling chipped off to render it more martial. So began the cult of rough stone exteriors, soon to become all the rage as 'rubblemania'.

Ardkinglas, surrounded by a spectacular array of rhododendrons on the shores of Loch Fyne, gives the impression of an old tower-house sensitively restored along the lines of Kellie Castle. But, just like Formakin, Ardkinglas, this Edwardian sporting lodge, was built entirely out of the imagination of its architect. Lorimer was a practical romantic, so he fused his version of ancient crow-stepped gables, turrets and corbelled courses with all the conveniences of a modern country house. Inside, his recreations of oak-panelled Jacobean rooms were among the first interiors to be fitted out with electric light. Lorimer's many modern gadgets included a shower-cage specially designed to refresh Sir Andrew Noble's guests after a hard day's stalking on the hills. They could then step out on to the first-floor loggia to savour their drams, as the sun slowly sank into the tranquil waters of Loch Fyne.

Whereas Lorimer preferred the stark rubble walls of Scotland's past, his contemporary Charles Rennie Mackintosh sought to unify his walls with harling. In the rich man's burgh of Helensburgh on the Clyde Coast, local building regulations demanded that houses be built in stone. Mackintosh wanted the harled look for his client, the publisher Walter Blackie, so instead of inexpensive brick he had first to build Hill House (1902-3) in stone, and then, as a rather impractical romantic, he had the masonry harled over in the manner of the seventeenth century.

To grow up in Hill House would just destine you to be an architect. And so it was with the young Kenneth Lawson. As a child he could appreciate Mackintosh's scaled-down fittings in the playroom. Its famous white bedroom of stylised doves and the skinniest ladder chairs made a profounder impression on him than on his parents, who could never bring themselves to sleep there. He saw how Mackintosh had pollinated Scottish building styles with other traditions. He found that the

  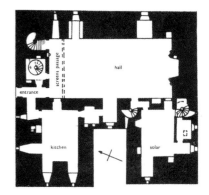

Top: The Salk Institute, La Jolla, California, Louis Kahn, 1901-74. Kahn's deployment of the 'served and servant spaces' in his buildings arose through his knowledge of medieval Scottish buildings like Borthwick Castle, 1430. Kahn's plan of Borthwick reveals how the service rooms, embedded in the walls, served the great banqueting hall, inspiring the deployment of the studies around the laboratories of the Salk Institute.

The New Museum of Scotland, Benson & Forsyth, 1991-9. The thick-walled architecture of Scotland's past, combined with late works of the Swiss architect Le Corbusier, were central to Graham Benson's design. He endorses Kahn's ideas about Scottish castles by creating spiral stairs between walls and sinking display cabinets into their deep masonry. To face the traffic of five streets Benson derived this proud tower not from mediaeval castles, but from the broch as a homage to the origins of Scottish architecture over 2000 years ago.

The Broch of Mousa, 100 BC, Shetland Isles. Of elegant drystone construction with double-walled internal stairs, brochs are unique to Scotland. As symbols of power they dominated the seaways. Ruins of over five hundred brochs dot the Scottish Atlantic coastline.

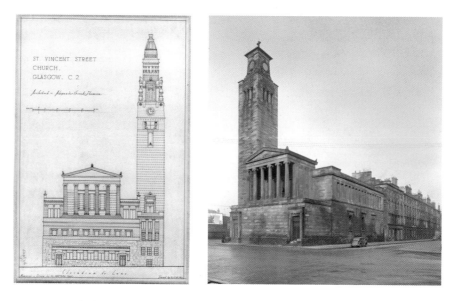

Left: St Vincent Street United Presbyterian Church, Glasgow, 1857-9, by Alexander Thomson, 1817-75. The last surviving church of this master of romantic classicism.

Right: Caledonia Road Church, Glasgow, 1856-7 by Alexander Thomson. Thomson's first masterpiece. His raised temple portico stood side by side with a tall elegant clock tower that could never have come out of ancient Greece. The superb interior, with a magnificent open roof of painted beams, was torched by vandals in 1965. Now cruelly isolated by city planners on a traffic island, the architect's first major work survives as a romantic ruin.

seats around the windows in the drawing-room and the fireplace ingleneuk were inspired by what Mackintosh had sketched in the English West Country. The white bedroom, showing his understanding of Japanese building traditions, is an astonishingly sparse room, considering the cluttered interiors of Mackintosh's era. Outside there are no crow steps, no fortified turrets, no sign at all of historical details, yet the random layout of the windows and the balanced asymmetry of his plan clearly draw inspiration from old fortified keeps.

The early fifteenth-century castle of Borthwick in the Scottish Borders had a profound effect on Louis Kahn, one of the most influential architects of the mid-twentieth century. Its thick walls and wide vaulted spaces talked to the American architect. He saw how the deep walls provided small rooms for a variety of ancillary services; how the central banqueting hall of Borthwick was serviced by the surrounding small rooms embedded within the walls. From this Kahn derived his concept of rooms being either 'served' or 'servant' spaces. What he had experienced in that dark medieval Scottish castle he brought to vibrant twentieth-century life under the bright sun of Southern California. With their rugs and oak tables his studies were the servant spaces where the scientists could hatch their experiments before testing them in the stainless-steel served spaces of the laboratories. 'I separated the studies from the laboratory and placed them over gardens,' said Kahn.

If he had learnt from Scotland for the layout of the Institute's interiors, the two flanking laboratories facing an open piazza of travertine also evoked the massive ruins of Hadrian's Villa outside Rome, which the architect had studied as a young man. By combining these memories with a total rethinking of what a campus could be, Kahn created his cliff-top masterpiece at La Jolla, under the California sun. 'Architecture is the masterly, correct and magnificent play of volumes brought together in light,' wrote Le Corbusier, which was just what Kahn built at Salk.

The thick-walled architecture of Scotland's past, combined with late works of the Swiss architect Le Corbusier, were central to Benson & Forsyth's design for

the New Museum of Scotland. Graham Benson endorsed Louis Kahn's ideas about Scottish castles by creating spiral stairs between walls and sinking display cabinets into their deep masonry. To face the traffic of five streets he devised a round entrance tower, with inserted cuts in deference to Le Corbusier. But he derived this proud tower not from medieval castles, but from the broch, as a homage to the origins of Scottish architecture over two thousand years before.

Climbing the stairs inside, a deeply framed window directs your eye to Edinburgh Castle, with its round moon battery echoing Benson's evocation of a broch. The roof garden is held up by an arc of white concrete, which itself mirrors the circumference of the drum of the MacEwan Hall of Edinburgh University. Benson's aim was to make a suitable setting for the artefacts of Scotland's history in an armature of contemporary design. He drew in elements from Charles Rennie Mackintosh and merged them with later forms derived from Le Corbusier. By marrying elements of the Scottish vernacular with European Modernism this new museum expresses an international outlook.

The Doric austerity of the Royal High School, Edinburgh (1825-9), designed by Thomas Hamilton, was 'unquestionably one of the finest buildings in the kingdom' – the claim of the Glasgow architect Alexander Thomson (1817-75). Although he was nicknamed 'Greek' Thomson, there was little Greek precedent for the numerous buildings he provided Victorian Glasgow with. These included multilayered tenements and highly original churches. But such innovative ideas as glazed street arcades were never realised. Thomson's aim was to throw all history into the crucible, reduce it to fluid thought, and then distil its essence. He became a bold experimenter and one of the outstanding Scottish architects of his day.

St Vincent's Street Church is Thomson's vision of Solomon's Temple. In his many inventive villas he drew on the whole of architectural history, including Egyptian and even Indian building forms. He looked to the leading architects of Europe, especially the great German neoclassicist Karl Friedrich Schinkel. Yet he

Glasgow School of Art, west front, 1909. Mackintosh's greatest building, the School of Art, begun in 1896, still stands like a castle above Glasgow's Sauchiehall Street on Garnethill. Winning the competition for the new school at twenty-seven, Mackintosh was able to expand his original plan during its decade of construction.

'The Hen Run' was the affectionate name given to Mackintosh's inventive solution to connect the last phase of the arts school at the upper level to the library wing of 1909.

took Schinkel's ideas further, disguising windows so that they disappeared as dark recesses within façades of receding and advancing planes.

Thomson had set the course in Glasgow, whose architects continued to innovate in the classical style well into the twentieth century. Even as late as 1906 when the British Museum decided to extend its galleries, the trustees had to fall back on the expertise of the Glasgow architect J.J. Burnet. No London architect had either Burnet's flair or his classical knowledge.

Beyond Glasgow's classical tradition the talented young architect Charles Rennie Mackintosh was hatching plans that owed little to Greece, though he would soon owe much to 'Greek' Thomson. Mackintosh was an accomplished artist who loved to draw the 'Scottish chateaux'. He saw how their unadorned lower walls were often capped with exuberant upper storeys. Here there was no fearful classical symmetry. Windows were placed where they were needed, yet in their overall layout he saw that they still retained a pleasing sense of balance. For Mackintosh the 'Scottish chateau' represented 'the only architecture that we can call our own'. The most talented student of his day at the Glasgow School of Art, he won the Alexander Thomson travelling competition, which allowed him to study architecture across Europe.

> Bless'd too is he who, midst his tufted trees,
> Some ruin'd castle's lofty towers sees,
> Imbosom'd high upon the mountain's brow,
> Or nodding o'er the stream that glides below.
> Richard Payne Knight

'If I am lonely in a foreign country, I search for ruins,' writes Christopher Woodward in his thought-provoking book *In Ruins*. So I wonder what he would

St Peter's seminary, Cardross, 1958-6, closed 1980. Gillespie, Kidd & Coia, lead architects Isi Metzstein and Andy MacMillan.

Opposite: The chapel of St Peter's – then and (left) now.

'My voice sticks in my throat; and, as I dictate, sobs choke my utterance. The City which had taken the whole world was itself taken.' – 'The Sack of Rome', St Jerome, 395 AD.

think of Scottish culture if he stumbled unknowingly on the ruins of St Peter's, Cardross? St Peter's is not a ruin of an early church, but it can be glimpsed amidst tufted trees, and the stream that glides below is the mighty River Clyde. Astonishingly, this ruin is barely fifty years old.

St Peter's seminary, consecrated in 1966, marked a climax of the enlightened patronage of modern architecture by the Roman Catholic Church in postwar Scotland. This once great Modernist masterpiece was created by Isi Metzstein and Andy MacMillan, working seamlessly together in the office of Gillespie, Kidd & Coia. Jack Coia had hired them both when they were still students at the Glasgow School of Art. In 1956 he gave them their first key commission, a church for the New Town of Glenrothes in Fife. In the design of St Paul's, the church buildings of this enterprising practice took a radical new direction as Metzstein and MacMillan looked to contemporary Europe for inspiration.

This small church initiated many others as the New Towns expanded across Scotland. The practice grew, providing schools, colleges, hospitals, offices, housing and university buildings, but the masterpiece was St Peter's, Cardross. Colin St John (Sandy) Wilson, architect of the British Library, has commented:

> The church and campanile of East Kilbride was of its time without rival in Great Britain and was a match, dare one say, even for Le Corbusier himself at Ronchamp…Much later, the same quality of carved mass and ebulliently unpredictable detail is present in the seminary at Cardross and Robinson College in Cambridge…Their buildings were serious, passionate and utterly memorable.

Clearly Le Corbusier's priory of La Tourette near Lyons was the primary inspiration, but St Peter's also shows the influence of Charles Rennie Mackintosh, whose importance was still to be rediscovered in Glasgow in the early Sixties. The challenge for Metzstein and MacMillan as secular architects was to create 'sacred space' – how to translate the ecclesiastical traditions of a thousand years into a modern language? They looked to Mackintosh's Glasgow School of Art (1897-1909), where they had met and trained, to lead them out of mainstream dogmatic Modernism towards more expressive forms.

Today St Peter's is a derelict wreck, stranded in such vandalised decay that not even the most passionate ruinist would see it as in anyway 'bless'd'. The vertical thrust of the Scottish baronial tower of Kilmahew House, around which the college pivoted, was burnt down by vandals and demolished in 1986. The sense of enclosure so created is now lost for ever, isolating the main study bedrooms, the chapel and the refectory. The adjacent teaching and recreational building, where once large windows reflected the turrets and crow-stepped gables of the Victorian house, lies wrecked.

St Peter's was deconsecrated by the archdiocese of the Roman Catholic Church, not, as many believe, as a result of the changes wrought by Vatican II but because of the expense of running an uneconomic building when the price of heating oil soared during the oil crisis of the Seventies. What can now be done? Given the highest category of listing by Historic Scotland, the Church still owns the ruins. What does it say of our culture that the one masterpiece of the late twentieth century was left to disintegrate like this? Even at this late hour St Peter's could yet be rejuvenated into a centre for young musicians and year-round festivals. It still lies among ravishingly beautiful grounds with exotic shrubs and trees imported by the Glasgow shipping magnate James Burns of Kilmahew.

For the young Glasgow-born James Stirling, too, Mackintosh's work would have the greatest significance. As a 2nd Lieutenant with the Black Watch in the Maryhill barracks during World War II, he often got asked by the girl students to the Saturday night hops in the School of Art. 'I was fascinated by the building,' he said, 'and got to explore its nooks and crannies with the ladies, who were somewhat adventurous with young officers on the eve of the second front.' Such accommodating little crannies, and the great spaces that opened beyond them, fired his imagination. Parachuted ahead of the D Day landings, Stirling miraculously survived with only severe wounds to his left hand. Invalided out of the war, he was left to recuperate in a temporary hospital ward in the requisitioned Harewood House. When lying flat on his back in the sumptuous gallery at Harewood, he later recalled, 'looking up at the Robert Adam ceiling I made the decision to become an architect.' So what Mackintosh had suggested, Adam confirmed, and James Stirling would become one of the greatest architects of the late twentieth century.

When Stirling's Staatsgalerie opened in Stuttgart in 1984 it was immediately recognised as a masterpiece, making him an overnight hero in Germany, something he never achieved in his own country. Waiting for the London release of *Highlander*, I was amazed to catch a television commercial for a Rover car pulling up in front of Stuttgart's banded masonry with its pay-off line: 'Britischer Auto. Britischer Architekt.' 'Do you feel that you are a more European or an

Anglo-Saxon architect?' Stirling was asked at the opening. 'Scots,' was his abrupt reply. I liked that.

No one was more extravagant in their praise of the Stuttgart gallery than the critic Emilio Ambasz, who said that it took Stirling 'to sing with marble voice the legitimate cravings of the German soul for a secular chamber to celebrate a Te Deum in quiet grandeur'. 'It's no longer enough to do classicism straight,' said Stirling. 'In this building the central pantheon, instead of being the culmination, is but a void – a room like non-space instead of a dome – open to the sky.'

Neue Staatsgalerie, Stuttgart,1977-82, by James Stirling. This circular arena, inspired by the Lake of Canopus at Hadrian's Villa, is one of the great open spaces in contemporary architecture.

Page 148: The Great Hall, Syon House, Isleworth, 1760-69, Robert Adam, with a replica of *The Dying Gaul*. After studying Roman architecture for close on five years, Robert Adam embarked on reinventing classicism by remodelling Syon House in 1760. 'Finished in a style to afford variety and amusement,' was the promise the young architect gave his client, Sir Hugh Smithson, the future 1st Duke of Northumberland. At Syon the revolutionary Adam Style was born. But the architect's masterstroke, of enclosing the great courtyard with a Pantheon-like rotunda, was never realised.

Page 149: Neue Staatsgalerie Stuttgart, open rotunda, 1984, James Stirling. 'It's no longer enough to do classicism straight,' Stirling said at the opening of his own revolutionary approach, 'in this building the central pantheon, instead of being the culmination, is but a void – a room like non space.' This visionary architect was too innovatory for St Andrews, where Stirling's plans for an arts centre were thwarted by conservationists, leaving his half completed university residences there as his only work in the country of his birth.

10 SCOTIA DEPICTA
From Picts to pictures and sculpture

There's no art
To find the mind's construction in the face.
                                            Macbeth

Painting, for my wife Micheline, has been the devouring passion of her life. Her portraits go well beyond the surface of appearance. 'I am particularly interested in expression,' she says, 'especially in the eyes. The eyes, as we say in France, are the mirror of the soul.' Micheline's sense of exuberant colour still amazes me, especially in the portraits that I have sat for. Perhaps that's all down to her Mediterranean upbringing; certainly, it's a long way from the grey world where I grew up in 1930s Edinburgh. 'It only takes a little talent to paint a likeness,' she believes. 'It takes much more to catch the emotional energy of a person, but if you capture that you will reveal the mind.' Micheline opened my eyes to portrait-painting in Scotland. At the Edinburgh Festival exhibition of Allan Ramsay, one of the greatest eighteenth-century portraitists, Micheline amazed me with the insights she could draw out of these pictures about Scottish character.

Micheline has strong views on contemporary art and never holds back in expressing them. Sometimes this has its amusing consequences. When Michael Ovitz, one of Hollywood's top bananas, invited us round for dinner he was intrigued to know what Micheline would make of a painting he had just recently acquired. On the way over I asked her to hold back if she really hated what she saw. 'I shall say nothing if he doesn't ask me,' she said. 'But if he does I shall just tell him what I think.'

As soon as we arrived we were swept upstairs to Michael's teak-lined rooftop gallery. Facing us was a large all-white canvas – a square, seemingly, of absolute nothingness. Micheline braced herself and stood back in shock.

'So what do you think?' he asked her.

'I think that this is the best work of art you have ever bought.'

'You know,' said Michael, 'the artist achieved this effect with over fifty separate layers of white.'

'Of course, it makes all the difference,' Micheline said, realising that Michael was experiencing something of an irony deficiency. 'I think the painter is a genius. The director of the gallery is a genius too. But you know, I think the man who bought it is an absolute idiot.'

Dinner was now going to start with a challenging agenda, especially after Micheline delivered her *coup de grâce*: 'If at the bottom of your nothing painting the artist had quoted the French poet Paul Valéry's comment on literature, that "a blank page could be a beautiful work of art", that at least would have given some nobility to your white shit.'

A month later we were at the Centre Pompidou in Paris and to our amazement there was the same painting side by side with another all-white canvas. Micheline couldn't resist calling up Michael Ovitz to tell him where she had seen his painting.

'Well,' he said, 'since you thought so little of it, I sold it.'

A few years later Micheline was persuaded by a close friend to see a play in Paris, even although she has never been too crazy about French theatre. But Yasmina Reza's *Art* captivated her immediately. Centred on a white painting which one of the characters even calls 'white shit', the play hit her with an extraordinary sense of *déjà vu* along with all the arguments as to whether it was art or not affecting the friendship of three guys. After *Art* Micheline had dinner with one of the actors, who gave her Yasmina Reza's phone number, and next day they met. 'Listen, I fell in love with your play and simply adore it,' Micheline told Yasmina, who had come along with her agent. 'Sean and I would love to buy the English-language rights.' The agent interrupted to say that they were already in discussion with the London producer Cameron Mackintosh, who had quite liked the play. 'But Micheline adores *Art*,' Yasmina said. 'She doesn't quite like it, she really loves *Art*, so why don't we go with her?'

So Micheline and I acquired the English-language stage and film rights and commissioned Christopher Hampton as translator. The result was the critically acclaimed 1996 West End production starring Albert Finney, Tom Courtenay and Ken Stott, who all added telling touches to the script. *Art* went on to win both the *Evening Standard* Drama Award and the Laurence Olivier Award for Best Comedy. But this didn't impress Yasmina Reza, who thought she had written a tragedy. When the final West End curtain dropped in 2004, the play had gone through twenty-six cast changes and celebrated its eighth birthday. In New York *Art* ran for six hundred performances and won the Tony Award for the Best Original Play, and it has since been translated into thirty-five languages. According to the magazine *Business Week*, *Art* has accrued over £150 million from its worldwide travels.

I discussed the film opportunities with my old friend Sidney Lumet. Our friendship extends back over forty years and five movies, beginning with *The Hill*, which saved me in 1965 from bondage fatigue between *Goldfinger* and *Thunderball*.

Ken Stott, Tom Courtenay and Albert Finney at the opening night of the West End production of Yasmina Reza's *Art* with a proud producer.

Previous pages: Being painted by Micheline in 1978 on the terrace at Malibu, our Marbella home for many years in southern Spain.

Yet despite our efforts Yasmina Reza insisted that *Art* should first be produced in French. Sadly, we are still waiting.

Reza's minimalist white painting neatly bookends the art of the twentieth century as a negative of the famous *Black Square* painting by Kasimir Malevich of 1915. But the Russian artist's negation of a painting expresses much more. It was first exhibited in a gallery at ceiling height, just as an icon is displayed in an Orthodox Christian home, where traditionally an all-protecting Mother of God looks down from the 'beautiful' or 'holy' upper corner of a room. For over a thousand years the painters of icons, or 'holy pictures' as they prefer them to be called, captured the living likenesses of the early saints through their faces, enlightened by the faces 'streaming down to them from God to guide their hands'. But could you expect such divine help if you were asked to paint the portraits of long-forgotten mortal kings? That was the problem we pondered in the Great Gallery of the Palace of Holyroodhouse when David Murray and I were making our film on Edinburgh. Arranged all around us were portraits of Scotland's ancient monarchs: nearly ninety portraits of mostly legendary kings, receding back into the deep time of unrecorded history.

When Charles II decided to celebrate his newly 'United Kingdom' after the Restoration of 1660, he invited the Dutch artist Jacobus de Wet to glorify his descent from an impossibly long line of over one hundred Scottish monarchs stretching back into the mists of time. Memorialising their legendary past was a Stuart failing, one which Shakespeare went out of his way to flatter. By having his witches confront Macbeth with a line-up of eight Scottish kings (including the probably mythical Banquo) he was clearly aiming to curry favour with the recently crowned James I of England, the grandfather of Charles II.

Jacobus de Wet's problem was that nobody knew what most of those kings looked like. There were a number of likenesses of the recent monarchs, but then what? The artist's solution was to paint the face that he knew best – his own. And then, in a masterful touch, he gave each of them Charles's prominent Stuart nose to distance the regal faces back into history. When we rapidly dissolved all the portraits together, one after another, in our film, it was only then that we realised that the economical artist had also saved on props. A handful of unlikely hats kept being recycled over the monarchs' heads. Jacobus de Wet must have held headgear in high regard, for at Glamis Castle he even featured Jesus in a Homburg, which must make it one of the few Christs in Western art to have been painted with a hat.

There was a precedent for painting the real and mythical kings of Scotland. When Charles I was finally shamed into returning to the land of his birth to celebrate his long-delayed coronation in 1633, the accomplished painter George Jamesone was chosen to glorify his stately entrance to the capital of Scotland. As a loyal subject Jamesone embarked on producing over a hundred portraits of Scottish monarchs, all the way back to King Fergus. He too had to invent face after face. Despite having spent most of his life in England, Charles must have delighted in seeing his royal pedigree stretch all the way back to the ancient Pictish kings.

Born in Aberdeen towards the end of the sixteenth century, the young George Jamesone was influenced by contemporary Dutch artists. When a number of

Christ with Mary Magdalene by Jacobus de Wet, 1688, Glamis Castle chapel. Here the Risen Jesus, dressed as a gardener, has the curious attributes of a wide-brimmed hat and a shovel.

Jamesone's royal portraits came to auction in the 1960s few gave them a second glance and they went for very little money. Two young art historians spotted them for what they were and bought as many as they could afford. One of the lucky bidders was Duncan Thomson, a future director of the Scottish National Portrait Gallery. The other was Duncan MacMillan, the author of *Scottish Art, 1460-1990*.

The impossibility of capturing the likeness of ancient kings brings us to the essence of portrait painting during the Scottish Enlightenment. When Henry Raeburn met the accomplished Gavin Hamilton in Rome, Hamilton's advice to the aspiring young artist from Edinburgh was never to paint from memory, but to engage with his subject sympathetically. Years later, when Raeburn exhibited his first painting in London of Sir John and Lady Clerk of Penicuik, its sensational success encouraged him to move his studio south.

The Scottish monarchs of Jacobus de Wet, 1684, the Palace of Holyroodhouse. Just 20 of the 111 royal portraits. Only a few were derived from originals by George Jameson painted for Charles I some sixty years earlier.

Sir Walter Scott, 1822, Sir Henry Raeburn, 1756-1823. The author of the *Waverley* novels is caught by the artist at the height of his powers. Even though Raeburn had only a few more months to live, his portrait is charged with life and painted with great forcefulness.

Mr and Mrs Chalmers-Bethune and their daughter Isabella, 1804, David Wilkie, 1785-1841. The smothering presence of this ruddy-faced patriarch makes us ponder the daily dilemmas faced by his daughter and wife.

Sir John and Lady Clerk of Penicuik, 1792, Sir Henry Raeburn. This evocatively back-lit portrait of Sir John and Lady Clerk established the artist as the leading painter of the Scottish Enlightenment. 'Sir Henry painted standing, having his palette set he began at once to a portrait without previous chalking out,' a sitter observed. 'By a few bold and skilfully managed touches he produced striking effects.'

Pitlessie Fair, 1804, David Wilkie, 1785-1841. This all-encompassing portrait of the annual May Fair in Pitlessie village was painted when the artist was just nineteen.

Edinburgh at this time was a forcing-ground of intellectual inquiry, well described as a 'hot-bed of genius' by the wry Scots writer Tobias Smollett in his last great novel, *The Expedition of Humphry Clinker* (1771). From the 'lad o'pairts' who had advanced himself from lowly beginnings in the countryside to the good and the great of the Scottish Enlightenment, Raeburn was there to chronicle them all. That he did this not in a series of commissioned likenesses but through insightful portrayals of character made him one of the most accomplished painters of his time. Raeburn's last study was of Sir Walter Scott, a fitting end to a career which had owed so much to the writings of that 'Wizard of the North'.

By remaining in Scotland, Raeburn was an inspiration to up-and-coming artists like David Wilkie, whose insightful triple portrait of the Bethune family was clearly influenced by the master. 'An excellent painter can tell, not only what are the proportions of a good face, but what changes every passion makes in it,' was the philosopher Thomas Reid's definition of a great artist. And Wilkie goes further than Raeburn in his close study of expressions, as Duncan MacMillan reveals:

Having attended Bell's Edinburgh lectures on the anatomy of expression, Wilkie was well armed to capture the expression of a caring mother's tender pride. Just as poignantly he expresses the lively innocent curiosity of her daughter. In contrast the ruddy-faced father, framed by his huge girth, expresses an awkward suspiciousness and perhaps even hostility to the young artist who is in the process of painting him.

In *Pitlessie Fair*, painted in 1804, the young Wilkie embarked on a portrait of his home village. 'Most of the figures,' he said, 'are portraits of the inhabitants of a small village in Scotland where the Fair is annually held.' These included his own father and many members of his extended family. 'The painter must study the traits of human expression,' the surgeon Charles Bell wrote. And here in this remarkable painting Wilkie delivers these thoughts in paint.

A war-wounded soldier dying from tetanus. Charles Bell, 1774-1842, Royal College of Surgeons, Edinburgh.

Illustration from *The Anatomy of the Brain, Explained in a Series of Engravings*, 1802, Charles Bell, 1774-1842. As much an artist as an anatomist, this brilliant Edinburgh-born surgeon published a series of innovatory textbooks co-authored with his brother John Bell.

There's no art
To find the mind's construction in the face:
He was a gentleman on whom I built
An absolute trust.

Macbeth I.iv

King Duncan responded in *Macbeth* to the news that the Thane of Cawdor had faced his execution for treason as though death 'were a careless trifle'. Whether the face could express one's inner thoughts or not became one of the great controversies of the Scottish Enlightenment. It was a debate provoked by Thomas Reid in Aberdeen – that other great centre of learning in mid-eighteenth-century Scotland. 'How are sensations of the mind produced by impressions on the body?' was the gauntlet Reid threw down to scientists. 'How does the body act upon the mind or the mind upon the body?' It was a challenge that was more than met by Charles Bell and his brother John, also a surgeon, who employed art in the daily pursuit of their science. 'As I proceeded in writing a book on anatomy,' wrote John Bell, 'I felt the necessity of giving plates to it, for a book on anatomy without these seemed to me no better than a book of geography without maps.'

Curiously at this time, artists actually studied anatomy more than anatomists did. To accurately convey anatomical detail, Bell maintained, art and science must go hand in hand. Charles Bell, who had studied painting under the artist David Allan, followed his brother's lead in writing and illustrating a series of publications on the anatomy of the brain and its expression in painting. Bell demonstrated that Reid was right, that sensation and expression were the result of a direct physiological system of communication provided by two distinct sets of nerves, sensory and motor – the one applicable to sensibility and the other to motion. It became one of the fundamental discoveries of modern science. Bell's own drawings became a vital instrument in his anatomical research; his art linked the originality of Reid's philosophy with the beginnings of modern neurology

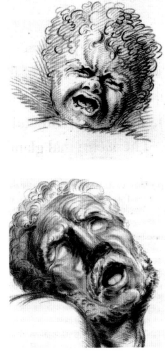

and subsequently psychiatry, paving Edinburgh's future reputation in these fields. As a field doctor, Charles Bell attended the wounded of the Napoleonic Wars, including at the Battle of Waterloo. Working continuously for three days and nights, his heroic action in treating both British and French casualties saved many lives. He even found time to sketch the gruesome wounds inflicted on the soldiers by sword and gunshot. Later he developed his rapidly executed drawings into demonstration paintings to record their clinical conditions. And there, two centuries later, they are still on display in Edinburgh's Surgeons' Hall. We view them today just as we would contemplate Goya's *Disasters of War*, as art deploring man's inhumanity to man. Yet these paintings record the clinical effects of traumatic wounds with medical accuracy. One of the most moving captures the unbearable agony of a tetanus-infected soldier, his spine doubled up in a seizure known as 'the hysteric arch'. Bell's illustrations of extreme pain in his *Anatomy and Physiology of Expression* profoundly influenced Géricault when he came to paint *The Raft of the 'Medusa'*, illustrating a most morbid chapter of French history. Géricault revealed to a shocked public how this desperate shipwrecked group, marooned on the open seas, was driven by thirst and hunger to murder and cannibalism.

'It is from Scotland that we receive rules in taste in all the arts,' wrote Voltaire in 1762. When the great French philosopher and author praised Scots for their taste in the arts he was surely thinking of the works of his friend David Hume, 'le bon David', who wrote his influential *Treatise of Human Nature* in France. Hume was

The Raft of the Medusa, 1819, Théodore Géricault, 1791-1824. Géricault drew on many anatomical drawings of Charles and John Bell to depict with accuracy the agony of the desperate survivors of the French frigate *Medusa* lost on a raft at sea.

Facial Expressions of Pain, Charles Bell, from *The Anatomy & Physiology of Expression as Connected with the Fine Arts*.

one of the key players of the Enlightenment in Scotland, that period of light and learning when the arts and sciences blossomed together. It was a time when Scots philosophers influenced progressive thought in both Europe and America. Artists played their part too, for new directions in painting followed philosophy. Voltaire probably also had in mind the genius of Allan Ramsay who had painted Hume, as well as his contemporary Jean-Jacques Rousseau.

Ramsay, along with many fellow Scots, had studied with masters in Rome. In their clarity and humanity Ramsay's portraits epitomised the cultural confidence of his time. Ramsay's father, the poet and author of *The Gentle Shepherd*, proposed that the effete modern taste should be abandoned for the art of the 'good old bards', for they could provide a model of 'natural strength of Thought and Simplicity of Style our Forefathers practised'. This became a search for the bards of the classical world exemplified by Homer and his incomparable *Iliad*.

Heroic canvases on classical themes won for the Lanark-born painter Gavin Hamilton a European reputation. His paintings aimed to reflect the new philosophy of moral sensibility. Hamilton and the philosopher Adam Smith had been students together at Glasgow University. As Adam Smith argued in his *Theory of Moral Sentiments* (1759), society at large depended not on reason, but feeling. Smith maintained that sympathy depended on imagination, and that the feminine sensibility played a key role in the evolution of society. Remaining for much of his life in Rome, Hamilton's approach influenced the up-and-coming generation of artists. Jacques-Louis David's heroic painting *The Oath of the Horatii* clearly owes much in its inspiration and composition to Hamilton's *Death of Lucretia*.

When the Venetian ambassador showed Antonio Canova's sculpture of *Daedalus and Icarus* in Rome in 1780, it was 'Il Gavino Amilton' who praised it first. Hamilton persuaded the Venetian sculptor to abandon his early baroque style and to learn from antiquity. Canova was so inspired by Hamilton's heroic

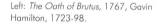

Left: *The Oath of Brutus*, 1767, Gavin Hamilton, 1723-98.

Right: *The Oath of the Horatii*, 1784, Jean-Louis David,1759-95.

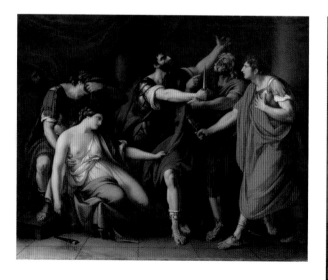

depictions of classical history that a father-and-son relationship developed. Once Hamilton introduced Canova to the studios of Bartolomeo Cavaceppi and Francesco Antonio Franzoni, restorers of Roman sculptures, the true Canova style was born.

Apart from being a champion of neoclassicism, Gavin Hamilton was also a highly successful archaeologist, collector and dealer in sculpture. Among the extensive ruins of the Emperor Hadrian's villa at Tivoli he discovered a few fragments of a gargantuan vase and embarked on one of his most ambitious creative reconstructions. With much enterprise he acquired a ten-ton block of Carrara marble and had his friend Giovanni Piranesi re-invent, with much artistic licence, the vase's many missing sections. Soon the costs far exceeded the artist's pocket, so Hamilton quickly involved his friend Sir William Hamilton, 'Envoy Extraordinary to the Kingdom of the Two Sicilies' in Naples. Sir William had the Enlightenment's thirst for knowledge in the arts and sciences; his great passion was collecting ancient Greek vases, then being unearthed in large numbers from hillside tombs all around the Bay of Naples. Hamilton published his collection in what would become one of the most beautiful and influential illustrated books of the eighteenth century.

It was from one of William Hamilton's vases that another Edinburgh-born artist, Alexander Runciman, drew his inspiration for his *Origin of Painting*. This vase was supposed to be a record of the original primitive moment when a girl drew her lover's profile on the wall as he slept – a fantastically improbable but imaginatively potent idea. Thus Runciman glorifies the first artist as a woman and the first painting as made by her under the guidance of love; a defining moment at the dawn of civilisation, triumphing the feminine principle. For art, as celebrated by Runciman, was born of love, sympathy and imagination. When he returned from Rome as an accomplished artist, he persuaded his patron Sir James Clerk to abandon his original commission for murals on classical themes.

The Origin of Painting, 1773, Alexander Runciman, 1736-85.

Left: Alexander Runciman's sketch for the central oval of the Penicuik ceiling of the blind Ossian playing his harp.

Right: A Pictish harper carved on the Dupplin Cross, Forteviot, c.800.

Opposite page: A Pictish warrior as imagined by John White based on his observations of drawing the inhabitants of North America in the late sixteenth century.

Runciman's dazzlingly coloured ceiling of Celtic heroes attending the blind harp-playing Ossian, with his great hound at his feet, became a wonder the Scottish Enlightenment.

When the artist John White dreamt up his fierce vision of a Pict, he had recently returned from Virginia with Sir Walter Raleigh. Images of tattooed American Indians clearly came to colour White's imaginative recreations of Scotland's early people. His grotesquely decorated ancient warrior, wielding a shield and grasping the hair of a severed head, has muddled our perception of the Picts ever since.

Such mythical Hollywood-like depictions contrast with the very ordinary figures portraying Picts on Roman slabs. But who were the Picts? We know them only from their Roman or Latin name, Picti, the painted ones. We also know what they were called in Old English, in Old Norse, in Old Irish and in Old Welsh. But we don't know what they called themselves. Their name may be forgotten but their existence, through their art, puzzles us to this day. It is an art unique to Scotland, yet its masterpieces are scattered across small museums and are often inadequately displayed. As the essential enigma of early European art they deserve much better.

Few have done more to rescue the Picts from the enveloping mists of fanciful fakelore than Isabel and George Henderson, who have spent a lifetime connecting the scattered symbol stones with manuscripts, metalwork and other surviving artefacts to paint the most rounded picture yet of our elusive ancestors. They now live in the northeast of Scotland near the cross-slab of Nigg, one of the true masterpieces of Pictish art and closest in its intricate carving to the illuminated designs of the Lindisfarne Gospels and the Book of Kells. Despite the erosion and mutilations of centuries, many of the surviving stone carvings are works of incomparable power. Isabel Henderson has done much to reveal the visual messages of salvation and damnation that these monuments convey with their early Christian symbols and the stranger, more secular, Pictish emblems which are still largely beyond our understanding.

George Henderson makes convincing claims that Pictish art inspired the picture pages of such masterpieces of illuminated art as the Book of Durrow and the Echternach Gospels. The famous Book of Kells, made in the monastery of Iona founded by St Columba, is full of reminiscences of the brilliant ornamental designs still to be seen on Pictish sculptures. That not a single Pictish manuscript has survived is no surprise to Henderson, since the iconoclasts of John Knox's fanatical Reformation would have destroyed them. In that era of national self-hatred even the effigies of the Scots kings were thrown into the sea off Iona, and nearly every medieval manuscript perished. Isabel Henderson's research on the late-eighth-century St Andrews Sarcophagus has shown that the Picts were cosmopolitan. In this work, the flowing drapes and the nuzzling dog could have been inspired, she thinks, by a Byzantine ivory from Constantinople. The figure of the biblical David bears a Pictish knife but is cloaked in a gown, which also shows clear influences from abroad.

By the tenth century the Picts in the east had amalgamated with the Scots in the west, and their literature and history ceased to be relevant to the later medieval chroniclers of Scotland. They left behind their remarkable carvings, the only traces of a lost people: as mysterious to Scots as the Etruscans are to Italians. The Pictish symbol stones remain the enigma of early medieval European art. It is the one art that is unique to Scotland. Displayed across the country on so many free-standing stones, it's an art that we might eventually lose, as the carvings are eroding through a drastic increase in acid rain. Victorian photographs and casts now reveal details that have been irrevocably lost. With our new ability to make precise reproductions, surely these stones should be protected for all time and replicas placed at their original sites.

An imaginative scheme to re-display the most important collection of Pictish stones, in an old schoolhouse at Meigle near Forfar, was commissioned by Historic Scotland in 1996. In this little museum three outstanding carved slabs, including a massive cross-slab over 2.5 metres tall, combine early Christian symbols on one side with secular hunting scenes and a whole range of enigmatic Pictish symbols on the other. A key part of the new layout called for a mirrored wall to reflect back a Calvary of stones and so allow the two scenes to interact, the pagan with the Christian. Sadly, the expense of this was deemed unprofitable, given the number of expected visitors. So this important European collection remains laid out with all the imagination of a garage sale. Once again culture has to take a back seat to commercialism, under the aegis of an organisation originally set up for preservation but now given by the government the impossible task of augmenting its funds on the basis of ticket sales.

The Museum of Scotland's rather arbitrary display of their small collection of symbol stones only hints at what a dedicated centre of Pictish art could be. I still remember the overpowering thrill that the Jacob Epstein exhibition gave me in the old Waverley Market during the Edinburgh Festival of 1961. The exhibition was devised by Richard Buckle with much help from the Festival director the Earl of Harewood, who had rescued a number of Epstein's masterpieces from an appalling situation. *Adam*, the sculptor's monumental nude alabaster of male sexual energy,

Pictish symbol stones, the Meigle Museum, near Forfar, Angus.

The Nigg stone, c.780 compared with the interlacing of the *Book of Kells,* c.800.

This incisively carved wolf seems to have stalked off his Pictish stone from Ardross, Rosshire, to lurk between the lines of the *Book of Kells.*

Perhaps a Gospel Book, illuminated as richly as the *Book of Kells,* could have been displayed on the altar of some great Pictish church such as St Andrews.

and other dynamic religious works were being touted by a Blackpool fairground barker; a shilling purchased a glimpse of their alleged erotic thrills. As you circled around this reclaimed sculpture lit against the darkness of Waverley Market, *Adam*'s essential spirituality returned as though he were set high on a hill in Judaea. 'Here was inspiration indeed,' wrote Neville Cardus in the *Guardian*. 'Here was art greater than life, and not, as with nearly all art today, as small as life.' Such skilful settings could breathe new life into a progression of Pictish symbol stones displayed with equal imagination in a dedicated centre, to celebrate the foundation of art in Scotland as a key part of European patrimony.

In 2003 I was enthralled by an imaginative plan to convert Edinburgh's former Royal High School into a centre for photography. The photography proposal had much going for it. David Octavius Hill & Robert Adamson, the first true artists of photography, had their studio in Rock House perched up on the cliff just above the school. One of the first photographs depicted Thomas Hamilton's Greek Revival masterpiece of 1828 from the vantage point of his choragic monument to Robert Burns. The National Galleries of Scotland promised their superb collection, and the combined photographic holdings of Scotland could be available for exhibition there.

When I became the collection's patron I suggested that they call it the Hill Adamson instead of the Scottish National Centre for Photography, or even worse, land it with the unpronounceable ugly abbreviation of SNCP. Since I had worked with Sony on films and knew Howard Stringer, its energetic chief, we immediately got generous sponsorship. And then silence from Scotland. I found it interesting that a Welshman and an international Japanese company found this project sufficiently stimulating to put up sponsorship but that the Scottish Executive failed to show even a flicker of enthusiasm. There have been six ministers of culture in Scotland in ten years and, apart from Rhona Brankin, they don't seem to have achieved anything. They couldn't grasp the potential of this visitor destination, a superb collection in a building of world significance, which will be internationally rewarding for the whole city. 'Who is Hill Adamson?' one of them asked, believing that those pioneering Scots were a single person. Clearly large conversion costs will be involved, and my hope is that with support and a sensitive architect the Hill Adamson will go ahead and be housed in Hamilton's Athenian masterpiece.

Science and art went hand in hand in the development of photography as a new way of capturing portraits. The St Andrews University physicist David Brewster was a close friend of Fox Talbot, the inventor of the calotype, the first negative-positive photographic process. Brewster, together with the chemist John Adamson, produced the first calotype in Scotland, an event which was to have far-reaching

Panorama of Edinburgh, from the Crown of St Giles, Robert Barker, begun 1796.

consequences. His brother Robert Adamson perfected the technique and set up as a calotype photographer in Edinburgh in 1843.

Apart from being a pioneering scientist, Brewster was also an ardent believer in the democratic right of churches to elect their own ministers. This was at a time when landowners had the legal right to overrule church elders with their own appointments. In 1843 the issue came to a head when over a third of all the Church of Scotland ministers dramatically walked out of their annual assembly to create their own Free Church. 'There has not been such a subject since the days of John Knox,' said D. O. Hill, an artist as well as a photographer, who gave himself the task of painting the portraits of the great multitude in one gargantuan canvas. 'I got hold of the artist,' wrote Brewster to Fox Talbot, 'shewed him the calotype and the immense advantage he might derive from it, getting likenesses of all the principal characters before they disappeared to their respective homes. He was at first incredulous, but went to Mr. Adamson, and arranged with him all the preliminaries for getting all the necessary portraits. They have succeeded beyond their most sanguine expectations.'

Although a painting that set out to combine the individual portraits of nearly five hundred people could hardly be expected to result in anything other than a crowd scene, it propelled Hill into one of the most successful collaborations in the history of photography. Hill and Adamson created some fifteen hundred expressive 'sun pictures', as they called their calotype photographs, before their four-year collaboration came tragically to an end when Robert Adamson died, aged twenty-seven, in 1848.

Before the discovery of photography, capturing realistic records of the world around us in large-scale painted panoramas was the driving force behind the work of Robert Barker in Edinburgh. To make observers imagine themselves feel they are really on the spot was how Barker described his patent, which aimed to capture his all-surrounding 'total view'. Visitors would enter a specially constructed building along a dark corridor before reaching a viewing platform, where the whole of Edinburgh would surround them, as an all-enveloping panorama, through Barker's ingeniously curved perspective. Even the word 'panorama' was the Irish-born Barker's invention – from the Greek *pan* meaning 'all' and *orama*, 'view'.

Calotype photographs c.1845 by David Octavius Hill, 1802-70 and Robert Adamson, 1821-48.

Left: The 159 St Andrews golf group – the first golfing photograph.

Centre: David Octavius Hill.

Right: James Linton, his boat and bairns, Newhaven harbour.

The Wealth of Nations, 1993, Eduardo Paolozzi, 1924-2005, Royal Bank of Scotland, The South Gyle, Edinburgh Park. Inscribed with a quotation from Einstein, 'Knowledge is wonderful, but imagination is even better.'

'Tis evident that all the sciences have a relation, greater or less, to human nature; and that, however wide any of them may seem to run from it, they still return back by one passage or another.' – David Hume

'Knowledge is wonderful, but imagination is even better,' runs in block capitals along the base of Eduardo Paolozzi's colossal *Wealth of Nations* bronze sculpture below a tangle of cast body parts in search of a figure. The quotation is from Albert Einstein but it could just as easily have come from Adam Smith, although the clasping hands here are huge, in contrast to the economist's famous invisible hand that promotes ends beyond one's intention. The sculpture's inventive presence of fragmented limbs and DNA-like coils guards the entrance to the offices of the Royal Bank of Scotland in Edinburgh, a potent reminder that the true wealth of nations lies in the imagination of its people.

In St Mary's Episcopal Cathedral, Paolozzi's soaring windows now illuminate the Victorian Gothic of Gilbert Scott with shafts of coloured light. Nearby the Dean Gallery houses a tidied-up replica of his Chelsea studio along with the vast holdings donated by this most prolific artist. Paolozzi's close friend the author J.G. Ballard once said: 'If the entire twentieth century were to vanish in some huge calamity, it would be possible to reconstitute a large part of it from Paolozzi's work.' In a long and fulfilled life Paolozzi's inventive mind experimented with many of the major art movements of the last century, from Surrealism to Cubism through Art Brut, Conceptualism and Geometric Abstraction to Pop – although, as a diehard old Surrealist, he always denied being a Pop artist, wittily scotching the claim many had made that he was the father of British Pop. 'Pop art for me,' Paolozzi said, 'is like diving into a barrel of Coca Cola bottles.'

Paolozzi was brought up on Leith Walk in an Edinburgh he never forgot. The son of Italian immigrants who ran an ice-cream parlour in Albert Street, the young Paolozzi never lacked visual stimulation. Near his old jazz club next to St Mary's Catholic cathedral, his great bronze assemblage of fragments called *The Manuscript of Monte Cassino* is a memorial to his father, deported during the war only to be torpedoed at sea by a German U-boat.

Newton, 1995, Eduardo Paolozzi, in the courtyard of the British Library. Derived from William Blake's print of 1795. Paolozzi's commanding sculpture illustrates Isaac Newton's belief that mathematics now determine how we view the world.

BUNK! – *Evadne in Green Dimension*, screenprint, Eduardo Paolozzi, 1972.

As Is When, *Wittgenstein at the Cinema Admires Betty Grable*, Eduardo Paolozzi, 1965, screenprint. Paolozzi shared the philosopher Ludwig Wittgenstein's interest in engineering and cinema. In the early Seventies he created innovative posters for the Edinburgh Film Festival.

The Conan Doyle Memorial, Picardy Place, Edinburgh, sculptor Gerald Laing, b.1936. Sherlock Holmes is holding his famous Petersen pipe. Or is it a pipe?

Opposite: *Truth or Consequences*, 2006, Gerald Laing.

An American Girl, 1977, Gerald Laing. Galina was the artist's model.

Across the street the caped figure of Sherlock Holmes stands contemplating the comings and goings of Leith Walk, holding his famous Petersen pipe which bears the inscription of Magritte's disclaimer, 'Ceci n'est pas une pipe.' If you aren't athletic enough to reach up and read that, then there are the huge paw prints of the Hound of the Baskervilles to feel in the bronze base beside the famous detective's feet, interspersed for contrast with those of Phoebus, the sculptor's Jack Russell. The maker of this wry memorial to Conan Doyle, in front of his home in Picardy Place, is the artist Gerald Laing. Curiously, Edinburgh's road planners dictated that this one-and-a-quarter-lifesize statue should turn its back on the pedestrians of Picardy Place to face the passing traffic.

Laing's dot paintings of Anna Karina and Brigitte Bardot became instant icons of the Sixties and established him in the forefront of the Pop Art movement when he worked in New York. His romance with the American Dream within a few years turned to disillusion, to be followed by a flight into abstraction. Returning from his five-year stint in New York as an accepted artist whose work had even been included in the American Pavilion of the 1967 São Paulo Biennale, Laing re-earthed in the north of Scotland. At Kinkell he rebuilt a late-sixteenth-century tower house into a work of art with his new American wife, Galina Golikova. In 1973 Laing abandoned abstract art and began modelling figures in clay for casting into bronze. Nearly all were modelled on Galina, in elegant forms echoing the Cubism and angularity of the great sculptor Archipenko of the interwar years.

Laing's long-term ambition to create a gargantuan hilltop memorial to the Highland Clearances was thwarted, but in 2007 the same group of displaced Highlanders was erected in Helmsdale. Although reduced from the original plan which would have had the figures reach over five metres tall, this emigrating family are by no means insignificant. A second casting was installed above the Red River in Winnipeg, Canada, where it is celebrated more optimistically as *The Settlers*. Both were cast by Laing's son Farquhar, in his Black Isle Bronze foundry, which is now one of the most successful in the country.

The first night of vicious bombing over the living city of Baghdad shocked the artist who had started his career as a Sandhurst-trained officer. It sent him back to painting in the spirit of his New York days. Using early Pop Art techniques, Laing's *Shock and Awe* series questions the quality and truth of the American Dream. Most controversial of all was his *Truth or Consequences*, exhibited at Chelsea's National Army Museum in 2007. Painted on both sides of triangular slats, the piece made a smiling Tony Blair, standing by the London bus bombing of 7 July 2005, morph into George Bush with the city of Baghdad in flames behind him.

John Bellany and his fellow Edinburgh art student Sandy Moffat saw themselves as Expressionists and were deeply critical of the grip abstraction had on painters. Spurred on by their friend the poet Alan Bold, they nailed their Alan Davie-inspired figurative and Expressionist paintings to the railings outside the Royal Scottish Academy summer show in 1962.

John Bellany was born in 1942 at Port Seton near Edinburgh into a family of fishermen and boat-builders. There the sea held less the pleasure of summer swimming than the dread of death by drowning. He grew up in a deeply superstitious community of God-fearing Presbyterians fraught by evil, all rich seams of anguish that Bellany would later mine as themes for his startling canvases. As a postgraduate student at the Royal College of Art, he was overwhelmed by the 1965 Max Beckmann exhibition at the Tate. Invited to East Germany, he became aware of the work of Otto Dix and other artists of the Neue Sachlichkeit, or New Objectivity movement. But it was his visit to the site of the Buchenwald concentration camp that moved Bellany to despair. 'The dour early subjects became blacker,' Moffat recalls. 'After Buchenwald Hell obsessed him.'

In the years ahead Bellany would forge an art of deep symbolic meaning. Anchoring his vision around the harbour and seas of Port Seton, he began to address universal themes – *The Ship of Life, The Wheel of Fortune, The Crucifixion, The Dance of Death*. Symbolic fish and seabirds would often temper his growing awareness of fate and doom, sometimes with much ironic humour, as with his puffin painted as a comical mask. Then, fuelled by the demon drink and giddying success, Bellany plunged into ever deeper despair through the Seventies, as many of his near-demented self-portraits reveal. Leaving his wife Helen and family he married Judith, who was herself ill. When Bellany was recovering from a near-fatal illness he explored his predicament in an allegory called *The Presentation of Time*.

Boats as symbols of human life and a deep respect for fishermen pervade the very different art of Will Maclean. From washed-up flotsam and jetsam, harvested from the tideline tangle of the Isles, Maclean creates beautifully crafted assemblages. These haunting elegies evoke a lost seafaring world of hunters still in touch with nature, listening for fish at sea in the dead of night.

One of the most popular yet officially misunderstood artists in Scotland also has a great affinity with the sea. George Wyllie, the ex-Royal Navy officer and sometime customs officer of the Waterguard, uses humour in his art with deadly serious effect. But can an artist who uses humour be serious? Of course, but few in the art establishment seem to think so. Although Wyllie's work has been acquired by the Arts Council of England and many collections abroad, not one piece has been acquired for the national collections in Scotland. It doesn't worry Wyllie, who stays well away from the chatterers in the art world, clinking their wine glasses at private views. He prefers his art out of doors in the public domain.

Through the Richard Demarco Gallery, Wyllie met and soon collaborated with the German artist Joseph Beuys on his many forays to Scotland. Beuys made him think big, literally. And so began a series of public sculptures which connected with a wide public, though strangely not with the gatekeepers of the national collections. Wyllie's later series of spires, slender tripods pivoting their counterweighted central arms in the landscape, would be a homage to Beuys, who spoke of the urgent need for balance in our relationship with nature. Public sculpture for Wyllie is art that the public can't avoid.

Wyllie's full-scale replica of a Glasgow-built steam locomotive made in straw captured the imagination of everyone who saw it. His *Straw Locomotive* hung

Sad Self-Portrait, 1976, John Bellany, b.1942.

Opposite page: *The Presentation of Time – Homage to Rubens.* The grateful artist has gathered his friends and the symbols of life around him, as the owl of death visits his mortally ill second wife. Bellany nudges aside the dog of evil as the time of life is presented to him by his first wife, Helen. The beam of a lighthouse turns sunset into dawn. The glow of life returns. Soon John and Helen will re-marry and their lives will continue together again. His friends here include the artist Alan Davie whose paintings had so long inspired Bellany. In turn Davie encouraged Bellany to retain his 'Nordic mystical power'. I am the one with the fish on my shoulder; I must remember to ask him why.

The Sabbath of the Dead, Will Maclean, b.1941. Maclean was one of the first recipients of a Scottish International Education Trust grant.

over the Clyde from the Fineston crane, which once had dispatched nearly twenty thousand steam engines to the railways of the world. There it was, poised over an empty river, as much a potent symbol of the city's industrial decline as a promise of Glasgow's regeneration through a renewed awakening in the arts. No gallery or museum thought it worth preserving Wyllie's internationally acclaimed requiem for the age of steam. So the artist defiantly torched it in a Viking funeral near the ruins of the derelict engine sheds, witnessed by many of the men and women who once worked there. When the flames died down, there in the belly of its burnt-out boiler was a great Wyllie touch – the silhouette of a large iron question mark. The self-styled scul?tor likes to put the question at the centre of his art.

His next public art spectacular was a giant floating *Paper Boat*, which sailed the Clyde, Forth, Thames and Hudson. The great bascules of Tower Bridge lifted in its honour as Captain Wyllie sailed up river to Westminster. When the peak of the *Paper Boat* parted to reveal a giant question mark, to the skirl of the bagpipes, there wasn't a dry eye in the Houses of Parliament. Wyllie ended the tour by dropping anchor in New York under the World Financial Center, the symbolic capital of capitalism. Next day the *Paper Boat* made a real splash in the *Wall Street Journal*, under a quote from Adam Smith's *Theory of Moral Sentiments*. Not for nothing was the artist once a customs officer, dealing with the comings and goings of the wealth of nations. *Le Douannier* Wyllie is Scotland's most popular artist, but unlike Henri Rousseau, who was merely a clerk, Wyllie was a real exciseman, just as Robert Burns and Adam Smith were before him. And it shows.

When David Harding arrived at the Glasgow School of Art in 1986 to set up the Environmental Art Department he inspired his students to make their work site-specific, for the context to be half the work. Harding had been the first town artist of Glenrothes, one of Scotland's first New Towns, set up in 1948. When he

Hippos emerging from the River Leven, Glenrothes by Stan Bonnar, b.1948.

The Paper Boat, 1990, George Wyllie, b. 1921. The Paper Boat sailed the Clyde, Forth, Thames and Hudson, finally anchoring at the World Financial Center. There it earned an accolade from the *Wall Street Journal*, quoting Adam Smith's 'Moral Sentiments', which greatly pleased the artist as an ex-customs officer.

arrived in 1968 he found no glen there as a foil for the bleak postwar housing; in fact there was 'no there there', as Gertrude Stein famously said of Oakland, California. Harding changed all that by creating, along with several young Art School graduates, nearly a hundred works large and small which gave the people of Glenrothes a sense both of place and of playfulness. Harding helped to launch another new wave of artists, which included Douglas Gordon, Christine Borland, Louise Scullion, Ross Sinclair, Clare Barclay, David Shrigley and Jim Lambie.

Douglas Gordon is known for projecting Hollywood features like Alfred Hitchcock's 110-minute *Psycho* over twenty-four hours (although I wonder if the projection runs during the night for the guards when the gallery is closed). Harding was invited to the opening few frames of Gordon's glacially slow frame-by-frame unspooling of John Ford's *The Searchers*, which he has timed to unfold over five years in the desert north of Palm Springs.

In the 1960s Ian Hamilton Finlay and his wife Sue took over Stonypath, a smallholding at her father's farm in the Borders. Together they set about creating a garden from very sparse beginnings. Only one wind-battered tree stood against the house in an otherwise bleak landscape. Today it's a place apart. With its temples and well placed one-word poems, the Stonypath garden evokes as much a classical past as a revolutionary present. 'Certain gardens are described as retreats,' said Finlay, 'when they are really attacks.' By integrating sculpture with words and phrases inscribed on stone he created his symbolic garden. 'You can change a bit of the actual world by taking out a spade of earth.'

At the centre of the garden is a temple dedicated to Apollo. Its inscription – 'his music, his missiles, his muses' – suggests all manner of latent meanings for this multi-tasked god of ancient Greece and Rome. The oveworked deity's other concerns included music and architecture; and now, ever since NASA instigated the Apollo missions – outer space. Because religious buildings are exempt from land tax, Finlay disputed the district council's demands when it taxed his temple as an art gallery. And so began the first of many Battles of Little Sparta. Finlay renamed Stonypath 'Little Sparta', because Sparta was traditionally the enemy of Athens and Edinburgh was the Athens of the North. Despite being nearer Edinburgh, through some bureaucratic quirk Little Sparta was taxed from Glasgow. When the sheriff's officer swooped and in lieu of taxes carried off art belonging to American museums, this whole Ealing comedy became an international incident. It was one that the resolute Finlay finally won.

Ultimately, Finlay's aim was to plant poetry in the natural world. He wished his work to be taken as 'something that can be used by society'. From ideas grown in the garden of Stonypath his works have blossomed across the world. 'I feel on the edge as regards the Scottish scene,' he once said, 'but as regards the world I feel in the centre. I seem on the edge because I'm in the centre.' It was a spiritual retreat, or rather attack, that Finlay never left.

Richard Demarco always reminds me that we first met when I modelled for the Edinburgh College of Art life class when he was a student. I am afraid that he may

The World has been empty since the Romans, 1985, Ian Hamilton Finlay, 1925-2006.

Apollon Terroriste, 1988, Ian Hamilton Finlay, 1925-2006. The golden bust of Antoine Saint-Just, instigator of the 1794 Paris reign of terror, has the inscription 'Apollon Terroriste' engraved across his forehead bonding cruelty with the idealism of Apollo, in Ian Hamilton Finlay's garden of attack. Finlay's inscription quotes the ruthless Saint-Just, but it equally echoes the sentiments of Sir John Clerk of Penicuik who held that the Roman remains in Scotland were 'the last tangible links with civilisation'.

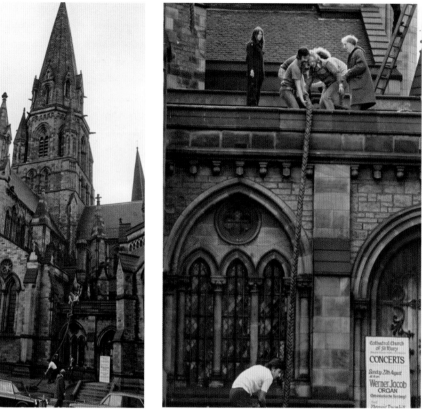

Magdalena Abakanowicz, b.1930, festooning St Mary's Episcopal Cathedral, with a long red rope as her contribution to the Polish Exhibition at the Edinburgh Festival of 1972.

have the paintings to prove it. Twenty years later our paths crossed again when he was livening up the arts in Edinburgh. I left to join the Navy in 1947, the year of the first Edinburgh Festival. Ricky has been at every festival since and soon became a major participant in the Fringe. He co-founded the Traverse Theatre in 1963 in an old doss-house off the Royal Mile. I liked his approach, for he saw no barriers in the arts and immediately created a gallery there. But it quickly outgrew the Traverse walls so he moved over to the New Town in 1966, where he met the Edinburgh establishment head-on. I remember meeting up with him there as the Polish artist Magdalena Abakanowicz was clambering up ladders at the end of Melville Street, attaching great swags of red rope over the buttresses of St Mary's Episcopal Cathedral.

Ricky had been invited to Poland by the Communist state, but instead of selecting work from the official party list, he famously went down into the cellars of the cities. Leaving his official list crumpled provocatively on the floor, he chose to meet a new generation of mostly dissident artists. Abakanowicz was one of those, and part of his invited exhibition of over forty Polish artists which very nearly didn't happen. Demarco's chairman, Jean Polworth, had been kept in the dark over the scale of the show, although the trucks had already left Warsaw. 'You realise that there's nothing in our budget to cover this exhibition,' Lady Polworth explained to His Excellency the Polish Ambassador in London. 'But of course we do,' he said. 'We know that. It's Ricky Demarco.' To his credit, the Poles were happy to pay; in 1972 no official UK organisation would have invited such a show. But what worked for the Poles didn't suit the board of the Scottish International Education Trust, which had also contributed to this Polish exhibition at a time of heightened tension during the Cold War.

Our Trust had been born out of the collapse of the Upper Clyde Shipbuilders. The Conservative government had forced the Fairfield's yard to be part of that amalgamation, so the experimental working methods between workforce and management, forged there by Sir Iain Stewart and productivity expert Jim Houston, sank with it. *The Bowler and the Bunnet*, the film I made on Fairfield's, had brought us all round to the idea of creating a fund to help young talents with initiative and ideas to remain in Scotland (see p.189). The editor of the *Scotsman* Alastair Dunnett brought all his creative energy to it and joined my friend the world racing champion Jackie Stewart as vice chairman, under the chairmanship of Sir Samuel Curran, the first principal of Strathclyde University.

To get our Trust up and running I decided to go back on my word and do another James Bond picture. By donating my entire fee of over $1 million from *Diamonds are Forever* the Trust got off to a flying start. One of the first projects we sponsored was the establishment of a visiting fellowship in drama and the appointment of a director of drama at Strathclyde University. We rented an office at the top of the Richard Demarco Gallery and made Ricky our first director, thinking that his enthusiasm for practically everything made him the man for us.

The Polish art exhibition was a great success, but it would be Tadeusz Kantor's *The Water Hen* that would be the sensation of the 1972 Festival. 'Edinburgh's resident cultural bandit has done it again,' said the theatre critic Michael Billington, who heaped praise on Ricky for capturing Kantor's Polish Cricot-2 theatre group and finding a remarkable home for it in a derelict former city poorhouse.

Kantor was a sculptor before he became a set designer. Born of 'happenings', Kantor's 'Theatre of the Impossible' had developed out of secret performances during the Nazi occupation of Poland. His aim was to fuse the individual crafts of dancer, actor, mime artist and musician into what I can only define as three-dimensional animated painting. Kantor became an immediate liberating force for change in the staid British theatre of the time. By blurring the boundaries between drama and art he sent shock waves from Edinburgh across the stages of the English-speaking world.

I caught up with the excitement in Kantor's Festival performance of *Lovelies and Dowdies*. It was one of the most extraordinary theatrical events I have ever experienced. First our coats were taken away by over-officious cloakroom attendants with the persistence of airport security guards today. We were then bundled through two opening and closing doors into the mayhem of the room beyond. There, brooding over a table of bizarre objects, was the stern figure of Kantor himself dressed in black, ordering the now bemused theatre-goers this way and that like a sinister ringmaster. As I came through the doors he leapt forward to divert me into a side area. He had chosen me to be one his forty 'Mandelbaums', a bunch of religious fanatics whose purpose, we were told, was to

Lovelies and Dowdies had me pinned behind a canvas drape with Tina Brown and Auberon Waugh to experience Kantor's 'Theatre of the Impossible' at the Edinburgh Festival Fringe.

Left: Tadeusz Kantor and Richard Demarco at a rehearsal in the Edinburgh Poor House, 1972.

Right: Backstage with the Kantor cast and a bewildered Sandy Nairne.

trample to death the Princess Abenceraga. For this privilege I was corralled behind a stretch of cloth, where I found myself next to two journalists, Tina Brown and Auberon Waugh. I had come as a spectator to enjoy a play, and now I was to be part of the action in the worst-paid acting role of my life. But what an experience.

In front of us erupted a whirl of dramatic energy marching to the beat of strident music. Artists clad in dusty suits and shabby bowler-hats manipulated sculptural mannequin versions of themselves as they hobbled past us. Mouldering, dusty dresses and rags clung to the women. A figure with two heads, his second swinging between his legs, swaggered between identical twins. Another strained under the weight of a door followed by the grimmest reaper who ever played Death. For much of the time Kantor would remain frozen, staring back amidst the mayhem. This was a theatre like none other. The demented actions of these players still haunt me to this day, like a nightmare painting of Hieronymus Bosch come to life.

During the Cold War Ricky crossed over into the Eastern Bloc nearly a hundred times. By 1972 he found himself under the scrutiny of MI6, the British Secret Service. They asked him why he was always lurking around the Polish Embassy. He explained that he had to apply each time for a visa to visit his artists. When they eventually realised that he was of no threat to British national security, they asked Ricky if he had ever thought of working for his own country. He explained that was just what he thought he was doing through the art exchanges between Poland and Scotland. Ricky then handed them his Scottish International Education Trust calling card with his name as director alongside mine. 'Now there's someone who could work really effectively for you,' he said. 'Why don't you recruit the world's most effective agent in defence of the free world?' They had a drink on that one.

As far as our Trust was concerned, Ricky soon proved what a one-man band he was. Money was spent as fast as he talked. You couldn't get a word in because he

Left: Lady Roseberry, one of the original founders of the Edinburgh Festival, with the inventor of the geodesic dome, Buckminster Fuller, and the arts shaman, Joseph Beuys. Who else in the world could have brought these three together other than Ricky Demarco?

Right: 'Strategy Get Arts', the palindrome banner being installed at the Edinburgh College of Art, August 1970.

was a walking tape. The fact that what he was giving away was hard-earned cash seemed of little concern to him. He would promise money without any discussion with our board. Regrettably, we had to let him go. He found it very hard to accept from me that he was being fired.

Few in Edinburgh have ever come to terms with Ricky Demarco. In an era of mass-marketing, those creative forces who can capture what is new and vital as it flies past them often fall foul of the funding bodies with spreadsheet brains bent on business-plan projections for three years ahead. What cannot be taken away from Ricky is his dynamism and his ability to perceive new beginnings in art, theatre and beyond before they happen. At his invitation, Joseph Beuys led the *Strategy: Get Arts* event from the Kunsthalle Düsseldorf, which occupied the Edinburgh College of Art in August 1970. His old beat-up Volkswagen van blocked a corridor, and together with a trail of little sleds equipped with survival kit of rolls of felt, pieces of animal fat and torches was exhibited as *The Pack*. In the entrance hall Klaus Rinke installed a jet of water for visitors to negotiate. In a large life studio Beuys performed *Celtic (Kinloch Rannoch), Scottish Symphony*, applying gobs of gel to the walls as a film of Rannoch Moor ran to a score by Henning Christiansen and Rory McEwan (see also p. 254). Gotthard Graubner created a mist room in a space near the Sculpture Court. Daniel Spoerri staged *The Bananatrap Dinner*, which reversed everyone's expectations of a banquet, with strange switches like desserts consisting of meat. The college's grand entrance staircase was scattered with Stefan Wewerka's broken chairs, above which Beuys's favourite young artist, Peter Schwarze, who renamed himself Blinky Palermo, painted a mural of thin parallel stripes of colour.

If the art-going public was confused, the college and the art establishment were mostly outraged. The event was condemned by the Scottish Arts Council for bringing dishonour to the meaning of art. The director of the National Gallery of Modern Art resigned as the chairman of the Friends of the Demarco Gallery. The mural was judged 'an insult to the ethos of the college', and as soon as the show left town the school was fumigated and purged of any trace of the exhibits. In a last act of rejection, Palermo's mural was painted over with white emulsion. Over recent years there have been moves to re-instate the mural since Palermo died young and few of his works of this scale exist. One estimate puts the worth of the Edinburgh mural at £300,000. A two-day conference was called to discuss the possibilities. 'This is the only major work of Palermo's outside Germany,' said Professor Alan Johnston of the Edinburgh College of Art. 'It was a scandal that it was painted over.' But instead of meticulously restoring the mural by delicate paint scraping, Johnston ordered in decorators to paint new stripes over the emulsion, over the original Palermo. This outraged lecturers and archivists at the Kunsthalle Düsseldorf as well as art historians at the Institute of Art History, Bonn. For Anne-Marie Bonnet, who now teaches at Yale, it was an irresponsible decision for an art institution to have taken. By painting new stripes over Palermo's original, which now lies even deeper under an extra layer of paint, all that has been achieved is an inauthentic pastiche – or, in other words, a worthless fake.

Joseph Beuys would be a frequent visitor to Scotland throughout the 1970s, becoming known as much for his extended lectures as for his provocative 'aktions'. *I Like America and America Likes Me* of 1974 involved him being transported from his plane directly into a New York Gallery, wrapped up in felt, where he shared a space for three days with a coyote. Such a confrontation explored for Beuys the dilemma of an animal revered in Native American lore yet despised by America's immigrant settlers. When it was restaged by the Demarco Gallery at the Edinburgh Festival a man stepped forward at the end of the performance. 'I am that coyote,' he said to Beuys. It was Jimmy Boyle, who had been let out on day release from Glasgow's notorious Barlinnie Prison. After the death penalty was abolished in the UK, long-term and often violent prisoners were offered the alternative of 'the Special Unit', a suite of rooms in the centre of Barlinnie where there were few of the constraints of a prison cell. Boyle had been one of the most dangerous prisoners in the maximum-security wing of Porterfield Prison, Inverness, where his protest took the form of living naked like a caged animal. In Boyle's case the experiment was so successful that he has since established himself as a sculptor and now has an international reputation, living in the South of France.

Beuys's influence on artists in Scotland has been considerable, but perhaps on no one more than on George Wyllie. He collaborated closely with Beuys on the installation of Edinburgh's *Poorhouse Doors* by Johannes Cladders for the München Gladbach Museum in Germany. One of Wyllie's biggest regrets was when Giovanni Caradente invited the Demarco Gallery, in association with the Scottish Sculpture Trust, to select artists for the 1990 Venice Biennale. Sadly Wyllie's work was passed over. Just imagine that white *Paper Boat* floating gently along the Grand Canal.

Memories came back to me of my days as a coffin-polisher in Haddington as we drove south down the A1 to see Ricky Demarco's great barn full of art on a headland south of Dunbar at Skateraw. The enlightened seed merchant Johnny Watson had heard on the radio of Ricky's eviction from his offices in Edinburgh's

Royal High School. He offered him immediate refuge for his vast collection in a humidity-controlled seed barn that he had recently erected. Sandra and Johnny Watson's Skateraw farm lies on some of the most fertile land in Scotland in a beautiful coastal landscape of environmental importance. Through his study of the rock formations at nearby Siccar Point, the farmer James Hutton, who in the eighteenth century became the father of geology, realised that the cliff's red sandstone, overlying the vertical layers of grey shale, could be explained only by the action of stupendous forces over vast periods of time. Science and the arts still interact at Skateraw. On the walls of the nearby Torness nuclear power station an endless film by Ken McMullen, *Lumen de Lumine* ('Light of Lights'), played at the opening of the Skateraw archive in 2006.

In the spirit of Joseph Beuys, Ricky's mentor, this great barn, straddling a landscape of such historical importance and under the shadow of controversial scientific advances, indicates a new kind of gallery for the twenty-first century. 'New beginnings,' as the shaman said, 'could be in the offing.'

Ricky Demarco, our first director of the Scottish International Education Trust, at our last meeting in the SIET office above his enterprising gallery.

Pages 182/3:My reward for such lunatic leaps around Ken Adam's inspired moonscape set for *Diamonds are Forever* was the founding of the Scottish International Education Trust, to help young talents in the arts and sciences find their feet in Scotland.

11 RIVER OF INVENTION
Workshop of the world

Lord, send a man like Robbie Burns to sing the Song o' Steam!
Rudyard Kipling, 'M'Andrew's Hymn'

You often learn the strangest things, sometimes even about your own country, during the making of a film. This was especially true in the production of *The Name of the Rose*. The director Jean-Jacques Annaud had assembled a refreshingly diverse cast, which included Austria's best-loved cabaret artist, Helmut Qualtinger. This multi-talented man played the role of Remigio da Varagine, the jovial monk who gets severely scorched. We got into conversation about the Vienna he knew after World War II. Helmut had co-authored a controversial book with the provocative title *From the Third Reich to the Third Man*, which had set many a Viennese hat feather fluttering. He told me that the first structure in Vienna to be restored after the war was the *Riesenrad*, or Ferris Wheel, which provided that memorable scene with Orson Welles in Carol Reed's *The Third Man*. Today it stands as the last true Ferris wheel in the world, designed by George Washington Gale Ferris for the Columbian Exposition of Chicago in 1893.

But I wonder how many people know that the Viennese version was assembled on the spot in 1897 from parts manufactured entirely by Glasgow companies. The massive axle was forged in the foundries of W. Beardmore & Co., which developed the heavy armour-plating for the Royal Navy's dreadnoughts. All the girders, spokes, wheels and linkages were fabricated by Arrol's, the same company which provided all the steel for the construction of the Forth Bridge. This was an appropriate feat, since a Ferris wheel is in effect the arcs of two suspension bridges joined together to form a circle.

A century later, when the 'London Eye' was assembled on the Thames to mark the Millennium, not a single structural component was shipped from Scotland. The Czech Republic supplied the hub and spindle, which runs on German bearings. The French built the capsules, which are tensioned on the spokes of Italian cables. And it was all craned into position by Dutch engineers. What became of Scottish innovation and industrial enterprise?

Just as the industrial base of the country was falling apart in the 1960s, there I was as James Bond, promoting British inventiveness, armed with advanced technologies and increasingly innovative gizmos. Although the Bond gadgets were far-fetched gimmicks, I did have hands-on experience of real precision engineering when I served in the Navy, training on the battleship HMS *King George V*. The ease with which the hydraulic machinery enabled her massive 14-inch guns to sweep and pivot so smoothly in their four gun turrets was uncanny and never ceased to astound me.

For well over a hundred years the workshops and shipyards of the west of Scotland led the world in ship design. Yet after World War II governments, unions and management seemed increasingly locked into unsolvable conflict. Through a remarkable chance encounter at a golf club dinner I met Sir Iain Stewart, one of the truly innovative captains of industry on the Clyde. He told me about the successful experiment he was pioneering at the Fairfield Shipbuilding and Engineering Company at Govan, mentioned in the previous chapter, following its threat of closure.

On 15 October 1965 at 4.15 p.m. on a Friday afternoon, half an hour before the workers were to leave work for the weekend, the Fairfield's yard manager had summoned the shop stewards to tell them that the firm was bankrupt and closing down. Three and a half thousand were to lose their jobs. Stewart was encouraged

Pages 182-3: My reward for such lunatic leaps around Ken Adam's inspired moonscape set for *Diamonds are Forever* was the founding of the Scottish International Education Trust, to help young talents in the arts and sciences find their feet in Scotland.

Opposite: In the monastic gloom of *The Name of the Rose* the witty cabaret artist and writer Helmut Qualtinger casts a wry look back at F. Murray Abrams and me.

Left: Vienna's Glasgow-made *Riesenrad* of 1896.

Centre: The London Eye of 2000, made entirely from overseas structural components.

Right: Q's instructions on the use of the James Bond gadgets were a fun part of the early Bond films. Some of them even worked in reality, like this jetpack, which got me over a wall into the safety of my Aston Martin DB5 in *Thunderball*, 1965.

Aboard HMS *King George V* fronting one of the formidable gun turrets. This battleship was considered an elite posting, creating much scorn from other less fortunate recruits.

A ship takes shape at the Fairfield Shipbuilding and Engineering Company at Govan on the Clyde. Founded in the 1860s as Randolph, Elder and Company, Fairfields pioneered many innovations including the invention of fuel-efficient multiple-expansion engines.

by the then Labour Prime Minister Harold Wilson to save the yard with a radical new plan. Together with Jim Houston, the trouble-shooting productivity expert with American know-how, they set out to bring the bosses and workers together. Houston still remembers the astonishment of the Fairfield trade unionists when they were invited to participate with the management for the chance 'to run a better railroad'. So the 'Fairfield Experiment' was born, and a unique partnership between government, private capital, management and trade unionists was launched. All at once ships were built on time – or even ahead of time. Strikes were drastically reduced, and eventually eliminated. Wages were increased. And the Fairfield yard began to make a profit.

Iain Stewart invited me to come and see for myself what had already been achieved. I found the shipyard abuzz with activity. Workers were getting on amicably with an equally enthusiastic management. There was no hint of the dreaded *them* and *us* attitude which had so soured working relations on the Clyde. It seemed obvious to me that the Fairfield Experiment had cracked the nut of British industrial malaise and its success should be more widely known. As I watched the circling cranes and the agility of the welders, the idea for a film swung into my mind. I decided to fly the flag for Fairfield's revolutionary new shipbuilding methods and took a month off from the London scene to direct a documentary, for no pay. Iain Stewart invited me to stay and I soon came to know many of the shipbuilders, playing soccer with them at their lunch-break. The timing was good as we were able to film the launch of the *Atlantic City*, the first ship made under the new agreement.

Ten years earlier, Hilary Harris had directed his flag-waving paean of praise for Clyde shipbuilding, *Seawards the Great Ships*. The young American had been inspired by a treatment for a visually driven film written by that great talent scout and social engineer, John Grierson. Grierson was by then a seemingly slumbering presence on the board of Films of Scotland. *Drifters*, his highly manipulated and imaginative first film on deep-sea trawler-fishing, had aerated the dull waters of British documentary in the 1920s. Grierson's ambition was that Harris should do the same for the Clyde. Urging him to reach for the stars, he told Harris, in his disarmingly gruff Scots-Chicagoan accent, that his film would succeed if it answered a question, one which had always puzzled him: 'Why do the eyes of ship workers, standing on the slipway, well up with tears when the last rope is cast off from the ship they've just built?' Harris's reply was *Seawards the Great Ships*. Grierson, not a man known to be loose with his praise, was more than satisfied with his answer. *Seawards* went on to win Scotland's first Academy Award. It inspired a new generation of film-makers in Scotland, but ironically Hilary's triumphant film gave no hint of the closures soon to befall the great shipbuilding river of the Clyde.

Since the Glasgow writer Cliff Hanley had written Harris's narration ten years before, he seemed the perfect choice to write the script for the film I had in mind. It was a good match. We both believed in breaking down the demarcations which had come to bedevil shipbuilding on the Clyde. Even as late as the Sixties, what you

Hilary Harris, directing *Seawards the Great Ships*, 1958.

Sir Iain Stewart, whose experiment at Fairfield's inspired *The Bowler and the Bunnet* in 1967.

wore on your head still defined your place in the yards. The managers still sported bowlers and the ship workers flat 'Andy' caps or 'bunnets', and never the twain did meet. There was a lot of fire in Cliff's belly as we honed down the opening narration in broad staccato brush-strokes.

Scotland
The country of the extremes
Love of life
Hatred of life
Poets and murderers
Rigid temperance and savage drinking
John Knox and Johnny Walker
Prosperity and poverty

Vast empty landscapes and the most congested slums in Europe
Warm hearts and idiot violence
A country of sturdy democracy and savage class hatred side by side

Always the division
The gulf between opposites

The bosses and the workers
Them and us
The Bowler and the Bunnet

Seeing *The Bowler and the Bunnet* after all those years, during my retrospective at the 2006 Rome Festival, made me think how much we have lost since those fraught years of industrial strife. There I was, up there on the screen, wearing my bunnet, analysing the problems of the Clyde, freewheeling through the shipyards on a grocer's bicycle to 'Land of Hope and Glory', hoping that the film would be a force for change. When it was first broadcast in 1967, it was damned with faint praise in the Scottish press. 'Showmanship spoils Clyde documentary,' was the line the *Scotsman* took, which was a lot better than Glasgow's *Herald*, which failed to review the film at all. Both Tory and Labour focus groups asked to see it, but it must have failed to focus either party's policy on shipbuilding because I never heard back from either of them. Any hopes I had of influencing politicians and injecting new thinking to help reverse the decline of the Clyde came to nothing. The Fairfield Experiment seemed born to die.

In 1968 Harold Wilson's Labour government forced Fairfield's to merge with five other yards to form the Upper Clyde Shipbuilders. Three years later I was with Iain Stewart at the bar in London's Dorchester Hotel, when the UCS chairman walked over. 'How's it going?' asked Stewart. 'Great guns,' he replied. The Upper Clyde Shipbuilders went into receivership the very next week. The then Tory government under Edward Heath had refused it a £6 million loan. This time the shipbuilders didn't strike. They took over the yards to complete the ships as a work-in. Led by

Directing *The Bowler and the Bunnet* in 1967. Scottish Television only showed the film once. Had our efforts received a wider distribution I still think it could have been politically influential. The media then seemed more caught up in the Swinging Sixties than in the reality of Britain's industrial collapse.

The more exotically titled *La bombetta e il berretto* was screened during my retrospective at the first Rome film festival in 2006.

such charismatic union shop stewards as Jimmy Reid, their campaign caught the public's sympathy, winning widespread support in Scotland and beyond. At one massive fund-raising rally on Glasgow Green, after the ex-Clyde ship welder Billy Connolly had entertained the 80,000-strong crowd of supporters, Jimmy Reid told them that their campaign had just received a £5000 contribution from Lennon.

'But Lenin's deid!' a shout came back.

'How can you compete with that?' said Billy, turning to Reid as he dropped his guitar. 'Guys like that are funnier than comedians – that's why I left the shipyards.'

Although *The Bowler and the Bunnet* rose without trace in Britain, a print reached Moscow and played a significant role in inviting me to star in Mosfilm's *Krasnaya Palatka* ('The Red Tent'). The Politburo had long believed that I shared the 'dangerous imperialist tendencies' which Soviet apparatchiks had perceived to be the driving force behind the James Bond films. My film helped to scotch that by reassuring the appropriate committee of my 'unimpeachable proletarian credentials'. The director Mikheil Kalatozishvili had worked with Sergei Eisenstein, as had many of his talented technicians. So it was an eye-opening experience to be a part of such a well oiled team, one which worked so effortlessly to bring off the complicated camera moves with all the imagination and precision of top midfield soccer players.

The friendships won over the Fairfield's debacle made us think that we should combine our forces to further the aspirations of all those young Scots who were so often driven out of Scotland for lack of work. The Trust to help them was born via my fee from *Diamonds are Forever*. In hopes it would become a sizeable endowment, in 1970 the gift got the Scottish International Education Trust off to a flying start. Thanks to prudent investments by our first chairman Jim Houston and our board since then, the SIET has since awarded grants approaching £3 million to thousands of aspiring youngsters in the arts and sciences who live in Scotland. Let's hope that all the really successful ones can now do the same for others.

Pages 190-1: The Falkirk Wheel, 2004, is the spectacular centrepiece of the £84.5 million 'Millennium Link', the UK's largest canal restoration project. Developed by British Waterways to reconnect the Union Canal with the Forth and Clyde Canal. There can be few more heroic or greater demonstrations of Archimedes' principle. Since floating objects displace their own weight of water, the wheel is kept in perfect balance when the boat enters. This allows it to rotate through 180° in four minutes, consuming an astonishingly eco-friendly 1.5 kilowatt-hours, roughly equivalent to boiling eight kettles of water.

Here's a recent Scottish engineering achievement to raise our spirits in the tradition of the Scottish Enlightenment – the Falkirk Wheel. What once took eleven slowly operated locks to link the eighteenth-century Forth and Clyde Canal to the more meandering nineteenth-century Union Canal is now accomplished for the twenty-first century in one fell swoop by the world's first rotating boat lift. In the early days of the Millennium Lottery Fund the Dundee architects Nicoll Russell dreamt up a functioning lifting wheel, but for the funders that was not exotic enough in its practical design. So other architects were brought in who believed that form must follow fantasy. Neither those giant beak-like blades, nor the hoop-like structures along the last high section of the canal, have any other function than to catch the eyes of motorists and lure them down the bewildering back roads. How those great Scots geometers, canal builders and early entrepreneurs would have smiled. The Falkirk Wheel should be saluted not only for its extravagant engineering solution to a mundane problem, but also for the fun of its essential madness in the great tradition of Scottish Surrealism. Now let's hope it pays.

The tradition of invention goes back a long way in Scotland, especially in shipbuilding. The *Great Michael* of the Royal Scottish Navy was the largest warship in Europe when she was launched in 1511, equipped with massive artillery which may even have included Mons Meg, the greatest-calibre gun in history – and it's still to be seen in Edinburgh Castle.

The practice of mechanical engineering at Glasgow University dates back at least to the 1760s, when James Watt worked as a mathematical instrument-maker and developed his far-reaching improvements to steam engines. In 1840 Glasgow was the first British university to appoint a chair in Civil Engineering and Mechanics. William Thomson was only twenty-two when he was appointed in 1846 to its chair of Mathematics and Natural Philosophy, a professorship which he would hold for over fifty years, latterly as Lord Kelvin. He and his colleague the theoretical scientist James Clerk Maxwell practically predicted the twentieth

Lord Kelvin, 1824-1907, with binnacle compass. To take account of the constant variations in an iron-hulled ship's retentive magnetism, Kelvin's adjustable binnacle compass was first patented in 1876. This immediately created the new profession of compass adjusters.

Kelvin made the Atlantic telegraph feasible in 1866, after several expensive failed attempts. The project was rescued through the invention of his iron-clad mirror galvanometer. This delicate instrument made the transmission of messages possible by detecting the very small currents passing along the telegraphic cable on the Atlantic seabed joining the old world with the new world.

century with their inventions and scientific discoveries. In electricity and magnetism Kelvin's innovations extended in every direction, on land and sea. His magnetic binnacle compass was renowned for its accuracy and made modern marine navigation possible.

Science, engineering and education advanced hand in hand in the West of Scotland. Glasgow's Anderson's Institution opened as early as 1796 to offer 'a place of useful learning, a university open to everyone, regardless of gender or class'. In a little over a hundred years it grew to become the most innovative technical college in Europe, launching the careers of many eminent engineers and scientists. By 1910, as Anderson's University, it had built the largest facility in Europe dedicated to technical education. In 1964 it became the University of Strathclyde.

Allan Glen, a successful Glasgow tradesman, endowed a school in his name in 1850, 'to give a good practical education and preparation for trades or businesses, to between forty to fifty boys, the sons of tradesmen or persons in the industrial classes of society'. Although the school was notionally fee-paying, it offered a large number of bursaries to pupils from all social classes based solely on their academic ability. Beneficiaries of this enlightened scheme spanned the arts and sciences and have included down the years the architect Charles Rennie Mackintosh, the sculptor George Wyllie and the television producer Gus Macdonald. Sadly, this innovative school was closed when Glasgow abandoned selective education in 1979.

Before Allan Glen's, Gus Macdonald attended the Scotland Street School, designed by Mackintosh. He remembers it was surrounded by engineering workshops, each specialising in the manufacture of different ships' components. Every street running down to the Clyde was devoted to the manufacture of different items, such as marine engines, hydraulic pumps and all the other essential machinery required when the Clyde was still an international force in shipbuilding.

When the fourteen-year-old Macdonald entered the shipyards as an engineering apprentice in 1954, the embers of the politically radical 'Red Clyde' still glowed. Many remembered 1919, when Churchill had ordered tanks into George Square, fearing that Glasgow might become the second Petrograd in the wake of the Russian Revolution. The Marxist John Maclean was even nominated by Moscow as Scotland's Soviet consul, though Lenin would later write that Communism must avoid the infantile leftism of the 'English' Maclean.

By the Fifties, shipbuilding on the Clyde was still riven by industrial strife, which drove Macdonald to become a radical and active trade unionist. In May 1960 he led a strike of the engineering apprentices, along with Alex Ferguson, the future manager of Manchester United, and the comedian Billy Connolly. Soon, apprentices in Newcastle joined in the strike. Although their Geordie comrades took some time to catch up with their witty rapid-fire Glaswegian patter, the combined demands of the apprentices were more than partially met. Macdonald went on to produce outstanding television programmes, like the multi-award-winning series *World in Action*, before entering politics and becoming a New Labour peer as Lord Macdonald of Tradeston.

The Great Eastern, 1858, designed by Isambard Kingdom Brunel, was the only ship large enough to carry the 7000 tons of cable long enough to connect Ireland with Newfoundland. Determining the depth of the ocean was essential to the laying of the transatlantic cable. Kelvin came up with an ingenious method of gauging its depth by using piano wire connected to a glass tube containing silver chromate, which changed colour when in contact with sea water. Seeing Kelvin surrounded in coils of piano wire the scientist James Joule asked what it was for.

'Sounding,' Kelvin replied.
'What note?' asked Joule.
'Deep C.'

James Watt and the Steam Engine, 1855, by James Eckford Lauder, 1811-69. The discoverer of economic steam power is imagined in a highly romantic Victorian perspective. Watt peers like a medieval alchemist at a model of a steam engine, perhaps dreaming of further refinements to his invention of the steam condenser.

How did the shallow, meandering Clyde become one of the great shipbuilding rivers of the world? Thanks to chance events during the Carboniferous era, Scotland was dealt all the natural resources for an integrated iron and steel industry. The ironstone and limestone of the Scottish Lowlands, the extensive coal measures to fire the furnaces and the abundant fire-clays to line the hearths, were all laid down over three hundred million years ago when the land was a luxuriant tropical swamp. When processes were developed to smelt iron with coke won from coal, instead of with charcoal from the now nearly nonexistent forests, Scotland rose to become a leading industrial power. Such Enlightenment figures as Dr John Roebuck, a physician turned manufacturer, in 1759 founded the Carron Ironworks, the first dedicated enterprise of its kind anywhere in the world. Roebuck's foundry manufactured a vast range of products, from cannons to elegant neoclassical fireplaces designed by his partner, the architect Robert Adam.

Only in Scotland could another new branch of science be revealed through watching the distilling of alcohol. By observing how heat from the fire under whisky stills was transferred through the spiral 'worms' submerged in the condenser water, the Scottish chemist Joseph Black deduced the concept of latent heat and so conceived the discipline of thermodynamics. This led in 1765 to Black's Glasgow University instrument-maker, James Watt, inventing the separate condenser to produce the first thermally efficient engine. James Watt had other

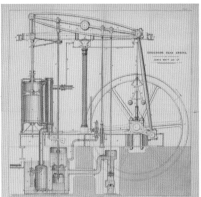

improvements in mind, but they didn't impress Dr Roebuck at the Carron Ironworks. Failing to be taken seriously, Watt turned his back on Scotland and joined forces with the enterprising ex-button maker Matthew Boulton in Birmingam, whose firm was one of the first to manufacture steam engines. With Watt's inventive mind and Boulton's great entrepreneurial salesmanship, the partnership prospered. By selling steam power to the world the enterprising firm of Boulton & Watt became literally the prime mover of the Industrial Revolution. 'We have what the world wants,' Boulton told the Russian Empress Catherine the Great. What we have is power.'

One of the largest shareholders in the Carron Ironworks was the eccentric landowner Patrick Miller. After making his fortune as an Edinburgh banker, he invented the Carronade gun for the Royal Navy. His formidable cannons can still be seen today on the deck of Nelson's *Victory* in Portsmouth harbour. Miller had always been interested in ships, and asked his friend the painter Alexander Nasmyth to draw up plans for a small double-hulled pleasure boat. It would be powered by hand-cranked paddles, which he had just invented and would soon patent. When his children's tutor, James Taylor, suggested that he should 'try out the power of steam' he had the paddles connected by chains to an onboard steam engine designed by a local engineer, William Symington. On 14 November 1788 she puttered across Dalswinton Loch, exceeding five knots, on Miller's estate in the Borders. Those on board included Miller's tenant, the poet Robert Burns,

Boulton and Watt steam engine. The Soho Works, Birmingham, 1780s. This enterprising company sold their engines by offering to install and service them free of charge. They would then demand a royalty of one third of the saving over the cost of the previous power supply.

A Carronade, on the deck of Nelson's flagship HMS *Victory*. To arm the Royal Navy's warships deadly Carronades were cast by the versatile Carron Iron Works. Their bewildering range of products ranged from huge castings to kilted Highlander doorstops and Benjamin Franklin's stove. Elegant fireplaces were designed by the architect Robert Adam, who was a director of the company.

Alexander Nasmyth and his artist son Patrick. Could there ever have been a more appropriate group than that to celebrate the union of the arts and sciences during the Scottish Enlightenment? But it would be William Symington's *Charlotte Dundas*, the fifty-eight-foot steam-driven paddle tugboat, which would really usher in the new age of the steamship. Powered by Carron Ironworks engines, the *Charlotte Dundas* proved her superior pulling power over the tow-horses by drawing, without resting, two fully laden barges along twenty-two miles of the recently opened Forth and Clyde Canal in 1801.

In America Robert Fulton launched his *North River Steamboat* (often mistakenly called the *Clermont*). With her paddles driven by a Boulton-Watt engine, he initiated a regular three-hundred-mile round trip on the Hudson between New York and Albany in 1807. The first practical steam-powered ship in Europe was the *Comet*, which sailed out of Port Glasgow in 1812. Steam engines quickly proved their worth in water transport, but their cargoes were limited by the amount of coal required on board to power them. As a result they were long confined to river or coastal trade.

Despite Watt's advances, an even more efficient engine was clearly needed. If they could use less coal, that would mean more cargo and therefore greater profits. The solution was found in what became known internationally as the 'Scotch boiler', which would later be augmented by compound multiple-expansion engines. The cylindrical boilers devised by the Clyde firm of Randolph Elder & Co. in 1862 allowed for a great increase of steam pressure. They replaced the rectangular marine boilers of the time, which could only operate safely up to twenty pounds per square inch pressure. The Scotch boiler immediately increased pressures to fifty pounds, and then by steady evolution engineers took them up to 250, giving ocean-going steamers greater flexibility in navigation and speed.

John Elder's developments in engine efficiency were almost as revolutionary as James Watt's. Elder's compound engine nearly halved a ship's consumption of coal by allowing higher steam pressures in multiple-expansion engines. These advances were based on a scientific understanding of the relationship of heat and work. Elder had studied at Glasgow University, which had founded the first British chair in Engineering. Scientific innovation and practical engineering skills were what made the Clyde the most famous shipbuilding river in the world.

As the demand for larger ships grew, the river needed to be drastically deepened if the yards on the Upper Clyde were to keep ahead of the competition. As early as 1824 steam dredgers began to extend the depth of the channel. An obstructing sill of volcanic rock was found at Elderslie and blasted out by a vast amount of explosives. It took over fifty years to remove over a hundred thousand tons of this intractable rock. By then some of the largest liners in the world were able to make their way down river from such world-famous yards as John Brown's on the Upper Clyde. The *Lusitania* of 1907 was followed by a fleet of other great ocean liners, including the *Queen Mary* and the *Queen Elizabeth*, the largest ships of their time.

From the start, Scots followed the Clyde-built engines on board as ships' engineers, who would soon be immortalised by poets and writers – none with more affection than by Joseph Conrad in his sea-going novels. The first time the

Charlotte Dundas, 1803. This first steam tug proved its worth by towing two 70-ton barges some 20 miles along the Forth and Clyde Canal to Glasgow, making her the world's first practical steamboat. Commissioned by Lord Dundas, the *Charlotte Dundas* was powered by a William Symington steam engine from the Carron Iron Works.

The *Charlotte Dundas* developed out of Patrick Miller's twin-hulled steamboat, with its patented paddle wheel, which made a successful cruise over Dalswinton Loch in 1788.

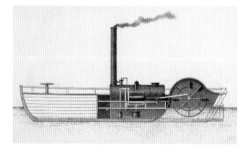

young Józef Teodor Konrad Korzeniowski had heard English spoken was in 'a strong Scotch accent' by the engineers of the St Gothard Tunnel. As a fifteen-year-old student the displaced Pole remembered that he 'could listen my fill to the sounds of the English language, as far as it is used at a breakfast-table by men who do not believe in wasting many words on the mere amenities of life'. Later, as he worked his way up from third mate on the *Loch Etive* to sea captain in the British Merchant Navy, Conrad would meet many more Scots ashore and aboard. In his novels he would later fine-tune the Scottish accents of his marine engineers with his friend, the writer R.B. Cunninghame Graham, whose own life of adventure inspired Conrad to write *Nostromo* (1904). When Conrad was down on his luck and sought to captain a ship again, Cunninghame Graham would write to the Clyde shipping companies to warn them against employing Conrad as it would be a dreadful loss to English literature.

To the rhythm of the pistons Rudyard Kipling banged the drum in 'M'Andrew's Hymn' for the canny Scots engineers who manned the huge 'slam-bangin'' engines in the bowels of ships. In this virtuoso performance of nearly two hundred lines

Compound Marine Engine, SS *Orient*, 1879, John Elder & Co. Following on the success of the high-pressure 'Scotch Boiler', this enterprising firm developed multiple-expansion engines which made transatlantic crossings and heavy cargo shipments economically possible.

George Wyllie's *Straw Loco*, 1987, hangs forlornly over the Clyde from the same Finneston crane that once shipped over 20,000 steam locomotives for the railways of the world. The *Straw Loco* and Anthony Gormley's *Sculpture for Derry Walls* were judged the two outstanding public sculptures of the TSWA commissions of 1987.

Opposite: The John Brown & Co. shipyard at Clydebank built some of the finest ocean liners of all time including the *Lusitania* and the *Queen Mary*.

The Bennie Railplane, 1930, LNER Poster of George Bennie's propeller-driven overhead railway as imagined racing northwards on the West Highland line.

Kipling even manages to relate the constancy of the ship's connecting rods with the predestination of John Calvin, before he makes a plea for 'a man like Robbie Burns to sing the Song o' Steam!'.

LORD, Thou hast made this world below the shadow of a dream,
An', taught by time, I tak' it so – exceptin' always Steam.
From coupler-flange to spindle-guide I see Thy Hand, O God –
Predestination in the stride o' yon connectin'-rod.
John Calvin might ha' forged the same – enorrmous, certain, slow –
Ay, wrought it in the furnace-flame – *my* "Institutio"…

'Mister M'Andrew, don't you think steam spoils romance at sea?'
Damned ijjit! I'd been doon that morn to see what ailed the throws,
Manholin', on my back – the cranks three inches off my nose.
Romance! Those first-class passengers they like it very well,
Printed an' bound in little books; but why don't poets tell?
I'm sick of all their quirks an' turns – the loves an' doves they dream –
Lord, send a man like Robbie Burns to sing the Song o' Steam!
To match wi' Scotia's noblest speech yon orchestra sublime.

Scottish engineering firsts could also be leaps into a future too far. My favourite vision of yesterday's tomorrow is George Bennie's 'railplane' (left) in an optimistic railway poster of the 1930s. This streamlined propeller-driven carriage, rushing into the Highlands suspended on an overhead monorail between trestle girders, was a triumph of ingenuity. The quarter of a mile of test track, opened outside Glasgow in 1930, attracted world attention. The streamlined aluminium carriage could be driven at speeds of up to 120 miles an hour by the four-bladed propellers at either end. Plans were afoot for a fast Glasgow–Edinburgh monorail link. But the timing was wrong. The Depression came and the track was dismantled in the 1940s for the war effort. Bennie's railplane was just an idea too far ahead of its time. Had it succeeded, there would have been no excuses for delays caused by the wrong kind of leaves on the line.

And who should be Homer Simpson's boss, in that most popular television series of all time, other than a wily Scots engineer? As the owner of the Springfield Nuclear Power Plant, Charles Montgomery Burns is as filthy-rich as he is wickedly mean. The brilliant animator Matt Groening takes nothing positive on board from the tradition of the reliable engineer Scot. Rather, he paints Burns as a miserly robber baron revelling in every negative Scottish stereotype, as evil as any character in Conrad's *Heart of Darkness*. But then, what are we to think of *The Simpsons'* much more famous grouchy groundkeeper Willie at the Springfield elementary school? That flaming-red-bearded janitor with his impossibly broad Scottish accent is now the most instantly recognisable Scottish voice in the world, even putting Billy Connolly into second place.

It seems that the legend of the Scots engineer will never falter and may even extend into the centuries to come, or at least until the twenty-third. 'To boldly go

where no man has gone before' in *Star Trek*'s universe you just had to have a Scot as engineer. The canny Montgomery Scott, the Chief Engineer of the starship *Enterprise*, became known to generations of Star Trekkies as Scotty. It was all down to the Canadian-born actor James Doohan, whose commanding words from the faster-than-light-generating propulsion unit were always delivered in Hollywood Scottish. This once confused the organisers of an engineering conference in Scotland who wanted to honour the intergalactic Scot, hearing that he had been born in Linlithgow. Reluctantly Scotty had to decline. 'You see I never fly,' he told them, 'and what's more I'm Irish.' If that exploded one myth, there was another to be scotched. Through the entire run of *Star Trek*'s three-year television series, no one ever uttered that now immortal line, 'Beam me up, Scotty.' But by the time the fourth *Star Trek* movie came along, the producers relented and allowed Captain Kirk to come quite close with 'Scotty, beam me up.' Doohan's last request for his ashes to be beamed up into outer space was realised for only a brief four minutes before the capsule dropped Scotty down into the mountains of New Mexico. If only he had passed on his skills driving warp-engines he might have been successfully teleported into eternity.

If Scottish engineering prowess lives on in fiction, how sad it is that much of Scotland's industrial prowess is now forgotten. Surely the greatest of the redundant steelworks and foundries could have been preserved as a glorious part of our lost heritage, like the massive Ravenscraig steelworks of Colvilles. The innovative cantilevers of the Forth Bridge were brought into reality by the pioneering use of steel smelted in the west of Scotland by Colvilles and fabricated in Arrol's workshops at Dalmarnock.

The success of this engineering wonder of its age won for Sir William Arrol & Co. the reputation of bridge-builders to the world. Despite this, when the firm was forced to close, its buildings were bulldozed into extinction. Filing cabinets were thrown out and thousands of engineering drawings, plans and photographs were strewn across the blasted site and scattered to the winds. Had it not been for such eagled-eyed industrial archaeologists as John Hume and his colleagues, who gathered up as much as they could, the entire record of Arrol's international bridge-building output would have been lost to the world.

Or take Glasgow's Saracen Foundry, which exported to the world a legendary variety of ironwork, from elegant railings for India to complete kits for opera houses in Brazil. Surely their ornate headquarters would have been a monument worthy of preservation? After all, we revere and guard all those crumbling castles of our feudal past. So why couldn't we have saved at least some of those engineering workshops to remind us of our once great industrial enterprise? Instead of the lore and gore of the Middle Ages, such centres could have celebrated the ingenuity of Scotland's pioneering engineers, steelworkers, locomotive- and ship-builders, at a time when they led the world. 'But who would visit them?' I hear some dry-stick guardian of our heritage ask. All I would say is just look at what has been accomplished in Germany on the Ruhr. Faced with the same collapse of its heavy industries, local enterprise there has regenerated its decaying steel mills and workshops into dazzling new entertainment venues.

Colville's 'Big Mill' at Ravenscraig surely deserved a better fate than to be blown sky high and left for years as an empty site to dream of shopping malls to come.

The innovative cantilevers of the Forth Bridge demonstrated by its engineers Sir John Fowler, 1817-98, and Benjamin Baker, 1840-1907. Their outstretched arms demonstrate how the weight of the bridge's central span, here symbolised by their Japanese assistant Kaichi Watanabe, is transmitted to the banks of the Firth of Forth through the diamond-shaped supports. The pull in Watanabe's supporters' arms indicates the tension in the ties, and the push in the lower struts stands for the compression in the tubes. Watanabe studied at Glasgow University under Lord Kelvin, returning to Japan as a pioneer of electric railways before becoming the president of the Ishikawajima Ship Building company.

The Forth Bridge immediately entered popular culture with postcards often conflating its high girders with the effects of strong drink. One of the great challenges for kids of an engineering bent was to build the Forth Bridge out of Meccano.

The once abandoned Ruhr steelworks at Duisburg in the Emscher region of Germany show how imagination can reverse the destiny of a rusting steelworks to celebrate industrial heritage with fun and great panache, turning dereliction to delight. The abandoned dead-tech of redundant industrial plant has been imaginatively deconstructed by Peter and Anna-Liese Latz into a playful reconstructed pleasure ground. Landscaped parks lead up to ponds on which lilies now float on water where once fire flamed up open-hearth smelters. Blast furnaces soar up as accessible follies, as magical as any tower in the City of Oz. Challenging plunge and swimming pools for kids have been plumbed into the gas storage tanks. Under spans of girders, auditoriums and stages have been created for dance, theatre and opera. At night the blast furnaces evoke an eerie beauty, as they loom out of the darkness in a changing light show devised by Jonathan Park, famous for his Pink Floyd and Rolling Stones illuminations. Now more people service these regenerated fun palaces than ever worked in the same spaces producing steel.

Yet back on the Clyde, what's left is an overriding sense of lost industrial pride. In the wry words of Billy Connolly, yesterday's shipbuilders must now bend the knee as a thousand wine waiters in Glasgow's refurbished bars.

In the 1960s there was enough local initiative in the Fife coalfields to preserve the first concrete winding-gear tower in the British Isles. It now provides a striking eye-catcher, and a monument to our innovative industrial past. The country park of Lochore Meadows was reclaimed from the scarred landscape of open-cast and strip mining. Although modest when compared with the large German parks, this imaginative reclamation showed early on how our industrial past could have been celebrated. Since all exhausted open-cast mining fields have now to be returned to some semblance of natural order, it gave the operators of the nearby Lochgelly mine the inspired idea of creating a new landscape in the spirit of eighteenth-century garden design. They invited the collaboration of the award-winning architect and designer Charles Jencks on the strength of the sweeping mounds and curved reaches of water that he and his late wife Maggie

Lochore Meadows Country Park preserved the innovative concrete winding gear tower as a worthy memorial to Fife coalmining.

Left: The redundant Thyssen steelworks at Duisberg in the Ruhr have been born again as imaginative entertainment complexes, with ever-changing light shows at night created by Jonathan Park.

Right: Landschaftspark Duisburg Nord.

Keswick created around her family home of Portrack in the Borders. Jencks's plan for the regenerated Lochgelly coalfields is drenched in meaning; his landscape aims to portray a microcosm of geographical Scotland.

When Maggie Keswick Jencks was told that she had an advanced form of cancer her despair was compounded by the bleakness of the hospital wards and corridors. She thought that hospitals should be designed as a progression of beautiful spaces to lift rather than to depress the spirits. Her idea of a caring centre, a life-enhancing and tranquil oasis where patients with cancer and their carers could meet and learn what options were available to them, was born. Maggie sought a building that would come to express and define her feelings in what she hoped would be an architecture of compassion rather than of terror. Before Maggie died in 1995 Richard Murphy was commissioned to design the first centre. It was built out of a derelict stable block in the grounds of Edinburgh's Western General Hospital on a very modest budget.

At Portrack in the Borders, Charles Jencks and Maggie Keswick created one of the most original landscapes of the twentieth century by damming the meandering River Nith, deepening ponds and creating sweeping landforms. Jencks plans to transform open-cast mining sites in Fife along similar lines.

The first Maggie's Centre was such an immediate success with patients and visitors alike that it encouraged the launching of a series of innovatively designed centres in other cities. Following Edinburgh, the firm of Page & Park converted the old gatehouse of Glasgow's Western Infirmary into a Maggie's Centre on two levels. The same firm won the 2006 Andrew Doolan Award, Scotland's most prestigious architectural prize, for the Raigmore Maggie's Centre in Inverness. Charles and Maggie's wide circle of friends included many of the world's leading architects, some of whom have designed jewel-like works as Maggie's Centres.

The pleated roof line of Frank Gehry's Dundee Maggie's Centre protects the welcome refuge from the bleak cliffs of Ninewells Hospital which loom behind. Astonishingly, Dundee's Maggie's Centre is the first building in the British Isles to be built by the architect of the Bilbao Guggenheim Museum and the Disney Hall in Los Angeles. Across the Tay, Zaha Hadid, another vibrant force in world architecture, has created her first UK building in Kirkcaldy. Backed against the Victoria Hospital's tower block, her Maggie's Centre sparkles on the outside like a black diamond, whilst the white curving spaces of the interiors look out over an expanse of life-affirming greenery.

These innovative Maggie's Centres offer spiritual uplift in their inventive design, in contrast to the dreary monochrome brutalism of most hospitals. Part temple, part art gallery and part home, the Maggie's Centres represent a new building type. Their universal success has confirmed Maggie Keswick Jencks's belief that caring within beautiful spaces raises the spirits of patient and carer alike. Challenging architecture, Charles Jencks believes, can raise your spirits and reinforce your resolve to face your illness. And what better definition could there be of great architecture than as a life-enhancing force?

I would like to end on a curious footnote, on how Scottish inventions are often the last to benefit Scotland. I was told this by Roderick Graham, one of the BBC's most imaginative and intelligent director/producers (*Z Cars*, *Elizabeth R* and Dennis Potter plays). When Graham was invited to head up drama production in BBC Scotland's Glasgow studios, being a keen sailor he chose to live on the Clyde at Helensburgh. He acquired a mooring for his boat and a house just a few streets along from where John Logie Baird, the inventor of television, was born. Imagine his surprise when he discovered that this was the only area in central Scotland unable to receive BBC television.

Maggie's Centres. Richard Murphy, Western General Hospital, 1996, extended 1999. This award-winning scheme for the first Maggie's Centre pivoted on a welcoming kitchen. By fusing architecture and furniture in his corridor-free plan, Murphy set the standard for all the Maggie's Centres to come.

Opposite top: Ninewells Hospital, Dundee, 2003, Frank O. Gehry.

Below: Victoria Hospital, Kirkcaldy, 2007, Zaha Hadid.

12 THE GEMMES
From Highland Games to Elephant Polo

Soccer was my abiding passion as a schoolboy. Each morning I'd kick a ball down the street from our home in Fountainbridge all the way to Bruntsfield Primary School in Edinburgh's West End. My classmates were just as soccer-crazy. We all dreamed one day of playing for Scotland, or at least for the Scottish or English leagues. Some of us, like Dave Mackay, actually achieved that heady aim and ended up playing for Tottenham Hotspur. Laurie Reilly played for the Hibs – Edinburgh's Hibernian. I never quite reached such stellar heights, but by twenty-one I was playing on the right wing professionally for Bonnyrigg Rose in the Scottish Junior League. For that I received my first and last professional fee for playing soccer.

I have already described how the good Robert Henderson rescued me from the playing fields of Manchester United during my tour of *South Pacific*. He no doubt saved me from being a forgotten player in professional league soccer. But it's never once dimmed my passion for the game. I've remained a fervent soccer fan ever since. In my early years of acting I played nearly every Sunday for the Show Biz Eleven, which raised large sums for charity. A team of celebrities was put together each week by the music promoter Jimmy Henney, who worked for the music publisher Chappell's. We would meet on a Sunday morning at the BBC and then be driven off in a charabanc to matches as far apart as Brighton and Yorkshire, where we would get quite big crowds. The line-up varied but could include Tommy Steele, Freddie Trueman, Glen Mason, Des O'Connor and Jimmy Tarbuck, Ronnie Carroll, Dave King, with Tony Daley on the wing and David Frost in goal. Dave King was the most flamboyant but was really not that gifted, and he didn't jive at all with Ronnie Carroll. Once when Ronnie placed the ball and walked back to take a penalty, Dave King rushed up and kicked it, nearly knocking out the corner flag. From time to time we were lucky to have real professionals like Wally Barnes, Billy Wright and Danny Blanchflower. It all depended who showed up. One Sunday

when most of the stars were working, thirty-five thousand fans had turned up in Sheffield to see the celebrities when we were well short of being a complete squad. Henney rose to the challenge by convincing the bus driver and one or two star-struck passengers to join us on the pitch.

One weekend before I had a London theatre opening, I went over on my ankle and left the ground on crutches. Wally Barnes, a veteran player, had the solution. 'Here's what you do, son. It's a surefire remedy. You plunge your ankle for a minute into a bowl of the hottest water you can stand, and then again for the same time into one of ice-freezing water.' I did that three times during the night and it was as painful as hell, but I made the stage the next day and was fine. 'Swelling is nature's way to rest the joint,' Wally told me. 'The hot and cold treatment takes

I played charity matches for the Show Biz Eleven whenever I could from the late Fifties onwards.

GRAVESEND AND NORTHFLEET FOOTBALL GROUND
STONEBRIDGE ROAD, NORTHFLEET

SAM ENGLISH'S BENEFIT MATCH

ALL STAR XI
v.
SHOWBIZ XI

MONDAY, 26th SEPTEMBER, 1960

Kick-off 7.15 p.m.

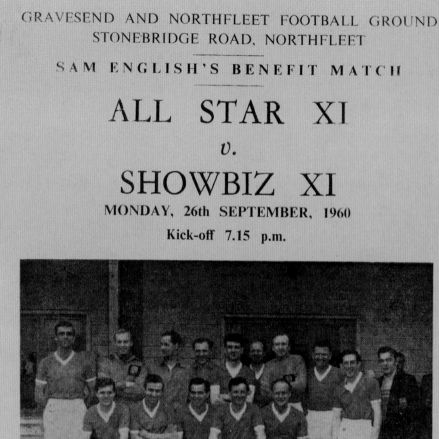

SHOWBIZ

Back row (*standing, left to right*) : Sean Connery, Ken Day, John Burgess, Pip Wedge, Peter Regan, Wally Barnes, Bill Cotton, jr., Dave King, Glen Mason, Bill Parry (masseur).

Front row (*seated, left to right*) : Ronnie Caroll, Des O'Connor, Jimmy Henney, Siggy Jackson, Franklyn Boyd.

SOUVENIR PROGRAMME

Price 6d

away that support, so you look out, and walk gingerly.' That's exactly what I did, treading the boards lightly on that Monday morning.

Scots can claim to have perfected, if not invented, the 'beautiful game'. Whatever you think, or whatever experts of the game now claim, soccer has been played in Scotland for centuries. The puzzle is which country really did invent the gemme, as we call it in Scotland. The strongest contenders range from the ancient Greeks and Mexicans to the Romans and Chinese. What's your hunch? Mine is China. After all, the poet Li Yu was writing poems about *cuju*, or 'kick ball', over a thousand years ago. And to cap this, frescoes have been discovered in China from the first century, but then those soccerers seem to have been all women.

The earliest Scottish contender is the ball game played every New Year's Day in the Orkney Islands. Orcadians (dropping their lls) call it 'the Ba'. The Ba is played up and down the streets of Kirkwall, with teams divided between the uptown and downtown, known locally as the Uppies and Doonies. When the cork-filled leather ba is hurled to the crowd around the old Kirk Green, it disappears immediately into a whirling scrum where it may not be seen again for hours. Most of the time nobody really knows where the ba actually is. The first side to either manoeuvre its hidden presence up the town to hit a designated wall, or down town into the water of the harbour, becomes that year's winner. It's not soccer as we know it, but there are beginnings of the game there. No one really knows the Ba's origins. It may date from the days when these northern islands were part of Norway. Is it symbolic of the Old Year fighting the New? Or does it have a more sinister Viking derivation, as a beheading game, with the ba symbolising the severed head of a vanquished foe? That more ghoulish source might lie closer to the truth, like that polo match played with a human head we re-enacted in John Huston's movie of Kipling's *The Man Who Would Be King*.

With no limit to numbers, mob soccer like the Ba, part sport, part riot, was played in Scottish towns throughout the country in the Middle Ages. Being rowdy affairs, they would often end in violence. By the end of the fifteenth century things had got so out of hand that Parliament decreed that 'no part of the realm should be used for soccer, golf, or other such unprofitable sports, but for the common good and the defence of the realm, bows should be offered for archery and targets made up as previously ordained'.

The idea that soccer and golf are 'unprofitable sports' would stagger many of the sports-obsessed members of the Scottish Parliament today. But five hundred years ago, defending the realm against England, the auld inemie, was a serious concern. Those urgent calls for archery training programmes have left us with one of the strangest mementoes of those times of trouble, the Kilwinning Papingo. With great foresight for the nation's safety, the deeds of the Ancient Society of Kilwinning Archers stretch all the way back to 1483, making it the oldest sporting club in the realm. 'Ding doon the doo!' the cry goes up below the tower of the old abbey, as the annual Kilwinning Papingo Contest gets under way. A group of sturdy archers are straining their bows, eyeing the battered papingo high above. 'What is a papingo?' I ask a wily bowman taking aim. 'Well, it's no a doo, or dove,' he tells me, as his arrow flies up past the battered wooden bird, swinging off a ten-

Opposite: Showbiz Eleven programme, 1960. Our ad hoc team often had to travel long distances out of London by bus, although this evening match took place at Gravesend, nearer home.

Below: Chinese Football – woodblock illustration from *The Three Powers, Sancai Tuhuia*, a Chinese encyclopaedia first published in 1609.

The Ba, Kirkwall Orkney. More civil war than sport, the Ba may be a survivor of the mob football played all over Scotland in the Middle Ages, perhaps not unlike Calcio Storico, the fight football of Florence.

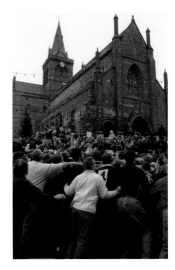

A shooter of the Royal Company of Archers at the annual Edinburgh target practice on the Edinburgh Meadows.

The Ancient Society of Kilwinning Archers annual contest is won when the first arrow hits the papingo, or parrot, high up on the tower of Kilwinning Abbey, Ayrshire.

The winner receives the Silver Papingo Award, known as 'Jingle Bells', to keep for a year.

foot pole a hundred feet above. 'It's a parrot,' he said. 'Centuries ago they had a real bird tied up there.' A flurry of arrows continues to miss their painted apology for a parrot, until finally the elusive papingo lurches sideways from a hit.

We hear the prize before we see it. With the tinkling of over three centuries of hanging medals, the ancient silver Papingo Arrow, known affectionately as 'Jingle Bells', is ceremoniously presented to the winner, who becomes Kilwinning's captain for the next year. Slipping on the scarlet 'benn', or sash of silk, over dark-green breeks, and capped by a tammy in circles of red, white and green to match the Kilwinning targets, the winner now looks all the part of a swashbuckling captain.

A much grander archery event provided a memorable sequence for the film we did on Edinburgh. We covered the Royal Company of Archers' annual tournament on Edinburgh's Bruntsfield Links. As for hitting the target, the smartly turned-out green-uniformed bowmen didn't fare much better than the Kilwinning boys. When the cameraman asked for a safe vantage point, one of the archers wryly suggested that he would be safest the closer he could get to the target. And so it turned out to be. Not one of the arrows struck the target that day, never mind hitting a bull's eye. 'This is the oldest sporting club in the country,' boasted one old boy, who was an Edinburgh lawyer in real life. 'Our origins go back to 1676, you know.' Sadly there was no one there from Kilwinning to challenge that.

The Royal Company of Archers owe much of their presence to the fictions of Sir Walter Scott. Their uniforms match the description of the Lincoln-green bowmen at the Ashby de la Zouch tournament in *Ivanhoe*. With its colourful evocation of medieval archery it was no surprise that Scott, an archer himself, would put this company centre stage for the royal visit he stage managed in Edinburgh for King George IV in 1822. This was an event of some significance, for it was the first time a British monarch had visited Scotland in over two hundred years. To celebrate this royal visit, the King elevated his green archers by renaming them the 'Sovereign's Body Guard in Scotland' for all time to come. The long circling bonnet feathers of the Royal Archers now remain a comforting reassurance of Her Majesty's presence at each August's Royal Garden Party in the grounds of Holyroodhouse. But as for being an effective bodyguard, I'm not so sure. Left to these green-uniformed bodyguards, the defence of the realm would seem to be in the same parlous state it was over five hundred years ago.

Beyond the targets of the Royal Archers on Bruntsfield Links that day, old men were golfing on a public course where the game has been played continuously since the early 1400s. Not far from them kids were enjoying a game of knockabout soccer, with jackets thrown down as goalposts. What memories that brought back for me – playing soccer with what you've got; especially when I learnt that the boys were nearly all from my old primary school beyond the Links.

As long ago as 1636 an Aberdeen Grammar School master, David Wedderburn, devoted a section of his popular teach-yourself Latin primer *Vocabula* to a vivid description of soccer. This little book caused something of a sensation during the Soccer World Cup in 2006 when an edition from the National Library of Scotland was displayed as a key exhibit in the *Fascinating Soccer* exhibition at Hamburg, Germany. 'The influence of this book is quite tremendous,' Professor Wulf Koepke of the Museum für Völkerkunde said. 'It rewrites part of soccer history. Passing wasn't supposed to have happened until the late 1860s and yet this Aberdeen book is talking about it centuries before.' English soccer historians were quick to challenge *Vocabula*'s early references to passing the ball, claiming the phrase *huc percute* which was translated as 'pass it here', really means 'strike it here' and that *repercute pilam* means 'strike it back again'. Well, I'm sorry, as a professional soccer in my youth, if that's not a definition of passing, what is?

Wedderburn's description of the game may not be as defining as the *Rules of Association Soccer* published in England well over two hundred years later, but at

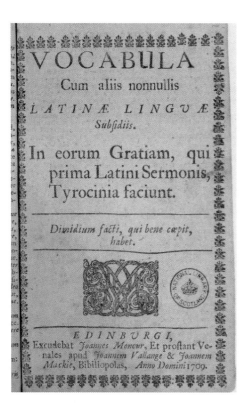

Vocabula, a teach-yourself Latin book with a lively description of early seventeenth-century soccer was first published around 1636 by David Wedderburn, a teacher at the Aberdeen Grammar School. Had I been at school then this lively account of playing soccer might have made me learn Latin.

least there's a reference to the goalkeeper, which failed to make the 11 Rules of 1863. In his fulsome introduction, the writer Melvyn Bragg raised this little rulebook to the status of one of the twelve most influential books in the English language. Too bad, then, that he suppressed any mention of the contribution that Scots have made to the game. This provoked Richard McBrearty, the curator of the Scottish Soccer Museum, to claim that *Vocabula* 'is the first evidence we have come across of a game with goalkeepers and players passing the ball to score'. Since Wedderburn's description ends on his home team's defeat, that in itself is proof enough for me that it describes soccer as we know it today in Scotland. Where's the conceit in that? The Celt, as that most ancient of traditions has it, must fall in battle.

Sortiamur partes; tu primum socium dilige; Qui sunt nostrarum partium huc se recipient; Quot nobis adversantur; Execute pilam ut ineamus certamen; Age, huc percute; Tu tuere metum; Praeripe illi pilam si possis agere; Age objice te illi; Occurre illi; Repercute pilam; Egregie. Nihil agis; Transmittere metum pila; Hic primus est transmissus. Hic secundus, hic tertius est transmissus; Repelle eum, alioqui, adversarii evadunt superiores; Nisi caves jam occupabit metam; Ni melius a nobis ludatur, de nobis actum est. Eia penes vos victoria est; Io triumphe. Est pilae doctissimus; Aeque eo fuisset, reportassimus victoriam…

Here's a translation by the Latin scholar and soccer aficionado Hamish McGrittie. He purposely omits 'passing'. Judge for yourself.

Select your side and team-mate. Let our team line up here. How many are against us? Start the game by kicking the ball. Strike it here. You guard the goal. If you can, seize the ball from him. Come on, block him. Retrieve the ball. Kick it back. Well done. But you are not shooting for the goal. There's the first shot – the second – the third. Block that man or our opponents will be the winners. Unless you're careful they will quickly score a goal. We have not played at our best yet. Hurrah, victory is in your hands. A triumph. He is very clever with the ball. Come on, do as I say. Up till now we have played better, haven't we, team? Come on, we still can win…

To cap it all, Scotland provided the Hamburg exhibition with the world's oldest soccer ball. Dating back to around 1550, this inflatable stitched leather ball was discovered during the restoration of Mary Queen of Scots' bedchamber at Stirling Castle. We know that Mary played tennis at Falkland and golf on Scottish links – could she have been a midfield player too?

To have your club battle for the Scottish Cup at Hampden is every soccer fan's dream in Scotland. It's the oldest soccer trophy in the world, played in the world's oldest soccer stadium. And the claims stack up. The world's first soccer international was played on 30 November 1871 when Scotland met England. Of course it had to take place on the home patch and, just as importantly, it had to be played on Scotland's national day, St Andrew's. Although this encounter was a great match, the result was a goalless draw. Despite that, the Scots astounded the English as they ran and passed the ball across the midfield in ballet-like moves. What passed for soccer in those days was a dribbling game. Players struck out on their own, ignoring their team-mates, running with the ball until they were tackled or scored. The 'Scotch Professors', as they were soon called, generously handed their more choreographed style to England. And soon the Scottish way of playing took over the world.

But even in those early days there was a downside to the gemme. I've always supported the team that I thought played the best soccer. For years it was Celtic, who were the first British team to win the European Cup in Lisbon in 1967. They beat the world-famous Internazionale Milan 2–1 in an all-out attacking style that changed the face of soccer. What is even more extraordinary in these days of international signings, all the players of this unbeatable Celtic team came from within thirty miles of Glasgow.

Over the years I've shifted my allegiance to Rangers. Why, as a once Celtic supporter, with its strong Catholic-Irish allegiances, should I cheer on a team known to attract extreme Protestants? Well, religious affiliations in sport mean nothing to me. It's the gemme I love. I deplore the bigotry of sectarianism that still blights soccer in Scotland, especially in clashes between Celtic, who field the emerald green of Catholic Ireland, and the blue of Protestant Rangers. Let's have the referee raise the red card to all bigots, be they blue or green, and send such mindless prejudice off the field for ever. Why can't we all come together to celebrate the soccer those Scotch Professors pioneered back in the early days — those great midfield players who opened up the gemme worldwide?

Despite its place in early soccer history, the Hampden stadium was falling into near-dereliction by the 1960s. To help restore it, I came up with an idea for an international friendly match between Brazil and Scotland. My friend the shipbuilder Sir Iain Stewart persuaded Sir Adam Thomson of British Caledonian Airways to donate twenty-two seats for the Brazilian team, including Pelé, then the world's greatest player. Celtic and Rangers would combine to field a select team. Entry would be half a crown – 30 old pence, less than half of that in today's money. Embassies were invited to contribute and fly their flags. I agreed to underwrite the whole event to the tune of £35,000. With Celtic and Rangers so strong at the time, this international friendly had all the promise of a phenomenal celebration of soccer. Yet despite all our backing, a wildly supportive press and doubtless the enthusiasm of thousands of soccer fans, Willie Allan, the Secretary of the Scottish Soccer Association blew the whistle on us. 'Soccer isn't showbusiness, son,' he told me, his lip curling into a dismissive sneer, to scotch our dream. I had been away from Scotland too long.

'The beautiful game' was what that Brazilian soccerer of genius, Edison Arantes do Nascimento, called the game he loved and lived to play. Better known to a wider world as Pelé, he became a legend in the 1960s. With astonishing speed and a near-miraculous control of the ball, Pelé scored over and over again, as though playing the ball dancing to a Samba beat. The silky soccer style of Pelé, now followed by the Portuguese Cristiano Ronaldo, can trace its origins back to Archie McLean, a

The Scottish Cup, or to give it its full title, the Football Association Challenge Cup, is the trophy awarded to the winner of the national football cup competition of Scotland. It dates back to the 1873-4 season which makes it the oldest national trophy in the world.

wily mechanical engineer from Glasgow with a passion for soccer. McLean was an accomplished twenty-year-old player with Ayr United and St Johnstone before he was sent out to Brazil in 1914 to help set up a new cotton-thread mill in São Paulo for the famous Paisley textile firm of J. & P. Coates. He was expected to stay three months, but ended up living there for forty years. Within weeks he had founded the Scottish Wanderers.

What I find so extraordinary is that there might never have been a Pelé, a Zico or a Ronaldo if it hadn't been for three Scots: Charles Miller who introduced the game to Brazil in 1894, Archie McLean who laid down the ground plan of Samba-playing Brazilian soccer, and the talented coach Jock Hamilton who developed it. But by introducing the notion of passing the ball between players, it was McLean who really transformed the Brazilians' crude game of kick and rush. Under his training the Scottish Wanderers were soon playing soccer at the top of the league with the same deft precision with which they manipulated their cotton-mill machinery. McLean's ideas were a revelation to the Brazilians, who had been playing the English-style dribbling soccer since it was introduced in the 1890s by Charles Miller who was schooled in England. Switching to what the Brazilians called the *tabelinha* – 'the little chart' – McLean encouraged his team to speed down the field with the ball to play a very fast, short-passing game. But no one was more nimble on his feet than McLean himself, who became a national hero in Brazil as *veadinho*, 'the little deer'. As a fervent soccer fan now in my late seventies, why has it taken me so long to learn about Archie McLean? And to think that he even shared my mother's maiden name.

Miller was the son of a Scottish engineer; he was born in São Paulo in 1875 and sent for schooling in England, where he developed a passion for soccer as a lethal striker. Returning to Brazil with two soccers, he campaigned to establish the game first among the British expats. On 19 June 1899, in front of a turnout of sixty spectators, Charles 'Nipper' Miller's São Paulo Athletic Club, the team which he founded and captained, won 1–0 against Mackenzie College on a field at Chacara Dulley, making it the first recorded soccer match in Brazil. Three years later Miller's São Paulo Athletic Club won the first Brazilian league title 2–1 in a play-off match against Paulistano. He died in 1953, five years before Brazil won the World Cup title for the first time. His pioneering place in Brazilian soccer is still celebrated, and there is a street in São Paulo named in his honour.

Jock Hamilton from Ayr was Fulham's successful coach in the early 1900s, before Brazil's Paulistano recruited him to promote what became wrongly known as the *sistema inglês*, or English system, given that Hamilton's fast ball control and midfield passing style was essentially Scottish – or the *sistema scozia*. South America gained greatly from itinerant Scots, who as often as not were engineers, and steely soccers in their downtime.

Uruguay, the first team ever to win the World Cup, in 1930, has much to thank John Harley, 'El Técnico', a Glasgow engineer who introduced the Scottish pass-and-move style when playing for the Montevideo team Peñarol before becoming their coach. Another Scot, Glasgow schoolteacher Alexander Watson, brought soccer to Argentina. He first coached his pupils at the St Andrew's School in

Buenos Aires in the early 1880s. A few years later he founded the first soccer league outside of the British Isles, which would grow into the Asociación Argentina de Soccer in 1912. It earned him the honorary title of 'Father of Argentinian Soccer'.

Scots were such skilful soccerers in the Victorian era that they played a key part in promoting soccer across the world. Their style of pass and run was a revelation to English teams, who hired a disproportionate number of athletes from Scotland. Since every player of Liverpool's team of 1892 was a Scot they were known affectionately as the 'Macs'. Soon 'Scotch Professors' were taking their skills all over Europe. Ex-Celtic player Johnny Madden coached teams in Czechoslovakia and George Smith MacGregor helped inspire an early version of the German Bundesliga.

Canada's first club, Carlton FC of Toronto, was founded in 1876 by Scots who also played a key part in the early soccer successes of the USA. In China, Glaswegian John Prentice's team, the Marine Engineers Institute FC in Shanghai, was affiliated to the SFA in 1888. Scots miners in Pachua initiated the first soccer club in Mexico. 'We taught the world to play the game,' once headlined Scotland's *Daily Record*, 'and then forgot how to do it ourselves.'

Illustrations from the Scotland vs England friendly of 30 November 1872, played at West of Scotland Cricket Club Ground, Partick, Glasgow. This was the first international football match played in Scotland under Football Association rules. The match resulted in a goal-less draw.

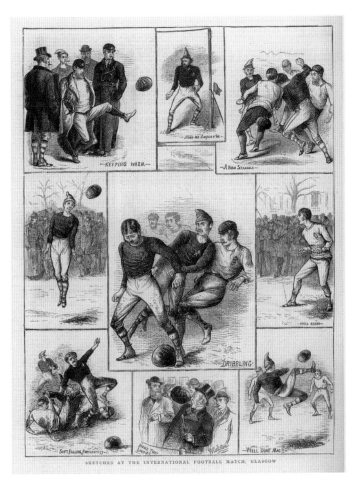

SKETCHES AT THE INTERNATIONAL FOOTBALL MATCH, GLASGOW

Statue of Donald Dinnie as William Wallace, 1889, Ballarat, Victoria, Australia.

Donald Dinnie, 1837-1916, strongman extraordinaire, was internationally famous as the nineteenth century's greatest athlete. Born near Aboyne in the Highlands, he won over 10,000 competitions in a career that spanned over fifty years.

They may not have put up a statue to Archie McLean in Brazil, but in Australia Donald Dinnie, the world's first sports superstar, was given this honour – though, rather bizarrely, not under his own name. So famous was this great athlete towards the end of the nineteenth century that he was chosen to model for William Wallace, the greatest Scottish patriot of them all. For those tough Scots Gold Rush freebooters who founded the city of Ballarat, north of Melbourne, there could be no better embodiment of the strength and endurance of Scotland's supreme hero than that chief of sporting chiefs, Donald Dinnie, the Highland Colossus, the Braveheart of his day. Always kilted, and dapper to the points of his waxed moustache, Dinnie cut a striking figure. 'His Clan Hay kilt seemed to swirl and fizz as he walked,' one observer wrote. 'I have never seen one who looked so clearly part of Scotland's story.'

Born in 1837 near Aboyne at Balnacraig, Donald Dinnie began his working life as an apprentice stonemason. His strength was legendary. When helping his father repair the old Potarch Bridge, Donald lifted and walked the bridge's ringed granite anchor stones. Now known as the 'Dinnie Steens', no one has manhandled them since. He could carry granite window lintels up ladders on his back. But he would swiftly down tools if there were Highland Games to compete in. Dinnie mastered all the events and went on to become the fastest runner, the highest jumper, and most surprising of all, the most elegant Highland dancer in the world. At sixteen he was winning wrestling bouts against all comers. Soon he was earning more at the games than he was paid for working as a stonemason. His fame soon spread abroad. Caledonian Clubs invited Dinnie to compete coast to coast across Canada and America. He won them all, winning up to sixteen events in a single afternoon. 'I had usually put in small effort to win,' he wrote back home to his folks in Aberdeenshire.

At the world's then largest and most lucrative games in Boston, Dinnie was declared the outright winner. 'Donald Dinnie is the champion of the world,' wrote the *Boston Herald*. 'He is a man of splendid physique, and although all the noted American athletes were present, they became diminutive when compared with him.' 'There goes another Donald Dinnie,' was the cry from the trenches in World War I, when the Royal Artillery named their deadly sixty-pound mortar after him.

Before he retired Donald had won over ten thousand athletics competitions worldwide, which made him for thirty years the uncontested all-round athlete of the world. All this was before the establishment of the Olympic Games, which is probably why so few know his name today. Back near where he grew up, his prowess is now celebrated annually when the elaborately chased Dinnie Cup is the coveted prize for the all-round winner of the Aboyne Highland Games. Amongst other contests, Donald Dinnie the invincible Highlander won 500 hurdling events; 2000 wrestling matches; 1800 'putting the stone'; 2000 hammer-throwing, 1800 high jumping, 200 weight lifting (in his kilt) events; and 1400 caber tosses.

Highland Games were the precursors of major sports events today, but no one really knows how they began. My guess is that they were originally recruiting drives organised by clan chiefs to hire the most skilful fighting men for their retinues. Turning a tree trunk over on its end in caber-tossing could have originated in heaving massive logs across ravines to make primitive bridges. And other events, like throwing the hammer, may derive from Highland crafts and their attendant necessities. Blacksmiths could have limbered up before forging iron on their anvils by throwing their hammers. Rounded riverbed stones may have provided ideal 'cleachnearts' for putting the stone. Re-enactments of such gatherings were the highlight of Queen Victoria's annual visits to the Highlands. She loved her 'mighty men of Deeside', as she wrote in her Balmoral diary of August 1848. 'It looked very pretty to see them, in their different coloured kilts, scramble up through the woods…We were all much pleased to see our gillie Duncan win.'

The early Scots monarchs were hunters, to a king. For King David in the twelfth century, hunting became a religious experience and the stuff of legends. Once, out riding in his Edinburgh park, he was thrown to the ground when his horse was startled by a stag. Then as the King looked up, framed between the animal's menacing antlers a crucifix began to glow. The King bowed. The stag dipped his head, before slowly retreating back into the shadows of the wood. For his miraculous escape King David founded the abbey of 'Holyrude', which means the holy cross; and the antlered cross, which can still be seen today on the gates of the Palace of Holyroodhouse, became its crest.

Over the centuries the hunts grew in scale and range and could last for more than a week, circling over moors and forests. They became known as tinchels, from the Gaelic *timchioll* meaning a circuit.

The heraldic cross or 'Holy Rude' in the antlers of a stag frames the Palace of Holyroodhouse, Edinburgh.

Five or six hundred men do rise early in the morning [wrote an English visitor to the Highlands in 1618], and they do disperse themselves divers ways, and seven or eight miles compass, they do bring or chase the deer in many herds [two, three or four hundred in a herd] to such or such a place as the Noblemen shall appoint them…. then all the valley on each side being waylaid with two hundred of strong Irish greyhounds, they were let loose as the occasion served upon the herd of deer so that with dogs, guns, arrows, dirks and daggers in the space of two hours fourscore fat deer were slain.

The young Mary Queen of Scots was a fearless rider who loved the excitement of the chase, or hawking in the Lomond hills above Falkland Palace. Her father James V had turned McDuff's dour Fife castle into a Renaissance palace to celebrate his marriage to Mary of Guise from France. Here Princess Mary spent some of her happiest days. Beyond the parterres of the garden, she could play real, or royal, tennis. Her Falkland court, which dates back to around 1539, still exists, and thanks to the enterprising Falkland Real Tennis Club it is the world's oldest tennis court still in play.

Real tennis, royal tennis, or court tennis evolved in the courtyards of castles and in the cloisters of monasteries in France. The game was probably first brought to Scotland in the early 1200s by Marie de Couci, the mother of King Alexander III. Then it was called 'caitch' from *cachier*, to play tennis, in the medieval dialect of Picardy. The courts were known as 'caichpules', but this word might also derive from the Flemish or Dutch for 'game of chases'. Certainly, the court at Falkland Palace follows the French pattern of a *jeu quarré*. Originally players in France played with their hands in a version of the game known as 'jeu de paume', meaning handball. Later came gloves, then short bats, before the present strung rackets out of which today's lawn tennis evolved in 1874.

At the Falkland Real Tennis Club, tennis is still played with a heavy asymmetric wooden racket shaped like a hand. The solid ball has half the bounce of a modern tennis ball. Because of Falkland's stone floor and roughcast walls they don't last long. The net is set two feet lower at the centre to encourage the cross-court shot. Extra points are won if the ball goes through one of the four square wall-openings known as 'lunes'. When 'Tenez!' – 'Look out!' – echoes around the court it's the warning that a serve is about to take place, and that's what gave the game its name of 'tennis'.

In the following centuries, the game in Scotland seldom reached the heights of Mary's royal tennis, until a young Scot took the Centre Court at Wimbledon by storm. Over the years I've seen many exciting matches, but I've never seen anything like the response the teenager Andrew Murray got from the crowd in 2005. I saw him win three straight-set games, before taking David Nalbandian to five sets at Wimbledon. For me Andy is as gifted as anyone who has ever played the game. He grew up in the sleepy town of Dunblane northeast of Glasgow. Sleepy, that was, until an insane psychopath broke into his primary school and shot sixteen of his schoolfriends and a teacher. The eight-year-old fled to the headmaster's room and survived. If there is anything positive to come out of the unimaginable

Opposite: *A Royal Game of Tennis in the Jeu de Paume, Versailles*, published by Charles Hulpeau, sixteenth century.

The Falkland Palace Royal Tennis Club promotes 'real' or royal tennis in a court constructed for James V of Scotland in the 1540s, which makes it the oldest tennis court in use today. The club celebrated the Falkland's court 450th anniversary with a tournament in 1989.

Andrew 'Andy' Murray, b.1987, charged on to the international tennis scene at Wimbledon in 2005, where I saw him give an extraordinary performance for an eighteen-year-old and I have followed his meteoric career ever since.

horror of such an appalling tragedy, it was Andy's resolve to persevere with his tennis. The game became his overriding passion. A year after the massacre his tennis had so improved that he reached the semi-finals of an under-11 event in France. His mother, Judy Murray, gave up her job as the Scottish National Tennis Coach to train her son full-time. When Andy won a place at the Sánchez-Casal Academy in Barcelona, he was well on his way to becoming a major international player. Although prone to injuries, the still-growing teenager had all the makings of a serious title contender. I encouraged him all I could, and it came as no surprise to me when he broke into the world's top ten in the spring of 2007. And to cap that, his elder brother Jamie finally emerged that year from under Andy's shadow as a most promising doubles player.

I hope that Andy's continued success will go some way to scotch that witty slur on our national tennis-playing talents, brilliantly perpetrated by my *Monty Python* friends long before I played King Agamemnon in *Time Bandits* for Terry Gilliam. In one of their most surreal sketches, a squad of tennis-playing blancmanges descend from outer space determined to win at Wimbledon. Knowing that Scotland is the worst tennis-playing nation in the world, they turn the entire population of England into Scots. In the final match at Wimbledon, the blancmanges are on the cusp of defeating their last kilted opponent when two sweet-toothed spectators rush on to the centre court and start to devour them with spoons. So watch out, Andy.

The oldest game of the Highlands is shinty. It's probably as old as the language brought to Scotland by the Irish over fifteen hundred years ago. Clan against clan, glen against glen, the mock yet fierce combat of shinty expresses its origins in the rivalries of warrior people. It's a very tough game. They are armed with curved hickory or ash sticks called 'camans', whose triangular-shaped hitting edge lofts the ball. There's as much aerial combat as footwork. Shinty is not unlike Irish hurling. It's similar yet different, just like the shared Gaelic language of the West Coast of Scotland and Ireland, which differs in some words although the grammar is much the same. So each year a Gaelic International is played out, under composite rules, between the pick of Scotland's shinty players and Ireland's finest hurlers.

Shinty's formidable wedge-shaped camans are not unlike the oldest golf clubs to survive. Although the Dutch game of *kolven* used similar clubs to drive balls across sheets of ice, the Scots were the first to think of sinking them in holes on grassy greens. After all, it's that elusive hole that makes it golf.

Golfers from abroad always find it strange when I show them that the rugged, windswept coast around St Andrews established the look and layout for golf courses for all time to come. Golf just yearned to be invented on land like that. The earliest courses were played on coastal 'links' from at least as far back as the fifteenth century. Apart from the land being of little use for farming, the links were far enough away from the centres of towns or villages to avoid too much scrutiny from the Kirk, especially on a Sunday. Those raised beaches of gorse and tough seaside grasses and their windblown, sandy hollows have been artificially recreated by bulldozers hundreds of thousands of times across the world. How generations of golfers must have cursed those stretches of rough, in imitation of the tough marine grass which grows along the St Andrews shore. I've seen the same variations of greensward, long-grassed roughs, bunkers or sandpits and stretches of water set down on every kind of landscape in the world, from cleared jungles to barren deserts, all attempting to replicate that rugged North Sea coastline. Even the Longreach Golf Club in the Australian outback conforms to the St Andrews pattern, though its drives are all sand framed by scrubland with 'greens' or 'yellows' of sandy earth stabilised by the underlying oil. Golf has even colonised the polar regions. At Uummannaq in Greenland, 373 miles north of the Arctic Circle, golf is defiantly played aganst the elements on greens that are icy-white and with balls of day-glow red.

The earliest references to golf in Scotland were, typically, all about banning the game. But the citizens of St Andrews in the fifteenth century were given the use of their links by right of charter, 'for golfe at all times'. This ordinance reversed King James II's efforts to ban the game by Act of Parliament in 1457. But the later Stuart kings took up golf with a passion. When our James VI went south to be James I of England he promoted the game at court. His French-educated mother, Mary Queen of Scots, was an accomplished golfer. To carry her clubs Mary brought her *cadets*, which the French-speaking Queen pronounced 'caddays'. So to this day those who carry the clubs and proffer golfing advice bear the honourable name of 'caddies' on every golf course in the world.

The game of golf just teems with words from Scots. A 'caddie' selects a 'mashie niblick', or iron. A 'duffer' sets down a 'tee' and sends up a 'divot' on the

Mary Queen of Scots playing golf at St Andrews with Pierre de Chastelard, 1563.

Four men playing a game of golf, from a *Book of Hours*, c.1520-30.

Oppositie: The Gentleman Golfers of Leith founded the first golf club in 1744 and petitioned the City of Edinburgh for a silver trophy to be won annually. Ever since then a silver ball has been attached to the award which records the name of each year's winner. This tradition still continues under the club's new name of the Honourable Company of Edinburgh Golfers.

'links', missing the flowing 'burn' but landing the ball in a 'bunker'. An iron, or 'irne' in Scots, means a sword or the blade of a plough. So thanks to Scotland, biblical swords can now be beaten beyond ploughshares into even more peaceful golfing irons.

For one of the earliest descriptions of golf in Scotland we must return to that sports-loving master of Aberdeen Grammar School, David Wedderburn, and his teach-yourself Latin primer *Vocabula*. Apart from describing Scottish soccer for us so forcefully, Wedderburn includes another sports section called *Baculus*. He connects the Latin word *baculus*, meaning a stick or staff, with the old Dutch word *kolf* meaning a 'club', to the word 'golf' in Scots. His description of the game includes mentions of golf balls, bunkers or sand traps, a bunker club, 'Good Shot' and the golf hole – although this reference to the all-important hole is not the earliest. The world's first mention of Scotland's unchallenged gift to the game of golf occurs a few years earlier, in 1625, when a local Aberdeen document discusses war games 'in the principal parts of the links betwixt the first hole and the Quenis [Queen's] hole'.

Golf really took off in 1744 when several 'Gentlemen of Honour', being 'skilful in the ancient and healthful exercise of Golfe', drew up the original thirteen rules. The Scots novelist Tobias Smollett writes about a game which ended swimmingly well on Leith Links in 1771:

> …a multitude of all ranks, from the senator of justice to the lowest tradesman, mingled together in their shirts and following the balls with the utmost eagerness. Such uninterrupted exercise, co-operating with the keen air from the sea, must steel the constitution against all the common attacks of distemper – despite many a player having gone to bed with the best part of a gallon of claret in his belly.

Despite carrying such a bellyful they called themselves 'the Honourable Company of Edinburgh Golfers' and petitioned Edinburgh city council to donate a silver trophy for an annual competition on Leith Links. The winner was declared 'Captain of the Golf' for the year, and a silver ball engraved with his name was ceremoniously attached to a silver club. There are now four such golf clubs, all garlanded with silver balls, given pride of place in the clubhouse of Muirfield at Gullane. Here on the coast south of Edinburgh The Honourable Company of Edinburgh Golfers had the great St Andrews golfer Tom Morris create a new course for them in 1891. In the years since, Muirfield has hosted fifteen Open Championships and their grand title still proudly defends their entrance gate.

I never had a hankering to play golf, despite growing up in Scotland just down the road from Bruntsfield Links, which is one of the oldest golf courses in the world. It wasn't until I was taught enough golf to look as though I could outwit the accomplished golfer Gert Frobe in *Goldfinger* that I got the bug. I began to take lessons on a course near the Pinewood film studios, and was immediately hooked on the game. Soon it would nearly take over my life. I began to see golf as a metaphor for living, for in golf you are basically on your own, competing against

yourself and always trying to do better. If you cheat, you will be the loser, because you are cheating yourself. When Ian Fleming portrayed Auric Goldfinger as a smooth cheater, James Bond had no regrets when he switched his golf balls, since to be cheated is the just reward of the cheater.

EXT. GOLFCOURSE – DAY

JAMES BOND spots GOLDFINGER cheating.

JAMES BOND
    You play a Slazenger 1, don't you?

AURIC GOLDFINGER
    Yes, why?

JAMES BOND
    This is a Slazenger 7.

JAMES BOND shows GOLDFINGER his own golf ball.

JAMES BOND
    Here's my Penfold Hearts. You must have played the wrong ball somewhere on the 18th fairway. We are playing strict rules, so I'm afraid you lose the hole and the match.

The Stoke Park Club at Stoke Poges stood in for Ian Fleming's Royal St George's for my movie encounter as 007 with Auric Goldfinger in 1964. It was a film that kindled my passion for golf which has never left me.

During the filming of *Goldfinger*, I learned the essential challenge of links golf in Royal Dornoch in the northeast Highlands. Ever since then I have been drawn to links golf and its enduring challenges, and I've learnt to play a variety of shots under constantly changing conditions. It's quite naked golf. There aren't many trees, or other features, to aid your alignment. Much is left to the imagination and to picturing the shot. Then there's the wind, always a factor on a links course. You're required to play run-up shots and to work the ball this way and that.

Within a few years of *Goldfinger*, my golf was good enough to play against professionals in competitions. I was invited to join one of Bing Crosby's show business amateur teams against professional golfers in America, which was an early forerunner of the Pro Ams. It gave me the idea of promoting a Pro Am tournament in Scotland to showcase our Scottish International Education Trust. Since one of its first board members, the shipbuilder Sir Iain Stewart, had fabulous connections in the world of golf, the planning of the event got off to a flying start. We settled on the out-and-back Ayrshire course of Royal Troon, and chose the week following the British Open. Since all the key players in the world would be congregating at St Andrews that year, travelling down to Troon from Fife would hardly be crossing the Atlantic. Because the Troon course had been having problems with encroaching tides and with crowd control, we recruited rugby players as volunteer policemen, who made a great job controlling the twenty thousand who came for the tournament. The amateurs included the comedian Jimmy Tarbuck, the soccerer Kenny Dalglish, the boxer Henry Cooper, along with Eric Sykes and me.

With Bing Crosby, Jackie Stewart and Phil Harris for my first International Pro-Celebrity Golf tournament at Gleneagles in August 1976.

Gathered around the prizes are Johnny Miller, Peter Alliss, Bruce Forsyth, Jimmy Tarbuck, Bing Crosby and Kevin Keegan.

Sponsors put up generous prizes and we allowed them to place their logo on the holes for £1000. Eagle Star Insurance took the first hole, which was a drivable par 4. But when two players in the first half-dozen holed out in an eagle 3 to each claim their prize of £500, Iain Stewart thought we'd all be left penniless. Fortunately only one more player holed out in 3. The tournament was a great success, with Christy O'Connor becoming the all-round winner, and it re-established Royal Troon as a venue for future Opens. In 1970 I won a trophy at a tournament in Morocco, La Coupe du Roi de Maroc. Then the next day I was drawn against a brilliant player who had won the women's trophy. That was Micheline Roquebrune. We were married one year later.

In the late 1960s, when I was mastering the game, a remarkable book came out, catching the spirit of the times. Michael Murphy's *Golf in the Kingdom* took the frustrations that often befall the average golfer and turned them into a mystical Zen experience. A young golfer takes lessons from a wily left-handed all-knowing professional called Shivas Irons. It's a name charged with meaning for the impressionable young man from California, straight out of college, on his way to seek enlightenment in India. Shivas is a seer who delivers golfing nuggets of Celtic wisdom in the spirit of a Zen master. His name comes from Aberdeenshire and could derive from the old Scots verb 'shiv', meaning to push or shove. Then there's the debatable phrase 'to be blown to smithereens', which he shifts to 'shivereens' so as to connect the name to Shiva – the ancient Hindu god of destruction. And redemption. So Murphy finds his shaman, not in an Indian ashram with his mystic guru Aurobindo, but out there on a golf course in the Scottish county of the Kingdom of Fife.

'Extraordinary powers are unleashed in a back-swing governed by true gravity,' says Shivas. 'If you practise the skill of the inner eye you put streamers of heart power for the ball to fly up on.' I thought Murphy was on to something. He was describing 'inner golf', that state of grace which every golfer aspires to but seldom reaches, when every stroke transcends past form. It's that feeling of a winning certainty which must happen in every sport when the player enters what Murphy calls 'the zone'. My friend Jackie Stewart confirmed this as a motor-racing champion, which I'll come to later.

As soon as I read *Golf in the Kingdom,* I thought of its visual possibilities on the screen. For years Clint Eastwood held the movie rights and serendipitously, in the spirit of the book, he had me down to play the enigmatic Shivas. For permission to film at the Royal and Ancient Golf Club at St Andrews I put him in touch with the Secretary, who Clint, given his title, may have thought held a more lowly position in this venerable club than he did. When he dropped in on the course by helicopter, the Secretary was less than impressed. This left little to discuss, and nothing much more was heard of Clint's plans. Sad, because a screen version of *Golf in the Kingdom* would have been a great double for me, combining my passions for golf and the movies, especially if we had been able to film at St Andrews. But as the hippy-trippy Sixties imploded into the cynical Seventies, *Golf in the Swingdom* – as one sneering reviewer in Scotland called it – Murphy's quirky vision, was soon lost in the rough for me.

Over the years golf has taught me much, and its implicit codes of conduct have provided me with the nearest I have ever come to religion. A golf player is on his honour to call a shot against himself and to be considerate to other players following up behind. I can illustrate this well from an incident I heard about when playing a round at Pine Valley, considered to be the finest golf course in America.

Cliff Robertson, a veteran golfer in his eighties who carried the whole history of Pine Valley on his shoulders, came up behind a foursome. Etiquette would have normally let him play through. He asked the caddie to ask permission for this from the foursome, but he returned to say that their answer was no. So he got on to his cart and went up to them.

'Before you say anything,' he told them, 'you have no standing. There is no one in front of you. Now *you* are not going through.' Then he turned to the caddie: 'Take all their bags back on the cart to the club house.'

'Hey, don't touch our clubs!' one protested.

'Who invited you?'

'Some member.'

'You will never set foot on Pine Valley in your lives again. And your friend is now barred from Pine Valley for a year. Now I would like to play through.'

What a marvellous lesson that was.

The Masters Tournament at Augusta National Golf Club has grown to be one of the finest golfing experiences in the world. It's reborn each spring with the blooming of the azaleas among its tree-lined fairways. The way the annual Masters is run is a model for golfers everywhere. There is no advertising on the entire golf course; not a placard to block the shrubs. Your cup of coffee costs you a dollar, for which you also get a piece of sausage and a bun subsidised by some company that's part of the golf course. Only six companies are allocated franchises there, and they don't advertise. It's a form of Utopia. The rules are fair. What does it create? Nobody has periscopes blocking the view. Spectators walk and never run. They are assigned a place and sit there with their chairs for the whole day. If someone moves, another can take that place. Nobody argues. It's how society should be, a lesson in community spirit which would have delighted Plato.

The Augusta National Golf Club was founded in 1934 in what was once a botanic plantation by Clifford Roberts and the legendary golfer Bobby Jones, who had won the Grand Slam in 1930 by winning the British Amateur, British Open, US Open, and US Amateur, all in the same year. Jones had a particular affection for St Andrews and the town in return made him a Freeman of the City, the second American to be so honoured after Benjamin Franklin in 1759. Emory University and the Georgia Institute of Technology in Atlanta now share a Bobby Jones scholarship programme with the University of St Andrews.

Bobby Jones first achieved fame at the East Lake Golf Club, which played a key role in the development of golf in America. But by the 1960s the surrounding community had become a victim of the civil strife that then enveloped Atlanta. Golfers began to be preyed on by drug-dealers, and thieves with guns would hold up players for money. Trapped in a cycle of poverty and crime, Eastlake became a veritable war zone, which the Atlanta police called 'Little Vietnam'. Then in 1993 Tom Cousins, a lifelong member of East Lake and one of the nation's top real-estate developers, created a charitable foundation. It purchased the dilapidated golf

Augusta National Golf Club, Georgia, USA. The Masters Tournament at Augusta National Golf Club has grown to be one of the finest golfing experiences in the world. It's reborn each spring with the blooming of the azaleas among its tree-lined fairways. The way the annual Masters is run is a model for golfers everywhere. There is no advertising on the entire golf course: not a placard to block the shrubs. Your cup of coffee costs you a dollar for which you get a piece of sausage and a bun subsidised by some company that is part of the golf course. Only six firms are allocated and they don't advertise. It's a form of Utopia. The rules are fair. What does it create? Nobody has a periscope blocking the view. Spectators walk and never run. They are assigned a place and sit there with their chairs for the whole day. If someone moves another can take that place. Nobody argues. It's how society should be, a lesson in community spirit which would have delighted Plato.

With Denis Zherebko and Sven Tumba ready to inaugurate Moscow's first golf course, during a break filming *The Russia House*, 1989.

club, and with much courage and extraordinary persistence Cousins and his foundation members set out to win the confidence of the community. Soon new homes were replacing the run-down tract houses built in the 1960s. The diverse mixed-income population now shares a common goal in bettering the community. With the East Lake Golf Club flourishing once again, the local community benefit from the proceeds of sponsored tournaments. The neighbourhood youth can now take part in a multitude of after-school opportunities. And in memory of Bobby Jones East Lake Golf Club sends £25,000 back each year to St Andrews.

I am always keen to slip away for a round of golf whenever a movie schedule makes it possible. When filming John le Carré's *The Russia House* in Moscow I was invited by that all-round sportsman Sven Tumba to play on the first golf course in the Soviet Union. This enterprising Swede had not only threaded his nine fairways around high-rise tenements within a ten-minute drive from Red Square, he had also founded a golf school. One of its most gifted students, the teenager Denis Zherebko, was ready to tee off with us to inaugurate the course in 1989. The Moscow City Club has since grown, with membership now every bit as expensive as its American counterparts. Having long banned the game in the Soviet Union for its bourgeois decadence, how Stalin would have scowled.

During the war, when the British Embassy was packed with Scots, the UK enjoyed remarkably close relations with the USSR. Bob Dunbar, the press officer who later ran the London Film School, told me how they would often break away from Foreign Office etiquette to sink a few drinks with such adversaries as the film director Sergei Eisenstein and even Stalin himself. The Ambassador, Sir Archibald Clerk Kerr, was a witty Australian Scot who had forged close relations with Stalin. When he left Moscow towards the end of the war he met his replacement, Sir Maurice Peterson, at the airport. 'How do you think you'll manage to get on with Stalin?' he asked the new Ambassador. 'Easy, old boy, I'll invite him out regularly for a round of golf.' In fact, this routine diplomat soon alienated the dictator.

Royal and Ancient Golf Club, St Andrews.

Fidel Castro in 1959 about to tee off for a round of golf in Cuba, as Che Guevara checks his swing. This revolutionary day was captured by Alberto Korda (Alberto Diaz Gutierre) whose photograph of Che remains one of the great icons of the twentieth century.

The nights of hard-drinking bonhomie were gone for ever. Stiff-upper-lipped diplomacy became the order of the day, as international relations began their slow freeze into the Cold War.

Not all Communists were so averse to golf. When President Eisenhower made the front page of the *New York Times* by hitting a hole-in-one, Fidel Castro was driven to ask Che Guevara to teach him the game. 'He had been a caddie once to earn some money in his spare time,' the Cuban President remembered. 'I, on the other hand, knew absolutely nothing about this expensive sport.' Expensive sport or not, Cuba now boasts a world-class eighteen-hole golf course at the beach resort of Varadero. Through an improbable international sports initiative, Cubans are now being coached by British golfers in exchange for Cubans training British teams in baseball. Whoever brokered that one must surely deserve promotion.

The Vatican of golf is the Royal and Ancient Golf Club of St Andrews because it established the rules of golf in 1754. Some ten years later the number of holes at St Andrews was reduced from twenty-two to eighteen, and slowly over the years golf courses around the world fell into line. With a worldwide membership of 2400, the R&A is among the hardest golf clubs in the world to join. Fortunately, when Sir Iain Stewart was Captain of the R&A he proposed me. I was able to do the same for my old friend the world-champion racing driver Jackie Stewart, who can now proudly sport the R&A necktie. Its emblem depicts St Andrew bearing the saltire cross on which he was crucified. 'Only the Scots would have thought of celebrating a national game,' said the golfer and broadcaster Alistair Cooke, 'with the figure of a tortured saint.'

Golf has greatly enhanced my life. Through golfing I have met remarkable people, some of whom have been truly inspirational. It was through golf that I met Sir Iain Stewart who pioneered new industrial relations on the Clyde, which opened my mind to the possibility of political change. I met the flying ace Douglas Bader

Douglas Bader driving off at Gleneagles.

on the golf course. He never let the loss of his legs affect his game, eventually getting his handicap down to an extraordinary five. Long before the aerial Battle of Britain he had lost both legs in a flying accident. To the Germans he became a legend, because every time they shot him down he escaped. His last camp commandant finally clipped his wings by locking away his prosthetic legs.

Once after a good round at Gleneagles, Douglas invited me for tea to meet someone very special. Marilyn Carr was sitting on a chair. I went forward and shook hands with her feet. She had no hands, no arms. She served us tea with her feet, warmly welcoming us at the same time, as though this was the most natural thing in the world to do. Marilyn told me how she had appeared with Douglas in the documentary film *Two of a Kind* in 1971. *Look No Hands!*, Marilyn's autobiography recounting her triumph over her disability, was published in 1982, the year that she played a key role in the creation of the Douglas Bader Memorial Garden in Cupar, Fife. Years later, on the day I was awarded the Freedom of the City of Edinburgh in 1991, there was an envelope waiting for me at the Usher Hall. Marilyn had sent me this most moving poem:

The honour you are receiving is one that is long overdue,
You are a credit to Scotland, I was so proud when I met you.
It was in a suite at Gleneagles, while playing your favourite sport,
You took time out to chat with me, a kindness I never forgot.
I know you won't remember, how could you, the people you meet,
One thing however may ring a bell, I wrote for you with my feet.
I'd love to be in the Usher Hall, as I have followed your career
But I'll be here in Dundee, so far, and yet so near.
I hope your day is wonderful from beginning to its end;
I wish for you on this special day, Good luck, Good bye, your friend
                                                            Marilyn Carr

The Douglas Bader Foundation had initiated a support system for those who had lost limbs, or had been born without them. When the young David Murray came round in hospital and found that he had lost both legs in a near-fatal car accident, the first outside offer of help came from Douglas. This meant so much to David that he eventually founded the Murray Foundation to help amputees lead the fullest life possible.

Whenever I come back to Edinburgh David meets me at the airport and usually takes me for a drive and a chat. Once he asked me if I wouldn't mind coming with him to visit someone very special at the Astley Ainsley Hospital.

'Oh, Olivia Giles is not here,' said the receptionist. 'She's down in the bar with her mother and granny.' When we entered the room, there was this tiny woman. She was sitting on a little box, with four wheels. Olivia was quite surprised that I knew her name. She had no hands and no feet, just stumps covered with socks. Looking at her I didn't think that she could survive. It was only three weeks since her operation. 'Get this,' David said. 'There's no fucking dignity.' God, that's brutish, I thought, but David had been there too. Without limbs, how do you function? Think of going to the toilet. How can you ever lead a normal life?

Olivia was a very successful lawyer in Edinburgh. One day she was struck by flu, or so she thought. She kept on working by taking pills. Her doctor failed to recognise that her flu-like symptoms, when combined with splitting headaches and itchy hands and feet, could lead to something far more sinister. When she collapsed into a semi-coma, Olivia was finally diagnosed with meningococcal septicaemia, a vicious form of B-strain meningitis. By the time she reached Edinburgh Royal Infirmary, her limbs had grown gangrenous. Amputation was the only way to prevent the disease spreading and so save her life.

Months after our encounter Olivia got back in touch to say how well everything was now going. Her boyfriend had stuck by her, and she was soon going to Rome to just walk around the city. With her prosthetic feet and hands she was happy to walk taller, as she now had longer legs. When Olivia heard that research into meningitis was starved of cash, she organised a Leap Year Ball and asked me to be its patron. Her 'Leap for Meningitis' Ball on 29 February 2004 was a huge success, raising around £500,000 for vaccine research.

The next time we met, Olivia had re-learnt to drive. She had recently passed her test and had bought a car – a Porsche. She was a little scared, to start with. But since it was the middle of the day, with not much traffic about, she took my advice and had an easy drive over the Forth Bridge to St Andrews. After a relaxing tea she drove back effortlessly.

Olivia now works tirelessly to raise awareness about meningitis. Fees from her many television and radio broadcasts continue to help fund research into this often fatal disease. Her courage in leading as normal a life as possible, after such a catastrophe, is an inspiration to everyone she meets. Her advice to anyone who suffers loss of limbs is, 'Be who you are first; don't let your disability define you.' I don't see her so often, but I hear from David that she cooks, gives dinner parties and lives the most normal life possible. 'I greatly admire David Murray,' Olivia told me, 'because nobody ever says that he has done well *as a disabled person*. He is thought of first and foremost as a successful self-made businessman.' In 2006 the Murray Foundation won the Queen's award for voluntary service. Each year it hosts the Scottish Amputee Open Golf Championships. Any golfer can enter who has suffered the loss of a limb, through accident, illness or birth. I think it's just great that golf is here to the fore again.

'It's extremely, extremely mental. It's a kind of winter golf,' said the Canadian writer William Mitchell, who had his own ideas on what makes curlers tick. Who knows when and where curling on ice arose? In medieval Scotland, when lochs would freeze over for at least four months each winter, it's not hard to imagine the thrill of sending river stones twisting and grumbling over uneven ice. The first stones were loofies, from 'loofy', the Scots for a palm, since they were no bigger than the size of a hand. Curlers would leave their stones on the ice and many were lost, only to be rediscovered centuries later. When an old pond at Dunblane was drained two stones emerged dated 1511, the earliest curling stones to be discovered anywhere. Known as 'kuting stones', they were larger than loofies with

Winter Sports on Duddingston Loch.
Charles Altamount Doyle's extraordinary painting of 1876 catches the chaotic fun of Victorian winter sports, where skaters buzz dangerously around curlers over the crowded ice on Edinburgh's Duddingston Loch. Perhaps with some detective work the painter's young son Conan Doyle can be picked out, pictured somewhere in this mêlée.

hollows on each side for a good grip to help propel them across the ice, although these crude stones would not have been able to curl to reach their marks. It was only when handles were added to skilfully crafted circular stones that any degree of accuracy in plotting curving or curling paths was achieved.

What makes a perfect curling stone? Apart from its shock-absorbing toughness and abrasion resistance, the stone must have negligible water absorption. Otherwise, the water-to-ice-to-water expansion and contraction would soon cause small granite particles to break off and pit the rock. That's why the little island of Ailsa Craig in the Firth of Clyde is so famous in curling circles. Its dense fine-grained granite is literally unbeatable.

For my grandfather Joseph Connery, along with so many others escaping poverty in rural Ireland, Ailsa Craig was known affectionately as 'Paddy's Rock', a milestone on his way to seek employment in the workshops of Victorian Glasgow. Its towering cliffs and ruined castle reveal Ailsa Craig to be a fortress island, a place of refuge through the ages for monks and smugglers. Today it's the haunt of sea-birds as its name suggests in Gaelic – 'Ailishair-a-Chuain', the rock of seabirds. John Keats wrote of it:

Hearken, thou craggy ocean-pyramid!
Give answer from thy voice – the sea-fowls' screams!…
…Drowned wert thou till an earthquake made thee steep;
Another cannot wake thy giant size.

Ailsa Craig is now a protected island. So many circular stones had been quarried from its cliffs and the little island was so holed out that it was in danger of looking like a giant Gruyère cheese. Now only the existing boulders can be shipped across the Firth. The south end of the island yields the common speckled granite, whereas the rarer 'blue hone' rock is collected with increasing difficulty from the north. Master masons at Kays at Mauchline on the Ayrshire coast then begin the long process of turning the tough granite boulders into curling stones. It is a difficult rock to work and distinctive enough to be given its own geological name, Ailsite. Unlike most granites, the fine-grain Ailsite splits in all directions. Once the stones are brought to an approximate finished weight, they are polished and the striking bands added. Each stone is carefully machined and balanced into masterpieces of tooled geology. After the aluminium goose-neck handles are fixed, the 42–44 pound stone leaves its workbench to slide magisterially over the ice, as a true-running, balanced, gold-medal Ailsa stone.

Rocks of Ailsite have landed up as far away as Wales, carried down by glaciers in the last ice age. Or could other, more dynamic, forces be at work? Ailsite stones are now found scattered across the world. When one of them curled across the ice to win a gold medal for four remarkable Scotswomen at the 2002 Winter Olympics in Salt Lake City, the world took curling to its heart. It made Scotland an international superpower in sports – well, at least for a day. Just what would Robert Burns and Sir Walter Scott have made of those winning women curlers, for both these powerful Scotsmen held the noble 'roarrring game' to be the most 'manly Scottish exercise'.

The noble ice sport is now the fastest-growing game in Canada, where over a million women and men of all ages curl. Given the chance, any one of them would consider selling their soul to the Devil to win the Brier, the top award in Canadian curling. That's the prize on offer in William Mitchell's hilarious story, *The Black*

Rhona Martin, the skip, surrounded by her gold medallists, Margaret Morton from Ayr, Debbie Knox from Fife, Fiona MacDonald and Janice Rankin from Inverness. Cheered to the skies on the Olympic ice of Salt Lake City in 2002, when the Scots team won Britain's first Winter Olympic medal in eighteen years.

The Winning Shot, Duddingston Loch, Charles Altamont Doyle.

Bonspiel of Wullie MacCrimmon. Wullie's only active religion is curling, which he plays fanatically in a small town in Alberta. One day on the curling rink, the Devil, a keen player himself, makes a Faustian pact with Wullie, promising him that he will win the Brier on his death if he'll come and curl with him in Hell. Wullie agrees on condition that he can save his soul if his rink can beat the Devil's rink in a challenge match. So Wullie and his friends, including the Reverend Pringle, take on the Devil's crew of Judas Iscariot, Macbeth and Guy Fawkes in a matter of afterlife and death. To discover what happens next, you must read Mitchell's book or visit the Red Deer centre in Alberta, where the ongoing saga surrounds the curling rink in witty murals.

In the days of long cold winters, Scotland could count on curling for four months a year on frozen lochs. Great competitions, known as 'bonspiels', mustered thousands on to the ice. The name bonspiel suggests that the game's origins derive from a continental melange of the *bon*, or good, of French with the *spiel*, or game, of Dutch or German. Whatever its origins, the bonspiel, or the good game, became Scotland's national sport.

Bonspiels in eighteenth-century Scotland celebrated the revolutionary slogans of the day – Liberty, Fraternity and Equality. Curling offered universal brotherhood, once you were initiated on to the ice by the Curlers' Court. A ceremony of clearly pagan origins continues to this day, where novices are 'made' curlers after negotiating a welter of bewilderingly inane indignities. Clutching curling stones, the kneeling supplicants first take an oath of allegiance. Then the Laird of the Ice, wearing his eagle-feathered tammy, demands that the blindfolded apprentice curlers navigate a number of bizarre challenges. They are forced to wear humiliating fancy dresses, each tailored to ridicule their professions.

The Dutch master Pieter Bruegel, 1525-69, features a sport very similar to curling in his well-known picture *Hunters in the Snow* which shows *eisschiessen* or 'ice shooting'. This game which originated in Bavaria was played with a long stick-like handle and is still enjoyed today.

The event can rapidly become a circus of Federico Fellini excess. An airline pilot is rushed down the ice for a phantom take-off, as his mocked-up aircraft wings waggle from his naked midriff. The arms of an electrician leap up when a hand-cranked electrical generator delivers shocks. When the Duke of Edinburgh volunteered to go through such an initiation in the Highlands, the unsettling demands made on him were so outrageous that he flew off the ice in raging disbelief.

When the Curlers' Court judges the by now humiliated candidates to have accomplished their tasks, the Laird of the Ice asks them all a string of unanswerable questions. Whatever they answer, he demands that each donates a fine to fill the curlers' 'stoop'. Finally, when everyone has drained a quaich of lethal 'curler's brew', the novitiates, now with their sight restored, are declared 'made' curlers. From then on they will all be considered as equals on the ice.

As curling grew ever more popular in Scotland, the Duddingston Club outside Edinburgh was the first to bring order to the often random chaos of an ever growing sport by laying down the first-ever rules of curling. They became the basis for the national rules drawn up thirty years later by the Grand Curling Club in 1838.

One of the world's last great bonspiels took place on the ice at Idaburn Dam at Oturehua in New Zealand. It brought to a glorious end the great communal activities of the Victorian bonspiel, which included skating, Highland dancing and general revelry around groaning boards of food and drink. From then on curling would retreat indoors. Curiously, it would be the desperately cold winters in Canada and the return of warm winters in Scotland that drove curling under roofs. Indoor rinks, combined with modern ice-making technology, brought the sport closer to an art form. Random ice-bumps and unpredictable snowfalls had always made curling more of a game of chance. It's now a game of skill enjoyed by millions. With its linear velocity the stone rushes forward, but the skill of the curler sends it into a spin. It's this angular velocity around its centre of gravity that gives the stone the 'hook' at the end of its run. A fast-spinning rock doesn't grab the ice surface as hard as a slowly curling stone – hence there's less curl.

The forces that make rocks curl depend on friction. The pressure of a heavy rock melts the ice surface, creating a thin film of water enabling the rock to move. The Zen of curling is about 'riding the pebble'. Before each game, a light spray of water droplets is applied to the surface of the ice to create a mosaic of tiny ice pebbles. The scatter of little ice pebbles means that only a portion of the stone is in contact with the ice, enabling it to follow predictable paths. Apart from clearing the path of any debris, forceful sweeping in front of a running stone warms the ice slightly, allowing the stone to travel and curl further by reducing friction. The idea is to end up with one or more stones closest to the 'button', or bull's-eye, at the far end of the ice sheet. This is accomplished by deft 'throwing' (sliding) and, more important, by guarding one's position against 'take-outs' (hits from your opponent's stones). The best games are decided by the final, sometimes dazzling, multiple carom shots, which suddenly knock apparent winners out of contention and leave new stones on or near the button.

Whatever mysteries of the game others might hold dear, nothing could have been more confounding than what the young Queen Victoria and her consort Prince Albert witnessed on a hot summer's day at Scone in 1842. For there in the long gallery of Scone Palace the carpet had been lifted to provide a curling rink. No stone had ever been thrown in such luxurious surroundings as it slid its way down the polished floor past the ancestral portraits of the Earls of Mansfield. The ancient game won the highest accolade a monarch could bestow. Scotland's once mere Grand Curling Club would now be known as the Royal Caledonian Curling Club. And it remains the curling governing body to this day. The day the Queen and Prince Albert were initiated into the mysteries of Scotland's ancient winter game at Scone Palace was a day not without irony. For it was from here in 1296 that her predecessor, King Edward I, stole Scotland's ancient Stone of Destiny over which the kings of Scots were crowned. Edward carried it off to London and had it installed in Westminster Abbey under the Coronation Chair.

Jacob got up early in the morning and took the stone that he had placed under his head. He stood it up as a pillar and poured oil on top of it. He named the place God's Temple (Beth El).

Genesis 28: 18–19

Scone's most ancient legend makes the crowning stone the pillow on which the Old Testament patriarch Jacob slept before communing with God in a dream. Another myth claims that the stone was brought from Ireland in the sixth century as the travelling altar of St Columba. On firmer ground it's held that the kings of Scotland were crowned on it at Scone outside Perth ever after the coronation of Kenneth MacAlpin in 847. When I received an honorary degree from the University of St Andrews I learnt that a former professor of geology had analysed the present Stone. In a learned paper he described it as 'coarse sandstone with porphyry inclusions', and even matched it to an outcrop two miles up the hill from Scone. Does this scotch the claims for its origins in the Holy Land, or merely add weight to the conspiracy theorists who claim that the real Stone was switched when King Edward took it south to Westminster in 1296?

Then there was the great heist of Christmas Day 1950 when four Scottish students broke the Stone out from under the Westminster Coronation Chair and spirited it back to Scotland in two pieces. The Stone was soon repaired in Glasgow's Sauchiehall Street by Robert Gray of Gray's Monumental Sculptors (not even Henry Moore ever called himself that). After leading the police on the wildest of goose chases, the Stone of Scone was placed on the altar of Arbroath Abbey from where the famous Declaration of Arbroath had asserted Scottish independence in 1320. For years Bob Gray used to amuse his friends by rattling a fragment of the true Stone in a Bluebell matchbox. Could he too have swapped the Stone of Destiny before its return? When asked, all he ever gave back was a wry smile. Although the students were all eventually rounded up no charges were ever brought. The law student Ian Hamilton argued that in order for a successful prosecution the Crown would first have to establish its rightful ownership. Nearly

The Long Gallery, Scone Palace, Perthshire. Queen Victoria and Prince Albert asked the Earl of Mansfield about the mysteries of curling on a summer's day in 1842. With a lack of ice and great ingenuity, the polished floor of Scone Palace's long picture gallery was pressed into action for a demonstration of the roaring game. As a result of this bizarre display the Queen granted a charter to the Royal Caledonian Curling Club, the mother club of the sport and the governing body of curling in Scotland.

The Stone of Destiny returns to Scotland in its hastily fabricated Stone Mobile in November 1996 escorted by Royal Archers.

The Stone of Destiny, Edinburgh Castle. Surely the destiny of the Stone, yearning for the throne over which the kings of Scotland were crowned, deserves better than this. St Edward's Chair in Westminster Abbey now lacks the Stone of Destiny it was designed to enthrone, ever since King Edward stole it south in 1296. Wouldn't it be courteous to send the chair, which had held the Stone for over eight hundred years, up to Scotland too?

fifty years later the Scottish Secretary of State Michael Forsyth thought that the return of the Stone might help to reverse the destiny of the Tory party in Scotland, which by 1996 was at an all-time low in the dying embers of John Major's government. With the permission of the Queen and to the fury of the Dean of Westminster Abbey, the old stone of fortune was levered out from under King Edward's chair and taken north.

So on 15 November 1996, with great pomp and somewhat questionable circumstance, the Stone of Destiny was processed up the Royal Mile towards Edinburgh Castle in a hastily put together 'Stonemobile'. Many in the crowd of ten thousand were puzzled as it passed, for how do you cheer or applaud a passing stone? Once it was installed on its castle cheeseboard, Prince Andrew welcomed the Stone's safe return to Scotland after over seven hundred years in a ceremony which owed much to a Marx Brothers' extravaganza. Rufus T. Firefly of Freedonia comes to mind. A twenty-one-gun salute then thundered from the battlements of the Moon Battery, to be echoed by HMS *Newcastle* lying anchored off Leith in the Firth of Forth. Few invent traditions as innovative as the Scots.

But what about that other roarrring game? 'As you accelerate down the straight, faces in the crowd cease to blur and appear to hover in front of you as you fly past them,' is how the three-times world champion Jackie Stewart describes the phenomenon. 'It's that inner force again, an almost transcendental moment when you know that you're driving at your unbeatable best. Somehow the clarity of those frozen faces signals that you're powered up to win. A little slower, a little faster, and you lose them.'

Cars were Jackie's passion at school before he left at sixteen to work in his father's garage at Dunbarton near Loch Lomond. At school he struggled to keep up with the other pupils, but under the hydraulic jacks, working with the other motor mechanics, he began to regain his confidence. "You see, I thought I was just stupid, dumb or thick because I couldn't spell or read like others,' Jackie remembers. 'It wasn't until my two sons Paul and Mark were both assessed as dyslexics that I realised, at the age of forty-two, the reason for my perceived "stupidity".' Since then Jackie has campaigned to raise awareness of 'word blindness'; diagnosing it early can greatly boost a youngster's confidence. He became president of the charity Dyslexia Scotland in 2004, which the Scottish government helped to fund. 'We still have a long and winding road to go,' said Jackie at its launching. 'No one should go through the educational dramas in their life that I did.'

Jackie was inspired to get into international motor racing by Jim Clark. 'Jimmy Clark was one of my best friends,' Jackie continued. 'He was also the best racing driver that I ever raced against. He was a natural, a mild and modest but extraordinarily talented Scotsman. He combined smoothness, precision and persistence. For me he was the complete racing driver; a driver's driver. The complete gentleman to race with.' As well as being world champion and winning twenty-five Grand Prix races, Clark was the first Scot to win the Indianapolis 500, in 1965. This was a feat that no foreigner had achieved in nearly fifty years. For the next four years Clark dominated international racing. And when he wasn't on the

Known as the Flying Scot, Jim Clark is still the only driver to win both the Formula 1 championship and Indianapolis 500 in the same year.

circuit he would return to farm in the Scottish Borders.

In 2007 another flying Scot, Dario Franchitti, would follow Jim Clark's feat by winning the Indianapolis 500. 'When I didn't win in '05, forty years after Jimmy Clark's great win, I was so upset,' Dario told the packed Indianapolis press conference. 'Especially since my old boss Jackie Stewart was there. But today I am in shock. Especially when I see all those names on that Indy trophy and all the great guys that should be on there. It's a humbling experience.' And to think that Dario won that race fuelled on alcohol – 100 per cent renewable energy.

Phil Hill, America's first and only world racing champion, admired the assurance of the quiet, shy Scot. 'Jimmy was a most naturally talented driver,' Phil told me as we snaked around California's Pebble Beach in his 1928 Bugatti. 'Jimmy combined craftsmanship with a mastery of race strategy. In close racing you knew his intentions at every turn – overtaking or slipstreaming on a high-speed circuit.' Then in that fateful year of 1968, taking part in a meaningless race on the badly maintained Hockenheim circuit in Germany, Clark's Formula Two Lotus careered off into a copse of fir trees at 150 miles per hour. He died instantly. He was just thirty-two.

Jimmy Clark was not the only friend Jackie Stewart lost in those dangerous years of open-wheeled Formula One racing of the late Sixties. As you left the pits the nervous reply to 'See you later' was always 'Hope so.' 'To be a racing driver between 1963 and 1973 was to accept not the possibility but the probability of death,' Jackie recalls in his autobiography. He nearly lost his own life, trapped in his crashed BRM and drenched in petrol during the 1966 Belgian Grand Prix. Jackie insisted, often against powerful commercial interests, on introducing car and circuit safety measures. Car seatbelts, full-face helmets, flame-protection tracksuits and circuit guard-rails are now mandatory, largely as a result of his relentless campaigning.

Up until he retired in 1973, Jackie Stewart was Formula One racing. His twenty-seven Grand Prix wins even eclipsed Clark's extraordinary run. What's

Jackie Stewart competed in Formula 1 between 1965 and 1973, winning three World Championships.

Dario Franchitti, winning the 91st Indianapolis 500 at the Indianapolis Motor Speedway on 28 May 2007.

always intrigued me is how Jimmy Clark and Jackie Stewart would have fared on the world racing circuits had the Hockenheim tragedy not intervened. When Stewart entered Formula One racing, Clark was at the very top of his form. What a spectacle that would have been, with a run of double Scots Grand Prix.

Thomas Lipton's magnificent obsession was competitive sailing. His life's ambition was to win the America's Cup; to wrest the 'Auld Mug' – as he called it – from its plinth in the New York Yacht Club. Born in Glasgow in 1850 to impoverished Irish immigrant parents, Thomas Lipton left school at ten. At fifteen he stowed away on board ship to America. When he returned five years later, brimming with American business flair, he set up a grocery empire which was so successful that by thirty he was a millionaire. He made his fortune by acquiring tea estates in Sri Lanka. Lipton's Brisk tea brand was as great on taste as on price. By cutting out the middle-man he made tea Britain's national tipple. And then to cap it all, he discovered the teabag. It made him the first tea tycoon. 'I knew as much about tea-planting,' he said, 'as Euclid knew about motoring.' But beyond his brilliant business sense, what he really knew most about was sailing.

Although he was knighted by Queen Victoria and became a frequent sailing buddy of King George V, the Royal Yacht Squadron continually blackballed Lipton's membership of this strictly gentlemen's club. 'There goes the King's grocer,' said one naval bigot from the Cowes clubhouse, as the *Britannia* sailed past them with Lipton and George V on board. But the defiant Tommy, as the Americans called him, sidestepped such mindless snobbery. To challenge the America's Cup he became a member of an Irish yacht club, the Royal Ulster, and ordered another J Class yacht from his fine shipbuilders Camper & Nicholson. He called them all *Shamrock*, for Irish luck, and ordered a fifth at the cost of £30,000.

Thomas Lipton's J Class yacht *Shamrock V* in full sail.

'I will try again,' said Sir Thomas Lipton after failing for the fith time to win the America's Cup or 'The Auld Mug', as he called it affectionately. Nevertheless he was hailed in American yachting circles as 'the world's most cheerful loser'.

When the 125-foot *Shamrock V* was launched in 1929 she had a crew of nineteen. But his tea fortune was no match for the oil and railway millions of a Rockefeller or a Vanderbilt. 'Never Despair. Keep pushing on,' was Lipton's defiant motto.

For his five heroic attempts to win the America's Cup and for being such a great sport, Cornelius Vanderbilt presented Tommy with a gold souvenir trophy, paid for by public subscription.

'In defeat lies the test of the true sportsman,' said Vanderbilt. 'You have proved to be a wonderful sportsman; quite the finest it has ever been our good fortune to race against.'

'Although I have always lost,' replied Tommy, almost too choked for words, 'you make me think that I've won. But I will try again. Yes, I will try again.'

Now, even Cowes relented and the great challenger was finally made a member of this exclusive club, just a few months before he died in 1931. Sixty years later the Thomas J. Lipton Company bought back *Shamrock V*, and after a four-year refit presented her to the Newport Museum of Yachting in Rhode Island. Now *Shamrock*'s towering sails can unfurl again. This most graceful of yachts may not have been the fastest, but she was certainly the most beautiful J Class yacht ever built. *Shamrock V* can now be yours, fully crewed for a week, for much the same sum Tommy shelled out to have her built way back in 1929.

Although Scotland may now have sunk low in the world's soccer ranking, perhaps we can take some credit, in the name of Archie McLean, that Brazil is still at number one. But hope is not lost. Our tradition of invention has brought a new sport into being, which allows me to end this chapter on a triumphant note. Scotland is now the world's most frequent top nation in elephant polo, a game that James Manclark, a Scots landowner and former bobsleigh and toboggan champion, developed as long ago as 1983!

Elephant polo was developed by James Manclark, a Scots landowner and former bobsleigh and toboggan champion. With his friend Jim Edwards, the owner of the Tiger Tops safari estate in Nepal, they adapted the rules of equestrian polo to allow four aside elephants to play two chukkas of ten minutes each. Local riders or 'mahouts' steer the elephants with their feet, as they ride ahead of the players leaning over the wide girth of the elephant swinging a 12-foot polo stick.

13 FILM
The heart in darkness

Film comes from the Celtic 'Felmen' – the cream of the milk.
Paul Knoche, *Der Rohfilm*, 1922

It has always amused me that the American cinema was born of a sniff-and-snuff movie. The sniff was *Fred Ott's Sneeze* (1894), a brief five seconds of cinematic wonder in the wake of a pinch of snuff. Known to film historians under its less catchy title of the *Edison Kinetoscopic Record of a Sneeze*, its director was William Kennedy Laurie Dickson. Although he was born in France, his Scottish ancestry stretched all the way back to that seventeenth-century beauty Anna Laurie, the 'Bonnie Annie Laurie' of fame and song.

Dickson had been developing his camera and projection system for the Edison Company in New Jersey since 1883, and took his first bow on screen in 1891 in what is now the earliest surviving American motion picture screened publicly. His many cinematic innovations include the 35mm celluloid strip with twin sprocket holes, which remains the film standard to this day. When Thomas Edison returned from Europe in 1895, Dickson even surprised him with a sound film.

Although a short film survived of Dickson playing his violin, the sound was lost and some thought that it had never existed. But when a broken wax cylinder was found in the early 1960s in a canister in the Edison music room and skilfully pieced together, a melodious violin was heard above the cracks and hissing. Later in 1998, with much digital ingenuity, Walter Murch, that Oscar-winning film editor extraordinary, miraculously married the music to the surviving film. For the first time in over a century Dickson's violin could now be heard as well as seen, playing one of the hits of the day in the world's first film musical, all of twenty-two seconds long.

Not only has this minifilm been claimed as the first sound film but it has also, rather more controversially, been outed as the first gay film. To show the stunning

effect of movement when combined with sound, Dickson played his violin as two of his Edison colleagues danced around in a circle. In his book *The Celluloid Closet*, Vito Russo sees those two men waltzing as the first evidence of homosexuality on the screen. Gay or straight, we'll never know, for the cinema like all the arts is open to endless interpretation in the eyes of viewers. When caught short of female company on an all-male dance floor in Morocco, during a night off during the making of *The Man Who Would Be King*, I asked Michael Caine if I could dance with his driver, since mine was no Nijinsky. I now wonder how our dance would have been interpreted had it ever been filmed?

Scotland provided the subject for America's first feature film, *The Execution of Mary Stuart*, with Mary played by a man, at least up until the final cut. This created a far greater shock on its first screening in 1895 than Lumière's train achieved that same year when it puffed into a French seaside station in front of a sophisticated Paris audience in a Champs Élysées café. It was one thing to fear a steam locomotive crashing into your room; quite another to believe that an actor had literally died on stage for your cinematic pleasure.

Dickson's *Fred Ott's Sneeze*, which he followed with his acclaimed sequel *Fred Ott Holding a Bird*, came to represent a film genre which John Grierson, some thirty years later, would call 'documentary'. From Mary's disturbing execution a cinema of the imagination would emerge, with actors, soon to be extended into feature films. As film production developed, these two strands of film-making would run in parallel to make a genuine evening of entertainment at the cinema. Documentaries, newsreels, cartoons, trailers, serials, short films, both

Opposite: *Fred Ott's Sneeze*, 1894. The first motion picture copyrighted in the United States was one of Thomas Edison's assistant's sneezing filmed by William Kennedy Laurie Dickson, 1860-1935.

Left: The Arrival of a Train at La Ciotat Station, filmed by the Lumière Brothers, 1895.

Right: Experimental Sound Film, 1895, William Kennedy Laurie Dickson. In this short Kinetoscope–Kinetophone film developed by the multi-talented Dickson, the sound was derived from a cylinder-playing gramophone. Dickson was an accomplished violinist and played the bacarolle from the once-popular comic opera *The Bells of Normandy* by Robert Planquette.

Left: Frank Lloyd, 1886-1960. One of the most prolific directors in early Hollywood, the Glasgow-born Lloyd was a co-founder of the Academy of Motion Picture Arts and Sciences, and a recipient of three of its first Oscars.

Right: Charlie Chaplin,1889-1977, often cast himself against the formidable Eric Campbell, 1878-1917, who fully filled the role of a menacing Scots bruiser.

factual and fictional, along with a second feature, or B movie, would run before the main attraction.

Many Scots were in at the beginnings of Hollywood. Charlie Chaplin's menacing fall-guy in many of his early shorts was the gigantic bearded Eric Campbell from the West of Scotland. Tragically, Campbell died in a head-on car crash before he was forty at the height of his fame. This almost forgotten comedy star was profiled in *Chaplin's Goliath* (1996), one of Kevin Macdonald's early documentaries.

Scotland's most prolific film director was Frank Lloyd. Born in 1886 into a music-hall family in Cambuslang, Glasgow, and a performer on stage by the age of fifteen, by 1913 he was acting in Hollywood, where he soon began to write and direct silent films. His early successes, featuring the star of the day William Farnum, included *A Tale of Two Cities* and *Les Misérables*, which established him as a dependable director. Lloyd was one of the founders of the Academy of Motion Picture Arts and Sciences in 1927. Within two years he had won an Oscar for his Nelson and Emma Hamilton biopic *The Divine*, and by 1935 he had won two more for Noël Coward's *Cavalcade* and *Mutiny on the Bounty*. Later he produced such notable titles as Alfred Hitchcock's *Saboteur* (1942). What is so astonishing is that Lloyd, who made a staggering 157 films earning fourteen Oscar nominations, is now a largely forgotten figure. And to think that he was famous for forty-five years.

From the earliest days of cinema a fascination with Scottish historical themes fed the appetites of Hollywood. Macabre shockers, or what Robert Louis Stevenson called 'regular crawlers', were especially popular. Not counting numerous shorts, five feature versions of *Dr Jekyll and Mr Hyde* were produced in

Whisky of his Ancestors, 1898, stole a scene from Gilbert and Sullivan's *Ruddigore* to become Dewar's most successful whisky commercial. As a kilted laird in his castle reaches for his bottle, the portraits come alive and climb down from their frames to share his ancestral dram. 'Keep advertising and advertising will keep you,' was the whisky distiller Tommy Dewar's philosophy. He commissioned the first-known drink film commercial which featured dancing Scotsmen in full Highland dress. When projected high up in New York's Herald Square, it brought traffic to a standstill.

Hollywood between 1912 and 1941, though none surpassed Fredric March's Oscar-winning performance and his menacing facial transformation in Rouben Mamoulian's production of 1931.

Scotland's ever-searching film ferret, the indefatigable archivist Janet McBain, lists seven *Macbeth*s produced in the first two decades of the twentieth century, nine titles based on Walter Scott's *Waverley* novels, and at least twenty kilted loonies of which my favourite title is *McNab's Visit to London* of 1905. In a dazzlingly daft burst of music-hall surrealism, a Highlander dives after his lost golf ball only to emerge kiltless from a fireplace to bamboozle a maid. The earliest Scottish music-hall artist to have survived on film is not Harry Lauder but his mentor, the kilt- and plaid-bedecked W. F. Frame, who was known on the Glasgow stage as 'yon wee daft particle'.

The tempestuous life of Mary Queen of Scots became the subject of many sequels. Ever since I first saw John Ford's romanticised *Mary of Scotland*, with the glamorous Katharine Hepburn playing the lead and Fredric March as Bothwell, I've harboured a soft spot for the doomed queen. But just like Shakespeare's *Macbeth*, which has also spawned numerous features, the realities of history have never hampered the imaginative vision of directors, especially beyond the English-speaking world, from Russia to Japan.

Alexander Mackendrick, the director of such classics as *The Ladykillers* and *Sweet Smell of Success*, spent years trying to bring his own gritty vision of 'Mary Queen of Scots' to the screen. Few films had been produced in Scotland up to that time without a heady draught of sickening schmaltz. Mackendrick always dreamed of correcting this, of making a historical film which would explore the dichotomies of Scottish life in the traumatic wake of the Reformation and the dilemmas faced by the Catholic Queen in John Knox's Protestant Scotland. Finally, after many false starts Mackendrick, armed with a well carpentered screenplay by James Kennaway, got the green light from Universal Studios in 1969.

Mackendrick wanted to recreate the impoverished Scotland of the grim sixteenth century where, far removed from the scenes depicted in tapestries on castle walls, the poor scuttled searching for food over filthy middens. Kennaway, whose adaptation of *Tunes of Glory* – on the class conflicts within a Scottish regiment – had already won him an Oscar nomination, shared Mackendrick's vision of a country tearing itself apart over a religious divide. But casting the American Mia Farrow as Mary Stuart raised the hackles of the press in Scotland. 'How will she manage a Scottish accent?' one reporter asked. 'Mary was educated in France and her first language was French,' said Mackendrick. This conference wasn't going anywhere, even before Kennaway brought it to a dramatic close. When asked what line his script would take, 'We shall surround this civilised young woman,' he said, 'with lots and lots of nasty fucking wee Scotsmen.'

Just as Mackendrick and Kennaway were all ready to go, with the cast under contract, the Scottish locations found and sets built at Shepperton, Universal Studios abruptly axed their European operation and the film was pulled. Mackendrick was advised to sue. 'I'll be paid for making films,' he said, before adding with unfashionable probity for Hollywood, 'I won't be paid for not making films.' After Mackendrick's dark portrait of a devious showbiz columnist mordantly played by Burt Lancaster in his masterful *Sweet Smell of Success*, there were few Hollywood hacks big enough to rally to his defence. Neither Mackendrick nor Kennaway, who died shortly afterwards in a motorway crash, would ever make another film.

James Kennaway's screenplay *Tunes of Glory*, 1960, directed by Ronald Neame, drew on Kennaway's own experience as a subaltern in the Queen's Own Cameron Highlanders during his National Service. The conflict in this Oscar-nominated screenplay pivoted on the fact that ever since the Jacobite Rising of 1745, English officers have been layered between Scots in Highland Regiments to help prevent any future insurrections. Here the self-made Scot, Major Jock Sinclair, played by Alec Guinness, is pitted against John Mills, the rich and privileged English Battalion Commander, Lt Col. Basil Barrow.

Encouraged to accept the challenge of directing the British Film Institute, which at the time was wallowing in self-destructive political correctness, Mackendrick was blackballed by a BFI governor who thought he would be too disorganised for the job. Now we can only imagine what Mackendrick would have brought to that stricken organisation in the Seventies, which continued to falter throughout the decade. Instead, Mackendrick became the dean of film and video at the California Institute of the Arts. Under his long tenure, CalArts grew into arguably the most creative film school in the world, with Mackendrick as its most inspiring hands-on teacher. 'Yet Sandy was an even better film-maker, and should have done more,' Charles Crichton said, before directing John Cleese's *A Fish Called Wanda* – 'He was head and shoulders over all of us at Ealing.'

Anyone contemplating a film career could do no better than read Mackendrick's book, *On Film-making: An Introduction to the Craft of the Director*. It offers the lifetime experience and thoughts of one of cinema's greatest masters. 'Speech involves rationalising our feelings and impulses, something film directors of the silent period discovered they could catch at first hand,' he writes. 'They found that the camera can, uniquely, photograph thought…Actions and images speak faster and more to the senses, than speech does.' I wholeheartedly agree with that. A silent gesture can convey more in a flash than a minute of spoken dialogue. Unlike most actors who resist directors cutting their lines, I have spent my whole career filleting mine. There are few directors who have not seen my cuts as improvements. Steven Spielberg paid me the ultimate compliment on *Indiana Jones and the Last Crusade* by adopting nine out of ten of my ideas which traded dialogue for added visual interaction. This is the very essence of Mackendrick's teaching, which he articulates so well in his chapter called 'The Pre-verbal Power of Cinema'.

Towards the end of his life Mackendrick was lionised by young film-makers during his retrospective at the 1990 Quimper Film Festival in Brittany. 'Are you an American?' a film student asked of the Boston-born director. 'I'm a Scot,' he said, 'the Mackendricks are a "sept", or branch, of the clan Henderson', as he tugged proudly on his Henderson tartan scarf. His parents had eloped from Scotland and through the weirdest of coincidences he was conceived in Hollywood, which must have instilled in him an early warning of the perils of the place. The young Mackendrick was soon dispatched to Kelvinside in the West End of Glasgow to be brought up by his Presbyterian grandmother. His family roots there included Thomas Annan, the pioneering Victorian photographer of the closes and houses of Glasgow's doomed medieval quarter, before it was demolished in the wake of a devastating cholera outbreak in the mid-nineteenth century.

In Scotland Mackendrick is still best known for his first film *Whisky Galore*, which he always put down as a mock-documentary on an amateur outing. Yet that was surely its strength. Filmed entirely on the Isle of Barra during the wet summer of 1948, the fledgling director was forced to augment his London cast with islanders. 'This taught me something that I have used ever since, which is how to take professional actors, trained actors, and put them up against the amateur.' Mackendrick explained: 'The result is that they feed off each other.

Whisky Galore, 1949, directed by Sandy Mackendrick. Compton Mackenzie's light entertainment, based on the whisky-looting islanders plundering the wreck of a US bound cargo ship during the war, gained much from the tension between producer and director. The romantic Russian-born Monja Danischewsky saw the islanders triumphing over interfering bureaucracy, Mackendrick's Presbyterian work ethic saw them more as a bunch of spongers. Yet the result was a triumph, a fusion of local talents with a professional cast and Ealing crew, all marooned together during a long wet summer.

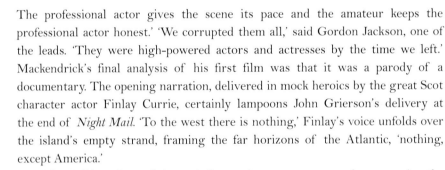

Left: *Night Mail*, 1936. Grierson's GPO film crew included Harry Watt as director, the poet W. H. Auden, Benjamin Britten as composer and the talented Brazilian film-maker Alberto Cavalcanti as the creative sound recordist, to create one of the true masterpieces of the early documentary movement.

Right: *Drifters*, 1929, directed by John Grierson, premiered at the London Film Society ahead of Eisenstein's *Battleship Potemkin*. Filmed in a small fishing village in Northern England, on board a herring boat at sea and through aquarium tanks to heighten what Grierson called 'the creative treatment of actuality'.

The professional actor gives the scene its pace and the amateur keeps the professional actor honest.' 'We corrupted them all,' said Gordon Jackson, one of the leads. 'They were high-powered actors and actresses by the time we left.' Mackendrick's final analysis of his first film was that it was a parody of a documentary. The opening narration, delivered in mock heroics by the great Scot character actor Finlay Currie, certainly lampoons John Grierson's delivery at the end of *Night Mail*. 'To the west there is nothing,' Finlay's voice unfolds over the island's empty strand, framing the far horizons of the Atlantic, 'nothing, except America.'

Night Mail (1936) was Grierson's first major success as a producer running the General Post Office Film Unit. The popular success of its national cinema release came as a spectacular vindication of Grierson's ability to assemble creative horses for courses. With Harry Watt and Basil Wright as directors, he invited the young composer Benjamin Britten to score the film and W.H. Auden, who was teaching at the time, to write poetry to the rhythm of the train hurtling north.

This is the Night Mail crossing the border
Bringing the cheque and the postal order.

The poetry only began when the night mail crossed the border; Grierson saw to that. As a romantic expat he always talked of the bump he experienced as the train bounced over the tracks entering Scotland. A stanza after:

Pulling up Beattock, a steady climb:
The gradient's against her, but she's on time.

Grierson now recites in his own gruff Chicago-Scots:

Dawn freshens, the climb is done. Down towards Glasgow she descends, towards the steam tugs yelping down the glade of cranes, towards the fields of apparatus, the furnaces set on the dark plain like gigantic chessmen. All Scotland waits for her in the dark glens, beside the pale-green sea lochs men long for news.

And as the film ends over shots of Glasgow, Edinburgh and Aberdeen, Grierson concludes in his rolling prose:

Thousands are still asleep dreaming of terrifying monsters, or of friendly tea beside the band at Cranston's or Crawford's. Asleep in working Glasgow, asleep in well-set Edinburgh, asleep in granite Aberdeen, they continue their dreams, and shall wake soon and long for letters, and none will hear the postman's knock without a quickening of the heart, for who can bear to feel himself forgotten?'

Norman McLaren, 1914-87. Invited by Grierson to join the Film Board of Canada, McLaren flourished and created some of the greatest masterpieces of animated cinema. He believed that 'animation is not the art of drawings that move, but rather the art of movements that are drawn.'

Neighbours, 1952, Norman McLaren. This Oscar-winning stop-animated film, in which two men either side of a picket fence fight over a flower, was judged as hopelessly naive by Grierson. But to the pacifist McLaren, it was the very naivety of his film's tabloid anti-war message that triumphed with audiences in the grim era of the Cold War.

Such sentiments would colour Scottish documentaries for at least forty years to come, especially award-winning films like *The Big Mill* and *The Heart of Scotland* by Eddie McConnell and Laurence Henson for Films of Scotland in the Sixties.

'Documentary' was the name given to factual film-making by Grierson when reviewing Robert Flaherty's *Nanook of the North* in 1921. Yet he never meant the term to describe the genre factually. After all, Flaherty had filmed *Nanook* in a specially built oversized igloo with no roof and a whole section missing for the camera, at a time when most Eskimos on the Labrador coast were living in tin huts. 'The creative treatment of actuality' was how Grierson memorably came to define documentary.

The most original film-maker to emerge in Scotland in the 1930s was Norman McLaren, whose increasingly abstract films were produced at the Glasgow School of Art. *Colour Cocktail* caught the eye of Grierson, who awarded it first prize at the 1935 Scottish Amateur Film Festival. The following year Helen Biggar, a postgraduate sculptor student of radical politics, collaborated with McLaren on *Hell Unlimited*, which creatively integrated animation graphics with anti-fascist Glasgow parades. On the strength of this McLaren was invited by Ivor Montagu to shoot his *Defence of Madrid*.

On his return from the Spanish Civil War McLaren worked for Grierson at the GPO Film Unit, creating such classics of creative propaganda as *Love on the Wing*. In this rather oblique promotion for the Royal Mail, white abstract forms shapeshift to music against multiplane coloured backgrounds. As the war clouds gathered in 1939 Grierson was invited to become the creative director of the National Film Board of Canada. McLaren, whose brief flirtation with Communism was soured by his experience of the Spanish Civil War, joined Grierson's new team as a pacificist. Despite his ethical position McLaren made several innovative propaganda films for the war effort, before creating the Film Board's experimental unit. In his Oscar-winning *Neighbours* (1952) he pioneered a live-action animated technique in which two territorial disputants were filmed a few frames at a time as they battered each other, arguing over the position of a picket fence. McLaren rewarded the creative freedom he enjoyed in Canada by producing startlingly imaginative films, which made him one of most awarded film artists in history.

After Grierson's success in setting up the National Film Board of Canada, which, most agree, became the best film agency in the world, he was offered the role of executive producer of Group 3, one of the co-operative film production enterprises set up in 1950 to receive government loans. Most of the films were light-hearted comedies tailored to raise spirits in the tough postwar years, but *The Brave Don't Cry*, directed by his friend the documentary film-maker Philip Leacock, was a true Grierson inspiration. Coalmining and its dangers were never far from his mind, having grown up in Stirlingshire.

Grierson's production of *Coal Face*, directed by the talented Brazilian Alberto Cavalcanti, had been an ambitious failure, despite its madrigal by W. H. Auden set to music by Benjamin Britten. This time Grierson focused on the mining disaster at the Knockshinnoch pit in Ayrshire, when over a hundred miners were trapped under ground. With a superb cast from the trail-blazing Glasgow Citizens' Theatre – 'the best gang I ever worked with' – this film could have been the beginning of feature film making in Scotland. Chosen to open the 1952 Edinburgh Film Festival, it was an immediate hit. But the Rank Orgnisation was against government participation in film production and relegated Grierson's success to a support feature. Further commercial pressures eventually put Group 3 out of business. Of its many stillborn projects none were closer to Grierson than his long-term ambition to bring the nineteenth-century novelist James Hogg's *The Confessions of a Justified Sinner* to the screen.

In Scotland new beginnings were in the offing in the late Sixties, to borrow the mantra of the German artist Joseph Beuys who was to become a frequent Edinburgh visitor. Much to his amazement, Mark Littlewood, who had been chosen on the strength of filming evocative landscapes, was driven by Ricky Demarco to a desolate peat bog on Rannoch Moor where Beuys directed him to shoot a static shot. The result was projected at the Edinburgh College of Art as a key part of the Kunsthalle Düsseldorf artists' 1970 show at the Edinburgh Festival called *Strategy: Get Arts*, with its enigmatic title craftily embodying a palindrome (see p. 179).

Parallel to such encounters in Edinburgh, the Film Festival began to feature the work of young Scottish film-makers, short films made without a shred of tartan. Johnny Schorstein's *KH-4* (its enigmatic title came from the cheap black and white East German Orwo film stock it was shot on) was all about the annihilation of Victorian Glasgow, when whole districts were being flattened without any regard to their architectural distinction. The city planners seemed to be in thrall to the Luftwaffe; although, to be fair, the German bombers of the World War II were far more selective and much less destructive. As swirling dust envelops a collapsing tenement in the talented Schorstein's imaginative film, a lone black-coated figure slowly turns towards us. Prophetically, for the future of film in Scotland, it was Bill Forsyth.

KH4, 1969, Jonathan Schorstein. At a time when many film-makers in Scotland were diverted into celebrating the destruction of Glasgow in bland sponsored documentaries, this little film of cultural resistance kept us all honest. As a promising graduate of the National Film School, Johnny's tragic early death was an unbearable loss to cinema in Scotland, at a time when Bill Forsyth, who is pictured here as his town falls around him, was determined to pioneer feature films in Scotland.

Forsyth's Edinburgh Festival film that year was *Waterloo*, which he had ingeniously stitched together by culling short ends of film from BBC soccer coverage along with scraps of magnetic sound. This was all too advanced for the Festival projectionist, as Forsyth's film met its own Waterloo in fragments on the floor. That night some key festival delegates gathered to watch a hastily patched-up re-run.

'Why did you start with five minutes of black spacing?' asked Sam Fuller, that year's featured director.

'I couldn't think what to put there, Sam,' said Forsyth.

'Young man,' replied one of the great masters of narrative cinema, grasping his arm, 'what an insult to your audience.'

Both Schorstein and Forsyth were selected by the National Film School in its first year, 1971. The director, Colin Young, had already made waves running the UCLA film school in Los Angeles. But it was not his international reputation so much as his gently reassuring West of Scotland manner that finally persuaded the Scottish education authorities that film was a proper educational pursuit for grant-aiding. Young was almost embarrassingly successful. Out of the first year's intake of twenty-five students, five came from abroad and five won grants from Scotland. Sadly, the creative Schorstein died too young to fulfil his promise. Forsyth left the National Film School after only one year, making him the its most successful drop-out. To his credit Forsyth's next Edinburgh Festival entry would be *That Sinking Feeling* (1979); and on that gallus-caper movie, produced by Paddy Higson, with much fun and little mun, Scotland's feature-film future was born.

When Peter Watkins assembled a band of amateur actors from Inverness on Drummossie Moor in 1964 to film his BBC re-enactment of the massacre of Culloden, he made television history. He interpolated the techniques of present-day war correspondents, while dressing his reporter in eighteenth-century clothes and having him speak live, as it were, from the battlefield. Such running commentaries brought home in terrifying detail the carnage caused by the cannonfire and grapeshot of the Hanoverian army against the swords and muskets of the ill-prepared Jacobites. Watkins also had an eye for casting non-professionals in leading roles, what the great Russian director Eisenstein called 'typage'. So *Culloden* has such well lived-in Highland faces as the doomed Keppoch, memorably played with much local resonance by George MacBain, Inverness's well kent Registrar of Births, Marriages and Deaths. Extra tension came from staff recruited from the local tax office, who played redcoats under Butcher Cumberland's Hanoverian command.

Watkins's *Culloden* came as a welcome antidote to the romanticising of Bonnie Prince Charlie and as a wake-up call to those sponsored Scottish film-makers sinking deeper in the tartan kitsch of tourist documentaries. When I read that the National Trust for Scotland was building a 'state-of-the-art £9m visitor centre' on Culloden Moor in which 'visitors will enjoy an immersion experience in the form of a groundbreaking audiovisual spectacle', I immediately thought of the Peter Watkins documentary. But no. The self-proclaimed 'spectacle' turns out to be an expensive re-enactment 'filmed on Lauder Moor', of all places, 'in the Borders'.

Culloden, 1964, Peter Watkins, b.1939. This tour de force of creative film-making interpolating twentieth-century reporting techniques into the carnage of eighteenth-century war, rejuvenated television documentaries in the Sixties. To heighten the realism of this civil war, Watkins recruited unknowns, what Eisenstein called 'typage', casting with an emphasis on types, representative of social groups, rather than individuals. Sadly Scottish Equity, the actor's union, condemned this masterpiece to the archives and it has never been shown since on British television.

But why? How effective it could have been, had the NTS extended its account of 1746 by embracing television history of the 1960s with that world-famous anti-war masterpiece. But then, what would the design consultants get out of that?

Growing up in a wartime mining village on the fringes of Edinburgh must have been grim enough. What the film-maker Bill Douglas brought to such an experience was indeed 'the creative treatment of actuality'. Many have thought that his remarkable trilogy was autobiographical. As Andrew Noble notes in his insightful introduction to *Bill Douglas: A Lanternist's Account*, 'Bill constantly reiterated Chekhov's maxim that memory was a creative filter employed not for factual recall but to make art, and that such art, deeply aware of its own formal means, should speak to and for our common condition.' 'Bill Douglas – was – is the kind of filmmaker who has always been rare in Britain,' said the director Lindsay Anderson. 'He was not attracted to cinema because he wanted to make a career for himself, or because he wanted to please an audience. He made films from the heart, and from his experience of life.'

Fortunately, in the late Sixties the British Film Institute production fund had an imaginative director and a board of sympathetic film-makers. Mamoun Hassan, to his eternal credit, made sure that Douglas received a sufficient budget out of a pitifully small fund and initiated the production of *My Childhood*, in which Jamie, Douglas's alter ego, plays out the dynamic story of his bleak upbringing in Newcraighall. Although it shouldn't be forgotten that the previous director, the enthusiastic Australian Bruce Beresford who did so much to spark up film production in Scotland, had already singled it out from the BFI's massive script pile. Originally shot in Eastmancolor, the film would attain its essential bleakness when released in black and white. The production was fraught. When the production manager, Iain Smith, realised that he had to arrange permission to film the scene with Jamie's mother in the same hospital where Douglas's own mother was then confined, it was just the start of his problems. He found out the day before shooting that there was no one cast to take her role, so he promptly drove over to Glasgow and had his own mother fill the hospital bed. Her low-key performance was appreciated by Douglas because he had spent much time with the professional actors teaching them to be unactorish. Smith later balked when directed to kill a neighbourhood cat for an essential scene and spent a morning scouring vets for one that had died of natural causes. Sadly, he didn't last the pace and was fired before the production ended. Despite this inauspicious start Iain Smith became one of the most efficient on-line producers I've ever worked with, and certainly *Entrapment* wouldn't have happened the way it did without him.

On his return to London, Hassan was shocked to find that Douglas had impetuously killed off Jamie in the train scene which ended the film. Douglas may have thought that there would be no chance for a sequel, never mind a trilogy, but was much reassured when funds were found to re-shoot that last sequence.

The further two episodes were even more fraught, as the level of creative intensity increased. When the sound recordist missed what Douglas had judged to be the perfect take he became suicidal and threw his typewriter out of the hotel window. Hassan, now affectionately known to the crew as MacMoun, was summoned again, and threatened to phone his chairman Michel Balcon to cancel the production. After a melodramatic scene where Douglas wound the telephone cable around his neck, the storms passed and the filming continued. The trilogy was finally completed, and remains one of the finest achievements of Scottish cinema. Douglas not only had the eye for a shot – the 'verb of cinema' as he called it – but he also had the passion to fight for his vision, however unpopular that made him.

Fortunately, before he died so young in 1991, his last film *Comrades* was brought to the screen with indefatigable persistence by Simon Relph. Commissioned by David Rose at Channel 4, its production was backed way beyond the Channel's means by Jeremy Isaacs, who felt that a British Film Industry that wouldn't back Bill Douglas was one that was not worth having. The comrades were six Dorset farmers, transported to Australia for forming a union to win a living wage, who became known as the Tolpuddle Martyrs. Into his elliptical retelling of their plight Douglas introduced a number of theatrical scenes, which included the magic lantern and early persistence-of-vision devices.

Douglas's obsession with illusion, which lies at the very quick of cinema, led to his unrealised feature on the life of the photographer Eadweard Muybridge, 'Flying Horse'. Douglas went back a decade before Dickson's pioneering inventions to Muybridge's successful experiments in photographing movement, including his photographic proof that a galloping horse really did have all four hooves off the ground at the same time. Parallel to Muybridge's pioneering photographic sequences, which would lead to the invention of cinema, Douglas's screenplay for 'Flying Horse' would not be without melodrama. A key scene would re-enact Muybridge's return from a camera outing in California's High Sierras, when he found his wife in bed with a friend and shot him.

My Childhood, 1971, director Bill Douglas. Jamie on the Newcraighall stair from the first film of a trilogy which would take another seven years to complete.

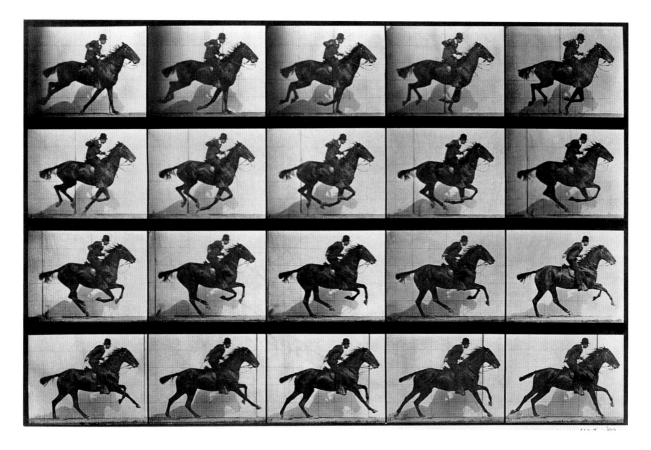

Eadweard Muybridge, *Flying Horse*, 1878. This famous horse-racing sequence was ingeniously achieved by the triggering of twelve consecutive cameras. It finally proved that all four hooves of horses leave the ground at a gallop.

How can such talents be quantified? Douglas certainly made films from the heart. The tragedy of film and television commissioning in Scotland today is that there are few people like Mamoun Hassan to judge the work of film artists. The early days of Channel 4, under the creative leadership of Jeremy Isaacs, jump-started production in Scotland, because his brief was that he, and his commissioning editors, would be interested only in projects that directors were passionate to make. Today it's seemingly the film and television commissioners who vie with each other for work, conforming their own ideas to what a juvenile public wants. Film artists who have fire in their belly, with no ambition to make their fortune building film and television conglomerates, are dismissed by commissioning editors as hobbyists. I have found that the same inept attitude is now increasingly present in Hollywood. Throughout my film career it has been my fortunate privilege to collaborate with such talents as Alfred Hitchcock, John Huston, Sidney Lumet, Dick Lester, Steven Spielberg and many others who had the 'vision thing'. I stopped acting in movies when what Billy Connolly calls 'a bunch of effing foetuses in three-piece suits' began to call the shots. Surely Scotland can learn from that.

Passion, and an eye on the lookout for new talent, collided to bring the breakthrough black comedy *Shallow Grave* to the screen. David Aukin, Head of Drama for Channel 4 and one-time adviser to Edinburgh's Traverse Theatre, was captivated by John Hodge's original screenplay, breathlessly promoted at the

Edinburgh Festival by a young producer called Andrew MacDonald. Aukin matched his enthusiasm with the talent of Danny Boyle, an ex-deputy director of the Royal Court Theatre who had recently brought off a cult television mini-series, *Mr Wroe's Virgins*, with great visual flair. In turn Boyle invited Brian Tufano, the ever resourceful and inventive cameraman of that series, to be director of photography. His casting included Kerry Fox, one of the stars of Boyle's series, and Ewan McGregor from Bill Forsyth's little-seen *Being Human*. Thanks to Aukin's policy of encouraging original contemporary stories and his disdain for the old-style British heritage movie, *Shallow Grave* was a critical and commercial success, getting its money back, and more, in Britain. Although set in Edinburgh and praised for its sense of place, much of *Shallow Grave* was filmed in Glasgow because of the £150,000 put up by the Glasgow Film Fund. There's probably a joke in there somewhere.

The Boyle-Hodge-McDonald-Tufano team had an even greater success with *Trainspotting*, latching on to the tearaway success of Irvine Welsh's scabrously funny non-judgemental film on the drug abuse of a bunch of Edinburgh heroin addicts. *Trainspotting*, with its tripped-out surrealism, went on to be the most successful British film of 1996 and was soon to earn £80 million worldwide. No further vindication was needed of Aukin's belief in the production of films for home audiences, instead of attempting to ape Hollywood, where, of course, a dubbed *Trainspotting* met with considerable success.

I am not an advocate of film-making in Scotland as a spur to tourism. No doubt Americans of Scots ancestry were driven to the land of William Wallace by Mel Gibson's *Braveheart*, even though, through more generous Irish tax concessions, it was largely filmed in Ireland. Tourists to Scotland, sophisticated enough to realise that *Brigadoon* never existed outside a Hollywood back lot, were confused over Bill Forsyth's *Local Hero*. Having found the fictional fishing village of Furness at Penman on the rocky northeast coast, they were astonished to find that the film was shot bi-coastally and that the village's nearby sandy beach was in the real world some 150 miles far off on the West Coast, at Camusdarrach. Tourist agencies may have seen little profit in *Trainspotting*, but there are now tours of the film's low spots in Leith.

Perhaps there will soon be similar excursions to the film locations of Alexander Trocchi's *Young Adam* around the Union Canal at Fountainbridge near where I grew up. The director David Mackenzie has as good an ear as he has an eye. Having spent months with different writers attempting to write a screenplay for Trocchi's *Young Adam*, he decided to have a go himself. Trocchi's novel was the Glasgow-born writer's first literary success before he blazed a path through the Beat world of the Fifties to become an addled smack-dependent. His erotic existentialist thriller of murder and meaningless sex is set adrift on a barge plying the no-man's-land of the Forth and Clyde canal in the grim postwar years of the late 1940s.

In the early 2000s Mackenzie was renting a flat with the writer Alex Linklater, now the deputy editor of the influential magazine *Prospect*. He had introduced Mackenzie to Trocchi as Scotland's one genuine Beat writer, master of egotistical

With John Huston, director of *The Man Who Would Be King*. 'By Gad, sir, you are a character. There's never any telling what you'll say or do next, except that it's bound to be something astonishing.' Sydney Greenstreet's description of Humphrey Bogart in *The Maltese Falcon*, written and directed by John Huston, is just how I remember one of the greatest directors I ever worked with and an even greater friend.

Above: *Young Adam*, 2003. Writer and director David Mackenzie. Peter Mullan and Ewan McGregor at the stern of their canal barge, the *Atlantic Eve*. A film that so well evoked the grim era of Alexander Trocchi's Beat classic with its uncanny sense of place.

Below: *The Ideal City*, 15th-century School of Piero della Francesca, The Ducal Palace, Urbino, Italy: a Renaissance lesson on how well a circular building can grace a square.

existentialism and self-styled cosmonaut of inner space. Together they shared a love of French cinema, which would come to haunt the film with its heightened sense of place and time. The de-saturated colour photography of Giles Nuttgens is awash with memories of Jean Vigo's *L'Atalante* (1954), as Joe, along with the captain and his wife, chug and creak their way between the grim wharves of the Forth and Clyde Canal on a barge called the *Atlantic Eve*. As Trocchi's alter ego, Joe, played by Ewan McGregor, is a thwarted writer at odds with the world. He spends most of the film with his eyes on Ella, the wife of the cuckolded captain Les, played with heroic dourness by Peter Mullan. To the echoing clomps of Les's boots pacing the metal deck above, Ella makes love to Joe down below in the grimy hold. For Tilda Swinton, who so poignantly portrays Ella in all her weaknesses, it's one of the most affecting performances of her career. What attracted her and Ewan McGregor to David Mackenzie's screenplay were its brave sparseness and its pared-down dialogue, which made it for both of them one of the most successful cinematic translations of any novel to the screen. Joe's loneliness as an alienated intellectual and the disillusioned Ella have left the pages of Trocchi's semi-autobiographical cult classic to live again in this most memorable film.

I was thrilled when Tilda Swinton accepted my idea of becoming an honorary patron of the Edinburgh International Film Festival in 2007. I have held the role since 1991 and felt that it was time to hand on the baton. The Festival was founded in 1947 by John Grierson, along with the leading lights of the Edinburgh Film Guild, who all felt passionately that the cinema should be an essential part of the world's largest arts festival. Then, with few other rivals, its reputation grew to make Edinburgh synonymous, in Hollywood and the wider world, with the movies. This was especially true in the late Sixties when the festival filled its screens with such independent movies as Dennis Hopper's *Easy Rider* and featured retrospectives of such undervalued American talents as Samuel Fuller and Douglas Sirk. It was then that I first became aware of the event, run on a shoestring by a youthful team out of a cramped New Town office in Randolph Crescent. Later it would expand into a converted church across from the Usher Hall, which was never my idea of Saturday night at the movies.

Despite Edinburgh's reputation I found that there were few on the city council who realised that Edinburgh had an international reputation in the wider world of cinema. Government agencies in Scotland and London were also reluctant to fund the festival adequately. Clearly, a dedicated cinema complex with pizzazz would go a long way towards showing local commitment and make Edinburgh a true film centre. After years of indecision, Richard Murphy, one of Edinburgh's most innovative architects with an international reputation, was persuaded to devise a scheme, thanks to the generosity of one of his key patrons. Inspired by that vision of an *Ideal City* painted by Piero della Francesca, Murphy's theatrical solution was to drop a circular cinema into Edinburgh's most deserted plaza, the inappropriately named Festival Square, to balance the Usher Hall across Lothian Road. His beautiful model became a talking-point of the 2004 Venice Biennale, but years later his enterprising scheme still awaits taking up in Edinburgh.

If Murphy's quite brilliant design were built I believe it would become an immediate beacon to movie-goers worldwide. Apart from the Festival, it could mount exciting film events in Edinburgh throughout the year. To help publicise the project I was persuaded to lend the new filmhouse my name, which, for one born on the other side of the tracks in nearby Fountainbridge, was a great honour.

I have been involved with this film festival for a long time. My old friend John Huston called it the only one worth a damn. Over the years many of his major films were premiered at Edinburgh, including *Moby Dick*, *Fat City* and one of which I am especially fond, *The Man Who Would Be King*. What can I now say other than to wish the proposed theatre all success, and that it would be fun to see it up and running in my own lifetime.

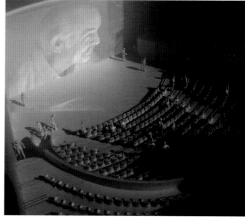

Richard Murphy's model for the projected Sean Connery cinema complex in Edinburgh's Festival Square would not only bring life to the dullest square in Edinburgh, but would also echo the rotunda of the Usher Hall on the other side of the street.

14 WHIT A LAFF
You must be joking

In the beginning was the pun.
  Samuel Beckett, *Murphy*

'It requires a surgical operation to get a joke well into a Scotch understanding' was the assessment of the Englishman, the Reverend Sydney Smith, who in 1802 was the first editor of the *Edinburgh Review*. Maybe he took his pleasures a little too seriously, or had he too many Edinburgh legal friends? Obviously Smith never ventured far enough west to experience the wild surrealism and patter of Glasgow wits.

I believe that humour is a most serious way of approaching life. So I am not drawn to film directors who don't do jokes. 'The nearer humour approaches seriousness, the funnier it will be,' said John Glashan. 'Humour is seriousness in disguise.' Glashan's dark, brooding and totally hilarious cartoons bear this wittiest of Glaswegians out. I offer his art, and the evidence of all the comedians who follow, as wry rebuttals to Sydney Smith's surgical requirements. Scottish humour can be cutting enough.

To plumb the historical well of Scottish wordplay we must go back over a thousand years to that merry evening when Charles the Bald, the ninth-century King of France, was banqueting with Scotus Eriguena, or John the Scot. Deep into his cups, the King leaned across the dinner table and asked the erudite philosopher-priest in the universal language of the time.

'Quid distat inter Scottum et Sotum?' (What separates a Scot from a Sot?)
'Tabula Tantum.' (Only a table.)

This is the first recorded Scottish joke, as far as I know. It could also be claimed to be the first Irish joke, as in the early Middle Ages all Scots were Irish. The Scots, you see, were an Ulster tribe who made Scotland their first colony. I've no problem with that, since a thousand years later my father's family also came from Ireland. Scot or Sot? My worry is, as a Scot, how close is that to a sot?

I met this chap at the Olympics. 'Excuse me but are you a pole vaulter?'
'No, I'm German,' he said. 'But how did you know my name was Walter?'

Opposite: *A Bonnie Heiland Laddie*, 1900s, Andrew Allan, detail of a chromo-lithographic postcard. This guileless smile inspired the poster for the Scotch Myths exhibition, devised by Barbara and Murray Grigor, initiated by the Crawford Centre for the Arts, St Andrews, and enlarged for the 1981 Edinburgh Festival.

Chic Murray, 1919-85, with Maidie, b.1922. The Tall Droll and the Small Doll.

This witty wordplay may not leap immediately off the page, but if you had heard it delivered in a stage German accent by Chic Murray at an Edinburgh Variety Show as I did in the 1950s, you would never have forgotten it. In a cascade of puns, which my French wife Micheline says gets much closer to its true meaning as *jeu de mots*, or play on words, Chic would leave half the audience in fits of laughter and the other half in total despair. You either got it or you didn't. Chic Murray's brevity really was the soul of wit. His storytelling had all the logic of a shipwrecked dream. His jokes plunged into the subconscious only to reappear as streams of finely honed nonsense. His humour condensed logic to displace the real world. Chic's plays on words revelled in a rush of purposefully confusing ambiguities.

A hen in kilts could referee better than that.

Postcard, Millar & Lang, 1900s, Glasgow. One of a series of wry cartoons by Andrew Allan who was a director of Millar & Lang, Glasgow's most prolific postcard company. Allan was a graduate of the Glasgow School of Art and was surely a surrealist way ahead of his time.

I've never understood why people groan when a great pun is cracked. Maybe it is because a rather unsuccessful eighteenth-century playwright, John Dennis, once said that puns were the lowest form of wit. This was scotched eloquently at the time by the great punster friend of Robert Burns, Henry Erskine, who was the wittiest Lord Chancellor we ever had. 'Puns are the lowest form of wit,' Erskine said, 'because they are the foundation of all wit.' I agree with that. To have fun with words is perhaps more Celtic than English, if my Scots-Irish family is anything to go by. I don't mean the Celtic Twilight of the fey Victorian Romantics, which James Joyce, punmaster that he was, called the Cultic Twalet. *Finnegans Wake* was one of the set books my mentor Robert Henderson had me read when we were on the road together in *South Pacific*, way back in 1952. It was part of his plan to educate me to be an actor. This bewildering book had me seeking words that dictionaries never knew, until I surrendered to the sheer inventiveness of Joyce's tortuous wordsmithery. Many of the allusions escaped me, so it was a great relief to meet others who had also failed to fathom the meaning of great chunks of *Finnegans Wake*. Yet my attempts at making sense of words which offered unexpected meanings opened up a whole new world for me, especially the sheer fun of a pun.

I found the Irish writer Jonathan Swift to be a master of the witty pun. He had no time for the small-minded and stunted pun-haters of the eighteenth century. From *A Modest Defence of Punning*: ''Tis true, some are *longer* and some *shorter* at Punning, and if a *Pig may* Pun as our *Detractors* affirm, then certainly a *Pigmay* can.'

Humour for Chic Murray was never confined to the stage; it enveloped every moment of his life. Even as a young engineering apprentice at Kincaid's shipyard in Greenock, his excuse for being late to work one day was that he had been brutally attacked by a gang of landscape gardeners:

I went to the butchers to buy a leg of lamb.
'Is it Scotch?' I asked.
'Why?' asked the butcher. 'Are you going to talk to it or eat it?'
'In that case, have you got any wild duck?'
'No,' he said, 'but I've got one here that I could aggravate for you.'

As a young soccer fan on the terraces I would often hear shouts approaching Chic's surrealism, especially if Glasgow Celtic were playing in Edinburgh. Once when the ref had clearly missed a foul, a yell went up: 'A hen in kilts could referee better than that.' What kind of fowl was that? It was only much later, when I discovered Chic's droll absurdities on the radio, that I realised his humour was anchored to West of Scotland traditions. Chic could make a quite ordinary observation and shift it into extraordinary daftness. Take the wedding in Blackpool he attended of that unfortunate much married bride, the one with the very long nose. 'She caught my eye,' Chic would tell his audience with something of a benign smile. 'To avoid embarrassment I nodded to her. She nodded back and cut the cake.' Billy Connolly told me that he could never have imagined that you could make a career out of

comedy. As a teenager, Billy was watching Chic on television one evening when he laughed himself off the sofa. 'It was a blinding flash on the road to Damascus,' Billy said. 'I knew that there was nothing else for me: that nothing else would do. As the years rolled by, when I had indeed taken up comedy as my livelihood, I was lucky enough to befriend Chic and had many a laugh over a pint with this clever and witty man.' Billy just loved Chic's weird wordplay. It inspired him to develop his own stream of patter, to see the strange in the familiar. But instead of Chic's ten-minute walk-ons as a 'front-of-tabs' man, as the Variety Show scenery was changed behind him, Billy soon pioneered his own lusty scatological no-holds-barred humour which could last over three hours on stage.

Ever since he left the shipyards as a welder to become a singing banjo-player in a band called The Humblebums, it was more what Billy said, than what he sang and played, that quickly made his name. He wrote and performed his own songs in *The Great Northern Welly Boot Show*, the Fringe hit of the 1972 Edinburgh Festival. This burlesque on the demise of Clyde shipbuilding, with its mix of politics and songs, brought together poets, musicians, artists and a cast of energetic young actors, some of whom went on to found the touring 7:84 Theatre Company with the playwright John McGrath.

With Billy Connolly and a moustached Pamela Stephenson in their Highland home, not far from Queen Victoria's Balmoral. Her trusty Highland ghillie was brought to life in a memorable performance by Billy in the movie *Mrs Brown*.

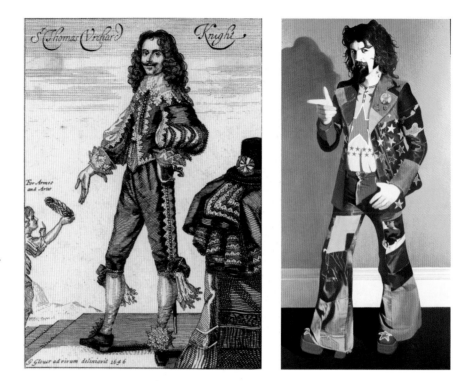

Left: Sir Thomas Urquhart of Cromarty, 1611-60. The 11th Chief of Clan Urquhart was the wittiest man of his age, master of word play, minter of new words, inventor of a universal language (lost at the Battle of Worcester) and translator into English of Rabelais's *Gargantua and Panatgruel*, which was even more outrageous than the author's wildly lewd French original.

Right: Billy Connolly, b.1941, by his friend John Byrne, b.1940.

In the long term it would be Billy's genius of acute observation, extracting humour out of the everyday rather than telling one-off jokes, that would create his huge international following. Astonishingly he achieved this in the patois of Partick, the Glasgow district of his childhood, which instead of restricting him to Glasgow clubs took him on to the world stage at a time when provincial accents normally guaranteed entertainment death. Now Billy is the grand master when it comes to delivering torrents of unrepeatable anecdotes.

If we said Billy Connolly's humour was Rabelaisian we'd be close to the mark, for two reasons. Thanks to a miraculous quirk of evolution, Sir Thomas Urquhart, the wittiest Scot who ever lived, translated into English the greatest work of humour ever written, Francois Rabelais's *Gargantua and Pantagruel*:

When Yolande saw her spouse all armed for fight
And, save the codpiece, all in armour dight,
My dear, she cried, why, of all the rest,
Is that unarmed which I love the best?

But to call Urquhart's version a translation comes nowhere near to describing the brilliance of the Scotsman's own verbal inventions, which went far beyond translation into elaborations that were transformations, in some instances three times longer than the original. What we know today as 'Rabelaisian' in English should really be called 'Urquhartian'. His threefold mission in life was to collect books, to learn foreign tongues and to uphold against all comers the glory of his native Scotland. Urqhuart's erudition chimed with Rabelais's.

Sir Thomas Urquhart of Cromarty was the laird of a crumbling estate in the Highlands, who claimed that he sprang from an unbroken line dating all the way back through 153 generations to Adam and Eve. Those who ridiculed this outrageous claim fell for his elaborate mockery of those pompous aristocrats who claimed their descent from kings. Sir Thomas had the wildness of Billy Connolly and the weirdness of Chic Murray. This earthiness may be universal, but I'm reminded of the graffiti on the penny-in-the-slot door of the Fountainbridge public lavatory I saw as a boy: 'Here I am broken hearted, spent a penny, and only farted.' Urquhart spoke many languages and, as a forger of words across many tongues, both ancient and modern, few could keep up with him. He was knighted by Charles I for supporting the Royalist cause in the northeast of Scotland at an uprising known as the Trot of Turriff in 1639, a bizarrely named encounter which initiated the Civil War.

Urquhart professed an overriding obsession that all the nations of the world should talk together in one language:

My Universal Language is a most exquisite jewel. It hath eleven genders, seven moods, four voices, ten cases, besides the nominative, and twelve parts of speech; every word signifieth as well backwards as forwards; and it is so compact of style that a single syllable will express the year, month, day, hour and partition of the hour.

Then at the Battle of Worcester in 1651, when the Scots contingent of Royalists was defeated, three thousand pages of Urquhart's universal language were blown

Left: Pantagruel by Gustave Doré, 1832-83. *Gargantua and Pantagruel* by François Rabelais, 1484-1553, was published in 1532 under the pen name of Alcofribas Nasier, an anagram of François Rabelais. Gargantua and Pantagruel are two giants, father and son, whose wild adventures are spun out over five satirical novels. With pages filled with crudity, scatological humour and violence, Rabelais's fantasy of the life of his times runs the whole gamut of human experience, from love to uncontrolled bodily functions, from war to peace. Religion is mercilessly satirised by this lapsed Franciscan monk in one of the greatest comic masterpieces of literature. 'Bring down the curtain, the farce is over.' were the last words of François Rabelais. How his great translator Sir Thomas Urquhart would have smiled.

Drollerie, 1581, Preston Grange painted ceiling. To show that the spirit of Rabelais was afoot in Scotland long before Urquhart, this challenging 'drollerie' was part of a group discovered during a renovation in 1962. Now installed in the boardroom of Merchiston Castle, part of the Napier University campus. Having such Pantagruelian excesses above must surely be a spur to academic discussion below.

to the winds, or so he claimed when captured and clapped in the Tower of London. All, or nearly all, was lost of this great work, but miraculously a few sheets survived, snatched out of the throes of battle by its author. At least there was enough for the silver-tongued knight to convince the Great Protector, Oliver Cromwell, that his universal language was essential to the future of the Commonwealth. Thus the great man of many words talked himself out of jail. Finally, promising to return to Cromarty to sort out his derelict estate, Urquhart escaped to Holland, where he lived for the rest of his life. On hearing of the restoration of King Charles II in 1660, legend has it that he died in a fit of uncontrollable laughter.

Not all humorous Scots were monks or knights. Sometimes the very lowly would elevate themselves to be lords of wit. For centuries odd-job retainers doubled as court jesters to the lairds of Highland castles. Jamie Fleeman, the 'Laird of Udny's Fool', was the embodiment of a jester, a fool who was wise, a challenge to the over-virtuous, a critic of the world. In Russia he could have been a holy fool to a tsar, where the tradition goes back for centuries. If Scotland can't lay claim to the first holy fool it can certainly make a claim for Jamie, who was the last kept fool in Europe. From his wise sayings, published after his death as *The Laird of Udny's Fool* (Aberdeen, 1833):

'Whose fool are you?' a stranger asked Jamie.

'I'm the Laird o' Udny's feel. And fa's feel are ee?' [And whose fool are you?] asked Jamie.

'Is that your brother?' the stranger said, looking down at Jamie's donkey.

'Na na, jist a casual acquaintance. Just like yersel.'

'Where are you going?'

'A'm gaun tae hell, sir!'

'What do they do in hell?'

'Ye ken – jist the same's they're daein here, sir, lattin' in the rich fouk an' keepin' oot the peer.'

'What said the devil to you?'

'Oh, he said na muckle to me, sir, but he was speerin' sair aboot ye!' [Oh he said nothing much to me, sir, but he was quizzing me hard about you!]

Jamie's last words were 'I'm a Christian, dinna bury me like a beast.' Locals from miles around raised a subscription for his memorial and had those words carved in granite on his grave.

Highland life gave rise to many humorous jibes, as tourists confronted native wits. Cartoons of ghillies and 'southron' toffs filled the pages of Victorian magazines like *Punch*. But then came an extraordinary revelation. Three-quarters of Mr Punch's anti-Scottish jokes, pivoting on such negative stereotypes as thriftiness, meanness, Sunday observance and the effects of whisky, were sent down from Scotland. Most amazing of all, the highest percentage of mean jokes came from Aberdeen, the Scottish city on which the grip of tight-fistedness had somehow fallen. One such cartoon has an American visitor lean out of his carriage to ask a lone figure in the otherwise empty street:

THRIFT.

Peebles Body (to Townsman who was supposed to be in London on a visit). " E—EH, MAC! YE'RE SUNE HAME AGAIN ! "

Mac. " E—EH, IT 'S JUST A RUINOUS PLACE, THAT ! MUN, A HAD NA' BEEN THE-ERRE ABUNE TWA HOOURS WHEN—*BANG*—WENT *SAXPENCE ! ! !* "

Mr Punch in the Highlands, Charles Keene, 1823-91.

In the wake of Queen Victoria and Prince Albert's annual forays to Balmoral, *Punch* magazine's autumn editions filled with cartoons ridiculing Highland traits; yet passed equal scorn on Sassenach swells bungling their chances in front of their kilted ghillies. Mr Punch's advice for the chinless shooters, bent on bagging stags and game birds in the Highlands with their twelve-bore gas-pipes, was never to pun on the word bore.

Punch's most famous Scottish joke, 'Bang went saxpence', was the creation of Charles Keene. This now largely forgotten joke on Old Mac's parsimony was so popular that it was made into a best-selling toby jug. Although Keene was an Englishman he was fed a constant supply of Scottish jokes by the artist Joseph Crawhall, who was one of the 'Glasgow Boys'. As a result well over 200 Scottish jokes by this talented engraver filled the pages of *Punch*. Their success no doubt encouraged Keene, as an honorary Scot, for he became an accomplished player and collector of bag-pipes.

'What's the name of this town?'
'Gie me saxpence an I'll tell ye.'
'Drive on. It must be Aberdeen!'

But why are so many of the most negative stories told about Scotsmen conceived and circulated by the Scots themselves? Over a hundred years ago Mr Punch could write: 'There's a quaint belief that somewhere in that grey Northern city of Aberdeen there's a joke factory where workers are tirelessly engaged in evolving anecdotes concerning small financial matters and sending them South!' But why is this? What makes Scots still laugh at themselves? Where do all these jokes about canniness, thriftiness and downright meanness come from? Perhaps humour is a

Opposite: *The Tay Bridge Disaster.*
Thomas Bouch's nearly two-mile-long
girder bridge was carried away in a storm
with the loss of 75 lives in 1879, which
would 'be remembered for a very long
time'. The Court of Enquiry found many
shortcomings in the bridge's construction.
But let William McGonagall have the
final word, with the last verse from one
of his most famous poems.

I must now conclude my lay,

By telling the world fearlessly
without the least dismay,

That your central girders would
not have given way,

At least many sensible men do say,

Had they been supported on each
side with buttresses,

At least many sensible men confesses,

For the stronger we our houses do build,

The less chance we have of being killed.

William Topaz McGonagall, 1825-1902,
was a self-educated hand-loom weaver
from Dundee who found his métier as
poet of banal rhymes and wildly
abandoned scansion. Much ridiculed
in his lifetime, his verses have been
trumpeted by such wits as Spike Milligan
and Billy Connolly. Today they are still
recited by Scots at home and abroad.

Faithfully Yours
William McGonagall
poet and Tragedian.

way of pre-empting despair, a strategy of self-disparagement to disarm a better-off neighbour? Our comic stereotypes have an uncanny ring with that other self-mocking culture. What is it that makes Jewish and Scottish humour so similar? Why are Scots, like Jews, both contenders for the title of 'the People of the Joke'? The Jewish beggar stories about schnorrers seem to be the double of Glasgow's shachlie wee bauchles (knock-kneed wearers of old shoes).

Well, how about asking a stand-up comedian who is both Scottish and Jewish, and who started life as a canny chartered accountant. Step forward Glaswegian Arnold Brown, who sees comedy as a kind of revenge. 'I can offer two racial stereotypes,' he proposes 'for the price of one.' Having been told by his Glasgow classmates that all Jews were wealthy, he recounts how he ran back home to spend a weekend ripping up the floorboards. Close on Arnold's heels is Mark Bratchpiece, a quick-witted raconteur from a shtetl in deep Lanarkshire. He said he would visit the wailing wall, 'but only for a wee greet'. Faither Bratchpiece now bills his three sons, Bratchy Junior, Martin and the Wee Man, as a four-man stand-up family show 'that ain't suitable for the family!'

What would that family make of Jerry Sadowitz? The Prince of Darkness, with funereal lum-hat and tousled hair, this Jewish Glaswegian is a Rabbi Burns with fire in his belly, a satanic versifier, who surely must rank as the world's number one shocker. But as he shocks he astounds, by performing brilliant tricks of close-up magic; with the most accomplished sleight of hand he slights his audience with tsunamis of outrageously bigoted patter. He can send up Charlie Chaplin as Adolph Hitler doing a viciously wicked imitation of Billy Connolly. And to think it was Billy who first put him on to me as one of the most brilliant comedians he had ever met.

Poverty yoked to a life-long campaign against strong drink was certainly a driving force in one of the most unconsciously funny men.

I hope the day is near at hand,
When strong drink will be banished from our land.
Cease from drink
And you will likely do well
Then there's not so much danger of going to hell.

No one is quite sure where William Topaz McGonagall was born. Some say Edinburgh, but it maybe was Donegal. Widely held as the writer of the best worst poetry in the world, the great tragedian won fame for his tortuous rhyme and flagrant disregard for metre:

I hail from the banks of the beautiful silvery Tay,
Which flows from Perth to Dundee and back again every day
I am sir, the greatest poet, versifier and tragedian
That Dundee has ever seen…

His 'Tay Bridge Disaster' is one of the few Scottish poems that Scots can recite more than a line of; so it's certainly destined to be remembered for a very long time.

Beautiful Railway bridge of the Silv'ry Tay
Alas! I am very sorry to say
That ninety lives have been taken away
On the last Sabbath day of 1879
Which will be remembered for a very long time.

It's remembered today precisely because of McGonagall's appalling rhyme. Like the crude woodcuts which illustrated Victorian broadsheets, McGonagall's verses often chronicled such disasters. McGonagall was encouraged to extend his range, even taking his verses to the gates of Balmoral to seek an audience with Queen Victoria.

I've a poem here for her Majesty
And I've walked all the way.
That's why I'm here at her castle near the Dee
Where the rabbits and hares do sport with mirthful glee
To see the Empress of India and Laird of Balmoral
So tell her I'm here, her humble and obedient servant
William Topaz McGonagall.

Rejected, but not dispirited, McGonagall sought refuge on the stage. His performance as the 'worst' Macbeth became legendary. McGonagall's Macbeth just never gave up. His swashbuckling fight scene with Macduff at the end of Shakespeare's tragedy must have been the most protracted in all history. While some actors specialised in dying, McGonagall preferred to give his audiences a good duel and roar on to the last syllable of recorded time.

Left: W.F. Frame. Before Harry Lauder this versatile tartan-clad comic and sometime clanvestite made his first appearance on the Glasgow stage in 1867 and toured America in 1898. 'W. F. Frame, the noted Scots comedian, is giving a concert in Saltcoats next week,' proclaimed an advertisement in the *Ardrossan & Saltcoats Herald* of 5 July 1904, adding: 'Doctors rest a week after Frame's visit.'

Right: Dundee of the future, postcard, 1900s by Cynicus, the *nom de guerre* of Martin Anderson, 1823-91. In contrast to Harry Lauder's urban view of the Highlands comes this bitingly critical eco-warning of unchecked industrial 'progress' by Cynicus. His view of Dundee as it yet might be is pictured from the Tayport Cynicus publishing house, across the once 'silvery Tay'.

McGonagall may have been an accidental comedian, but Glasgow's W. F. Frame was the really genuine music-hall article. Frame was the first Scots comedian to be immortalised on film. He was also among the first to be featured on postcards, where his crude stage acts were reproduced in exquisite colour by skilful Glasgow chromolithographic printers. Frame was also among the first to turn a buck mocking the tartan. He devised a true tartan horror show in which he wiggled and waggled his kilts and plaids. In drag he caricatured himself beyond the wildest excesses of the tartan-obsessed Victorians. He took his whole clamjamfry to America, years before Sir Harry Lauder tapped his crooked stick on the boards of Broadway and beyond.

When I lived in Edinburgh Harry Lauder's kilted wee mean 'mannie' and his vision of knobbly-kneed Scots could still find followers at the Edinburgh Empire Variety Theatre. For me, and most of my friends, Lauder's act was as appealing as it was appalling. If you ventured into Milne's Bar then you might have heard the poet Hugh MacDiarmid thundering against Lauder's 'chortling wut' peddling Scottish 'hokum' to the world. The bard even went so far as holding Lauder responsible for debasing popular taste and making the work of serious art impossible. In *To Circumjack Cencrastus* (1930) he wrote:

It's no' sae easy as it's payin'
To be a fule like Lauder.

MacDiarmid may have disparaged the wee man in print but he must have mustered some affection for him, as one of his prized possessions was Lauder's briar smoking-pipe. Not without some irony his widow Valda sent it off for auction to aid the Langholm MacDiarmid memorial sculpture fund. The auctioneer for the Scottish Sculpture Trust, in the guise of Chic Murray,

made great play of that when the successful bidder gave his name as Adam: 'I'm so sorry Mr Adam,' dropping his hammer. 'I didn't recognise you with your clothes on.'

Although his background was in mining in the Scottish Lowlands, Lauder's wee Heilan' mannie even set the stereotypical Scotch heather ablaze abroad. He caricatured every mean penny-pinching Scottish trait. Tom Shields, one of Glasgow's best-loved journalists, accurately describes the consequences of Lauder's international impact:

> He was vastly popular in England and the USA, but his persona of the tight-fisted, maudlin', pawky Scot in bizarre Highland dress gave the world the impression of Scotland as a country roamin' in the gloamin' forever in search of a wee deoch an' doris afore we gang back to the but an' ben. The tyranny of the tartan persisted in Scottish entertainment until relatively recent times with Andy Stewart filling the Empire Theatre in Glasgow for months at a time with comic songs such as 'Donald Where's Yer Troosers' and 'Campbeltown Loch I Wish Ye Were Whisky'. Curiously, the kilted Stewart would also perform passable impersonations of Elvis Presley and Louis Armstrong.

Lauder's legendary canny thriftiness was exploited to boost savings during World War I when he appeared on US War Savings stamps, along with his friend Charlie Chaplin. In Hollywood they were filmed together in a cross-dressing life swap, Harry in the garb of the scruffy hobo and Charlie as the tartan loony. Lauder was so successful in America that William Morris signed him up as his first client, founding his international talent agency on the swagger of his kilt. Lauder became the first international superstar. Meanwhile, Harry's cult of the Scot as a drunken sot kept right on round the bend:

Harry Lauder both photographed and caricatured on postcards. Which came first, reality or fantasy? Taking his creation onto the international stage the world's perception of Scotland was forever changed.

Right: Harry Lauder and Charlie Chaplin met in Hollywood. Shortly after this photograph was taken they exchanged costumes. A film clip survives of Charlie's wiggle and waggle of the kilt as Lauder attempts to strut like the tramp. Both Lauder and Chaplin appeared on US Savings Stamps, during world war 1. Although Chaplin organized his own business affairs, Lauder became the first client of William Morris, founder of the famous talent agency. Buying up all his contracts Morris paid Lauder $3000 per week provided that he always wore the kilt. Their handshake was the only contract they ever made and it was never broken.

And I'm fou the noo! absolutely fou!
But I adore the country I was born in.
My name is Jock McGraw and I dinna care a straw
for I've somethin' in the bottle for the mornin'!

'I Belong to Glasgow', Will Fyffe's great anthem to a city that was 'goin' roun' and roun', was much more my kind of song, as it was sung from the heart without any hint of mocking. The story goes that Fyffe met an affable wee man the worse for drink late on a Saturday night in Glasgow's Central Station. He was 'genial and demonstrative' and 'laying off about Karl Marx and John Barleycorn with equal enthusiasm', according to Albert Mackie's *The Scotch Comedians*. Fyffe asked him: 'Do you belong to Glasgow?' and he replied: 'At the moment, at the moment, Glasgow belongs to me.' So was launched that memorable anthem to the city, a song that sings the praises of Alcoholics Unanimous. It's all the more appropriate in today's Glasgow, where so many of the city's banks and shipping offices have been reincarnated as pubs and wine bars.

While Harry Lauder was happy being a stage Scotchman, Will Fyffe drew his characters from the grassroots. He could personify a Highland ghillie taking the rise out of the toff on the hill. Or pivot on one of Billy Connolly's wee drunk rubber men staring out a chip as he asks you, 'Are you all right, Jimmy?' Will Fyffe's drunk was an equally recognisable character on a Glasgow Saturday night. 'I may be under the affluence of incohol,' Fyffe would falter on the stage with perfect imperfect timing, 'but I'm not so think as you drunk I am'. Once for a bet he entered a lookalike Will Fyffe competition to sing 'I Belong to Glasgow' disguised as himself. He only came second.

I belong to Glasgow,
Dear old Glasgow town;
But what's the matter wi' Glasgow,
For it's goin' roun' and roun'!
I'm only a common old working chap,
As anyone here can see,
But when I get a couple o' drinks on a Saturday,
Glasgow belongs to me!

Even nature conspired to glorify Lauder's act. A hazelnut tree grew to mimic his wiggly waggly walking stick and survives today with the twisted scientific name of *Corylus avellana* L.'contorta'. 'As crooked as Harry Lauder's walking stick' soon became a catchword for bent businessmen at home and abroad.

With crooked stick and in full Highland fig, Harry is pictured with his sweetheart Ann Vallance who was soon to become 'Nance', his wife.

What Will Fyffe caught in song the artist John Glashan drew in brooding visions of alcoholic excess remembered from his native Glasgow. One of his favourite characters was Methylated Jim, a wee barfly of a man lost in one of those rough Glasgow boozers reserved for 'connoisseurs of the morose', as Hugh MacDiarmid so aptly put it in a memorable poem on Glasgow. In splodges of drab colour the artist splashed up a rack of grim bottles on a fish-and-chip wrapper before inking in the labels of such unpotable drinks as 'Methylated Spirits Nouveau'. With a scratchy pen he then floated his Methylated Jimmy into swirling washes of dire gloom. As the soggy picture of despair took shape, Glashan remarked on the cruel absurdity of such a place; one which provided its victims with all the chemical means of inebriation, only to throw them back into the street, once they had reached the state of grace for which they had paid the bar so handsomely.

All this was for the benefit of a BBC Scotland television series in which artists were invited to paint a work, as they talked about their life and art. It was a well known perk that the producer, W. Gordon Smith, got to keep the final artwork for his private collection. 'What should be done with this then?' Glashan asked the camera, as he held up his still damp finished barscape of blootered Glaswegian barflies. To the film crew's amazement he struck a match on the zinc counter and set his art-work alight. Through the flickering blue flames wee Methylated Jimmy wriggled and curled in his death throes. In a touch of genius, Glashan had used methylated spirits instead of water. As the wry Glashan ordered drinks all round (of a less undrinkable vintage), Gordon Smith must have sorely regretted that it would now never adorn his walls.

Glashan had excelled as an artist at the Glasgow School of Art. In a few bold sweeps of fluid watercolour, often coagulating into impressionist swirls and blobs on resistant surfaces, dark brooding shadows would take shape, pierced by shafts of light often achieved by the confident flick of a palette knife. Glashan would then ink in his cast of characters. They could include the *ménage à trois* of Anode Enzyme, the world's greatest genius (IQ 12,790 – formerly 12,794, but 4 were lost watching television); Lord Doberman, the richest man in the world, along with the supermarket manageress, Bechamel Lecithin, pictured naked on an elegant chaise longue. This whole mad fantasy of the absurd would then be framed in lines of neat handwriting, a combination reminiscent of those hand-coloured relief etchings of William Blake.

Will Fyffe, 1885-1947. Glasgow's famous comedian was actually born in Dundee.

John Glashan, 1927-99. Triumphing in the morose, John Glashan's cartoons captured the gloomy zeitgeist of postwar Britain.

The body doesn't store alcohol — You've got to keep replacing it...

Would you like to send the wine back, sir?

Glashan was fully conscious of the prejudices of art historians, who have seldom given credit to such great cartoon artists of the past as Cruikshank, Gilray and Rowlandson. The often bitter narratives which played around Glashan's creations may have reflected his own experience in attempting to win commissions as a portrait painter at the beginning of his career. His father Archibald McGlashan (the minimalist in Glashan dropped the Mc) was an accomplished but undervalued portrait painter, who always reminded his son that they shared the heritage of Velázquez, Rembrandt and Michelangelo.

> I have never been a devoted follower of truth.
> Truth beneath the lyre is my emblem.
> Cynicus (Martin Anderson)

Opposite: Lord Doberman dining at Mollusc Hall by John Glashan. 'Would you like to send the wine back, sir?'

With one of his most famous postcards, the laird of Castle Cynicus poses.

In the decade before the self-mockery of the Harry Lauder school of national self-deprecation came another lone comic artist with cynical satire in his belly. Martin Anderson, under the *nom de guerre* of Cynicus, elbowed his way into the complacent world of double standards that was London of the 1890s. The biting industrial-strength irony of his caricatures had not been seen since the satirical excesses of Rowlandson and Cruikshank. Although Anderson was brought up in St Andrews, he had witnessed the rampant squalor of Glasgow's mean streets as an art student. But perhaps it was his experiences in Paris which turned his ambitions away from being an artist and towards the profession of masterful caricaturist and social commentator. The opening of the first Honoré Daumier retrospective coincided with his visit there. Daumier's searingly observed caricatures of nineteenth-century society must surely have inspired *The Satires of Cynicus*, Martin's first collection of acerbic cartoons. Satirising the law, the Church, politicians and every aspect of Victorian complacency, there were few targets which Martin didn't ridicule. His works became bestsellers. The Martin publishing empire grew. Soon he was employing a whole village back in Fife to hand-tint editions in colour washes, which immediately became collectables. Martin then went on to invent the comic postcard single-handedly. Soon his cynical commentaries, articulating the fears and aspirations of society at large, were broadcast on postcards to homes across the land.

The Cynicus postcards became so commercially successful that Martin began to build himself a dream castle at Balmullo, near the Fife village where he was born. Castle Cynicus was as eccentric as its creator. He built a long picture gallery and museum to entertain and educate local farmworkers and miners. His generosity to the underprivileged did not go unpunished. By entertaining local workers Martin soon began to draw the wrath of his snobbish and mean-spirited neighbours. His final wish for Castle Cynicus to become a retreat for workers was denied him. When he died, one of the most vindictive local critics bought Castle Cynicus and razed every trace of it to the ground. The artist had his posthumous revenge, for the vandal died soon after the last swing of his wrecker's ball. Now nothing remains of Scotland's strangest castle, save for a few sepia postcards and the commemorations of one of the most remarkable comic artists of his time.

'Who said Bannockburn?', 1900s, by Andrew Allan.

'Would you like to sit on my knee?'

Edinburgh, Princes Street Gardens, 'crayograph' by Andrew Allan, one of a postcard series, published by Millar & Lang, Glasgow, 1900s. Apart from his caricatures of Scots, Andrew Allan developed a process he called crayographs for a series of city scenes and landscapes, but it would be his kilted caricatures that would sell in thousands. It is hard to believe that Allan was the same artist of the combative 'Who Said Bannockburn?'.

As the artistic director of Millar & Lang Allan had a fine art training at the Glasgow School of Art when the architect Charles Rennie Mackintosh was a night student there. It is tempting to think that Allan's art nouveau lettering owed something to Mackintosh, as he saw himself first as an artist, but made his living as a talented caricaturist.

Other postcard companies in Scotland lasted longer, though none had the cutting edge of Cynicus, preferring instead to peddle uncritical McClichés. One of the most successful of these companies was Millar & Lang, which brought out streams of self-mocking postcards devised by Andrew Allan in beautifully printed chromolithography. Although Allan had trained as an artist at the Glasgow School of Art, it wouldn't be his meticulously drawn landscapes that would make their mark but rather his ribald, toothless, pawky Highlanders. It was a tension that would later make him take his own life.

'The Broons' and 'Oor Wullie' were brought to life by Dudley Watkins in the Fun Section of the *Sunday Post* in 1936, and they've been with us ever since. Not only were they the brainchild of the editor Robert Low, but they were also modelled on his immediate family. Maw and the bunnet-wearing pipe-smoking Paw Broon were based by Watkins on Low's own folks, who lived above him in the same Dundee tenement. Low's playful eight-year-old son Ron was the real-life Oor Wullie, right down to his dungarees, bucket and spiky hair.

Once Watkins got into his stride, the editors at D.C. Thomson would send the storylines to his home in Broughty Ferry, where he would ink up the cartoon characters with wry humour. Apart from these Scottish favourites, Watkins created many icons of comic art in the *Beano* and *Dandy* comic weeklies. His characters included the nation's favourite cow-pie-munching strongman, Desperate Dan, now memorialised in bronze on a Dundee street complete with his dog, Dawg.

Despite the rough-and-tumble of D.C. Thomson's freewheeling thick-ear school of comics (as the style soon became known), Watkins saw himself as a religious

artist, and his lifelong ambition was to illustrate the Bible. When an exhibition of his life's work opened at the Dundee Art Gallery such heartfelt pictures as *Jesus with His Disciples on Lake Galilee* bore uncanny resemblances to his much loved characters in the Broons. After all, Watkins was only following that long tradition in Western art of deriving the faces of his holy subjects from the locals.

Being in two places and two time zones at once was heady stuff in the late 1940s, when Billy Neill recreated himself as Bud and brought Glasgow's long-held Wild West dreams to surrealist life with Lobey Dosser, the cowboy sheriff of Calton Creek. Lobey Dosser took his name from the homeless who used to doss in the lobbies of Glasgow tenements to sleep rent-free. Apart from his famous Lobey Dosser strip, Bud created thousands of pocket cartoons complete with pithy captions. These raised Glaswegian patter to new heights of linguistic lunacy, rivalling even the punning inventiveness of James Joyce. In line and word no one ever caught the look and the patois of the West of Scotland so imaginatively as did Bud Neill. The brilliance of his wit inspired a whole new generation of comedians and pantomime dames.

I like to keep in touch on the Internet with some of the stranger goings-on in Scotland through the *Glasgow Herald*'s witty and idiosyncratic Diary. On the run-up to Glasgow's year as European City of Culture in 1990 its then editor, Tom Shields, decided to wave the flag for his local hero and promote a public sculpture to the memory of Bud Neill and his one-eyed sheriff of Calton Creek. It became one of the longest-running campaigns in Scottish journalism. At the height of the campaign the Diary was receiving over five hundred letters a week, as Tom Shields writes:

The Broons – the Dundee tenement family born in the late 1930s and still going strong today. Ironically the most Scottish of all strip-cartoon characters were illustrated by the English artist Dudley Watkins, who was talent-scouted at the extraordinarily early age of eighteen by D. C. Thomson, the family-owned newspaper company in Dundee.

Oor Wullie strip by Dudley Watkins inked up for the *Sunday Post*, 24 September 1944.

Bud Neill, 1907-70. Astride the flailing two legs of his 'wee lassie foal' El Fildeldo, Sheriff Lobey would ride the purple plains of Glasgow's Partick, as he dodged the baddie Rank Bajin (an upper class twit who talked posh) through the dull grey post-war world of the A bomb menace, stranded GI brides, Korea, sweetie rationing and much, much less.

Bud Neill not only had an eye for the absurd but an ear to snatch the fineries of the Glasgow dialect as they flew past him. Apart from Lobey Dosser, Bud provided witty pocket cartoons for Glasgow's *Evening Times*, the *Daily Record* and the *Daily Express*. Since nearly all of his original work was binned by these newspapers, we have to thank Yvonne Barron and Ranald MacColl, aficionados of the range, who painstakingly re-inked his cartoons from poor-quality newspaper cuttings.

Lobey Dosser sculpture by Tony Morrow with Nick Gillon, Woodlands Road, Glasgow, 1992.

The statue of Lobey Dosser in Woodlands Road, Glasgow, can lay claim to two firsts. It is the world's only two-legged equestrian statue. It is the only statue in Britain since Victorian times to be erected by public subscription. The above claims may or may not be accurate but what is true is that it is Glasgow's best-loved statue. The wee horse's nose is shiny from the many friendly pats it has received since it was unveiled in 1992. Lobey astride his faithful steed El Fideldo brings a smile to the faces of all who pass by and is thus a fitting tribute to newspaper cartoonist Bud Neill. Many weans have been photographed sitting on Lobey's knee. Students use it as a backdrop for their graduation pictures. Whether or not Neill would approve of the statue, we do not know. But we think he might be entertained by the reaction to it. We think he might like the fact that this cheeky stookie is the first thing the faithful from the nearby Free Kirk see when they come out of their services.

What Bud Neill wrote and illustrated Stanley Baxter brought to life in his television educational series, *Teach Yersel Glasgu*. This master of mimicry would pitch such seemingly impenetrable phrases as 'Na ah'll no borra wi a barra choclit, Clara' before interjecting its translation in the haughtiest English accent of pure cut crystal: 'No, I shall not bother with a bar of chocolate, Clara.' 'Giesa annara barra tamarra' – 'Give me another bar tomorrow.'

During the Depression of the 1930s in Scotland's inner cities, poor Jewish immigrants scraped a living alongside their equally poor native Scots. Perhaps because of some deep-seated affinity between the Low German roots of Yiddish and the North German origins of Lowland Scots, a new street lingo was born, Scots-Yiddish. According to the historian David Daiches it was destined to be the shortest-living dialect in world history, for it had all but died out after Hitler's war.

> You think that everything I say is funny
> just because I've got a funny voice.
>
> Ivor Cutler

If there was one humorist who emerged from this dual world and survived, it was Ivor Cutler. Born in 1923 into a Jewish immigrant family who lived within sight of Glasgow Rangers' soccer grounds at Ibrox, he loved to claim that his first scream was drowned by fans cheering a goal. Cutler's childhood experiences growing up in those bleak years eventually fed into such hilarious books as *Life in a Scotch Sitting Room* (1984) and *Glasgow Dreamer*. Introducing his stage performances with whingeing hymn-like chords on a wheezing harmonium, Cutler would deliver episodes from these recollections enunciating each word with the righteous authority of a Free Presbyterian minister's Sabbath sermon.

Trained as a teacher, Cutler had no stomach for the sadistic punishment, administered in Scottish schools, of thrashing the hands of children with a tawse. He had suffered 'the tingle of the tawse' over two hundred times as a schoolboy. I can feel for that, as we had a Mr Brown in our Edinburgh school who wore a tawse permanently between his waistcoat and jacket, ready to whip out on the slimmest

Ivor Cutler, 1923-2006. The unassuming master of surrealist humour whose eccentric take on the world was embedded in the Scotland he had to flee. 'Imperfection is an end,' he said, 'perfection is only an aim.'

See me! screamed the old woman and tottered off the cliff. The sharp wind up her coat revived her interest in life for a few bitter-sweet seconds.
Ivor Cutler 1981

Occidental Pearl
'Two balls ran down a hill. One landed on its side, the other, upside down.'
—Ivor Cutler

obtuse angles go home

pretext. I was once the target of his fury, singled out in front of the class as a reprisal for some mild joint misdemeanour, before being belted one hand after another with calculated ferocity. And to think that this was the same man who had peaceably drummed into me Pythagoras's theorem.

The implement of torture was also known as a Lochgelly, from the little Fife village where the most sought-after tawses were made. The enterprising saddlers, John Dick & Sons, designed them in various weights and sizes as a lucrative sideline to harness- and saddle-making. Tooled to a high standard by skilled leather craftsmen, the firm's 'Lochgelly' enjoyed a steady export market to France. This puzzled the Fife firm, since corporal punishment in French schools was outlawed in 1881. Over the years this niche-market Scottish export had become the whip of choice much loved by masochists as *le fouet écossais*. In a dramatic gesture Cutler chopped his up, and handed out the leather pieces to his bewildered pupils, before turning his back on the land of the tawse for good. 'Leaving Scotland,' he would always say, 'was the beginning of my life.'

The innovative teacher A.S. Neill, himself a refugee from Scottish teaching methods based on fear, offered Cutler a place at Summerhill, his free-thinking school in Suffolk which fostered the belief that freedom nurtured learning. After enjoying the confidence and ideas of the Summerhill children, whom he treated as his equals, Cutler left to teach the less privileged in inner-London primary schools. For over twenty-five years he taught dance, music, African drumming, movement, drama and poetry, before finally liberating himself full-time as the grand old master of the surreal.

Being a humorist I'm naturally a lugubrious kind of bloke.
Ivor Cutler

Singing simple nonsense verses to ever-increasing audiences drawn from all walks of life, Cutler's act was like no other. In spontaneous outbursts of mild abuse, often directed at latecomers or fidgeting weans in the front row, he would weave magical tales out of the totally mundane. In time his fan base extended from the philosopher Bertrand Russell to the Beatles, Billy Connolly and Franz Ferdinand's Alex Kapranos. Cutler was performing to capacity audiences up to a year before he died at eighty-three in 2006. Thanks to numerous recordings and a shelf-full of little books with such witty names as *Cockadoodledon't!*, *Is That Your Flap, Jack?* and *Scots Wa' Straw*, the dazzling and dour world Ivor Cutler created lives on.

By Geck or by goak
I'll be Faust in this boke.
Carotid Cornucopius

If Bud Neill's observant eye could match his attentive ear, the poet Sydney Goodsir Smith could create vivid imagery from words. Like Rabelais before him, Sydney came to things through words, rather than to words through things. His Rabelaisian *Carotid Cornucopius* was subtitled a 'Drammantick, backside, bogbide, bedride or badside buik in-containuentingshreehunder and sixty-five fitts'. For the poet Hugh MacDiarmid *Carotid* was 'as alive as an hilarious old tinker – a fine reeking haggis of a book in the tradition of Sir Thomas Urquhart'. 'If a composite of all the conversations proceeding at any given time in all the pubs and public conveniences and disorderly houses of Edinburgh could be secured,' wrote MacDiarmid, 'that composite would be amazingly similar to one of Mr Smith's fitts.'

Sydney Goodsir Smith was no mean drinker. He once found himself on a hungover Saturday Edinburgh morning desperately seeking an emergency entrance to a pub. Somewhat unsure of his immediate surroundings, Sydney wandered through the handsome doors. Reassured by the ornate brass fittings along the counter, he ordered a stiff drink. Whatever look there was on that bankteller's face in the 1950s, it's Sydney, that wise old auk of the Canongate, who now has the last laugh. That yon bonnie bank, like so many venerable Victorian temples to Mammon, is now an opulent Edinburgh bar and bistro. Surely only a bard of Sydney's prophetic genius could have foretold its glorious future. Slainte!

Just to show that the fun of wordplay is still a popular pastime in Scotland, when Inverness Caledonian Thistle (known to generations of soccer fans as Caley) beat Celtic 3–1 in 2000 for the Scottish Cup, the headline in the *Scottish Sun* ran: 'SuperCaleygoballisticCelticareatrocious'. Oh, Julie Andrews, where's your Supercalifragilisticexpialidocious the noo?

But before we raise a glass to our comic heritage, let the last lesson come from Bill Duncan's *Wee Book of Calvin*: 'The road tae the pub is the short-cut to Hell.' And to think a friend sent me that grim wee reminder with this seasonal inscription: 'In case you're having a merry Christmas, just remember where you came from.' Now for me that really nails the bollocks to the mast.

Opposite: A.S.Neill, founder of Summerhill in 1921, talking to children on equal terms in the 1930s. The school still flourishes in Leiston, Suffolk, under the care of Neill's daughter, Zoe Redhead.

Left: The Dome, née Royal Bank of Scotland, George Street, Edinburgh. It took this bank over forty years to morph into the bar intuited by the poet Sydney Goodsir Smith one hungover Saturday morning in the Fifties. Finding an emergency entrance to a pub through ornate doors and reassured by the elelgant brass fittings, he ordered a stiff round of drinks at the teller's counter. What poetic prescience is that.

Right: From Carotid Cornucopius, 1947, by Sydney Goodsir Smith, 1915-75, a New Zealand-Scottish poet, artist, dramatist and novelist who wrote poetry in literary Scots. In this illustration by Randell Wells Carotid rejoices as the Great Auk of the Canongate in kilts.

15 WAVERLEY

Or 'tis sixty years hence

This was the full title Sir Walter Scott gave to his first historical novel of 1814, distancing it back in time to the defeat of the Jacobite Rising of 1745. Now it's sixty years since I left Edinburgh in 1947 and the noble name of Waverley Station is prefixed by 'Edinburgh'; a needless change, but certainly not among the worst alterations my hometown has suffered over these last sixty years. 'Edinburgh,' wrote A. J. Youngson in *The Making of Classical Edinburgh*, 'owes its singular character to the late and sudden flowering of Scottish culture.' Such a singular character was recognised by UNESCO in 1995 when the Old and New Towns of Edinburgh were listed as a World Heritage site. But it's an accolade Edinburgh could soon be in danger of losing. When Dresden proposed an inappropriate development in the form of a bridge, UNESCO threatened to delist the city as a World Heritage site.

Each time I return to the city I am shocked at the mediocre quality of the new architecture. And now even the cobbles of the New Town are being asphalted over, street by street. The planners should look to Copenhagen to see how a World Heritage site is preserved. Those who now administer and plan developments in what they still claim to be the Athens of the North might stop and ponder the oath taken by the Athenians of ancient Greece: 'I will leave my city not less, but greater and better than I found it.' Apart from two recent public buildings, the New Museum of Scotland and the Parliament, and some innovative housing down the Royal Mile, there has been little built since the war that leaves Edinburgh a greater or better city.

Glasgow's accolade of European City of Culture in 1990 was awarded for the promise of its imaginative programme. But what confirmed the jury's decision over Edinburgh and other UK cities was that a renewed cultural pride in the city was apparent even at a domestic level. When the jury was invited to the home of Lucy Parr and Graeme Shearer, who were in the process of rejuvenating their

Victorian flat on Park Terrace, the judges were astonished at what these two young architects had already achieved. As the setting sun bathed the gilded angels in the restored drawing-room overlooking Kelvingrove Park, a meal was being prepared out of an innovatively designed kitchen and study. Exposed metal beams supported a mezzanine level inspired by the Venetian architect Carlo Scarpa, as a striking contrast to the *belle époque* grandeur of the room next door. This brilliant partnership was tragically cut short when Lucy died soon after the birth of their first child, leaving her inspiration on how to complement the old with the new as a challenge for architects to come.

The Year of Culture left many creative footprints in Glasgow. Peter Brook's staging of the *Mahabharata* in an abandoned tram shed left the new performance space and gallery, the Tramway. In 1999 Glasgow received a second honour as the UK City of Architecture and Design. But despite many initiatives, including a new building programme on Glasgow Green and an exhibition on Alexander 'Greek' Thomson in the newly fitted out architecture and design centre, the Lighthouse, Glasgow's record of destroying its built heritage shows no sign of lessening, and few contemporary buildings of significance have arisen to take their place. Unlike Glasgow, Edinburgh survived the attentions of the Luftwaffe during World War II nearly unscathed, but not those of such madcap postwar planners as Patrick Abercrombie, bent on driving motorways through Edinburgh's Georgian terraces. The demolition of houses along the Royal Mile was proposed in the interests of traffic. Fortunately such hare-brained schemes were resisted by the many articulate residents who still lived within the city centre along the paths of the planned motorways. Few were more forceful than the writer Robert Kemp, whose newspaper campaign in the end won the day for reason.

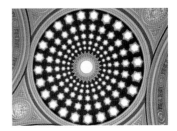

The Royal Bank of Scotland headquarters in St Andrews Square was originally the Dundas Mansion designed by William Chambers in 1774. The star-domed Telling Room of 1857 by Dick Peddie owes more than a nod to the German architect Karl Friedrich Schinkel's opera set for Mozart's *Magic Flute*.

Sadly, the remaining decades of the twentieth century dealt Edinburgh some of its worst buildings. As concrete parodies of Mies van der Rohe's elegant International Style minimalism, they rose across one of the most beautiful cities in Europe in brutish ugliness. None were as bad as the offices built by the self-sanctioning vandals of government. They were by law permitted to despoil Edinburgh's skyline without ever seeking planning permission, and could cock a snook at any reasonable request from conservation groups. Whereas God was in the details of the phosphor-bronze mullions of New York's Seagram Building (or so Mies always claimed), only the Devil could ever have lurked in such monsters as the government's Argyle House, with its rows of windows gaping like unsmiling teeth, locked in a brace of rotting concrete mullions.

The best buildings in Edinburgh's Princes Street fell like dominoes through the 1960s, despite the heroic campaigns waged by Colin McWilliam. In one last-ditch attempt to save the Life Association building of 1855, the indefatigable architectural historian confronted the wrecker's ball by lying down in front of this magnificent Venetian palace, but to no avail. It fell, only to be replaced by another concrete insult. Edinburgh continues to expand its share of overscaled blockbuster buildings in glass. The good people of the Canongate and the Royal Mile have had the overscaled Caltongate development foisted on them, despite over two thousand petitions lodged against it. The application for a five-star hotel, breaching a hole in the Royal Mile, was passed through by Historic Scotland, an extraordinary decision for a body which is known to fuss over the retention of nondescript rubble walls instead of encouraging creative new work. The architect Allan Murray dismissed the numerous objections of local residents and such respected conservation groups as the Cockburn Association as showing 'a real ignorance of the city'. More an ignorance of the architects and planners, I would say.

Allan Murray's best building is his Under Fives Centre, sensitively scaled to the needs of pre-school kids and snugly lodged behind the Old Assembly Close off the Royal Mile, near where my grandparents lived. It has style, which I find quite

Argyle House, Grassmarket, Edinburgh, Architects, Michael Laird and Partners, 1966. Before Edinburgh was nominated as a World Heritage City, the capital of Scotland suffered grievously from the building of unregulated Government administration offices, from the late Fifties onwards. Argyle House was one of the worst, built in the historic Grassmarket under the ramparts of Edinburgh Castle. Its concrete mullions parodied the elegant phosphor-bronze 'I' beams of New York's Seagram Building by the architects, Ludwig Mies van der Rohe and Philip Johnson, 1954.

Other disfigurements of Edinburgh are too depressing to illustrate, such as the St James's Centre by Ian Burke & Martin, 1964. As a monster, spreadeagled over the site of James Craig's once-elegant square of 1775, the catastrophic impact of the St James's Centre was like a knife thrust into the heart of the elegant New Town.

Robert Adam's Edinburgh South Bridge proposal of 1785, would have made Edinburgh the greatest neoclassical city in the world. Computer-generated design by Sandy Kinghorn

Pulteney Bridge, Bath, 1773, designed by Robert Adam over the River Avon has shops on both sides, gives some hint at what Adam's great project might have been.

lacking in his many office buildings. I had high hopes, when those arid wall oven windows of the Sixties Midlothian building on the Royal Mile came down, that we would have a building of some architectural distinction as its replacement. The previous tenement on the site was a strong, characterful vernacular building which was a welcoming haven for us in the postwar years with its folk clubs and the great dive inside called Bungy's. What now stands on this important corner of the Royal Mile and George IV Bridge is neither good nor bad. It may tick all the planners' boxes for its use of stone, its deployment of windows and much else, but where's its sense of Edinburghness? How much more interesting this development would have been had its architect created a dialogue between past and present and designed a building of our time that complemented its neighbours.

Reassuringly, there are now a number of practices which have achieved outstanding work in Edinburgh, winning more than their share of national awards. Malcolm Fraser, Sutherland Hussey and Richard Murphy have all built imaginatively to complement Edinburgh's past. Fraser's Dance Base was carved out of a series of redundant spaces in the Grassmarket. It has practically no façade, but inside dancers can now leap towards stunning skylight views of Edinburgh Castle. For the Edinburgh Sculpture Workshop Sutherland Hussey has designed an ingenious series of studio spaces near the port of Leith.

Adapting old buildings to new uses is one of the greatest strengths of Richard Murphy's practice. He has brought new life to Stirling's ancient Tollbooth, out of courtrooms and even prison cells, to create Scotland's most popular centre for live music. A building that once convened a parliament in the reign of James VI now plays host to the kings and queens of jazz, from ceilidh bands to string quartets. Bars and cafés pivot off an engineering wonder of a spiral staircase, to link the ancient spaces to the music rooms, a perfect play of old and new, the hallmark of a Murphy-rejuvenated building.

Stirling Tolbooth Arts Centre, 2001, Richard Murphy Architects. A model of creative rejuvenation and a triumph of adaptive re-use. A seventeenth-century courthouse and jail were imaginatively turned into a vibrant arts centre pivoting around a daring spiral staircase.

This architect's most daring and imaginative proposal was for a stunning glazed Ring of Saturn to provide the Usher Hall with a rooftop bar. Having grown up next to MacEwan's brewery in Fountainbridge, I often wondered why the Scottish brewers, who paid for the MacEwan Hall, the Younger Hall and the Usher Hall, insisted that we should take our entertainments dry. Today most of us love a tipple before a concert. How wonderful it would have been had the Murphy plan gone ahead with its escalators up to the rooftop for an interval drink, with Edinburgh's eternal skyline as a backdrop. His scheme was vetoed in favour of a bulging blister on the rotunda for twice the cost, at £20 million. Murphy's rooftop Oloroso restaurant on George Street, with its stunning view of Edinburgh Castle, just hints at what concert-goers might have had. His practice may have won the most awards in Scotland and Murphy may be his name, but like the Irish stout, he's not bitter.

Usher Hall, Richard Murphy's rejected scheme for refreshment bars around the roof setback beside the dome. Such an innovative solution would have allowed concert-goers to glide up escalators to toast Edinburgh's incomparable skyline.

AFTERWORD

'Andy, everyone loves a winner.'
'Not in my country they don't.'
  Andrew Greig, *Preferred Lies*

Ever since the Treaty of Union between Scotland and England created Great Britain in 1707, England has always considered itself Britain. Where my mother was born in the Highlands, the rail timetables referred to Scotland as North Britain. But was there ever a South Britain? It was only recently that Edinburgh's North British Hotel was renamed 'The Balmoral'. Could London ever have named a major hotel 'The South British'? It's this inequality of attitude that has always irritated me.

In the mid-Sixties I became interested in politics in Scotland when Winifred Ewing was campaigning for the Scottish National Party in the Hamilton by-election against formidable odds. Since Labour had captured 71.2 per cent of the vote at the previous general election, Ewing's sensational victory in 1967 made headlines across the UK and sent shock waves through the other Scottish parties. Yet when she arrived in Westminster, MPs treated her deplorably. All I have ever campaigned for is to have Scotland considered an equal partner with England. I am for a Scotland that makes her own decisions, a sovereign state that will be a voice in Europe and around the world. I would also like to banish all aspects of feudality in Scotland. A couple of statistics substantiate my case: for example, only 4 per cent of all the companies owned in Scotland have their head offices in Scotland. The rest are in the south or abroad.

When I learnt that Edward Heath's government in 1973 had traded the extinction of the Scottish fishing industry in order to allow Britain's entry into the Common Market (as the European Union was then called), it convinced me that Scotland would always be so shabbily treated until she could manage her own affairs. Now, thanks to the release of government papers under the thirty-year rule, we learned that in 1975 Denis Healey, the then Labour chancellor, downplayed the vast oil profits gushing in from the North Sea. He feared Scots would demand independence, and so would plunge the rest of Britain into bankruptcy. What prosperity could Scotland have enjoyed had we retained control over our own oil reserves? In the nineteenth century we used our abundant coal to engineer inventions for export to the world. Yet our oil reserves were sold off as our industries were allowed to die. Look what Norway achieved with her oil policies during the same period.

For centuries Scotland has punched well beyond its weight in the world. When Arthur Herman flew from Washington DC to attend an Edinburgh symposium based on his book on the Scottish Enlightenment, *How the Scots Invented the Modern World*, over half the audience actually argued against the idea. The good-natured Herman, who has no Scottish family connections, put it all down to Scots contrariness. But why? Let's abandon this national cringe.

When I read a newspaper in Hollywood I've often thought that if the word 'success' dropped out of all its news reports and articles, the paper would just fall apart. So too in Scotland, but the word would then be 'failure'. For much of my life I've thought of exchanging the bogus bonhomie of California, forever wishing me a nice day, for the honest aggression of Scotland, where it's assumed that I've made other arrangements to get through my day. What is it in our culture that accentuates the negative and puts down our positive achievements? When I brought a contingent of ninety-five people over to Scotland for the world premiere of my movie *Entrapment* at the Edinburgh Film Festival, the tabloids put their heavies in the hotel just to upset me. Success is a red rag to them. They want to take you down. They just want you to fail so that they can report on your discomfort. That's why Billy Connolly refuses to have newspapers anywhere near his home.

The Alamo in San Antonio, Texas, is a very unAmerican monument. It celebrates defeat and failure over victory and success. It's a concept we would have no difficulty understanding in Scotland, where the country is strewn with ruins and sites of long-lost battles. Texas has other affinities with the land of the kilt, as it's the only state in the union I know which sports national dress. This takes the form of buckled levis, wide-brimmed Stetson hats and buckskin boots. On ceremonial occasions they arm themselves with holstered six-shooters, just as Scots wear jewelled black daggers, or sgian dubhs, tied under their knees by ribbons, or nickie-tams.

One of the most touching monuments inside the Alamo is a memorial to Robert Bontine Cunninghame Graham (the friend of Conrad mentioned in Chapter 12). In 1880 this Scots adventurer and writer had set up his ranch near San Antonio along with his exotically named wife, Gabrielle de la Balmondiere. It was only recently established that her real name was Carrie Horsfall, a tearaway doctor's daughter from Masham, Yorkshire. As ranchers they were heroic failures and doubly unsuccessful settlers, as their homestead was twice burnt down by marauding natives. Returning to Scotland to look after the

The victorious Winifred Ewing at the Hamilton by-election, 1967. Winifred Ewing became only the second Scottish Nationalist MP to be elected to Westminster. Nationalists, in the wake of Ewing's unexpectedly large majority over a Labour stronghold, forced the Conservative leader Ted Heath to make a commitment to devolution in his 1968 'Declaration of Perth'.

crumbling estate of Gartmore outside Glasgow, Cunninghame Graham became a radical Liberal MP, promoting the underclass by defending workers' rights. He encouraged Keir Hardie to stand for Parliament under the banner of the Scottish Labour Party, which they had founded together. The first membership card emblazons both their portraits. Under the coalminer Hardie unfurls the slogan 'No Monopoly'. Under Cunninghame Graham, who was descended from the kings of Scotland, it reads 'No Privilege'. Now there was a true socialist, unlike Tony Blair.

Towards the end of his long life this remarkable man co-founded the National Party of Scotland, with support from such seemingly opposing forces as the Duke of Montrose and the Scots bard Hugh MacDiarmid, who saw no contradiction in extolling Graham as both a campaigner for workers' rights and a true aristocrat. I thought that was a wonderful assessment of a man who made his mark in Parliament, wrote superb short stories, and, not least of all, founded two political parties.

In 1995 I deposited $1.2 million in a bank account and donated the monthly interest of around $8000 to the Scottish National Party. This was curtailed in 2001 when new laws prohibited political parties from accepting money from people not on Britain's electoral register. As the honorary chairman of the American Friends of Scotland charity, I have helped to strengthen the connections between the US and Scotland as a reminder that nine out of the thirteen governors of the original thirteen States were Scots. To accentuate the positive, the Scottish International Education Trust, which I initiated and co-funded over thirty-five years ago, has since boosted the careers of many young talents in Scotland. But what's the purpose of this if our politicians don't follow suit?

When New Labour latched on to celebrities for its Cool Britannia image I was invited to Chequers, to be courted by Tony Blair and Gordon Brown. They were anxious to win my public support for their devolution referendum plans that September. Despite my impression that Scottish devolution was just an irritating irrelevance for Tony Blair, Cherie took me aside afterwards and said, 'Now you really will go to Scotland and campaign, won't you?' I found it quite insulting. I don't play the guitar. But in the end I went. It resulted in a photo opportunity featuring Gordon Brown and me crossing the Forth, framed against the cantilevers of the Forth Bridge. Gordon had the decency to send me a thank you fax. I never heard a word back from either Cherie or Tony Blair.

I was as critical as anyone when the Royal High School, on its commanding site, was passed over as the new Scottish Parliament and a new building was fast-forwarded into construction before all its requirements were known. But at the opening I forgave what the First Secretary Donald Dewar had commissioned, for I was thrilled with what the Catalan architect Enric Miralles had achieved in that remarkable complex of buildings at the end of the Royal Mile. Despite the Greek tragedy of their early deaths, Miralles and Dewar's posthumous achievement has been endorsed by the people. Within a year of its opening the Parliament was one of the most popular visitor destinations in Scotland. Unlike the cost overruns of Blair's vacuous Millennium Dome, at least here we had a happy ending. If the

Scottish Labour membership card. The miner Keir Hardie and the land-owning radical Robert B. Cunninghame Graham were the co-founders of the Scottish Labour Party in 1888: the first Labour political party in Britain. The membership card displays Keir Hardie framed by the slogan 'No Monopoly' and Cunninghame Graham with 'No Privilege'.

Crossing the Forth with Gordon Brown in the lead-up to the 1997 Referendum on Devolution to promote Labour's 'yes-yes' campaign for Scottish Devolution.

Parliament cost over £400 million, consider that it will cost over £4000 million to half decommission the fast breeder nuclear reactor at Dounreay. Miralles's Parliament, against tough opposition, won the 2005 RIBA Stirling Prize, the UK's number one architectural award. Even the *Scotsman* newspaper, which had conducted a negative campaign against this building from the day of its announcement, reluctantly applauded. It's always puzzled me how newspapers in Scotland can be bought by outsiders to peddle their own agendas.

> Then let us pray that come it may,
> As come it will for a' that,
> That Sense and Worth, o'er a' the earth,
> Shall bear the gree, an' a' that.
> For a' that, an' a' that,
> It's coming yet for a' that,
> That Man to Man, the world o'er,
> Shall brothers be for a' that.

When the Queen opened the first Scottish Parliament in just under three hundred years, Sheena Wellington sang with much emotion 'A Man's a Man for A' That', Robert Burns's plea for world equality. But how else is the great poet and songwriter honoured in Scotland today? According to the Moffat Centre at Glasgow Caledonian University, the 'Burns brand', in hideous tourist-speak, now contributes over £3 million a week to the Scottish economy. It's hardly different from the marketing of Mozart in Austria. But there at least they know the world significance of their man.

Mozart, like Burns, satirised the pompous, spoke up for the underdog and promoted universal harmony. Wolfgang Schüssel, the Austrian chancellor, placed Mozart in his 250th anniversary year at the centre of an international conference to celebrate Austria's six-month presidency of the European Union in 2006. Condoleezza Rice, America's Secretary of State, attended a commemorative Mozart concert at Salzburg. So wouldn't it have been appropriate for Robert Burns to take centre stage during Britain's six months' presidency of the European Union, especially since the Gleneagles G8 conference was being held in Scotland? Yet the best the British government could do was to give the American President a plate of haggis. Could all those Scots in Blair's government not have done us prouder?

Burns was born in 1759 on 25 January and Wolfgang Amadeus Mozart was born in 1756, the same month but two days later. Both were freemasons. Brother Wolfgang Amadeus Mozart's Vienna lodge was of the Scottish Rites. If Brother Robert Burns could visit the colossal Temple of the Scottish Rites today – the headquarters of the Supreme Council of the Southern Jurisdiction of the 33rd Degree of the Ancient and Accepted Rite of Freemasonry in Washington, DC – he would be amazed to see that inside its granite walls its library houses the largest collection of his work outside the National Library of Scotland.

Like the poetry of Burns, Mozart's music can play any role you care to name – political or commercial; comic or spiritual; popular or high-brow; compassionate or bawdy. But what are we selling? Possibly we're selling Burns down the sweet Afton.

Flow gently, sweet Afton, among thy green braes,
Flow gently, sweet Afton, the theme of my lays…
My Mary's asleep by the murmuring stream,
Flow gently, sweet Afton, disturb not her dream.

Who are we celebrating? We're celebrating a great lyric poet. Robert Burns is one of the world's greatest songwriters. Bard. Bawd. A poet's poet. A poet for all seasons. But are we up to the essential genius of the man? For genius he was. Robert Burns lived and loved and wrote in the late eighteenth century, in that glorious period we now call the Scottish Enlightenment. He was an embodiment of that age of reason when Scotland held its intellectual head high, in Europe and the world. He was a poet of the vernacular who still speaks to the hearts of everyone. 'For my part,' Burns wrote to his publisher, 'I never had the least thought or inclination of turning poet till I got once heartily in love, and then rhyme and song were in a manner, the spontaneous language of my heart.' Burns embodied the virtues of that era of light and learning, when creative ideas flowed between the arts and sciences.

'Gie me a spark o' Nature's fire
That's all the learning I desire,'
    writes Burns.
'Scots steel with Irish fire
Is the poetry I desire,'

MacDiarmid replies.

It takes three hundred years to build an army that's admired and respected around the world. But it only takes three years pissing about in the desert in the biggest western foreign policy disaster ever to fuck it up completely.

Gregory Burke, *Black Watch*

During an interview at the 2006 Edinburgh Film Festival I was asked what film had made the greatest impact on me. My immediate response was *Black Watch*. That this was a play, and not a film, came as some surprise to the audience. But what a play. The shattered lives of a squad of young Scots returning from Iraq's Camp Dogwood was the runaway hit of that year's Edinburgh Festival Fringe, and would soon become the first international success of the new National Theatre of Scotland. Researched and written by the acclaimed Scottish playwright Gregory Burke, whose scenes of foul-mouthed bravado were worked up into a most heartbreakingly moving piece of ensemble theatre by John Tiffany, *Black Watch* reveals the emotional erosion on those young recruits lucky enough to have survived Bush and Blair's ill-fated 'war on terror'.

When Alex Salmond became Scotland's new First Minister in June 2007, I suggested that he should invite a performance of *Black Watch* at the opening of the Scottish Parliament. What an unforgettable evening that became. 'Can you imagine that happening in London?' said the director John Tiffany, turning to the post-theatre gathering. 'Talk about putting art at the heart of things.'

Given the play's depiction of a brutal war, bombarded with mortars of Fife expletives from the squaddies, a few Edinburgh heads may have turned when they saw that an eleven-year-old boy had been in the audience. But Connor Sinclair got

Black Watch, National Theatre of Scotland at Glenrothes, March 2008.

With Connor Sinclair, the eleven-year-old brother of Alister who served in Iraq, at the special Edinburgh performance of *Black Watch* when Parliament reconvened in 2007.

more than most out of *Black Watch*. Alister, his oldest brother, served in the Highland regiment in Camp Dogwood in Iraq for seven months and was medically discharged after he returned to Scotland. 'It gave Connor some understanding of what Alister had gone through,' his father told me. The young Connor is a keen bagpiper, so I wrote an encouraging letter to him. 'I am glad you liked my piping,' Connor replied. 'I am busy doing piping at the Highland Games. We have bought the oldest caravan in the world and are having great fun. Mum got the number plate printed with tartan letters and the message "Wee Bagpiper on Tour". Scotland for ever, Connor.'

'In the final marching sequence, as the men moved forward and stumbled in shifting patterns, I found to my surprise that I was crying,' wrote Ben Brantley, chief theatre critic of the *New York Times*. 'For this was no anonymous military phalanx. It was an assembly of men who, while moving in synchronicity, were each and every one a distinctive blend of fears and ambitions and confusion. They were every soldier; they were also irreducibly themselves. This exquisitely sustained double vision makes *Black Watch* one of the most richly human works of art to have emerged from this long-lived war.' For many in the audience that night in Brooklyn, the choreographed theatrical non-judgemental journey of *Black Watch* was the most inventive piece of theatre they had ever seen. The triumph of such a universal theme with a Scottish perspective was a glorious vindication for the National Theatre of Scotland. It answered all those MacJeremiahs who had prophesied that it would be inward-looking and parochial.

First thing each morning I turn to the *Herald* on my computer – first for its witty Diary, which helps keep my Scots sense of humour in tune. The *Herald* is not only Scotland's oldest newspaper, it is one of the oldest continuously published English-language newspapers in the world. It was first published in 1783, the year that America finally won her independence. How ironic then, that the *Herald* lost its independence in 2003 to the American publishing company Newsquest, a division of Gannett, which seems to run it as a cash cow.

'Newsquest's price-cutting policies…to make a few people rich in the USA [are] breaking a lot of hearts in Scotland,' wrote Roy Greenslade in the *Guardian*. 'Despite increased profits, with margins of 35 per cent, for three successive years,' he continued, 'Newsquest is accused of making job cuts that have undermined the paper's editorial quality and integrity.' A petition called on the owners to abide by the assurances they gave to the Competition Commission when they acquired the *Herald*, the *Sunday Herald* and the *Evening Times* that they would maintain the quality and level of coverage of Scottish issues and opinions. Such high-profile Scottish journalists as Robert Dawson Scott signed it, along with over a thousand others, in protest at Newsquest's colonial attitude. 'Your core assets are your staff,' he wrote. 'If you get rid of half of them and make the other half ill through overwork you won't have any profits at all.' 'A new deal between media owners and civil society is essential if good journalism is to survive in Scotland,' said Joyce MacMillan, Scotland's best-known drama critic. 'Essentially, the levels of return on capital being sought are not compatible with good ethical and professional practice in journalism, or with the proper representation of Scotland as a community. Politicians need to act to ensure that our toothless competition and takeover legislation has some real meaning, and that media corporations are compelled to honour the undertakings they give.'

When India won its independence in 1947 Jawaharlal Nehru, its first Prime Minister, legislated that there would be no foreign ownership of newspapers. 'Foreign owners see culture only as a marketplace and inevitably become a focus of resentment,' said Sir Harold Evans, under whose enlightened editorship the *Sunday Times* became a campaigning newspaper through the 1970s. But within a year of Rupert Murdoch's ownership he resigned over his compromising policies. Evans pointed out that most of the best newspapers in the world are not owned or managed by conglomerates but by families who regard them as a public trust. My deepest regret is that my friend Tony O'Reilly's Independent News & Media Group's bid for the *Herald* lost out to Newsquest.

Let us give, in the first place, what is necessary; secondly, what is useful; next, what is pleasant, and one should add, what is likely to last.

On Benefits by Seneca, sentenced to commit suicide by Nero in AD 65

For someone who is a private person who also happens to be a public figure, I am a very easy target. I've been accused of professing to give to charity to avoid tax. Yet I pay tax every time I work both in the UK and the USA, although I receive no state benefits from either country as I live permanently in the Bahamas. When Kevin Costner asked me to play a cameo role as Richard the Lionheart in his *Robin Hood* movie (just five lines of dialogue and one day's shooting for $500,000)

A patriotic moment with William Wallace
outside His Majesty's Theatre during my
South Pacific tour, 1954.

I decided to split the entire fee between the SIET and the universities of St Andrews, Dundee, Edinburgh and Heriot-Watt. When I announced this at an Edinburgh press conference there were sneaky comments inferring that my donations were a complicated tax dodge. This had happened before when I gave over $1 million to initiate SIET, won from round-the-clock work on *Diamonds Are Forever*. It happened again when I sent £50,000 to save the London Youth Theatre and $80,000 for a laser machine for the treatment of throat cancer in Manchester. When a notorious tabloid newspaperman accused me to my face of tax-dodging, I lost it. The idea that funding medical research would in any way line my pocket was despicable beyond belief. I told him to shut his face, and left.

My reward soon came. At Dundee we immediately struck gold. My donation was the very first received by Professor Sir Philip Cohen, the driving force behind the Wellcome Trust Biocentre at Dundee University, set up in 1997. Cohen was able to winkle out much more from serious medical funders who couldn't believe that this brilliant scientist's research programme had been jump-started by Robin Hood, Prince of Thieves. In the ten years since its foundation this innovative research centre has now passed the £100 million mark in research funding. Ranking alongside Oxford and Cambridge in the life sciences stakes, Dundee is now recognised as a hub of biomedical and life sciences research. More than 260 scientists and support staff have joined the Biocentre. Fifty-one different nationalities are represented amongst the 650 now working at the university's School of Life Sciences. Well, that's some success story.

Given my background, if anyone should vote Labour, it's me. So it came as a surprise to discover that I had been put up for a knighthood by two Conservatives, Michael Forsyth, the former Secretary of State for Scotland, and Virginia Bottomley, former Secretary of State for National Heritage. It was only after Labour's successful referendum, which I had done my best to support, that I found out that their own proposal had been 'considered' by the junior Scottish Office minister Sam Galbraith and eventually rejected by Scottish Secretary Donald Dewar. Why? Because there was too much publicity associating me with the nationalists. In 1998, a year after Scotland had so wholeheartedly endorsed the idea of a Scottish Parliament, the former Labour minister Peter Mandelson called me up to explain that there had been a 'misunderstanding'. What a load of old bollocks that was. I was eventually knighted by the Queen in the Palace of Holyroodhouse in Edinburgh in July 2000 in that same long picture gallery of Scottish monarchs which we had filmed twenty years earlier.

As my lifetime in movies unfolded on the sixty-foot screen in front of my family, close friends and colleagues, it brought back to me lots of terrific memories. Memories of people who are fun and industrious, gifted and enthusiastic – these are all the qualities that I find admirable. To receive the American Film Institute's Life Achievement Award, that magical evening in 2006, was quite humbling. 'You know, making movies is either a Utopia,' I told the many talents gathered in front of me in the Los Angeles Kodak Theatre, 'or it's like shovelling shit uphill. Tonight I propose we put down our shovels and remember the good times.'

Well, I've had many.

HOW IT ALL BEGAN

'Let's find out things that even the locals don't know,' was Sean's advice to me for the film we made together on Edinburgh, his home town, twenty-five years ago. 'Aim for something fresh, original, visual, but above all make it quirky,' was his brief. So instead of a predictable plod through the history of Edinburgh's eighteenth-century New Town, Sean related how its pioneering first inhabitants included an Irish dwarf and the hard-drinking Polish Count Barolowski, known locally as Count Barrel of Whisky. It's the same approach we've taken here as I've followed his requests down the byways of Scottish history up to the present. It was surely serendipitous that, as a fledgling actor in the cast of *South Pacific* in 1953, Sean faced the swashbuckling statue of William Wallace every day across the street from His Majesty's Theatre in Aberdeen. When he was asked by the New Museum of Scotland to present a favourite object for its contemporary gallery, Sean chose a facsimile of 'The Declaration of Arbroath'. It was from this 1320 manifesto of Scottish independence which he had quoted so effectively from on the eve of the successful Scottish devolution referendum. But there was a surprise; when the parchment arrived at the museum Sean had slipped the Declaration inside a milk bottle. It was at once a celebration of his loyalties, a touching memory of his milk-delivering schooldays, and a doorstep reminder to be read by tomorrow's politicians. It's just such quirkiness we hope you have enjoyed in *Being a Scot*.

Murray Grigor

The one who needs a haircut is Murray Grigor, as we hang out from my old family home in, Fountainbridge, for *Sean Connery's Edinburgh*, 1981.

With Murray writing home thoughts from abroad in my Lyford Cay garden in the Bahamas.

ACKNOWLEDGEMENTS

First gargantuan thanks to Micheline and Sean Connery for their ever-generous hospitality in and out of Out of Bounds, their Bahamas home, where Micheline has her studio and where Sean, after talking hours with me, could vanish through a garden hedge on to a sliver of reconstituted coastal Scotland, to revive himself on the golf course of Lyford Cay.

Then my very special thanks to all those who helped bring this book to birth. To the designer Teresa Monachino who first caught Sean's eye with her telling juxtapositions of imagery. 'Everyone in Hollywood thinks the pictures are great,' replied Sean, when he saw our lavishly illustrated proposal, 'but what about the words?' Now Teresa's happy marriage of text and illustrations and superb page layouts grace the chapters with much imaginative flair won from her deep knowledge of print history and the graphic arts. To the master of clarity, the film director Paul Almond, who took off valuable time from finishing his six-volume epic on his ancestors to offer us a poet's advice at a crucial time. To Andrew Hewson for steering us towards our hawk-eyed editor and publisher Alan Samson at Weidenfeld & Nicolson, his PA Miss Moneypenny, a star better known in the constellation of Orion as Carole Green, and his other stellar colleagues, Stacey McNutt, Lucinda McNeile, Michael Dover and David Rowley. To Emily Hedges who ferreted out so many elusive pictures. To the optical eye of John Reiach whose photographs sparkle throughout these pages. To Nancy Seltzer who has organised Sean's comings and goings with such grace ever since his days in Morocco filming John Huston's *The Man Who Would Be King*. To Colin McArthur who has unravelled so many myths of Scotland and analysed their effect on all of us who live here. To all the other scholars who helped steer us off the rocky roads of doubtful facts. For their deep knowledge of Scottish art, Duncan Macmillan and Murdo Macdonald. For architecture, Charles McKean and David Walker, Scotland's Mr Memory Man. For their deep understanding of the complexities of Scottish history, Tom Divine, and for their insights into the heights of the Scottish Enlightenment and the depths of its Endarkenment, Nick Phillipson and Bill Zachs. To Catherine Lockerbie and the mother ship of all book festivals, where the spirit of the yurt has guided us from start to finish. To my daughters Sarah and Phoebe who helped dream up this ambitious project and did so much to nudge it to completion. To the memory of my late wife Barbara whose work on Scotland Creates, an exhibition celebrating five thousand years of Scottish art and design, finds many echoes here. To my partner Carol for her love of words, brave defender of the apostrophe and stickler for clear prose, who even managed to steer me towards some reviving down time.

Murray Grigor, Inverkeithing, Scotland

INDEX

Furness, Horace Howard 42
Fuseli, Henry: *Macbeth and the Witches* 45
Fyffe, Will 274, *275*; 'I Belong to Glasgow' 274
Fyvie Castle 138

G

Galbraith, Sam 298
galvanometer, mirror *192*
Gandy, Joseph 137; *The Origin of Architecture* 137, *137*
Garbo, Greta 38
Gaudi, Antonio *81, 82*, 84
Geddes, Patrick *113*
geese, barnacle 54
Gehry, Frank 208, *208*
Gentle Shepherd, The 160
Gentleman Golfers of Leith 224, *224*
geology, early studies *51*, *53*, 54
George IV, King 69, *69*, 70, 76
George V, King 244
Géricault, Théodore: *The Raft of the 'Medusa'* 159, *159*
Gibbons, John 84
Gibbs, James 129, 133, *133*, 134; *Book of Architecture* 133
Gibson, Mel 74, 259
Gielgud, John 32, 37
Gilbert Scott, George 79, 168
Giles, Olivia 232-235
Gillespie Kidd & Coia 145, *145*
Gilliam, Terry 130, 222
Girodet de Rousy Trioson, Anne-Louis: *Ossian Receiving the Ghosts of French Heroes* 65
Glasgow 122, *143*; Anderson's Institution/University 193; Barlinnie Prison 180; Caledonia Road Church *142*; cathedral 127; as European City of Culture 72, 284-285; Hampden Park football stadium 214, *215*; Lighthouse design centre 285; St Vincent Street United Presbyterian Church *142*, 143-144; Shawlands House 132; Tramway gallery 285; as UK City of Architecture and Design 285; Western Infirmary, Maggie's Centre 206; Woodlands Road, 'Lobey Dosser' statue 281; *see also* University of Strathclyde
Glasgow Caledonian University, Moffat Centre 293
Glasgow Citizens' Theatre 254
Glasgow School of Art *82, 83, 143*, 144, 145, 146, 253, 275, 278, *278*
Glasgow University 192, 196
Glashan, John 263, 274-275, *275, 277*
Glen, Allan 193
Glencross 69

Gleneagles *226*, 234, *234*; G8 conference 294
Glenrothes 174-175, *174*; church 145
Glorious Days 29, *29*
Goethe, Johann von: *The Sorrows of Young Werther* 57
Goldfinger 224, 226, *226*
golf *213*, 222-224, 226, *226*, 228-229, *228*, 231-234
Golikova, Galina 170, *170*
Gone with the Wind 47
Gordon, Douglas 175
Gosnold, Bartholomew 106
Gothic Movement 114-125
Gowrie, Alexander Ruthven, 2nd Earl of 44
Gowrie, John Ruthven, 3rd Earl of *42*, 43-44
Gowrie, William Ruthven, 1st Earl of 43, 44
Gowrie Conspiracy *42*, 43-44
Goya, Francisco: *Disasters of War* 159
Graham, Roderick 206
Grand Lodge of Scotland 88
Grant, Mrs Elizabeth 62
Graubner, Gotthard 179
Gray, Alasdair 122, *122*; *Puir Things* 122-123
Gray, Robert 240
Great Eastern, The 193
Great Michael 192
Greene, Grahame 123
Greenslade, Roy 297
Greig, Andrew 290
Grierson, John 185, 247, 252-253, *253*, 254, 260; *Drifters* 185, *252*; *Night Mail* 252-253, *252*
Grigor, Murray 300, *300*
Groening, Matt 48, 49, 198
Grose, Francis 74
Group 3: 254
Guardian 166, 297
Guevara, Che 233, *233*
Guinness, Alec *250*

H

Haddington 27
Hadid, Zaha 206, *206*
Hadrian, Emperor 127, 135; Hadrian's Wall 127, *127*; *see also* Rome: Tivoli, Hadrian's Villa
Hamburg: *Fascinating Soccer* exhibition 213, 214; Kunsthalle 65
Hamilton, Gavin 153, 160-161; *Death of Lucretia* 160; *The Oath of Brutus* 160
Hamilton, Ian 240
Hamilton, Jock 216
Hamilton, Thomas 79, *79*, 80, 80, 143, 166
Hamilton, Sir William 161
Hampton, Christopher 151

Hampton Court Conference (1604) 108
Hanley, Cliff 185-186
Hardie, Keir 292, *292*
Harding, David 174-175
Hardy, Robert 38
Hare, William 119, *119*
Harewood, Earl of 164
Harewood House 146
Harley, John 216
Harmon, Vic 31
Harris, Hilary 185; *Seawards the Great Ships* 185, *185*
Harris, Phil *228*
Haslar Hospital 25
Hassan, Mamoun 256, 257, 258
Hay, Father 89
Healey, Denis 291
Heath, Edward 186, 290, *291*
Helensburgh 140, 206; Hill House 140, *140*, 142
Helmsdale, Highland Clearances memorial 170
Hemingway, Ernest: *A Moveable Feast* 33
Henderson, Isabel and George 162, 164
Henderson, Robert 31, 32, 33, 34, *34*, 208, 264
Henley, William 118, 119
Henney, Jimmy 208, 209
Henry, Buck 32
Henry, King of France 106
Henson, Laurence: *The Big Mill* 253; *The Heart of Scotland* 253
Hepburn, Katharine 249
Herald (Glasgow) 186, 296-297; *Diary* 279, 281, 296
Herman, Arthur 291; *How the Scots Invented the Modern World* 291
Hermitage, Dunkeld 61-62, *62*, 63
Heston, Charlton 37
Hewlett-Packard 17
Highland clans, repression of 55
Highland Games 218-219
Highlander 23, 146
Higson, Paddy 255
Hill, David Octavius 74, 166, 167, *167*; *The Land of Burns* 74; *Poet's Dream, The* 74, *74*
Hill, Phil 241
Hill, The 27, *27*, 151
Historic Scotland 127, 129, 130, *130*, *131*, 135, *135*, 146, 287, 289
Hitchcock, Alfred 112-113, *112*, 175, 256; *Marnie* 112, 113; *Psycho* 175; *Saboteur* 248
Hodge, John 258
Hogg, James 121-122; *The Private Memoirs and Confessions of a Justified Sinner* 121-122, 254
Holinshead, Raphael: *Chronicles of England, Scotlande, and Irelande* 42, 44-45

Hollywood 248-249, 250, 258
Holms, Johnnie *139*, 140
Holy Blood and the Holy Grail, The 87-88
Holy Island, Northumberland *81*, 83
Home, John 56
Homer: *Iliad* 55, 57, 160
Honourable Company of Edinburgh Golfers, The 224, *224*
Hopetoun, Earl of 133
Hopetoun House 80, 133
Hopper, Dennis 260
Horsfall, Carrie 291
Houghton Hall 133, 134
House of Lords 71
Houston, Jim 177, 185, 189
Houston, John Adam: *The Wonder of Sir Walter Scott in Rosslyn Chapel* 88
Howard, Ron 92
Howlett, Stanley 31
'Humble Petition' 62-63
Hume, David 159-160, *169*; *Treatise of Human Nature* 159
Hume, John 200
humour 261-275, 276-279, 281-283
hunting 219, 221
Hussey, Sutherland 288
Huston, John 90, *93*, 211, 258, *259*, 261
Hutton, James *51*, *53*, 54, 181; 'Theory of Rain' *51*; *Theory of the Earth* 51, 54

I

Ibsen, Henrik: *Hedda Gabler* 32
Independent News & Media Group 297
Indiana Jones and the Last Crusade 251
Indianapolis 500: 242, 243, *243*
industrial innovation 182-183, 185-187, 192-198, 200, 204-206
Ingres, Jean-Auguste-Dominique 65, 74; *The Dream of Ossian* 65, 74
Inter Milan football club 215
Inverness: Porterfield Prison 180; Raigmore Maggie's Centre 206
Inverness Caledonian Thistle FC 283
Irving, Washington 69; *Abbotsford and Newstead Abbey* 69
Isaacs, Jeremy 257, 258

J

Jackson, Gordon 252
Jacobite Rising 56, 69, 128-129
James I, King *53*, 54
James I, King of England *see* James VI, King

PICTURE CREDITS

The authors and publisher are grateful to the following for their permission to reproduce the photographs and illustrations. While every effort has been made to trace copyright holders, if any have inadvertently been overlooked, the publishers will be happy to acknowledge them in future editions of the book.

Picture Research: Emily Hedges

Key l = left, c = centre, r = right, t = top, b = bottom

Page 1 © Reuters/Corbis; 2 Sean Connery's personal collection; 4 Julie Hamilton/Rex Features; 6 Sean Connery's personal collection; 7 Kevin Winter/Getty Images for AFI; 9 PA Photos; 10-11 Sean Connery's personal collection; 12 l Columbia/The Kobal Collection; 12 r © The Scotsman Publ Ltd; 14 Sean Connery's personal collection, 16 t and b John Reiach; 17 l © The Scotsman Publ Ltd; 17 r Sean Connery's personal collection; 18 By permission of the Trustees of the National Library of Scotland; 19 www.eamonnmcgoldrick.com; 20-21 Julie Hamilton/Rex Features; 22 © The Scotsman Publ Ltd; 23 Sean Connery's personal collection; 24 l Kingston Films/The Kobal Collection; 24 r MGM/Ronald Grant Archive; 25 and 26 Sean Connery's personal collection; 27 MGM/7 Arts/The Kobal Collection; 28 tl and br Sean Connery's personal collection; 28 tr © Richard Demarco. With kind permission of The Demarco European Art Foundation; 28 bl Peter Stubbs, www.edinphoto.org.uk; 29 Sean Connery's personal collection; 30 and 31 Sean Connery's personal collection (Bill Green, Health and Strength Magazine); 32 l From the Mander & Mitchenson Theatre Collection; 32 r and 33 l Sean Connery's personal collection; 33 r and 34 From the Mander & Mitchenson Theatre Collection; 35-39 Sean Connery's personal collection; 40 and 41 Library and Archives Canada; 42 Mary Evans Picture Library; 43 Private Collection/The Bridgeman Art Library; 44 Petworth House, West Sussex, UK/The Bridgeman Art Library; 45 © The National Gallery of Scotland, Edinburgh/The Bridgeman Art Library; 47 l © Michael Jenner/Alamy; 47 r Hans Wild/Time Life Pictures/Getty Images; 49 'THE SIMPSONS' TM and © 1990 Twentieth Century Fox Television; 50 Mary Evans Picture Library; 51 t With permission of the Master and Fellows of Corpus Christi College ; 51 b Crown copyright: RCAHMS; 52 Piccolomini Library, Duomo, Siena, Italy, Ghigo Roli/The Bridgeman Art Library; 53 MGM/Ronald Grant Archive; 55 l Piccolomini Library, Duomo, Siena, Italy, Ghigo Roli/The Bridgeman Art Library; 55 r John Reiach; 56-57 Private Collection/© The Maas Gallery, London, UK/The Bridgeman Art Library; 58 Murray Grigor; 60 t and b By courtesy of the Trustees of Sir John Soane's Museum; 62 t By courtesy of Robert Clerk, Penicuik House; 62 b Murray Grigor; 63 l Calum Colvin; 63 r John Reiach; 64 Calum Colvin; 65 l Musée Ingres, Montauban, France, Lauros/Giraudon/The Bridgeman Art Library; 65 r Musée Nat. du Château de Malmaison, Rueil-Malmaison, France, Lauros/Giraudon/The Bridgeman Art Library; 66 l Image courtesy of The Herald & Evening Times picture archive; 66 r Courtesy of the University of St Andrews Library; 67 © Bettmann/Corbis; 68 and 70 © National Gallery of Scotland, Edinburgh/The Bridgeman Art Library; 71 United Distillers and Vintners/The Bridgeman Art Library; 72 © National Gallery of Scotland, Edinburgh/The Bridgeman Art Library; 73 l Photography © The Art Institute of Chicago. Joseph Winterbotham Collection, 1959.1; 73 r Don Price/Fox Photos/Getty Images; 74 St. Peter's, Vatican, Rome, Italy, Alinari/The Bridgeman Art Library; 75 By permission of the Trustees of the National Library of Scotland; 76 l Photograph by Madeleine Shepherd, Courtesy of the James Clerk Maxwell Foundation; 76 r Science and Society Picture Library; 77 t Courtesy of Penny MacDonald; 77 b Jeff Christensen/Reuters/Corbis; 78 © Scottish Parliamentary copyright material is reproduced with permission of the Queen's Printer for Scotland on behalf of the Scottish Parliamentary Corporate Body. Photography: Adam Elder; 79 l and c Murray Grigor; 79 r and 80 l John Reiach; 80 c StockImages/Alamy; 80 r Phoebe Grigor; 81 tl © John Brooks/Robert Harding World Imagery/Corbis; 81 tr, l of c, r of c and b © Scottish Parliamentary copyright material is reproduced with permission of the Queen's Printer for Scotland on behalf of the Scottish Parliamentary Corporate Body. Photography: Adam Elder; 82 far tl Anan Photographic; 82 tl of c Giovanni Zani; 82 tr of c and tr John Reiach; 82 l of c © National Gallery of Scotland, Edinburgh/The Bridgeman Art Library; 82 r of c and b © Scottish Parliamentary copyright material is reproduced with permission of the Queen's Printer for Scotland on behalf of the Scottish Parliamentary Corporate Body. Photography: Adam Elder; 84 l John Reiach; 84 r © Scottish Parliamentary copyright material is reproduced with permission of the Queen's Printer for Scotland on behalf of the Scottish Parliamentary Corporate Body. Photography: Adam Elder; 85 John Reiach; 86 l Judith Tewson/Alamy; 86 c John Heseltine/Alamy; 86 r © Fred de Noyelle/Godong/Corbis; 87 Sean Connery's personal collection; 89 t and b John Heseltine/Alamy; 90 t David Lyons/Alamy; 90 c and b John Heseltine/Alamy; 91 l Michael Booth/Alamy; 91 r Christopher Furlong/Getty Images; 92 Scottish National Portrait Gallery, Edinburgh/The Bridgeman Art Library; 93 Sean Connery's personal collection; 94 David McGrath; 95 Time Life Pictures/Mansell/Getty Images; 96 l and r By permission of the Trustees of the National Library of Scotland; 97 Mary Evans Picture Library; 98 © The Trustees of the National Museums of Scotland; 99 b Archive Photos/Getty Images; 99 t Sandro Vannini/Corbis; 101 Herve Hughes/Hemis.fr/ Getty Images; 103 By permission of the Trustees of the National Library of Scotland; 105 Scottish National Portrait Gallery, Edinburgh/ The Bridgeman Art Library; 107 Mary Evans Picture Library; 108 By permission of the Trustees of the National Library of Scotland; 110 Angelo Hornak/Corbis; 111 Crown copyright: Historic Royal Palaces; 112 Sean Connery's personal collection, 113 and 114 t John Reiach; 114 b Murray Grigor; 115 l Reproduced by courtesy of the University Librarian and Director, The John Rylands University Library, The University of Manchester; 115 r Mary Evans Picture Library; 117 © 2005, Photo Scala, Florence/BPK, Bildagentur fuer Kunst, Kultur und Geschichte, Berlin; 118 Paramount/The Kobal Collection; 119 t Mary Evans Picture Library; 119 b Private Collection/Bridgeman Art Library; 120 Murray Grigor; 121 Nifro UK/Alamy; 122 Courtesy the artist, Alasdair Gray, and Sorcha Dallas, Glasgow; 123 t© Hulton-Deutsch Collection/Corbis; 123 b Paul Rovere/Courtesy of The Age; 125 John Reiach; 126 © Macduff Everton/Corbis; 128 Panoramic Images/Getty Images; 129 l © Steve Austin, Papilio/Corbis; 129 r Murray Grigor; 130 and 131 tl and b John Reiach; 131 tr © Francis G. Mayer/Corbis; 132 John Reiach; 133 l John Bethell/The Bridgeman Art Library; 133 c worldthroughthelens-UK/Alamy; 133 r Natalie Tepper/arcaid.co.uk; 134 t David Gowans/Alamy; 134 b © Crown Copyright Reproduced by courtesy of Historic Scotland; 135 t© RCAHMS, Copied from 'Vitruvius Scoticus'; 135 b Crown copyright: RCAHMS; 136 Francesco Venturi/Corbis; 137 l By courtesy of the Trustees of Sir John Soane's Museum; 137 r Murray Grigor; 138 John Reiach; 139 t Image courtesy of The Herald & Evening Times picture archive; 139 b l Crown Copyright: RCAHMS; 139 b r John Reiach; 140 l Crown Copyright: RCAHMS; 140 r © The Scotsman Publ Ltd; 141 tl © Peter Aprahamian/Corbis; 141 above c Don Brownlow/Alamy; 141 c John Reiach; 141 b Jeremy Pardoe/ Alamy; 142 Crown Copyright: RCAHMS; 143 l © Michael Nicholson/Corbis; 143 r The Glasgow School of Art Archives and Collections; 144 Murray Grigor; 145 Dan Dubowitz; 147 t © Werner Forman/Corbis; 147 b Werner Otto/Alamy; 148 Roman von Gotz/Bildarchiv Monheim/arcaid.co.uk; 149 © Richard Bryant/Arcaid/Corbis; 150-151 © David Steen/Sygma/Corbis; 153 © James Peltekian/

Corbis Sygma; 154 photograph by John Reiach; 155 Graham Metcalfe (from the film 'Sean Connery's Edinburgh', 1981); 156 l Scottish National Portrait Gallery, Edinburgh/The Bridgeman Art Library; 156 tr National Gallery of Scotland (Sir David Wilkie, William Chambers Bethune and Family); 156 br Courtesy of the National Gallery of Ireland. Photo © National Gallery of Ireland; 157 National Gallery of Scotland, Edinburgh/The Bridgeman Art Library; 158 l Courtesy of Duncan Macmillan; 158 r John Reiach © The Royal College of Surgeons of Edinburgh (Charles Bell, Opisthotonus); 159 l Musée des Beaux-Arts, Rouen, France, Lauros/Giraudon/The Bridgeman Art Library 159 t and br Courtesy of Duncan Macmillan; 160 l Yale Center for British Art, Paul Mellon Collection, USA /The Bridgeman Art Library; 160 r Musée du Louvre, Paris, France, Giraudon/The Bridgeman Art Library; 161 By Courtesy of Robert Clerk, Penicuik House; 162 l National Gallery of Scotland (Alexander Runciman, Blind Ossian Singing); 162 r Crown Copyright: RCAHMS; 163 © The Trustees of the British Museum; 164 John Reiach; 165 tr and c The Board of Trinity College Dublin; 165 tl Andrew Dowsett; 165 bl Inverness Museum and Art Gallery, Highland Council; 165 br Teresa Monachino; 166 City Art C: City of Edinburgh Museums and Galleries; 167 l and c Scottish National Photography Collection; 167 r Courtesy of the University of St Andrews Library; 168 John Reiach; 169 t Jon Arnold Images Ltd/Alamy; 169 bl © Trustees of the Paolozzi Foundation, Licensed by DACS 2008. Image supplied by Yale Center for British Art, Paul Mellon Fund, USA/The Bridgeman Art Library; 169 br © Trustees of the Paolozzi Foundation, Licensed by DACS 2008. Image supplied by The Stapleton Collection/ The Bridgeman Art Library; 170 Sculpture by Gerald Laing, photography by John Reiach; 171 t and bl   Painting by Gerald Laing, photography by Ewen Weatherspoon; 171 br Sculpture by Gerald Laing, photography by John McKenzie; 172 and 173 t John Bellany; 173 b Will Maclean (Work held in private collection, Glasgow); 174 l © The Scotsman Publ Ltd; 175 Andrew Lawson; 176-179 From the Demarco Digital Archive, University of Dundee, Courtesy of Richard Demarco; 181 © The Scotsman Publ Ltd; 182-183 Rex Features; 184 Cristaldifilm/ Ronald Grant Archive; 185 l © Paul Almasy/Corbis; 185 c © Andrew Fox/Corbis; 186 t Sean Connery's personal collection; 186 b Hulton Archive/Getty Images; 187 t Scottish Screen Archive and the National Library of Scotland; 187 b © The Scotsman Publ Ltd; 188 and 189 Sean Connery's personal collection; 190-191 © Benedict Luxmoore/Arcaid/ Corbis; 192 l and r © Hunterian Museum and Art Gallery, University of Glasgow; 193 Musée de la Marine, Paris, France/ The Bridgeman Art Library; 194 National Gallery of Scotland (James E Lauder, James Watt and the Steam Engine); 195 l and br Mary Evans Picture Library; 195 tr Science Museum/SSPL; 196 and 197 Science Museum/SSPL; 198 t and b Glasgow City Archives; 199 t Central Press/ Hulton Archive/ Getty Images; 199 bl Murray Grigor; 199 br © Hulton Deutsch Collection/ Corbis; 200 Murray Grigor; 201 t © The Trustees of the National Museums of Scotland; 201 c © Grant Smith/ Corbis; 201 bl and r Murray Grigor; 202-203 Julie Hamilton/Rex Features; 204 t Murray Grigor; 204 bl VISUM Foto GMbH/Alamy; 204 br vario images GmbH & Co. KG/Alamy; 205 Charles Jencks; 206 l and r Richard Murphy Architects/Alan Forbes; 207 t Keith Hunter/ arcaid.co.uk; 207 bl and r Helene Binet; 209 and 210 Sean Connery's personal collection; 211 t © The British Library Board. All Rights Reserved (15024.a.1); 211 b Charles Tait; 212 tl © Jim Richardson/ Corbis; 212 r and bl Steve McCarthy; 214 By permission of the Trustees of the National Library of Scotland; 215 Allsport/Getty Images; 217 Mary Evans; 218 t Seamus McGarvey; 219 John Reiach; 220 Private Collection/The Bridgeman Art Library; 221 t Crown Copyright: RCAHMS; 222 © Leo Mason/Corbis; 223 Mary Evans Picture Library; 224 British Library, London, UK, © British Library Board. All Rights Reserved/The Bridgeman Art Library; 225 National Gallery of Scotland (David Allan, The Prize of the Silver Golf); 226 Everett Collection/Rex Features; 227 Danjaq/EQN/UA/The Kobal Collection; 228-230 Sean Connery's personal collection; 231 The Augusta Chronicle; 232 Courtesy of Sven Tumba; 233 l © Tony Roberts/CORBIS; 233 r © Bettmann/CORBIS; 234 Keystone/Getty Images; 236 © Christie's Images Ltd (Figures Ice Skating. Charles Altamount Doyle (1832-1893). Pencil, Pen, Ink And Watercolour, 1876); 237 l © Georgios Kefalas/epa/Corbis; 237 r © City of Edinburgh Museums and Art Galleries, Scotland/The Bridgeman Art Library; 238 Kunsthistorisches Museum, Vienna, Austria/ The Bridgeman Art Library; 241 t Courtesy of the Earl of Mansfield, Scone Palace; 241 bl © Colin McPhersoh/Corbis Sygma; 241 br © Crown Copyright, Reproduced Courtesy of Historic Scotland; 242 LAT Photographic; 243 l © Schlegelmilch/Corbis; 243 r Harry How/Getty Images; 244 l © The Mariners' Museum/Corbis; 244 r The Mariners' Museum, Newport News, VA; 245 Chaiwat Subprasom/ Reuters/ Corbis; 246 Library of Congress, Washington DC; 247 l Roger Viollet/ Getty Images; 247 r Library of Congress Washington DC; 248 l Ronald Grant Archive; 248 r Mutual/The Kobal Collection; 249 Murray Grigor; 250 Knightsbridge Films/Ronald Grant Archive; 251 Ealing/ The Kobal Collection; 252 l GPO Film Unit/The Kobal Collection; 252 r COI/The Kobal Collection; 253 t and b Ronald Grant Archive; 254 Murray Grigor; 256 l BBC/Ronald Grant Archive; 256 r Source: BFI; 257 BFI/Ronald Grant Archive; 258 Private Collection/The Bridgeman Art Library; 259 Sean Connery's personal collection; 260 t Recorded Picture Company/The Kobal Collection/ Davidson, Neil; 260 b Galleria Nazionale delle Marche, Urbino, Italy/ The Bridgeman Art Library; 261 l and r Richard Murphy Architects/ David Morris; 262 Murray Grigor; 263 Ronald Grant Archive; 264 and 265 Murray Grigor; 266 l Mary Evans Picture Library; 266 r John Byrne © The Bridgeman Art Library. Courtesy of the People's Palace, Glasgow; 267 l Bibliothèque Nationale, Paris, France/The Bridgeman Art Library; 267 r John Reiach; 268 Reproduced with permission of Punch Ltd; www.punch.co.uk; 270 Mary Evans Picture Library; 271 Hulton Archive/Illustrated London News/Getty Images; 271 tr and br Courtesy of the University of St Andrews Library; 272 l From the Mander and Mitchenson Theatre Collection; 272 r Murray Grigor; 273 l and c Murray Grigor; 273 r Ronald Grant Archive; 274 t Seamus McGarvey; 274 b Ronald Grant Archive; 275 t From the Mander and Mitchenson Theatre Collection; 275 b and 276 John Glashan; 277 t Courtesy of the University of St Andrews Library; 277 b Murray Grigor; 278 Murray Grigor; 279 Oor Wullie and The Broons © DC Thomson & Co. Ltd 2008, Used By Kind Permission; 280 cartoons by Bud Neill ; 280 br Murray Grigor; 281 t Corbis; 281 b © The Estate of Ivor Cutler. Courtesy of Jeremy and Daniel Cutler; 282 Courtesy of Zoë Readhead; 283 l John Reiach; 283 r taken from Carotid Cornucopius Sydney Goodsir Smith; 285 John Reiach; 286 tl, tr and r of c Phoebe Grigor; 286 bl and br Tom Piper; 287 l Sandy Kinghorn. 287 r Alfonsina Monachino; 288 Richard Murphy Architects/ Alan Forbes; 289 Richard Murphy Architects/ Alan Forbes; 291 Keystone/Getty Images; 292 Courtesy of the People's Palace, Glasgow; 293 © The Scotsman Publ Ltd; 294 and 295 The National Theatre of Scotland's Black Watch. Photography by Manuel Harlan; 296 Sean Connery's personal collection; 299 Sean Connery's personal collection; 300 l Murray Grigor; 300 r Murray Grigor;. 312 Sean Connery's personal collection.

First published in Great Britain in 2008
by Weidenfeld & Nicolson
10 9 8 7 6 5 4 3 2 1

Text © Sean Connery 2008
Design and layout © Weidenfeld & Nicolson 2008

All rights reserved. No part of this publication may be reproduced,
stored in a retrieval system, or transmitted, in any form or by any
means, electronic, mechanical, photocopying, recording or otherwise,
without the prior permission of both the copyright owner and the
above publisher.

The right of Sean Connery to be identified as the author of this work
has been asserted in accordance with the Copyright, Designs and
Patents Act 1988.

A CIP catalogue record for this book is available from the British Library.

ISBN: 978 0 297 85540 8

Printed by Printer Trento Srl and bound by L.E.G.O SpA, Italy
Colour reproduction by DL Interactive UK

Weidenfeld & Nicolson
The Orion Publishing Group Ltd
Orion House
5 Upper St Martin's Lane
London WC2H 9EA

An Hachette Livre UK Company

The Orion Publishing Group's policy is to use papers that are natural,
renewable and recyclable products and made from wood grown in
sustainable forests.

Mixed Sources
Product group from well-managed
forests and other controlled sources
www.fsc.org Cert no. CQ-COC-000012
© 1996 Forest Stewardship Council
FSC

CUMBRIA LIBRARIES

3 8003 03536 9669

CKL

Cumbria
County Council

Libraries, books and more . . .

COCKERMOUTH

- - SEP 2008

- 3 NOV 2008   CkL-)MVJL

oct 09/10

- 9 APR 2009   1 5 FEB 2011

2 1 MAY 2009   1 2 JAN 2012

Please return/renew this item by the last due date.
Library items may also be renewed by phone or
via our website.
www.cumbria.gov.uk/libraries

CLIC

Ask for a CLIC password

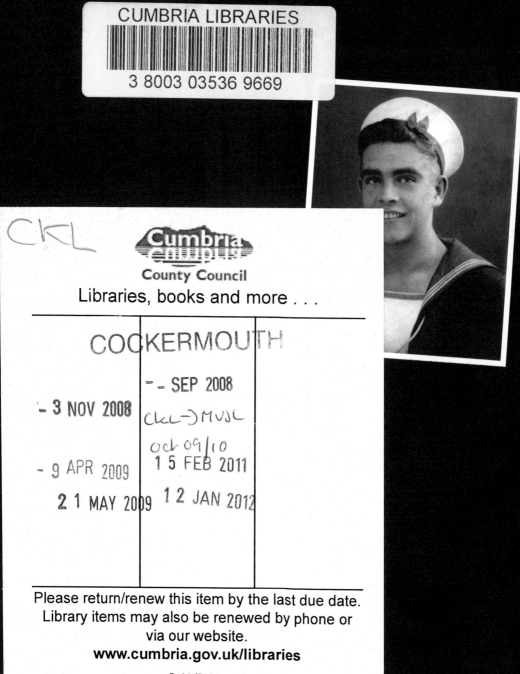